Improved Career Decision Making in a Changing World

EDITOR
Judith M. Ettinger

CONTRIBUTING AUTHORS
Dennis Engels, University of North Texas.
Judith Ettinger, Vocational Studies Center, University of Wisconsin-Madison.
Jean Jolin, Vocational Studies Center, University of Wisconsin-Madison.
Roger Lambert, Vocational Studies Center, University of Wisconsin-Madison.
Maile Pa'alani, Wisconsin Occupational Information Coordinating Committee.
Janet Pugh, Wisconsin Department of Industry, Labor and Human Relations.

DESKTOP PUBLISHING
Julie Peterson, Vocational Studies Center, University of Wisconsin-Madison.
Kimberlee Verhage, Vocational Studies Center, University of Wisconsin-Madison.

Organizations and individuals undertaking special projects funded by the U.S. Department of Labor for the National Occupational Information Coordinating Committee are encouraged to express their professional judgments. The interpretations and viewpoints stated in this document, therefore, do not necessarily represent the official position or policy of the U.S. Department of Labor, the NOICC members or their representatives, or the NOICC staff, and no official endorsement should be inferred.

```
        Library of Congress Cataloging-in-Publication Data


Improved career decision making in a changing world / contributing
   authors: Dennis Engels ... [et al.] ; editor, Judith M. Ettinger.
      p.    cm.
   Includes bibliographical references.
   ISBN 0-912048-95-6. -- ISBN 0-912048-94-8 (training manual)
   1. Career development.  2. Employee counseling.  3. Labor market-
-Research.  4. Minorities--Employment.   I. Engels, Dennis W.
II. Ettinger, Judith M.
HF5549.5.C35I57  1991
158.6--dc20·                                             91-29766
                                                            CIP
```

Copyright © 1991 Garrett Park Press

Published and distributed by the Garrett Park Press
PO Box 190-B, Garrett Park, MD 20896

ISBN Number 0-912048-95-6
Library of Congress Number
91-29766

ICDM Resource Group

Gary Crossley
ICESA
444 No. Capitol St., NW - Suite 126
Washington, D.C. 20001

R. V. Dorothy
National Veterans Training Institute
1250 14th St., Suite 650
Denver, CO 80202

Charlie R. Gertz
AT&T Bell Lab, Rm. 1D-640
101 JFK Parkway
Short Hills, NJ 07078

Nancy Hargis
Oregon OICC
875 Union Street NE
Salem, OR 97311

Gisela Harkin
U.S. Dept. of Education, OVAE, DVTE
Switzer Bldg. Room 4321
300 C St, SW
Washington, DC 20202

Joe McDaniel
Mississippi Dept. of Education
P.O. Box 771
Jackson, MS 39205

Chuck Mollerup
Room 301, Len B. Jordan Bldg.
650 West State St.
Boise, ID 83720

Daniel Marrs
North Dakota SOICC
1600 East Interstate - Suite 14
Post Office Box 1537
Bismarck, ND 58502

Mildred T. Nichols
Rhode Island SOICC
22 Hayes St.
Providence, RI 02908

Nancy S. Perry
P.O. Box 805
Augusta, ME 05332-0805

Mike Pilot
7223 Whitson Dr.
Springfield, VA 22153

Karen Reiff
Career Planning & Placement Specialist
Capital Area Career Center
611 Hagadorn Road
Mason, MI 48854

Charlotte Rodriguez
1902 14th Avenue
Greely, CO 80631

Pat Schwallie-Giddis
AACD
5999 Stevenson Avenue
Alexandria, VA 22304

Karen Wempen
IL Rehabilitation Services
623 E. Adams St.
Springfield, IL 62705

Counselor Educators Advisory Group

Loretta Bradley
Box 4560 COE
Department of Educational Psychology
Texas Technical University
Lubbock, TX 79409

David Jepsen
University of Iowa
N368 Lindquist Center
Iowa City, IA 52242

Lee Richmond
Education Department
Loyola College of Maryland
4501 N. Charles Street
Baltimore, MD 21210

Clemmie Solomon
3401 27th Avenue
Temple Hills, MD 20748

Howard Splete
Oakland University
522 O'Dowd Hall
Rochester, Michigan 48309

Table of Contents
Participant's Resource Guide

Page

Appendices

List of Figures

List of Figures continued

List of Figures continued

Foreword

Improved Career Decision Making in a Changing World (ICDM) is designed to help career development facilitators and their clients make wise decisions as participants in a labor market that is characterized by economic, demographic and technological change. As the United States approaches the year 2000, an older and more socially diverse work force must produce, trade and prosper in a global economy that is technologically advancing at a rapid pace. People of all colors, ages and cultures are seeking roles in the changing world of work--where and how do they fit into this modern mosaic of production and distribution?

The purpose of the *Improved Career Decision Making in a Changing World* Program is to help people find answers to career-related questions through the use of labor market information (LMI). The need for the answers--information--is greater today than ever before as more preparation is needed and competition becomes keener for the better jobs. We also move around more within the labor market. Most workers can expect to change jobs more than half a dozen times during their lives. We need information more than ever, but there is so much labor market information in today's "Information Age" that it is difficult for the average person to locate, sift through and interpret it to make intelligent career decisions.

The professionals to whom we often turn, career development facilitators, play a key role in career decision making and specifically, in the information-seeking process. They need to know how to help their clients find information, process it and use it effectively. The *goal* of the ICDM Program is to train career development facilitators to help their clients use labor market information to make thoughtful, responsible and enlightened decisions about occupations and careers.

Is helping clients in their career development and decision making important work? We certainly think so. Choosing one's career is no longer an isolated incidence that can be left to chance circumstances. Our work is too important; it is central to our lives; we are often identified by what we do. If we are happy, satisfied, and fulfilled in our work roles, these elements spill into our personal lives.

To provide our citizens with this important occupational and career information, the National Occupational Informational Coordinating Committee (NOICC) and the State Occupational Information Coordinating Committees (SOICCs) have accepted the mission to train career development facilitators to help their clients use labor market information. NOICC has sponsored the Improved Career Decision Making (ICDM) Program through cooperating SOICCs since 1981 and to date has trained over 30,000 career development facilitators. The training is provided through ICDM curriculum materials and workshops organized by the SOICCs with funding assistance from NOICC.

The ICDM Trainer's Guide and Participant Resource Guide are revisions of the original training materials, *Using Labor Market Information in Career Exploration and Decision Making*, published in 1986. This newer version is competency-based, using the counselor/staff competencies listed in the National Career Development Guidelines, also a NOICC Project. This ICDM curriculum is designed to be user-friendly. It can serve all population groups and it can be delivered in a variety of training modes and circumstances. It truly represents what is needed for *Improved Career Decision Making in a Changing World*.

In closing, I want to acknowledge the contributions of Roger Lambert and Judith Ettinger from the Vocational Studies Center at the University of Wisconsin, Maile Pa'alani, the Wisconsin SOICC Director, Walton Webb and Valerie Lloyd from the NOICC Office and the reviewers who took the time to contribute their expertise to the development of this publication.

Juliette Lester
Executive Director

Module 1
Introduction

National Career Development Guidelines-Counselor Competencies

Skills to assist individuals in setting goals and identifying strategies for reaching goals.

Knowledge of changes taking place in the economy, society, and job market.

Knowledge of education, training, employment trends, labor market, and career sources.

Introduction
Module 1

Introduction

"Hi, I'm Jane Cruz."
"Well, it's nice to meet you, Jane, I'm Tom Chen."
"You look familiar, Tom. I know I've seen you before. Do you work in this area?"

In many first time meetings such as this, the work we do is often our most descriptive label. How do we choose our work roles? Did she aspire to be in sales? Did he choose to become a nurse? How are these choices made? Are they the result of long-term planning or do we more frequently just stumble into the first job available upon graduation?

The decisions we make about our careers throughout our lives are crucial to our well-being. Yet, despite the importance of a career, the 1989 Gallup Survey found that less than half of today's adults made a conscious and informed career choice. Instead, chance and environment played an important role.

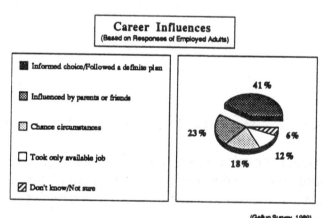

Figure 1.1

Career decision making is a complex process. During this process, clients typically analyze their personal traits, backgrounds and interests. One step in this process is to relate self-knowledge to the available opportunities in the world of work. Yet, because we are faced with a broad, rapidly changing spectrum of careers, we cannot assume a client or student will have the skills to locate, use and evaluate the most up-to-date and valid information effectively. Most people need "handles" to bring some order to the resources that help them. Some clients are capable of researching and using the available information to make good decisions; others may need help in locating and evaluating information to answer their questions. The *Improved Career Decision Making* training program will teach you about available resources that contain answers to many of these questions. This inservice program is designed to help you find, interpret and use career and labor market information with your clients.

The goals of the program are:

Goals of the
ICDM Program

Train career development facilitators to help students and clients:

1. Understand labor market information,

2. Use information to make career decisions,

3. Improve decision making skills, and

4. Develop an action plan to make more effective use of information in career decision making.

Figure 1.2

Career Decision Making and the Role of Information

What can a career development facilitator do to enable clients and students to make effective decisions? The National Career Development Guidelines, developed by the National Occupational Information Coordinating Committee, define competencies for staff who deliver career guidance and counseling programs.

National Career
Development Guidelines

Counseling

Knowledge of developmental issues individuals address throughout the life span.

Knowledge of counseling and career development theories and techniques.

Knowledge of decision-making and transition models.

Knowledge of role relationships to facilitate personal, family, and career development.

Knowledge of different cultures to interact effectively with all populations.

Skills to build productive relationships with counselees.

Skills to use appropriate individual and group counseling techniques to assist individuals with career decisions and career development concerns.

Skills to assist individuals in identifying influencing factors in career decision making, such as family, friends, educational opportunities, and finances.

Skills to assist individuals in changing biased attitudes that stereotype others by gender, race, age, and culture.

Skills to assist individuals in understanding the relationship between interpersonal skills and success in the workplace.

Skills to assist individuals in setting goals and identifying strategies for reaching goals.

Skills to assist individuals in continually reassessing their goals, values, interests, and career decisions.

Skills to assist individuals in preparing for multiple roles throughout their lives.

Information

Knowledge of changes taking place in the economy, society, and job market.

Knowledge of education, training, employment trends, labor market, and career resources.

Knowledge of basic concepts related to career counseling such as career development, career progression, and career patterns.

Knowledge of the changing gender roles and how these impact on work, family, and leisure.

Knowledge of employment information and career planning materials.

Knowledge of employment-related requirements such as labor laws, licensing, credentialing, and certification.

Knowledge of state and local referral services or agencies for job, financial, social, and personal service.

Knowledge of federal and state legislation that may influence career development programs.

Skills to use career development resources and techniques designed for specific groups.

Skills to use computer-based career information systems.

Individual and Group Assessment

Knowledge of assessment techniques and measures of skills, abilities, aptitudes, interests, values, and personalities.

Skills to identify assessment resources appropriate for specific situations and populations.

Skills to evaluate assessment resources and techniques related so that their validity, reliability, and relationships to race, gender, age, and ethnicity can be determined.

Skills to administer, interpret, and personalize assessment data in relation to the career development needs of the individual.

Management and
Administration

Knowledge of program designs that can be used in organizing career development programs.
Knowledge of needs assessment techniques and practices.
Knowledge of management concepts, leadership styles, and techniques to implement change.
Skills to assess the effectiveness of career development programs.
Skills to identify staff competencies for effective career development programs.
Skills to prepare proposals, budgets, and timelines for career development programs.
Skills to identify, develop, and use record keeping methods.
Skills to design, conduct, analyze, and report the assessment of individual and program outcomes.

Implementation

Knowledge of program adoption and planned change strategies.
Knowledge of barriers affecting the implementation of career development programs.
Skills to implement individual and group programs in a variety of areas such as assessment decision making, job seeking, career information and career counseling.
Skills to implement public relations efforts which promote career development activities and services.
Skills to establish linkages with community-based organizations.

Consultation

Knowledge of consulting strategies and consulting models.
Skills to assist staff in understanding how to incorporate career development concepts into their offerings to program participants.
Skills to consult with influential parties such as employers, community groups and the general public.
Skills to convey program goals and achievements to legislators, professional groups, and other key leaders.

Specific Populations

Knowledge of differing cultural values and their relationship to work values.
Knowledge of unique career planning needs of minorities, women, the handicapped, and older persons.
Knowledge of alternative approaches to career planning needs for individuals with specific needs.
Skills to identify community resources and establish linkages to assist adults with specific needs.
Skills to find appropriate methods or resources to communicate with limited English proficient individuals.

The Guidelines also include student competencies.

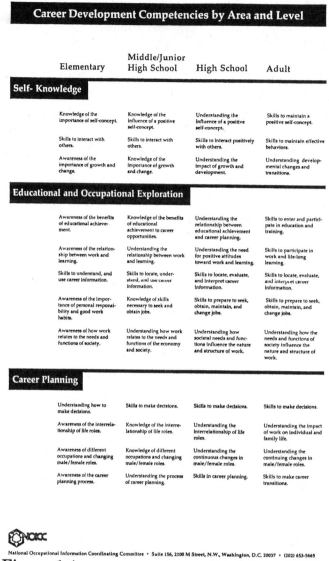

Career Development Competencies by Area and Level

	Elementary	Middle/Junior High School	High School	Adult
Self-Knowledge				
	Knowledge of the importance of self-concept.	Knowledge of the influence of a positive self-concept.	Understanding the influence of a positive self-concept.	Skills to maintain a positive self-concept.
	Skills to interact with others.	Skills to interact with others.	Skills to interact positively with others.	Skills to maintain effective behaviors.
	Awareness of the importance of growth and change.	Knowledge of the importance of growth and change.	Understanding the impact of growth and development.	Understanding developmental changes and transitions.
Educational and Occupational Exploration				
	Awareness of the benefits of educational achievement.	Knowledge of the benefits of educational achievement to career opportunities.	Understanding the relationship between educational achievement and career planning.	Skills to enter and participate in education and training.
	Awareness of the relationship between work and learning.	Understanding the relationship between work and learning.	Understanding the need for positive attitudes toward work and learning.	Skills to participate in work and life-long learning.
	Skills to understand, and use career information.	Skills to locate, understand, and use career information.	Skills to locate, evaluate, and interpret career information.	Skills to locate, evaluate, and interpret career information.
	Awareness of the importance of personal responsibility and good work habits.	Knowledge of skills necessary to seek and obtain jobs.	Skills to prepare to seek, obtain, maintain, and change jobs.	Skills to prepare to seek, obtain, maintain, and change jobs.
	Awareness of how work relates to the needs and functions of society.	Understanding how work relates to the needs and functions of the economy and society.	Understanding how societal needs and functions influence the nature and structure of work.	Understanding how the needs and functions of society influence the nature and structure of work.
Career Planning				
	Understanding how to make decisions.	Skills to make decisions.	Skills to make decisions.	Skills to make decisions.
	Awareness of the interrelationship of life roles.	Knowledge of the interrelationship of life roles.	Understanding the interrelationship of life roles.	Understanding the impact of work on individual and family life.
	Awareness of different occupations and changing male/female roles.	Knowledge of different occupations and changing male/female roles.	Understanding the continuous changes in male/female roles.	Understanding the continuing changes in male/female roles.
	Awareness of the career planning process.	Understanding the process of career planning.	Skills in career planning.	Skills to make career transitions.

NOIC

National Occupational Information Coordinating Committee • Suite 156, 2100 M Street, N.W., Washington, D.C. 20037 • (202) 653-5665

Figure 1.4

To master these competencies, a variety of self-awareness activities are completed. The next step is to relate self-knowledge to the many available careers.

According to Meyer (1988), the glut of information prohibits us from stopping once we locate the information. Information only has meaning if it is evaluated in light of what individuals know about themselves. Ensuring that it is collected in a manner that best serves the individual is the critical step. First, it is important for those seeking career information to sort out the relevant from the irrelevant. Second, as facilitators, we need to monitor the process of collection. Third, the information needs to be processed as it is collected so it becomes part of the decision about to be made. Fourth, the results of this processing need to be understood and integrated by the individual.

To illustrate, a student may be considering a career as a tobacco grower. The student wants to know what the job will entail. What will I do on the job? What will my income be? What kind of training do I need? The ICDM training program will teach you about available resources that contain answers to many of these questions.

Sample Questions to Ask of Information:

1. How will consumer behavior affect opportunities?

2. What public policies will impinge on this career?

3. How many workers are already in this field?

4. How many new workers will be needed in the future?

5. Where would I have to live to work in this occupation?

6. What will my work environment be like?

7. How will technology change the industry?

Figure 1.5

What Is Career and Labor Market Information?

It is information about jobs, workers, the work place and the preparation needed to work. It is readily available to the public through career information delivery systems (CIDS), printed materials, computer-based systems, videotapes, microfiche, current periodicals, newspapers and books.

A Changing Work Place

It is important for career development facilitators not only to understand the information about occupations but also to have knowledge about the broader issues that result in fluctuations in our social, political and economic systems, as well as changes in the occupational structures. For example, the composition of today's labor market has continued to change as the population shifts and our economy changes.

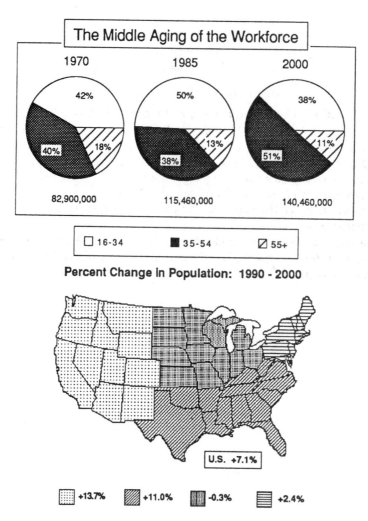

Figure 1.6

Another way to illustrate the importance of decision making is by examining our national priority for informed and skilled workers. They need basic skills, career education, and an understanding of the changing world of work.

Conclusion

The wealth of information may seem intimidating and the process for incorporating this information into career decision making may seem overwhelming. This inservice program, *Improved Career Decision Making in a Changing World*, will help you understand where to find information, how to make effective use of information and how to continually update your skills and knowledge through readily available resources.

Brown, D., & Brooks, L. (1991). *Career counseling techniques.* Boston: Allyn and Bacon.

Johnston, W. B., & Packer, A. H. (1987). *Workforce 2000: Work and workers for the 21st century.* Indianapolis: The Hudson Institute.

Meyer, H. E. (1988, May 15). Real-World Intelligence. *American way,* 54-65.

National Career Development Association (1990). *National survey of working America.* Washington DC: National Occupational Information Coordinating Committee.

Peterson, G. W., Sampson, J. P., & Reardon, R. C. (1991). *Career development and services.* Pacific Grove, CA: Brooks/Cole.

U.S. Department of Labor, U.S. Department of Education, and U.S. Department of Commerce (1988, July). *Building a quality workforce.* Washington DC: Office of Public Affairs, Employment and Training Administration, U.S. Department of Labor.

Notes

The Action Plan

National Career Development Guidelines-Counselor Competencies

Skills to use career development resources and techniques designed for specific groups.

Skills to implement individual and group programs in a variety of areas such as assessment, decision making, job seeking, career information and career counseling.

Skills to assist individuals in setting goals and identifying strategies for reaching goals.

The Action Plan

Nothing is more terrible than activity without insight."
Thomas Carlyle, 1795-81.

Change: A Personal Challenge

Most of us have heard the familiar saying, "There are people who make things happen, people who watch things happen, and people who wonder what happened." From personal experience, we admire people who "make things happen." Through our own efforts, however, we realize how hard it is to take action and make changes in our lives. We recognize what it takes to accomplish our goals--motivation, hard work, determination, tenacity, support from others, and sometimes, just plain luck.

Despite the personal sacrifices that may be required, many of us do want to change or improve certain aspects of our personal lives or work situations. We are motivated to make changes when we are exposed to new concepts and ideas that can improve or enrich our lives. As a result of these influences, we are charged with a mental and physical energy to change our behavior in some way--to quit smoking, to lose weight, to take a course in speed reading, or to develop a new program to better meet the needs of our students. Unfortunately, our motivation to act often withers, wanes and gradually subsides, due to factors such as the time needed to achieve change, the people who may be standing in the way, the money to implement our plans, the personal discipline that is necessary, or simply the pressures of daily life.

Needed: A Road Map

What is often missing is a "road map" to reach our destination. By studying persons who have achieved, psychologists have discovered that they have two common characteristics:

1. they set goals for themselves; and
2. they write them down.

In other words, they have **plans of action**, which serve as detailed road maps to their goals. The purpose of this section is to help you develop your own road maps, or Action Plans, of professional growth as a career development facilitator.

Some Barriers To Change

What prevents us from applying what we have learned? There are three distinct types of barriers that prevent the transfer of skills from an inservice program to the work site:

- **The participant.** Because of personal standards and ideas about how career facilitating should be accomplished, the participant may reject the values and concepts in the training course. Or, the participant may lack the confidence to use or apply the new skills developed during the training.
- **The participant's supervisor.** The supervisor may not encourage the participant to use the new skills or may not support the participant who applies what has been learned.
- **The organization.** The participant's new skills may not be accepted in the work environment due to time constraints, pay structures, incompatible office policies and procedures, or the lack of authority to act.

Overcoming Barriers: A Training Approach

To prevent these barriers from occurring, a comprehensive plan of action should be initiated before the training begins. We suggest the following approach:

Step 1.
The participant and supervisor develop mutual training objectives.

Your supervisor can work cooperatively with you by communicating his/her needs. The supervisor who has a voice in defining the skills that are needed will take a greater interest in the outcome of the training.

An example of a mutual objective might be:

To develop stronger ties between the school and the business community in order to place more students in work experience or internship programs.

Step 2.
Participant lists pre-training objectives.

Your first task in the training session is to outline what you wish to gain from the inservice. This enables the trainer to better meet your needs. Your objectives will be translated into an Action Plan at the conclusion of the training session. This Action Plan will contain activities and tasks to be completed back at your work site. A form for this purpose, "Program Hopes and Personal Change," is included in your guide.

An example of a participant objective might be:

To become skilled in how to access local labor market information to better advise students who wish to work in the community.

Step 3.
The training instills confidence in the participant.

In order to instill confidence, most modules will incorporate hands-on, work-related activities to develop your skills in the use of labor market information. A written form, the "Daily Planner" can be found in the guide. *It is important that you take at least five minutes to fill in the "Daily Planner" at the conclusion of each training module.*

An example of a practical training activity might be:

Role playing a career counseling session during which the counselor is showing the client how to scan and evaluate the help wanted ads in a newspaper to gain a broader understanding of the local labor market.

Step 4.
The training enables the participant to develop a supportive network.

Your work site may need to be modified in order to accomplish training goals. These modifications become components of your Action Plan.

An example of a training activity to enable the participant to develop a peer network would be:

A brainstorming session on how to develop ties between the school and the business community that results in the formation of interest or support groups among the participants that would continue beyond the training session.

Step 5.
An Action Plan is completed at the conclusion of training.

Your concluding activity will be the formulation of your plan of action. A two page worksheet, "My Action Plan," will help you create a specific outline with details, such as the resources needed and time frames required. When writing the plan, it is important that you consider the factors that will enable you to reach the Action Plan goals, as well as the obstacles that must be overcome. By doing so, you can develop realistic strategies to reach your objectives.

After the Action Plan has been completed, you will have time to discuss the plan with fellow trainees. Research has shown that group discussion is very valuable; the "talking it over" process creates a bond between you and your plan of action.

As a result of this training in Improved Career Decision Making (ICDM), you will be better informed about how the labor market works. You will develop skills in maintaining up-to-date information about its fluctuations and changes. You can utilize these skills by integrating information resources into your career counseling. It is critical that the skills developed during your training be transferred to the work place. By applying what you have learned, you can help your clients make the best possible career choices.

Your Action Plan is the culmination of the training session. Once you have achieved your training objectives, an Action Plan needs to be developed as a mechanism to assist you in making the important transfer of skills from the training session to your work environment.

It's Easy!

The creation of an Action Plan should not be intimidating, because the framework for your plan already exists. You have been formulating your plans from the very beginning of your training when you listed your hopes for the program and possibilities for change on "Program Hopes and Personal Change." During training, you have gradually added pieces to your plan. A review of your notes from each training module will reveal this information on your "Daily Planner." Your final Action Plan will combine:

- your original objectives as stated in "Program Hopes and Personal Change,"
- the actions listed in the last column of your module notes from your "Daily Planner," and
- any additional goals you wish to set for yourself and your organization.

A systematic approach to writing your plan is outlined on "My Action Plan." Once formulated, the Action Plan becomes a self-pledge; it is a commitment to engage in new behaviors as individuals and organizations as a result of the training.

The plan itself should be simple, realistic, and measurable. The plan defines what you want to do, how and when you will do it, what help you will need, and how you will measure what you have accomplished. An example can be found on the following pages.

Example Of An Action Plan

As a result of my training I plan to:

- set up a resource center called "Jobs in River City," with information on local employment opportunities;
- become active in the Chamber of Commerce in order to establish ties with community businesspersons; and
- work with other facilitators to establish a work study partnership between my organization or school and a local business or industry.

To illustrate the complete Action Plan process that is outlined on the participant's worksheet, we will use the first goal, **setting up a resource center on local employment opportunities**, as an example. Some of the services this center might provide would be:

- a Career Information Delivery System (CIDS) for career exploration and information;
- Federal, state, and local labor market information publications, such as the *Dictionary of Occupational Titles* (DOT), *Standard Occupational Classification* (SOC), *Occupational Outlook Handbook* (OOH), *Occupational Outlook Quarterly* (OOQ), *Standard Industrial Classification* (SIC), local newsletters, etc.;
- a list of the major employers in the community, with descriptions of their businesses or industries and the principal occupations found within them;
- telephone numbers of personal contacts that may be helpful, e.g., job telephone lines, human resource departments of governmental agencies and large employers, Job Service and JTPA contacts, private employment agencies, etc.;
- a chart showing the major occupational classifications within the local labor market, with information on qualifications, wages, hours and conditions of employment;
- cost of living information for River City: food, utilities, housing, etc.;
- information on tax deductions taken from paychecks, employee benefits and legal rights;
- a map showing where major employers are located, along with local public transportation services and schedules;
- video/audio tapes of local employers describing the qualifications they are seeking in prospective employees;

- a listing of postsecondary educational and training institutions, with catalogs of their offerings;
- a job bulletin board taken from the listings in the local newspaper or Job Service Office;
- a file of job postings from public institutions and any other large employers within the city;
- instructions for resume and cover letter writing; files of sample resumes and introduction letters;
- samples of common job application forms used by major employers in the area with instructions to follow; and
- a sign-up sheet for personal counseling services.

With this goal in mind, a Jobs in River City Resource Center, "My Action Plan" could be outlined in the following way on the worksheet:

I. Defining my concern

A. I have carefully reviewed my professional environment; the area that I would like to see improved relates to the lack of information our students have about job opportunities in River City.

B. I am concerned about this situation because:

1. many of our students wish to remain in River City and will be seeking work in this area;
2. national and state labor market information does not always apply to conditions in River City; and
3. our students lack job search skills.

C. The major facts that relate to this situation are:

1. sixty percent of our high school graduates remain in River City;
2. fifty percent have completed their education; they will not go on to a postsecondary program; they will be looking for work in River City;
3. students need information about where they can find work and how to get it;
4. "Education for Employment" is a goal of our school district; and
5. my principal supports school-wide efforts to educate for employment.

II. Seeking a solution

A. The elements of my situation most amenable to change are:

1. having the cooperation of most teachers and the school administration in setting up a Jobs Resource Center;
2. learning about the labor market in River City, thereby improving my career counseling skills; and
3. the frustration expressed by students looking for work; they have a need for a Jobs Resource Center.

B. The elements of my situation least amenable to change are:

1. the limited availability of time to set up the Center: finding materials, interviewing employers, developing handouts, etc.;
2. finding money in our budget to purchase some of the publications and computer software that would enhance the Resource Center;
3. convincing all staff members to support and contribute to the Resource Center; and
4. assuring that all students have access to the Resource Center.

C. I would use these indicators to consider my concerns to be satisfactorily resolved:

1. the completion of a Resource Center within three months;
2. the Resource Center will be used by at least 60% of the student body before the end of the school year as determined by a record keeping procedure;
3. students, staff members and administrators who use the Center will complete written evaluations of its effectiveness; and
4. the Center will establish working relationships with private and public employment agencies, such Job Service and JTPA;
5. the evaluations of the Center will be used to improve its future content and operation.

D. The forces that I see as unfavorable to (or blocking) the hoped-for change are:

1. coworkers who may not approve of the time that I will be spending to set up the Center;
2. teachers who may be unwilling to allow their students class time to use the Jobs Resource Center;

3. local businesses and industries that may be uncooperative; and
4. a lack of student awareness as to how the Center can help them.

E. The forces I see as favoring (supporting) the change are:

1. students looking for work;
2. the school district administration;
3. the library director;
4. special education teachers;
5. parents; and
6. local employers who envision the value of the Center.

F. The solution I see to my concern is:

1. to work closely with those persons who will support my efforts to establish the Center;
2. to communicate frequently with persons who may oppose or resent my efforts in order to address their concerns and enlist their support and cooperation;
3. to involve local business people in the planning of the Center; and
4. to ask my principal to appoint an ad hoc advisory committee composed of teachers, parents and local business people to assist in the planning and development of the Center.

III. An Action Plan to implement my solution

A. I see the time frame for the plan to be operative as follows:

1. Center established in three months;
2. student, staff and administrative evaluations of the Center in nine months; and
3. Center revisions in twelve months.

B. I will need the assistance of these individuals to implement my plan:

Name: Principal Sam Martinez
About: Administrative and financial support of the Center

Name: Library Director Helen Han
About: Help in finding information resources

Name:	Chamber of Commerce President Sue Young
About:	Getting cooperation from local businesses

Name:	English teacher Michael Feldman
About:	Sample resumes, cover letters and job applications

C. I will need to communicate the plan to:

Name:	Staff members, administrators and students
About:	Purpose/design/time frame for the Center

Name:	Local employers
About:	The purpose of the Center; their employment needs

Name:	Parents of students
About:	How the Center can help their child

Name:	Members of my own department
About:	Duties, responsibilities, time frames, etc.

D. I intend to follow up and evaluate the success of my plan by doing the following:

1. reviewing, tabulating and analyzing the evaluations of the Jobs Resource Center completed by the students, staff and administration by the end of the school year;
2. using the findings from the evaluations to set goals to improve the Center during the following school year; and
3. communicating these future plans to students, staff and administration.

Conclusion

As you can see by this example, your Action Plan can be a powerful instrument of change. Your plan outlines your goals and develops strategies to achieve, monitor and refine them. It is truly amazing what people can accomplish by simply setting realistic goals and writing them down.

Program Hopes and Personal Change

1. My hopes and expectations for this training are. . .

2. If my supervisors could have a goal for this training, they would want me to. . .

3. If my peers or associates could have a goal for this training, they would want me to. .

4. If the individuals that I supervise could have a goal for this training, they would want me to. . .

Adapted from *The Winning Trainer*, J.E. Eitington, Gulf Publishing Co., Houston, TX, 1990

ICDM   Action Plan-11

Second Component of Action Plan for _____
name

Directions: Notes should be taken by the participant on this worksheet at the end of each training session (allow 5 minutes). When the training is concluded this Planner is used to create the Action Plan.

Daily Planner

	Key Points of Module	Key Points Related to My Needs	Action I Intend to Take
Module 1			
Module 2			
Module 3			
Module 4			
Module 5			
Module 6			
Module 7			
Module 8			
Module 9			
Module 10			

Adapted from *The Winning Trainer*, J.E. Eitington, Gulf Publishing Co., Houston, TX, 1990.

Developing an Action Plan

I. Purpose

The final phase of this program is designed to give you an opportunity to apply the concepts and skills that you have learned to an actual on-the-job concern of your choice. This should provide real and lasting meaning to your training experience. It will also provide you with a maximum return from your investment of time and effort in the training session.

II. Procedure

A. Select a topic about which you have a genuine concern; that is, an area that requires some worthwhile improvement or remedial action. The concern may relate to management, an operational matter, an administrative change, a plan for self-improvement, an improvement in relations with others (supervisors, coworkers), etc. It may involve overcoming a deficiency or meeting a new challenge or opportunity. You alone know where a real need for change or betterment exists.

B. Individual work (20 minutes): Use the three-part *Action Plan Worksheet* to help you work through the details of your problem-solving activity.

C. Small group work (30 minutes): You will be assigned to a team of three (two other participants who share your concerns and yourself). Each of you will have the opportunity to present your concern and plan for action to the other two members for review, critique, feedback, and counsel. Each presenter will have ten minutes to secure help from the other two participants. Although this is your concern, objective "outsiders" can be of real help, because they may see things you might have overlooked. Feedback from your teammates will sharpen the issues for you and help you think through the steps outlined in your action plan.

Adapted from *The Winning Trainer*, J.E. Eitington, Gulf Publishing Co., Houston, TX, 1990

My Action Plan

I. Defining my concerns

1. I have carefully reviewed my "back-home" situation, and the area I would like to see improved relates to. . .

2. I am concerned about this situation because. . .

3. The major facts that relate to this situation are. . .

II. Seeking a solution

1. The elements of my situation most amenable to change are. . .

2. The elements of my situation least amenable to change are. . .

3. I would use these indicators to consider my concerns to be satisfactorily resolved.

4. The forces that I see as unfavorable to (blocking) the hoped-for change are. . .

5. The solutions I see to my concerns are. . .

6. The major facts that relate to my concern are. . .

Adapted from *The Winning Trainer*, J.E. Eitington, Gulf Publishing Co., Houston, TX, 1990

My Action Plan cont.

III. An action plan to implement my solution

1. I see the time frame for my plan to be operative as follows:

2. I will need the assistance of these individuals to implement my plan:

   Name: _____ about:_____

   Name: _____ about:_____

   Name: _____ about:_____

   Name: _____ about:_____

3. I will need to communicate the plan to:

   Name: _____ about:_____

   Name: _____ about:_____

   Name: _____ about:_____

   Name: _____ about:_____

4. I intend to follow up and evaluate the success of my plan by doing the following:

   Action taken: _____ Date: _____

   Action taken: _____ Date: _____

   Action taken: _____ Date: _____

   Action taken: _____ Date: _____

Adapted from *The Winning Trainer*, J.E. Eitington, Gulf Publishing Co., Houston, TX, 1990

My Action Plan cont.

III. An action plan to implement my solution

1. I see the time frame for my plan to be operative as follows:

2. I will need the assistance of these individuals to implement my plan:

   Name: _____ about:_____

   Name: _____ about:_____

   Name: _____ about:_____

   Name: _____ about:_____

3. I will need to communicate the plan to:

   Name: _____ about:_____

   Name: _____ about:_____

   Name: _____ about:_____

   Name: _____ about:_____

4. I intend to follow up and evaluate the success of my plan by doing the following:

   Action taken: _____ Date: _____

   Action taken: _____ Date: _____

   Action taken: _____ Date: _____

   Action taken: _____ Date: _____

Adapted from *The Winning Trainer*, J.E. Eitington, Gulf Publishing Co., Houston, TX, 1990

Notes

Module 2

Definitions of Terms and Concepts Related to Career Development and Labor Market Information

National Career Development Guidelines-Counselor Competencies

Knowledge of education, training, employment trends, labor market, and career resources.

Knowledge of employment information and career planning materials.

Definitions of Terms and Concepts
Related to Career Development and
Labor Market Information
Module 2

Terms and Concepts Related to Career Development

Career
Career is a life style concept that involves a sequence of work or leisure activities in which one engages throughout a lifetime. Careers are unique to each person and are dynamic, unfolding throughout life. They include not only occupations but pre-vocational and postvocational concerns as well as how persons integrate their work life with their other life roles. (Herr and Cramer, 1984)

Job
A group of similar, paid positions requiring some similar attributes in a single organization. (Super, 1976)

Work
Conscious effort, other than that having as its primary purpose either coping or relaxation, aimed at producing benefits for oneself and/or oneself and others. (Hoyt, 1991)

Occupation
A group of similar jobs found in different industries or organizations. (Herr and Cramer, 1984)

Skill
An attribute required of the worker in order to complete a work task. (Jepsen, 1991)

Task
An element of work to be completed. (Jepsen, 1991)

Career Development
The total constellation of psychological, sociological, educational, physical, economic, and chance factors that combine to shape the career of any given individual. (Splete, 1978)

Career Decision Making

The following steps constitute the decision making process:

- determine the concern to be acted upon,
- project possible alternative actions,
- review possible consequences of each alternative action,
- choose the best alternative at this time,
- decide how and when to implement the alternative,
- implement it,
- evaluate the results of the action, and
- determine whether a related decision needs to be made now or if further planning is needed.
    (Splete, 1978)

Career Guidance

A systematic program of coordinated information and experiences designed to facilitate individual career development and, more specifically, career management. (Herr and Cramer, 1984)

Career Education

The totality of experiences by which persons acquire knowledge and attitudes about self and work, and the skills by which to identify, choose, plan and prepare for work and other life options. (Herr and Cramer, 1984)

Developmental Guidance

Developmental Guidance is based on the premise that as children and adults mature, they pass through various developmental stages vital to their growth. Programs that systematically address the learning, personal/social, and career development needs of all individuals are the basis for this preventative approach to counseling and guidance. (Wilson, 1986)

National Career Development Guidelines

The National Career Development Guidelines are based on developmental guidance concepts and as a result are preventative, goal oriented and proactive in nature. (NOICC, 1989)

They reflect the national movement to improve career guidance and counseling programs throughout the life span and to support standard-setting efforts which:

- increase the understanding of lifelong career development needs, based on the conceptual framework of developmental guidance,
- expand the definitions of comprehensive career guidance and counseling programs,
- emphasize competency-based education and training,
- support program accountability efforts,
- heighten interest in achieving professional consensus on program guidelines and standards,
- renew legislative support for career guidance and counseling programs, and
- increase emphasis on certification of counselors, including career specialization.

(See Figures 1.2 and 1.3 for a listing of the Guidelines.)

Major components addressed in the Guidelines include:

- **Student Competencies and Indicators.** Guidelines for the outcomes of career guidance and counseling programs are the basis for program development. The competencies are stated as broad goals. The indicators describe specific attitudes, knowledge and skills related to career development. They are divided into five sequential levels: elementary, middle or junior high school, high school, young adult and adult. They are organized into three broad areas: self-knowledge, educational and occupational exploration, and career planning.
- **Institutional Capabilities.** This section provides a statement of the necessary commitment, structure, and support required for effective career guidance and counseling programs including administrative commitments, physical facilities, and supportive materials.
- **Personnel Requirements and Counselor Competencies.** This section provides a description of the roles of various staff members as well as specific competencies needed by counselors to deliver career guidance and counseling programs.

A basic understanding of the key concepts, vocabulary and measures of labor market information is essential to its effective use.

For those engaged in education, counseling, job development and job placement, an understanding of how to use labor market information effectively in career decision making is critical. Although one might not want, or necessarily need, technical knowledge of numbers and statistics, knowing the terms and concepts will help explain information found in the lay press or in technical reports.

What Is a Labor Market?

Labor markets bring together buyers and sellers seeking to exchange one thing of value for another. Sellers are individuals seeking work, and buyers are employers offering wages and other benefits in exchange for work. Through the operation of the market, employers obtain the labor needed to transform raw materials into goods and services, and workers earn an income to support themselves and others.

Labor markets are dynamic and constantly changing. They tend to be more complicated than other kinds of markets. There are many interacting variables that influence supply and demand in a labor market. The commodity being sold, the labor supply, is controlled by human beings with individual values and abilities who are free to make choices about education, training, occupation and geographical location. Moreover, workers can even choose to work for themselves and become their own employers.

What Is Labor Market Information?

Labor market information (LMI) is systematized data, produced on a regular basis, about employment, unemployment, jobs and workers. It includes information about people, jobs and employers.

Although many people may think of LMI as only basic employment and unemployment statistics, labor market information is, in fact, a wide array of employment related data on economic conditions and labor force characteristics, such as population, education, income, occupational descriptions and employment conditions.

Who Uses Labor Market Information?

The interpretation of labor market information contributes to the development of public policies and programs. Educators and students need data on occupational outlooks to make sound decisions about programs of study and careers. Young people need information about occupational descriptions, educational requirements, wages, and the employment outlook to make choices about careers and training. Managers of job training and retraining programs need labor market information to identify those most in need of training programs, to develop new curricula for vocational training, to design and implement appropriate programs and to place graduates in jobs. Employers use labor market information to set wages, design working conditions and evaluate alternative business opportunities.

Who Collects Labor Market Information?

The federal government is responsible for developing, maintaining and reporting labor market information and information about the nation's economy. The states collect this raw data for the federal government.

Several federal agencies are involved in the collection effort. They play a major role in data development by specifying a common methodology for data collection, processing and reporting that results in standard data available for each state. The major agencies are:

- The **U.S. Bureau of Labor Statistics (BLS)** collects and issues statistics on labor market conditions and social trends that affect the demand for labor. BLS is responsible for the methodology and procedures used by state agencies to collect data on the labor force.
- The **U.S. Bureau of the Census** collects a wide range of demographic, social and economic data. The Census also collects national, state and local data to describe the size, characteristics and status of the labor force.
- The **U.S. Office of Educational Research** collects and disseminates information about educational institutions, levels of enrollment, basic literacy skills attainment and information about school leavers.
- The **U.S. Office of Vocational and Adult Education (OVAE)** sets standards for spending federal vocational education funds. The planning requirements issued by the OVAE have a significant impact on the kinds of occupational information needed for vocational planning.

LABOR FORCE CONCEPTS

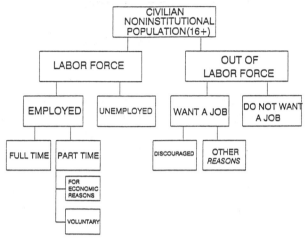

Figure 2.1

Civilian Noninstitutional Population
This group consists of all persons 16 years of age and older who are not members of the resident armed forces and who do not reside in institutions, such as nursing homes, prisons or mental hospitals. This is the group from which potential workers are available.

Civilian Labor Force and Labor Force Participation Rate
The group consist of the total number of civilians who are employed and unemployed. It does not include those persons employed by the armed forces. The proportion of the total civilian noninstitutional population, or of a demographic subgroup of that population classified as "in the labor force," is known as the **labor force participation rate**.

Employed
The BLS definition for employed are those people who:

- worked for pay or profit at any time during the payroll period which included the 12th day of the month;
- held jobs, but were temporarily absent from them for such reasons as a vacation, weather, personal illness or an industrial dispute; or
- worked without pay in a family-owned business for 15 or more hours.

The number of employed are estimated monthly through the Current Population Survey. The employed group includes three sub-groups of workers, wage and salary workers, self-employed workers and unpaid family workers.

- Wage and salary workers - People who work for wages, salaries, commissions, tips or pay in kind from a private employer, a non-profit employer or a governmental unit. Nonfarm wage and salary workers make up the major portion of this category.
- Self-employed workers - People who work for profit or fees in their own business, profession or trade, or who operate a farm.
- Unpaid family worker - Persons who work without pay for at least 15 hours a week on a farm or in a business operated by a household member who is related by birth or marriage.

Full-Time Employed
These are people who are employed 35 hours or more per week.

Part-Time Employed
These are people who are employed less than 35 hour a week. Part-time workers are further broken down into two groups: those who are part-time by choice, and those who are part time for economic reasons. The economic reasons include slack work, material shortages and the inability to find a full-time job. Some of these people are referred to as the "underemployed".

Unemployed
This group is defined by BLS as those persons who meet the following criteria:

- performed no work at all for pay or profit in the week of the 12th of the month;
- looked for a job at some point in the past four weeks; and
- were available for work in the survey week.

These people represent an unutilized but available labor supply.

Out of the Labor Force
This is a residual category of persons who are neither employed nor unemployed. These include people who are enrolled in school, those with family care responsibilities, persons with disabilities and those who are retired. Many of these people may move into and out of the labor force as economic or personal conditions warrant.

Want a Job

These tend to be the people who want a job, but who are not actively looking because they perceive there are no jobs available, or believe they are not skilled. They are sometimes thought of as "discouraged." This category may also include persons who want a job, but are not highly marketable, such as those lacking skills or who are differently abled.

Hidden Unemployment

These are discouraged workers, who for a variety of reasons think they cannot find work and sooner or later cease looking. Example: Unskilled workers in the ghettos of many large cities who, lacking education and/or transportation, often cannot find jobs and become resigned to life on the streets or on welfare.

Underemployment

This occurs when a worker is either overqualified for a job or works fewer hours than desired. Example: A college graduate in microbiology who can find no work in his/her field and ends up as a clerk in a department store.

Do Not Want a Job

These are people who have other responsibilities, such as schooling or caring for family members, as well as those persons who have already retired.

Frictional Unemployment, usually for a short duration, is caused when people are between jobs. Example: A waitress who quits a job to look for a position that offers better wages.

Structural Unemployment arises when there is a job skill mismatch such that the skills workers possess are not those that employers require. Example: A football player who has been released and who has no other job skills on which to rely.

Seasonal Unemployment is created when jobs are available for only a portion of the year. Example: Migrant workers who "follow the harvest" of various crops, but who have little chance of working in the colder months.

Cyclical Unemployment is caused by boom and bust cycles in the economy. Example: Oil field workers who enjoy plentiful and lucrative work when the price of oil is up and suffer economic setbacks as the price drops.

Unemployment Rate represents the number of unemployed as a percent of the labor force. The seasonally adjusted unemployment rate eliminates the influence of regularly recurring seasonal fluctuations which can be ascribed to weather, crop-growing cycles, holidays, vacations, regular industry model changeover periods, and the like, and therefore, more clearly shows the underlying basic trend of unemployment.

What Are Industries?

Industries are groups of firms that produce similar goods and services. Our economy has two basic kinds of industries: those that produce goods and those that provide services.

Industrial Sectors

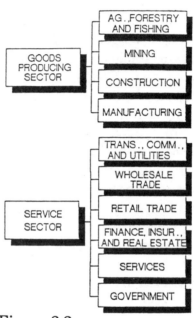

Figure 2.2

The **goods producing industries** supply everything from gasoline to drill presses to lamb chops. These industries employ less than one-third of U.S. workers. Major goods producing industries include:

- **Agriculture** (farming, food and fiber processing, and manufacturing of farm tools and fertilizers, to name a few elements of a basic industry)
- **Mining** (industries producing most of the basic raw materials and energy sources that industries and consumers use, including coal mining, metal mining, and oil exploration and processing)
- **Contract construction** (industries that build, alter, and repair

roads, bridges and structures, such as factories)
- **Manufacturing** (industries that manufacture goods ranging from miniature computer circuits to textiles to spacecrafts)

The **service industries** either provide services such as medical care or haircuts, or maintain and distribute the goods listed above. More than two-thirds of U.S. workers are employed in these major industrial groups. They include:

- **Transportation, communication and public utilities** (industries grouped together because they provide a public service. They are regulated and sometimes owned by public agencies, such as telephone companies, power companies, airlines, and truckers)
- **Trade** (industries involved in the distribution and sale of goods from producers to consumers, such as restaurants, wholesale textile dealers, and department stores. There are two divisions, one called wholesale trade and another called retail trade.)
- **Finance, insurance and real estate** (industries that provide financial services, protection, and property to businesses and consumers; among those in this group are banks, consumer credit agencies, insurance companies, and real estate brokers.)
- **Services** (industries engaged in providing a personal service to consumers, such as private hospitals, private schools, hotels, and the Girl Scouts)
- **Government** (national, state and local agencies including public schools, the postal service, police and fire protection, the Army)

There are several groups of industries in each division. For instance, under "services" one would find business services, legal services, educational services, health services, etc. Health services includes hospitals, offices of dentists, medical and dental laboratories, outpatient care facilities, nursing and personal care facilities. it is important to understand this type of industry breakdown because it provides a useful means for analyzing labor force activity.

Industries, like people, are highly dependent on each other. For instance, the trade industry depends upon the manufacturing industry to provide the goods it sells, and manufacturing depends upon the finance, insurance and real estate industries for the loans needed to buy goods and to expand. The manufacturing sector also depends on the finance industry for insurance and for the land and buildings needed for warehouses and stores. In turn, the trade industry relies upon public utilities industries for transportation, electricity, telephones, and so on.

Industry Definitions According to the Standard Industrial Classification (SIC)

In an economic context, industries are groups of firms that produce essentially the same goods or services. The **Standard Industrial Classification (SIC)** system of the U.S. Office of Management and Budget provides definitions and coding of industries based on their products or services. Narrower definitions of products or services are used to distinguish industries from one another at finer levels of detail. The SIC system is based on an ordering of products and services, arranged at increasingly greater levels of detail.

What Is an Occupation?

An **occupation** is a group of similar jobs found in different industries or organizations. With hundreds of thousands of meaningful differences existing in the overall marketplace, it is important to be able to recognize major categories of occupations when performing human resources planning, vocational counseling and economic development activities.

Data on occupational employment are needed to generate insights into the types of jobs held by workers, the characteristics of the job duties performed, and the skills and abilities required to function within the job in an acceptable manner.

Not only do jobs differ in their skill requirements, but all jobs are not available to all potential workers. Arising from attempts to restrict the entry of unqualified workers or other potential competitors, job qualification barriers reinforce the skill distinctions that exist naturally. Such barriers may include certification or registration guidelines, occupational licensing and apprenticeship requirements.

Occupational Shifts

Occupations undergo change. There are at least three designations to describe this change process.

1. A **new** occupation is an occupation in which major tasks, skills and duties are not included in any currently existing occupation, or in which tasks are combined in significantly different ways that preclude workers from other occupations performing the work without training beyond a short demonstration.
2. A **changing** occupation is an existing occupation that has

experienced change in duties, skills or tasks significant enough to require training beyond a short demonstration, but not significant enough to classify into another occupation, or to create a new occupation.

3. An **emerging** occupation is an occupation (defined by a reasonably well accepted descriptive phrase) that is growing rapidly from a small base either within an economy as a whole, or within a particular industry, and has significant education or training implications.

Occupational Definitions and Coding Systems

Occupational definitions and coding systems were developed for the purpose of assembling and simplifying detailed data on the skill and performance requirements of jobs. There are many ways to classify occupations. Each is designed for a different audience to meet a different need. Each system is based on functional differences in the work done and the work settings where work is performed.

The *Dictionary of Occupational Titles* (DOT) is probably the most familiar occupational classification system and contains the greatest level of detail. The DOT was first developed in the 1930s. It provides concise descriptions of job tasks for over 17,000 separate occupational titles. The system tries to describe jobs based on the nature and content of the specific tasks a worker needs to perform. Formal education and training requirements for individual occupations are also described.

The *Standard Occupational Classification* (SOC) system was developed by the U.S. Department of Commerce. The SOC provides a mechanism for cross-referencing and aggregating occupation-related data collected by social and economic statistical reporting programs. The system covers all occupations in which work is performed for pay or profit, including work performed by unpaid family workers. Occupations unique to volunteer settings are not included. The SOC is hierarchically structured on four levels: division, major group, minor group and unit group. Subsequent levels represent finer levels of detail. Residual categories are included where needed to handle groups of occupations that do not warrant separate identification or do not fit into one of the specific groups.

A third occupational classification system developed by the Bureau of Labor Statistics is the **Occupational Employment Statistics (OES)** system used in the OES survey. This schema is closely related to the SOC and is used to collect occupational staffing patterns from employers and to develop occupational projections. The OES contains over 750 job titles and definitions that specify job tasks and functions for individual occupations, sometimes on an industry specific basis. The OES system combined with benchmarked industry employment data, is capable of identifying and measuring the level of employment for specific categories of workers engaged in similar job tasks.

The OES helps to develop an accurate profile of occupational employment by industry, to provide basic data for projecting future occupational requirements, and to identify new and emerging occupations and declining occupations.

The OES survey is a mail survey which includes a sample of nonfarm establishments reporting to the state's Unemployment Insurance program. The survey collects data on both full- and part-time employees. The survey cycle covers a three-year period. Manufacturing industries are surveyed in one year, selected nonmanufacturing industries another year, and the balance the next year.

The primary source of occupational employment information is the OES/Matrix program generated with state and national data (Micro-Matrix). This program is designed to provide very detailed information on the occupational employment outlook for use in career guidance and planning employment and training programs. Outputs from the Matrix program show base year employment, projected employment in the target year, and the estimated number of average annual job openings. Job openings consist of new jobs expected to be created by growth--or job loss due to projected employment declines--plus openings likely to be created by mortality and labor force withdrawal. Matrices may be available statewide and for selected LMAs.

The projections are a key element in assessing the employment potential of different occupations and making an informed judgment on which training programs to provide. The projections show which occupations are expected to grow most rapidly and which are trailing or declining. The projections also provide estimates of the number of job openings likely to be created in each occupation. The number of future job openings is a function of the size of the occupation and the demographic and age structure of the workers in the occupation, in addition to projected economic growth.

In evaluating employment prospects, it is important to consider the level of job openings, as well as the growth rate of the occupation.

Sometimes, there is a preoccupation with growth in ranking occupations for training. This can be misleading since some slower-growth occupations may be generating a large number of job openings, or, alternatively, only a small number of workers may be employed in high-growth occupations. (For a fuller discussion of the projections, see Module 5.)

The survey questionnaire includes a list of occupations appropriate to each industry in the survey. Each surveyed employer is asked to give information about the number of full- and part-time employees for each occupation represented within the establishment. Employers are asked to list any occupations that do not fit under the titles provided in the questionnaire. Larger employers are asked to include information about new occupations in their firms that require substantial training or are emerging due to technological changes in the industry. This information provides valuable data for improving future occupational lists and for identifying occupations that are changing in nature or are new altogether. Currently, occupational employment estimates by industry are developed for approximately 750 occupations.

A fourth system for classifying occupations is used by the Bureau of the Census. This system over time has come to look much like the *Standard Occupational Classification.*

Definitions of Terms and Concepts Related to Career Development and Labor Market Information
Module 2
References

Herr, E. L., & Cramer, S. H. (1984). *Career guidance and counseling through the life span* (2nd ed.). Boston: Little, Brown & Company.

Hoyt, K. B. (1991, Winter). The concept of work: Bedrock for career cevelopment. *Future choices, 2*(3), 23-30.

Jepsen, D. (1991, May). *Personal communication.*

National Occupational Information Coordinating Council (1989). *National career development guidelines handbook.* Washington, DC: author.

Pietrofesa, J., Hoffman, A., & Splete, H. (1984). *Counseling: An introduction* (2nd ed.). Boston: Houghton Mifflin.

Splete, H. (1977). *Career development counseling.* Boulder, CO: Colorado Career Information System.

Super, D. E. (1976). *Career education and the meaning of work.* Monographs on career education. Washington, DC: The Office of Career Education, U. S. Office of Education.

Wilson, P. (1986). *School counseling programs: A resource and planning guide.* Madison, WI: Wisconsin Department of Public Instruction.

NOICC/SOICC ORGANIZATION

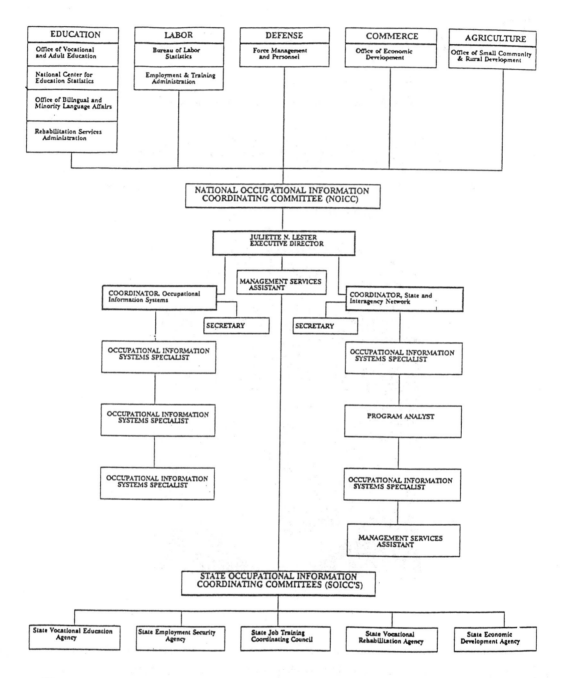

Figure 2.3

October 26, 1990

Module 3
Demographic Trends That Impact Career Decision Making

National Career Development Guidelines-Counselor Competencies

Knowledge of changes taking place in the economy, society, and job market.

Knowledge of changing gender roles and how these impact on work, family, and leisure.

Demographic Trends That Impact Career Decision Making

Module 3

Introduction

There are a number of relatively predictable factors that will have a direct bearing on the future labor force in this country. Many are demographic in nature; this refers to the number of births, deaths and the distribution of the population across the country. Demographics help us understand a great deal about the workers in our labor force: How many young adults will enter the work force over the next 10 years? How many workers are likely to retire during that period? Will there be a labor shortage or surplus? In this module, we will discuss demographic trends that can help answer these kinds of questions.

The three demographic trends that will be discussed are:

1. the maturation of America;
2. the increasing diversity of our population; and
3. the increasing number of women in the labor force.

Demographic Trend #1: The Maturation of America

There are few demographic forces at work in our society that are as powerful in their consequences and as predictable and certain in their outcome as the aging of our population. Over the coming decade, a shrinking pool of younger people will be available to enter the work force due to prior trends in lower birthrates. In addition, people are living longer; there is an increase in life expectancy.

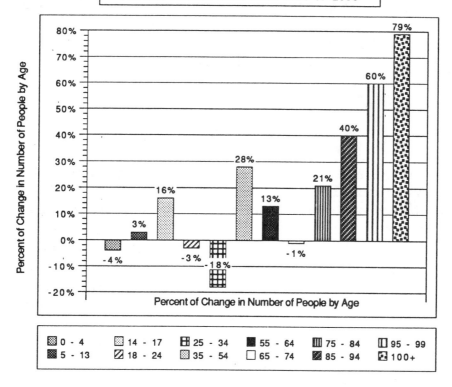

Source: U.S. Bureau of the Census, 1989

Figure 3.1

There are two separate components to this phenomenon. The first is the increasing number of people at the upper end of the age spectrum. This effects the age of the work force and also the occupations and industries that provide goods and services to the elderly.

The second component involves what is commonly referred to as the aging of the "baby boom" generation. Between 1946 and 1965, 75 million babies were born in this country; 70% more than the number in the preceding 20 years and around 25% more than the number in the 20 years following 1965. Since their arrival, this generation has placed enormous strains on the institutions of American society and will continue to do so.

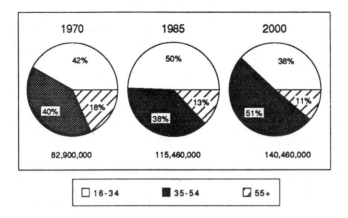

Source: Workforce 2000, 1987

Figure 3.2

Today the peak of the baby boomers is well into middle age. Right on the heels of the baby boom bulge is a much smaller generation sometimes referred to as the "baby bust." In this population lies the impending deficits in our work force.

This shortage will be with us during most of the 1990s. To add to the problem, many of the workers entering the labor force have a deficit in their basic skills. This will affect the labor market in several ways. There will be a greater need for training and retraining and new sources of entry level workers will come from segments of the population such as young minorities, older people, and persons with disabilities. Some say this labor shortage will be the number one factor guiding business decisions in the near future.

Demographic Trend #2: The Increasing Diversity of Our Population

Not only is the work force older, but its composition is changing. Blacks, Hispanics and other minorities will make up a larger share of the expansion of the labor force.

**NON-WHITES ARE A GROWING SHARE
OF THE WORKFORCE**
(numbers in millions)

	1970	1985	2000
Working Age Population (16+)	137.1	184.1	213.7
Non-White Share	10.9%	13.6%	15.7%
Labor Force	82.8	115.5	140.4
Non-White Share	11.1%	13.1%	15.5%
Labor Force Increase (Over Previous Period)	X	32.7	25.0
Non-White Share	X	18.4%	29.0%

Source: Workforce 2000, 1987

Figure 3.3

The small net growth of workers will be dominated by women, blacks and immigrants.

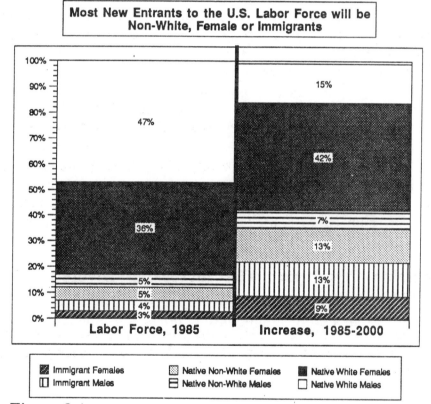

Figure 3.4

At the same time, it is expected that the passage of the Americans with Disabilities Act will result in an increased number of persons with disabilities in the work force.

By almost every measure of employment, i.e., participation rates, earnings, and education, blacks and Hispanics suffer great disadvantages. Of particular concern is the decline in labor force participation rates among minority males.

Smart managers who want to maintain a talented work force are beginning to court and train qualified but underutilized blacks, Hispanics, Asians, women and others who have often been discounted because of stereotyping or occupational segregation.

Demographic Trend #3: The Increasing Number of Women in the Labor Force

The last demographic trend discussed in this module is the increasing number of women in the labor force. By the year 2000, approximately 47% of the work force will be women. It should be noted that labor market activity has become the norm rather than the exception for most women today, and this is true for all colors and all marital statuses.

Women are a Growing Share of the Workforce
(number in thousands, except percent)

	1950	1960	1970	1980	1990	2000
Women in the Workforce	18,389	23,240	31,543	45,487	57,230	66,670
Female Labor Force Participation Rate	33.9	37.7	43.3	51.5	57.5	61.1
Female Share of the Workforce	29.6	33.4	38.1	42.5	45.8	47.5

Figure 3.5

Changes in women's work patterns have increased attention to issues such as dual career families, adequate child care and caring for aging parents. Despite the improved status of women in the work force, barriers still exist. For a discussion of these issues, see Module 8.

Summary

We live in a changing labor market. In order to make sense of the many changes, we need some "handles" to grasp. One of these handles is the body of information gleaned from a number of relatively predictable trends in our population. By understanding demographics, we can understand some of our labor force needs.

The trends discussed in this module are national in scope. Local trends may or may not follow these patterns. Understanding these trends and how they appear in a local, regional or state labor market is valuable when making career decisions.

Demographic Trends That Impact Career Decision Making
Module 3
References

Johnston, W. B., & Packer, A. H. (1987). *Workforce 2000*. Indianapolis: Hudson Institute.

Notes

Module 4
Theories of Career Development and Decision Making

National Career Development Guidelines-Counselor Competencies

Knowledge of developmental issues individuals address throughout the life span.

Knowledge of counseling and career development theories and techniques.

Knowledge of decision making and transition models.

Skills to use appropriate individual and group counseling techniques to assist individuals with career decision and career development concerns.

Knowledge of basic concepts related to career counseling, such as career development, career progressions, and career patterns.

Theories of Career Development and Decision Making

Module 4

Goal, Purpose and Scope

This module focuses on theories of career development and career choice, with special attention to information resources, decision making and career counseling. This discussion of theories and their uses for facilitating career development is designed for the purpose of stimulating and refining the knowledge and skill of practicing and aspiring career counselors, other career development professionals, paraprofessionals and their colleagues. In this module, career development and the role of the career development facilitator will be discussed. A rationale for using theories in the career development process will be presented. Highlights of selected theories of career development will be summarized. Finally, a career counseling model will be offered to provide an overview of the career counseling process and to serve as a tool to illustrate how various theories can help in the process of facilitating career development.

Introduction

In the United States and much of Western Society, people are expected and encouraged to work for a living. Substantial resources are directed to making education and work opportunities available and valuable to all citizens. Because numerous individual, social and other barriers may interfere with human and constitutional rights and ideals, people often need various forms of assistance to find work opportunities to enrich their lives.

What Is Career Development?

Career development has been defined as the interaction of psychological, sociological, economic, physical and chance factors that shape the sequence of jobs, occupations or careers that a person may engage in throughout a lifetime. Career development is a major aspect of human development. It includes one's entire life span and concerns the whole person. Career development involves a person's past, present and future work roles. It is linked to a person's self-concept, family life, and all aspects of one's environmental and cultural conditions.

What Is a Career Development Facilitator?

A career development facilitator is a person who is trained to assist people in their career development. Career development facilitators work with people of all ages; from young children, adolescents, their parents and teachers; through young, middle-aged and older adults; to others preparing to retire and retirees seeking vocational and avocational pursuits. To serve these diverse populations, career development facilitators work in a wide range of public and private educational, social and fraternal environments such as schools, Scouting, 4H, Young Men's and Women's Christian Associations, local chapters of the American Association of Retired Persons; in public and private sector agencies and private practices and in business and industry settings.

Career Development Facilitators Need to be Competent in Using Theories

Career development professionals and paraprofessionals have special competencies for planning, organizing, implementing and administering career development programs and services to individuals and groups in a wide variety of settings. Among the most important competencies of career development facilitators are knowledge of and skill in using career development theories.

What Are Career Development Theories?

Counseling theories are conceptual frameworks for describing or understanding complex human developmental processes. Theories describe, explain, generalize and summarize what we do in counseling to help clients make constructive changes that lead to success and satisfaction. Theories of career choice and development are points of view, conceptual tools, or road maps for counselors to use in working to help people choose, create, design, refine, develop and/or manage their careers.

Why Do Career Development Facilitators Use Theories?

The "why" we do something rather than the "how" we do it is explained through the use of theories. The reason we use theories is to help us reduce or manage uncertainty and make more responsible decisions.

In a field such as career development, where the unknown may outweigh the known, theory can help the counselor and client make informed efforts to reduce uncertainty and its impact (Herr, 1977).

How Do Theories Help Career Development Facilitators?

Theories help make sense of experiences; they bridge the gap between knowledge and the unknown. Career development theories offer rationales, guidelines, directions and goals for facilitating career development. While much professional knowledge in the field of counseling has been generated, there remains a great amount of uncertainty and undiscovered knowledge. The most dependable, efficient bridge to that potential knowledge lies in the realm of theory. Career development theory helps to:

- make sense of what we experience and learn;
- bridge gaps between knowledge and the unknown;
- summarize information;
- explain information;
- make predictions;
- point out relations between means and ends;
- formulate goals; and,
- stimulate research aimed at improving the knowledge and skill bases for career counseling.
  (Shertzer and Stone, 1974)

What Theories Do Career Development Facilitators Use?

There are many theories of career development and career choice. How does an understanding of career development theories help me as a counselor? How can theories help me use career and labor market information more effectively with individuals and groups? How do theories help me provide career exploration and decision making assistance? How do they help me work with individuals who need help finding a job? To answer these and similar questions, a brief description of some selected theories of career development and a model of the counseling process follow. The model is presented as one example of a structure to help career development facilitators in their work with clients. Additionally, the model provides a format for illustrating how theories can help with various aspects of facilitating career development.

Selected Career Development Theories

While there are many ways to categorize career development theories Jepsen (1984) has constructed a global classification system that will be used in this module. Career development theories can be divided into two major classes: Structural and Developmental. Numerous theories could be included in each area, however, coverage in this module will be abbreviated to highlight some major points of selected theories.

Structural theories focus on individual characteristics and differences among and between persons. The structural theories discussed in this module are: Trait and Factor Theory, Holland's Theory of Vocational Personalities and Environments, and Socioeconomic Theories.

Trait and Factor This theory originated with Parsons (1909) who believed that the best way to choose an occupation was to know one's self and the world of work and make a connection between the two sets of knowledge. Williamson (1939) and others expanded this theory through the use of tests and other assessment tools to measure people's traits and the traits required in certain occupations. Two major assumptions of trait and factor theory are that individual and job traits can be matched, and that close matches are positively correlated with job success and satisfaction.

Holland's Theory of Vocational Personalities and Environments Over a series of years, Holland (1966, 1973, 1985) presented his theory, which is based on assumptions that: people's occupations are extensions or manifestations of their personalities; that people working in an occupation have similar personality characteristics; and that human personalities and work environments can be classified into six categories of vocational personalities and environments. The six personality types and work environments are labeled: realistic, investigative, artistic, social, enterprising and conventional and share the acronym RAISEC. Holland suggests that people can function and develop best and find job satisfaction in work environments that are compatible with their personalities.

Socioeconomic Theory Sociologists and economists provide detailed explanations and descriptions of how one's culture, family background, social and economic conditions and other factors outside an individual's control, strongly influence one's identity, values, and overall human and career development. Socioeconomic theory is also known as the chance or accident theory. This approach to understanding career development suggests that many people follow the path of least resistance in their career development by simply falling into whatever work opportunities happen to come their way.

Developmental theories focus on intrapersonal differences across the life span of an individual's human development. The developmental theories that will be discussed are: Super's, Krumboltz's, Decision Making and Cognitive.

Super's Theory Super (1957) and other theorists of career development recognize the changes that people go through as they mature. Career patterns are determined by socioeconomic factors, mental and physical abilities, personal characteristics and the opportunities to which persons are exposed. People seek career satisfaction through work roles in which they can express themselves and implement and develop their self-concepts. Career maturity, a main concept in Super's theory, is manifested in the successful accomplishment of age and stage developmental tasks across the life span. Super pays close attention to the interrelationships among and between career stages and life roles, such as child, spouse, and parent.

Krumboltz's Social Learning Theory Krumboltz (1979) developed a theory of career decision making and development based on our social learning, or environmental conditions and events, genetic influences and learning experiences. People choose their careers on the basis of what they have learned. Certain behaviors are modeled, rewarded and reinforced.

Decision Making Theories Some decision making theories hypothesize that there are critical points in our lives when choices are made that greatly influence our career development. These decision making points are such events as educational choices, entry level job positions, changing jobs, etc. Other decision making theories are concerned with ongoing choices across the life span. The decisions that we make are influenced by our awareness of the choices that are available to us and our knowledge of how to evaluate them.

Cognitive Theories These theories of career development are built around how individuals process, integrate and react to information. The ways in which individuals process information are determined by their cognitive structures. These structures influence how individuals see themselves, others and the environment. Cognitive theories suggest ways to help clients build or refine a hierarchy of thinking skills and decision making skills that influence career development.

The selected theories that have been very briefly highlighted can be seen as representative of the majority of career development theories. At the same time, however, it must be noted that theory development and expansion need to continue to appropriately address the career development needs of specific populations, especially women and minorities.

Emerging Career Development Theories New theories must be developed that address the needs of specific populations, such as females, the gifted and talented, people of color, ethnic minorities, ex-offenders and persons with disabilities. It should be noted that while emerging theories exist and are being developed, they are beyond the scope of this module. Readers are advised to consult the works cited in the References List, most notably works by: Brooks (1990); Atkinson, Morten & Sue (1989); Greeley, (1975); Ivey, (1987); Pedersen, (1988); Gottfredson, (1981, 1984);

Schlossberg, (1984); Gilligan, (1982a, 1982b); Sue (1978, 1981); Heinrich, Corbine and Thomas (1990); and Lea and Richardson (1991); for coverage of these vital developments.

Promoting Decision Making in Life and Career Development

Knowing how to identify opportunities for choice and how to make responsible choices can empower people to enrich their lives and careers. Unfortunately, many people have neither taken the time nor made the efforts to logically think through and plan their career development. An abundance of research (Fredrickson, 1982: Isaacson, 1987: Zunker, 1986) indicates that the socioeconomic "chance" or "accident" theory is the single best descriptor of most people's career development. Many people fail to notice opportunities and responsibilities for choice in life or look to others to choose for them. Career development facilitators need to provide their clients with guidance and assistance in the decision making process.

The career development facilitator is frequently faced with clients who are unaware or ignorant of their career opportunities. Clients often say "tell me what to do" or "I want to take that test that will tell me what to do." Counselors do not tell their clients what to do. The goal of most counseling is to help clients become aware of opportunities for choice and to assist them in learning to make important choices. Therefore, most counselors are advocates for decision making; for informed, knowledgeable, responsible and wise choices as a primary means of positive self-governance.

The Process of Career Counseling: A Model

A number of writers have described what is involved in the career counseling process. Building on the work of these authors, especially Gysbers and Moore (1987), an outline of the career counseling process follows that has two major phases:

- identifying the clients goal or problem; and,
- resolving the goal or problem

The Process of Facilitating Career Development and Career Counseling

I. Client goal or problem identification
  A. Establishing a client-counselor relationship, including client-counselor responsibilities
  B. Gathering client self and environmental information to understand the client's goal or problem
    1. Who is the client?
      a. How does the client view himself/herself, others, and his/her world?
      b. What language does the client use to represent these views?
      c. What themes does the client use to organize and direct his/her behavior based on these views?
    2. What are the client's current status and environment?
      a. Client's life roles, settings, and events
      b. Relationship to client's goal or problem
  C. Understanding client self and environmental information by sorting, analyzing, and relating such information to client's goal or problem through the use of:
    1. Career development theories
    2. Counseling theories
    3. Classification systems
  D. Drawing conclusions-making diagnoses
II. Client goal or problem resolution
  A. Taking action with interventions selected based on diagnoses
    1. Counseling techniques
    2. Assessment, personal styles analyses
    3. Career and labor market information

B. Developing an individual career plan

C. Implementing an individual career plan

D. Evaluating the impact of the interventions used: Did the client accomplish the goal or resolve the problem?

    1. If goal or problem was not resolved, recycle.

    2. If goal or problem was resolved, close counseling relationship.

(Adapted from Gysbers, N.C. & Moore, E.J. (1987)

These phases and elements in the career counseling process may take place during one interview or may unfold over two or more sessions. While the steps logically follow one another on paper, in actual practice, they may not. There often is a back-and-forth flow to the process; some clients may only need limited counseling and may choose to terminate it at any point, preferring instead to work alone or with other resources.

Client Debriefing/Processing and Related Concerns
Goal of Problem Identification
Establishing the Client-Counselor Relationship
Gathering Client Self and Environmental Information
Understanding Client Self and Environmental Information
Drawing Conclusions - Making Diagnoses
Client Goal of Problem Resolution

Using Career and Labor Market Information in Career Counseling

In this phase of goal resolution or problem solving, career and labor market information can be used to:

- help clients gain current and accurate information about occupations and the world of work;
- instruct individuals about the realities of the work world;
- help clients expand their occupational and career horizons;
- help clients narrow their range of potential occupations;
- help clients obtain and interpret subjective career information, such as how it feels to work in career fields and specific occupations;
- motivate individuals to explore new options; and
- help individuals develop a balance between their needs and wants and occupational supply and demand in the labor market.

Developing, Implementing, and Evaluating an Individual Career Plan

When clients begin gathering and organizing information, they can relate and apply it to their career planning and decision making. By putting information together in certain ways and categories, relationships become more apparent. This tight focus can help clients identify and commit to clear career goals with specific objectives, such as the education, skills or training they will need. Clients can then draw up strategies and specific plans for accomplishing their goals.

The final phase of goal or problem resolution is assessing the behavioral changes that may have occurred during counseling and evaluating the impact of the interventions used during the process. One way to accomplish this is to have the client review and summarize what has taken place and generalize beyond the counseling process into the future. This is the point in the counseling process where maximum debriefing is essential, especially to tease out implications for future plans, actions and client success. Was the counseling effective? What steps have we taken toward the goal? Are we on the right track? Have we reached our goal? What steps could be taken in the future? Finally, the counselor and client can mutually review, summarize, and draw conclusions and implications from the counseling relationship and process.

How Do Career Development Theories Help in Making Diagnoses?

Diagnoses are based on all available client data and information, such as achievement tests, interest inventories, etc. In counseling, all available data are analyzed in terms of the models of human behavior, that best help the counselor understand the client's goals or problems.

The career development facilitator and client analyze the data through the lens of career development theory, searching for clues and ideas to help them identify goals or resolve problems. Human beings and their behavior, however, are highly complex. There is no exact science to define them. Nevertheless, theories are guideposts to human behavior.

Socioeconomic theories can also be helpful in making diagnoses. These theories provide ideas concerning what to look for in people's growth, development, and environment that will help in understanding how they discover, refine and maintain their identity. For example, an understanding of clients' family values could help us understand the value structure underlying their choices in terms of gender stereotyping and occupational selection.

How Do Career Development Theories Help in Setting Goals?

During goal or problem identification, clarification, and specification, Crites (1981a) suggests that "the client and counselor collaboratively identify the attitudes and behaviors in the career problem that are interfering with the decision making process and together they survey the range of possible solutions." During this period, career theories can be helpful.

All career development theories contain ideals and goals that can help to guide career development. For example, decision theories can help a client make a specific choice, such as a short-term goal. Decision theories also can help a client learn a process of decision making, which the client can use to set long-term goals to enrich all aspects of his/her life.

By inference, every career theory can be seen to have some concept of self-actualization, competence or career maturity that can serve as an ideal or long-term goal to aim for in counseling. Holland's concept of congruence, consistency and

identity, Super's concept of career maturity, and Miller-Tiedeman and Tiedeman's concept of being captain of the ship of one's "lifecareer" can serve as long term goals or ideals to aim for in career counseling.

How Do Career Development Theories Help Clients?

Crites (1981a) suggests that there are at least three major outcomes of career counseling - - making a choice, acquiring decision making skills, and enhancing general adjustment. Knowledge gained from theories can be helpful in dealing with each of these outcomes.

To enable counselors to help individuals make career choices, trait and factor theory offers interest, aptitude, values and career maturity assessment. Trait and factor theory helps clients assess their personality traits that might be desirable in certain careers. Personality and developmental theories also suggest possible patterns of previous behaviors that may facilitate or hinder choice making. Socioeconomic theory offers clients an understanding of possible environmental pressures (parents, peers, spouses) and how they affect career development. Cognitive theories provide insight into how individuals process and use information in choice making. Cognitive theories can illustrate the need for clients to develop skills in processing the information that is available to them. Decision theories and strategies provide clients with specific and general approaches to making choices and to overall decision making ability and responsibility.

The second outcome of the counseling process is acquiring decision skills. Counselors' abilities to assist individuals in acquiring decision making skills can be increased by the knowledge provided by career development theories. Decision making theory provides possible models to use and outlines and explains the decision making process so counselors can use and share this knowledge with their clients. While some clients may need direct help in seeing how to go about making a decision, others may need help in how they process information as they make decisions. In the latter cases, cognitive theories may provide some answers concerning how to help work with the problems clients may have in processing information.

The third outcome is general adjustment. Because work roles, work settings, and work-linked events play a substantial part in people's lives, attention to adjustment is crucial. A number of theories provide good insights into this issue. Holland's theory, especially his concept of congruence, can help one understand and assess relationships between personality and work environments. Developmental theories, such as Super's, can also be helpful, particularly the concept of developmental tasks at certain stages of life, such as selecting a mate, rearing children, etc. Understanding developmental tasks to be mastered at different ages and stages across the life span and how the person has performed them can provide insight into the nature and quality of a person's adjustment. A related developmental concept is career maturity, or, for adults, career adaptability. Instruments are now available to help obtain measures of career maturity or of the general adjustment and adaptability of individuals to their work roles.

Decision making theory can be helpful in promoting a person's general adjustment. Tiedeman and O'Hara's model examines the processes that lead up to choice as well as what happens once a person is on the job. Tiedeman and O'Hara use such terms as **induction, reformation,** and **integration** to describe the phases a worker may go through as he/she deals with job adjustment and advancement. Similarly, the concept of life career roles and role conflict can be useful to help explain and remedy life and job adjustment problems and issues.

Conclusion

In this module, discussion has focused on career development theories and their importance in facilitating career development. Career development theories were classified into structural and developmental categories. Highlights of selected theories from each classification scheme were briefly described. A model of career development was presented to offer some guidelines and structure for the process of career development facilitation. Illustrations of how career development theories fit into the counseling model were presented. Special attention was paid to decision making and career and labor market information as major aspects and tools in facilitating life career development.

Trait-Factor Theory

Brown, D. (1984). Trait and factor theory. In D. Brown & L. Brooks & Associates. *Career choice and development* 2nd ed. (pp. 13-36). San Francisco: Jossey-Bass.

Crites, J. O. (1981). Comprehensive career counseling: Model, methods & materials. In P.A. Butcher (Ed.), *Career counseling: Models, methods, and materials*. New York: McGraw-Hill Book Company.

Crites, J. O. (1981). Trait-and-factor career counseling. In P.A. Butcher (Ed.), *Career counseling; Models, methods, and materials*. New York: McGraw-Hill Book Company.

Kapes, J. T., & Mastie, M. M. (Eds.). (1988). *A counselor's guide to vocational guidance instruments* 2nd ed. Alexandria, VA: The National Career Development Association.

Osipow, S. H. (1983). Personality traits and career. *Theories of career development* (3rd ed.). Englewood Cliffs, NJ: Prentice-Hall, Inc.

Osipow, S. H. (1983). The work-adjustment theory-Loftquist and Dawis. *Theories of career development* (3rd ed.). Englewood Cliffs, NJ: Prentice-Hall, Inc.

Parsons, F. (1909). *Choosing a Vocation*. (Reprinted 1988). Garrett Park, MD: Garrett Park Press.

Holland's Theory of Vocational Personalities and Work Environments

Holland, J. L. (1985). *Making vocational choices: A theory of vocational personalities and work environments* (2nd ed.). Englewood Cliffs: Prentice-Hall, Inc.

Weinrach, S. G. & Srebalus, D. J. (1990). Holland's Theory of Careers. In D. Brown, L. Brooks & Associates (1990) *Career choice and development*, 2nd.ed. San Francisco: Jossey Bass.

Socioeconomic Systems

Borow, H. (1984). Occupational socialization: Acquiring a sense of work. In N.C. Gysbers (Ed.), *Designing careers* (160-189). San Francisco: Jossey-Bass.

Herr, E. L. (1984). Links among training, employability, and employment. In N.C. Gysbers (Ed.), *Designing careers* (160-189). San Francisco: Jossey-Bass.

Hotchkiss, L., & Borow, H. (1990). Sociological perspectives on work and career development. In D. Brown, L. Brooks & Associates, *Career choice and development* 2nd ed. (262-307). San Francisco: Jossey-Bass.

Super, D. E. (1984). Perspectives on the meaning and value of work. In N.C. Gysbers (Ed.), *Designing careers* (27-53). San Francisco: Jossey-Bass.

Roe's Theory of Personality and Occupational Behavior

Osipow, S. H. (1983). Roe's personality theory of career choice. *Theories of career development* (3rd ed.). Englewood Cliffs, NJ: Prentice-Hall, Inc.

Roe, A. (1972). Perspectives on vocational development. In J.M. Whiteley & A. Resnikoff (Eds.). *Perspectives on vocational development* (66-82). Washington, DC: American Personnel and Guidance Association.

Roe, A., & Lunneborg, P. W. (1990). Personality development and career choice. In D. Brown, L. Brooks & Associates. *Career choice and development* 2nd ed. (68-101). San Francisco: Jossey-Bass.

Ginzberg's Theory of Occupational Choice

Ginzberg, E. (1984). Career development. In D. Brown & L. Brooks (Eds.), *Career choice and development* (169-191). San Francisco: Jossey-Bass Publishers.

Osipow, S. H. (1983). The Ginzberg-Ginzberg-Axelrad and Herma theory. *Theories of career development* (3rd ed.). Englewood Cliffs, NJ: Prentice-Hall, Inc.

Super's Theory of Career Development

Osipow, S. H. (1983). Super's developmental self-concept theory of vocational behavior. *Theories of career development* (3rd ed.). Englewood Cliffs, NJ: Prentice-Hall, Inc.

Super, D. E. (1990). A life-span, life-space approach to career development. In D. Brown, L. Brooks & Associates. *Career choice and development* 2nd ed. (197-261). San Francisco: Jossey-Bass.

Super, D. E. (1985). Coming of age in Middletown: Careers in the making. *American Psychologist, 40,* 405-414.

Adult Career Development

Levinson, D. J., Darrow, C. N., Klein, E. B., Levinson, M. G., & McKee, B. (1978). *The seasons of a man's life.* New York: Alfred A. Knopf.

Neugarten, B. L. (1979). Time, age, and the life cycle. *American Journal of Psychiatry, 136,* 887-894.

Rodgers, R. F. (1984). Theories of adult development: Research status and counseling implications. In S.D. Brown & R.W. Lent (Eds.), *Handbook of counseling psychology* (pp. 479-519). New York: John Wiley & Sons.

Schlossberg, N. K. (1984). *Counseling adults in transition.* New York: Springer Publishing Company.

Sheehy, G. (1974). *Passages: Predictable crises of adult life.* New York: E.P. Dutton & Company.

Vaillant, G. E. (1977). *Adaptation to life.* Boston: Little, Brown & Co.

Decision Making

Miller-Tiedeman, A. & Tiedeman, D. V. (1990). Career decision making: An individualistic perspective. In D. Brown, L. Brooks & Associates, *Career choice and development* 2nd ed. (pp. 308-337). San Francisco: Jossey-Bass.

Mitchell, L. K., & Krumboltz, J. D. (1984). Research on human decision making: Implications for career decision making and counseling. In S.D. Brown & R.W. Lent (Eds.), *Handbook of counseling psychology* (pp. 238-280). New York: John Wiley & Sons.

Osipow, S. H. (1983). Tiedeman's developmental theory. *Theories of career development* (3rd ed.). Englewood Cliffs, NJ: Prentice-Hall, Inc.

Krumboltz's Theory of Social Learning

Mitchell, L. K., & Krumboltz, J. D. Social learning approach to career decision making: Krumboltz's theory. In D. Brown L. Brooks & Associates, *Career choice and development* 2nd ed. (pp. 145-196). San Francisco: Jossey-Bass.

Cognitive-Behavioral Theory

Gysbers, N. C., & Moore, E. J. (in press). *Career assessment and counseling: Skills and techniques for practitioners.* Englewood Cliffs, NJ: Prentice-Hall.

Keller, K. E., Biggs, D. A., & Gysbers, N. C. (1982). Career counseling from a cognitive perspective. *The Personnel and Guidance Journal, 59,* 367-371.

Kinnier, R. T., & Krumboltz, J. D. (1984). Procedures for successful career counseling. In N.C. Gysbers (Ed.), *Designing careers* (pp. 307-335). San Francisco: Jossey-Bass Publishers.

Krumboltz, J. D. (1983). *Private rules in career decision making.* Columbus, Ohio: The National Center for Research in Vocational Education.

Peterson, G. W., Sampson, J. P. & Reardon, R. C. (1991). *Career Development and Services: A cognitive Approach.* Pacific Grove, CA: Brooks/Cole.

New and Emerging Theories & Issues

Astin, H. S. (1984). The meaning of work in women's lives: A sociopsychological model of career choice and work behavior. *Counseling Psychologist, 12*, 117-126.

Atkinson, D. R., Morten, G., & Sue, D. W. (1989). *Counseling American minorities.* Dubuque, IA: Wm. C. Brown.

Betz, N. E. & Fitzgerald, L. F. (1987). *The Career Psychology of Women.* Orlando, FL: Academic Press.

Brooks, L. (1990). Recent developments in theory building. In D. Brown, L. Brooks & Associates, *Career choice and development*, 2nd. ed. San Francisco: Jossey-Bass.

Carlos Poston, W. S. (1990). The biracial identity development model: A needed addition. *Journal of counseling and development, 69*, 152-155.

Engels, D. W. & Dameron, J. D.(eds.). (1990). *The professional counselor: competencies, performance guidelines and assessment.* Alexandria, VA: American Association for Counseling and Development.

Farmer, H. S. (1985). Model of career and achievement motivation for women and men. *Journal of Counseling Psycology, 32*, 363-390.

Gilligan, C. (1982a). *In a different voice.* Cambridge, MA: Harvard University Press.

Gilligan, C. (1982b). Why should a woman be more like a man? *Psychology Today.* June, 68-77.

Gottfredson, L. S. (1981). Circumscription and compromise: A developmental t h e o r y o f occupational aspirations. *Journal of Counseling Psychology, 28*, 545-579.

Greeley, A. M. (1975). *Why can't they be like us? America's white ethnic groups.* New York: Dutton.

Hackett, G. & Betz, N. E. (1981). A self-efficacy approach to the career development of women. *Journal of Vocational Behavior, 18*, 326-339.

Hackett, G. & Campbell, N. K. (1988). Task self-efficacy and task interest as a function of performance on a gender-neutral task. *Journal of Vocational Behavior, 30*, 203-215.

Hansen, L. S. & Rapoza, R. S. (eds.). (1978). *Career development and counseling of women.* Springfield IL: Charles C. Thomas.

Heinrich, R. K., Corbine, J. L. & Thomas, K.R. (1990). Counseling Native Americans. *Journal of Counseling and Development, 69,* 128-133.

Ivey, A. E. (1987). Cultural intentionality: The core of effective   helping. *Counsleor Education and Supervision, 26*, 168-172.

Lea, D. & Liebowitz, Z. (1991). *Adult career development*, 2nd ed. Alexandria, VA: National Career Development Association.

Lee, C. C. & Richardson, B. L. (1991). *Multicultural issues in counseling.*Alexandria, VA: American Association for Counseling and Development.

Myers, J. E. (1989). *Adult children and aging parents.* Alexandria, VA:American Association for Counseling and Development.

Pederson, P. B. (1988). *A handbook for developing multicultural awareness.*Alexandria, VA: American Association for Counseling and Development.

Schlossberg, N. K. (1984). *Counseling adults in transition.* New York: Springer.

Sue, D. W. (1978). Counseling across cultures. *Personnel and Guidance Journal, 56*, 451.

Sue, D. W. (1973). Ethnic identity: The impact of two cultures on the   psychological development of Asians in America. In S. Sue & N.N.

Wagner (eds), *Asian Americans: Psychological perspectives.* Palo Alto, CA: Science and Behavior Books.

Sue, D. W. (1981). *Counseling the culturally different: Theory and practice.* John Wiley & Sons.

Abeles, R. P., & Riley, M. W. (1976-1977). A life-course perspective on the later years of life: Some implications for research. *Social Science Research Council Annual Report*, pp. 1-16.

Adler, A. (1929). *The practice and theory of individual psychology.* New York: Harcourt, Brace & World.

Bandura, A. (1977). *Social learning theory.* Englewood Cliffs, NJ: Prentice-Hall.

Borow, H. (Ed.). (1973). *Career guidance for a new age.* Boston: Houghton Mifflin.

Brim, O. G., Jr., & Kagan, J. (1980). "Constancy and change: A view of the issues." In O.G. Brim, Jr. & Kagan (Eds.), *Constancy and change in human development.* Cambridge, MA: Harvard University Press.

Brooks, L. (1984). Career counseling methods and practice. In D. Brown & L. Brooks (Eds.), *Career choice and development* (pp. 337-354). San Francisco: Jossey-Bass Publishers.

Brown, D. (1984). Trait and factor theory. In D. Brown & L. Brooks (Eds.), *Career choice and development* (pp. 8-30). San Francisco: Jossey-Bass Publishers.

Brown, D. & Brooks, L. (Eds.). (1990). *Career choice and development.* 2nd ed. San Francisco: Jossey-Bass.

Caplow, T. (1954). *The sociology of work.* New York: McGraw-Hill.

Career Skills Assessment Program. (1977). *Career decision-making skills, exercise booklet.* Princeton, NJ: Education Testing Service.

Center for Policy Research and Analysis, National Governors Association. (1985, May). *Using labor market and occupational information in human resource program planning* (Vol. I). Washington, DC: National Governors Association.

Crites, J. O. (1969). *Vocational psychology: The study of vocational behavior and development.* New York: McGraw-Hill.

Crites, J. O. (1981). *Career counseling: Models, methods, and materials.* New York: McGraw-Hill.

Dickens, C. (1852). London: Bradbury and Evans.

Dudley, G., & Tiedeman, D. V. (1977). *Career development: Exploration and commitment.* Muncie, IN: Accelerated Development.

Erikson, Erik. (1950). *Childhood and society.* New York: W.W. Norton and Co.

Frederickson, R. H. (1982). *Career information.* Englewood Cliffs, NJ: Prentice-Hall.

Freud, S. (1953). *The standard edition of the complete psychological works* (J. Strachey, Trans.). London: Hograth.

Gelatt, H. B., Varenhorst, B., Carey, R., & Miller, G. P. (1973). *Decisions and outcomes: A leader's guide.* New York: College Entrance Examination Board.

Gilligan, C. (1977). In a different voice: Women's conceptions of self and morality. *Harvard Educational Review, 47,* 481-517.

Gilligan, C. (1982). *In a different voice: Psychological theory and women's development.* Cambridge, Mass.: Harvard University Press.

Gilligan, C. (1982a). *In a different voice.* Cambridge, MA: Harvard University Press.

Gilligan, C. (1982b). Why should a woman be more like a man? *Psychology Today.* June, 68-77.

Ginzberg, E. (1972). Toward a theory of occupational choice: A restatement. *Vocational Guidance Quarterly, 20* (3), 169-176.

Ginzberg, E. (1984). Career development. In D. Brown & L. Brooks (Eds.). *Career choice and development* (pp. 169-191). San Francisco: Jossey-Bass Publishers.

Ginzberg, E,. Ginsburg, S., Axelrad, S., and Herma, J. (1951). *Occupational choice: An approach to a general theory.* New York: Columbia University Press.

Gordon, V. N. (1981). The undecided student: A developmental perspective. *The Personnel and Guidance Journal, 59,* 433-438.

Gottfredson, G. D., Holland, J. L., & Ogawa, D. K. (1982). *Dictionary of Holland Occupational Codes*. Palo Alto, CA: Consulting Psychologists Press, Inc.

Gottfredson, G. D. (1977). Career stability and redirection in adulthood. *Journal of College Student Personnel, 25*(4), 315-320.

Gottfredson, L. S. (1981). Circumscription and compromise: A developmental theory of occupational aspirations. *Journal of Counseling Psychology, 28*(6), 545-579.

Gottfredson, L. S. (1978). Providing black youth more access to enterprising work." *Vocational Guidance Quarterly, 27*(2), 114-123.

Gottfredson, L. S., & Becker, H. J. (1981). A challenge to vocational psychology: How important are aspirations in determining male career development? *Journal of Vocational Behavior, 18,* 121.

Gottfredson, L. S., Finucci, J. M., & Childs, B. (1984). Explaining the adult careers of dyslexic boys: Variations in critical skills for high-level jobs. *Journal of Vocational Behavior, 24,* 355-373.

Gysbers, N. C. (1983). *Create and use an individual career development plan.* Columbus, Ohio: The National Center for Research in Vocational Education.

Gysbers, N. C., & Moore, E. J. (1975). *Beyond career development - Life career development.* *Personnel and Guidance Journal, 53* (9), 647-652.

Gysbers, N. C., & Moore, E. J. (in press). *Career assessment and counseling: skills and techniques for practitioners.* Englewood Cliffs, NJ: Prentice-Hall.

Hansen, L. S. (1978). Promoting female growth through a career development curriculum. In L.S. Hansen & R. S. Rapoza (Eds.), *Career development and counseling of women.* Springfield, IL: Charles C. Thomas.

Hansen, L. S. "Promoting Female Growth Through a Career Development Curriculum." In L.S. Hansen & R.S. Rapoza (eds.), *Career Development and Counseling of Women.* Springfield, Ill.: Thomas, 1978.

Hansen, L. S., & Leierleber, D. L. (1978). Born free: A collaborative consultation model for career development and sex-role stereotyping. *Personnel and Guidance Journal, 56*(7), 395-399.

Hartz, J. D. (1977). *Career Program Resources.* Madison, WI: University of Wisconsin Vocational Studies Center.

Havighurst, R. (1952). *Developmental tasks and education.* New York: David McKay Co.

Heinrich, R. K., Corbine, J. L. & Thomas, K. R. (1990). Counseling native americans. *Journal of Counseling and Development, 69,* 128-133.

Herr, E. L., & Cramer, S. H. (1988). *Career guidance through the life span* (3rd ed.). Boston: Little, Brown.

Herr, E. L., & Cramer, S. H. (1988). *Career Guidance and Counseling Through the Life Span.* (3rd ed.). Glenview, Ill.: Harper-Collins.

Holland, J. L. (1985). *Making vocational choices: A theory of vocational personalities and work environments* (2nd ed.). Englewood Cliffs, NJ: Prentice-Hall.

Holland, J. L. (1966). *The psychology of vocational choice.* Waltham, MA: Blaisdell.

Holland, J. L. (1973). *Making vocational choices: A theory of careers.* Englewood Cliffs, NJ: Prentice-Hall.

Holland, J. L. (1974). *Self-directed search.* Palo Alto, CA: Consulting Psychologists Press.

Hoppock, R. (1967). *Occupational information.* (3rd ed.). New York: McGraw-Hill.

Hotchkiss, L., & Borow, H. (1984). Sociological perspectives on career choice and attainment. In D. Brown & L. Brooks (Eds.), *Career choice and development: Applying contemporary theories to practice* (Chap. 6). San Francisco: Jossey-Bass.

Hoyt, K. B. (1972). *Career education: What it is and how to do it.* Salt Lake City: Olympus.

Isaacson, L. E. (1985). *Basics of career counseling.* Boston: Allyn & Bacon.

Ivey, A. E. (1987). Cultural intentionality: The core of effective helping. *Counselor Education and Supervision, 26,* 168-172.

Janis, I., & Mann, L. (1977). *Decision-making: A psychological analysis of conflict, choice, and commitment.* New York: The Free Press.

Jaramillo, P. T., Zapata, J. T., & MacPherson, R. (1982). Concerns of college-bound Mexican-American students. *The School Counselor, 29*(5), 375-380.

Jepsen, D. A. (1984). Relationship between career development theory and practice. In N.C. Gysbers (Ed.), *Designing careers: Counseling to enhance education, work, and leisure* (pp. 135-159). San Francisco: Jossey-Bass Publishers.

Jones, G. B., Hamilton, J. A., Ganschow, L. H., Helliwell, C. B., & Wolff, J. M. (1972). *Planning, developing, and field testing career guidance programs.* Palo Alto, CA: American Institutes for Research.

Jordaan, J. P. (1974). Life stages as organizing models of career development. In E.L.Herr (Ed.), *Vocational guidance and human development.* Boston: Houghton Mifflin.

Jordaan, J. P., & Heyde, M. B. (1979). *Vocational maturity during the high-school years.* New York: Teachers College Press.

Kapes, J. T., & Mastie, M. M. (1982). *A counselors guide to occupational guidance instruments.* Washington, DC: National Vocational Guidance Association.

Keller, K. E., Biggs, D. A., & Gysbers, N. C. (1982). Career counseling from a cognitive perspective. *The Personnel and Guidance Journal, 60* (6), 367-371.

Kinnier, R. T., & Krumboltz, J. D. (1984). Procedures for successful career counseling. In N.C. Gysbers (Ed.), *Designing careers: Counseling to enhance education, work and leisure* (pp.307-335). San Francisco: Jossey-Bass Publishers.

Knefelkamp, L. L., & Sleptitza, R. (1976). A cognitive-developmental model of career development: An adaptation of the Perry scheme. *The Counseling Psychologist, 6,* 53-58.

Krumboltz, J., & Baker, R. (1973). Behavioral counseling for vocational decisions. In H. Borrow (Ed.), *Career guidance for a new age* (pp. 235-284). Boston: Houghton Mifflin, pp. 235-284.

Krumboltz, J. D., Mitchell, A. M., & Jones, G. B. (1979). A social learning theory of career selection. *The Counseling Psychologist, 6, 71-81.*

Lee, C. C. & Richardson, B. L. (1991). *Multicultural issues in counseling.* Alexandria, VA: American Association for Counseling & Development.

Levinson, D. J., Darrow, C. N., Klein, E. B., Levinson, M. G., & McKee, B. (1978). *The seasons of a man's life.* New York: Alfred A. Knopf.

Lewis, R. A., & Gilhousen, M. R. (1981). Myths of career development: A cognitive approach to vocational counseling. *The Personnel and Guidance Journal, 59* (5), 269-299.

Maslow, A. H. (1954). *Motivation and personality.* New York: Harper and Row.

Miller, D., & Form, W. (1951). *Industrial sociology.* New York: Harper and Row.

Myers, J. E. (1989). *Adult children and aging parents.* Alexandria, VA: American Association for Counseling and Development.

Naisbitt, J. (1982). *Megatrends.* New York: Warner Books.

National Career Development Association. (1991). The vocational/career counseling competencies, draft approved, January. Alexandria, VA: Author.

National Career Development Association. (1988). Ethical Standards. Alexandria, VA: Author.

National Occupational Information Coordinating Committees (1989). *The national career development guidelines.* Washington, DC: U.S. Department of Labor.

National Vocational Guidance Association. (1973). *Position paper on career development.* Washington, DC: National Vocational Guidance Association.

Neugarten, B. L. (1968). *Middle age and aging.* Chicago: University of Chicago Press.

Neugarten, B. L. (1979). Time, age, and the life cycle. *American Journal of Psychiatry, 136* (7), 889-894.

Osipow, S. (1969). What do we really know about career development? In N.C. Gysbers & D. Pritchard (Eds.), *National conference on guidance, counseling, and placement in career development and educational-occupational decision-making.* Columbia: University of Missouri. (ERIC Document Reproduction Service No. ED 041 143)

Osipow, S. (1983). *Theories of career development.* (3rd ed.). Englewood Cliffs, NJ: Prentice-Hall.

Osipow, S. (1983). *Theories of career development.* (3rd ed.). New York: Appleton-Century-Crofts.

Parsons, F. (1909). *Choosing a vocation.* Boston: Houghton Mifflin.

Pedersen, P. B. (1988). *A handbook for developing multicultural awareness.* Alexandria, VA: American Association for Counseling and Development.

Pedro, J. D., Wolleat, P., & Fennema, E. (1980). Sex differences in the relationship of career interests and mathematics plans. *Vocational Guidance Quarterly, 29*(1), 25-34.

Perry, W., Jr. (1970) *Intellectual and ethical development in the college years.* New York: Holt, Rinehart and Winston.

Reardon, R. C. (1984) Use of information in career counseling. In H.D. Burck & R.C. Reardon (Eds.), *Career development interventions.* Springfield, IL: Charles C. Thomas.

Rest, J. R. (1974). Developmental psychology as a guide to value education: A review of "Kohlbergian" Programs. *Review of Educational Research, 44,* 241-259.

Roe, A. (1957). early determinants of vocational choice. *Journal of Counseling Psychology, 4,* 212-217.

Roe, A. (1972). Perspectives on vocational development. In J.M. Whiteley & A. Resnikoff (Eds.), *Perspectives on vocational development* (pp. 66-82). Washington, DC: American Personnel and Guidance Association.

Schlossberg, N. K. (1984). *Counseling adults in transition.* New York: Springer.

Schlossberg, N. K., & Pietrofesa, J. J. (1978). Perspectives on counseling bias: Implications for counselor education. In L. S. Hansen & R. S. Rapoza (Eds.), *Career development and counseling of women.* Springfield, IL: Charles C. Thomas.

Sue, D. W. (1978). Counseling across cultures. *Personnel and Guidance Journal, 56,* 451.

Sue, D. W. (1981). *Counseling the culturally different.* New York: Wiley.

Sue, D. W. (1978). "Counseling the culturally Different: A Conceptual Analysis." *Personnel and Guidance Journal, 1977,55,* 422-425.

Sue, D. W., and others. (1982). "Position Paper: Cross-Cultural Counseling Competencies." *Counseling Psychologist, 10,* 45-52.

Sue, D. W. (1981). *Counseling the culturally different: Theory and practice.* New York: John Wiley & Sons.

Super, D. E. (1949). *Appraising vocational fitness.* New York: Harper & Brothers.

Super, D. E. (1957). *The psychology of careers.* New York: Harper & Row.

Tiedeman, D. V., & O'Hara, R. P. (1963). *Career development: Choice and adjustment.* Princeton, NJ: College Entrance Examination Board.

Vaillant, G. E. (1977). *Adaptation to life.* Boston: Little, Brown.

Wolfe, D. M., & Kolb, D. A. (1980). Career development, personal growth, and experimental learning. In J. W. Springer (Ed.), *Issues in career and human resource development.* Madison, WI: American Society for Training and Development.

Zingaro, J. C. (1983). A family system approach for the career counselor. *The Personnel and Guidance Journal, 62,* 24-27.

Zunker, V. G. (1986). *Career counseling: Applied concepts of life planning.* Monterey, CA: Brooks/Cole.

Zytowski, D. G. (1969). Toward a theory of career development for women. *Personnel and Guidance Journal, 47,* 660-664.

Module 5

What Is Information?
How Can It Be Accessed?
How Can It Be Used?

National Career Development Guidelines-Counselor Competencies

Skills to assist individuals in setting goals and identifying strategies for reaching goals.

Knowledge of changes taking place in the economy, society, and job market.

Knowledge of education, training, employment trends, labor market, and career resources.

Knowledge of basic concepts related to career counseling, such as career development, career progressions, and career patterns.

Knowledge of employment information and career planning materials.

Skills to use career development resources and techniques designed for specific groups.

Skills to use computer-based career information systems.

What Is Information?
How Can It Be Accessed?
How Can It Be Used?
Module 5

Introduction

Career decision making is a complex process. One step in the process is to relate self-knowledge to the available opportunities in the world of work. To do this successfully, one must be able to locate, access, evaluate and use information that defines options and opportunities. Career decision making using labor market information is based on the assumption that the more knowledge one can obtain about themselves and the world of work, the better the career choice.

We are surrounded by career and labor market information. Our challenge is to understand the information, help others understand their information needs, and integrate that information into the process of career decision making. In this module career and labor market information will be defined. Then the questions, how can it be accessed? and how can it be used? will be answered. At the end of the module, one kind of career and labor market information will be examined: labor force, industry, and occupational projections.

What Is Career and Labor Market Information?

In a very narrow sense, labor market information refers to data about people, jobs and employers. It can also include demographic, economic and educational data. It provides us with an understanding of the labor market and the economy.

Two Examples of Information

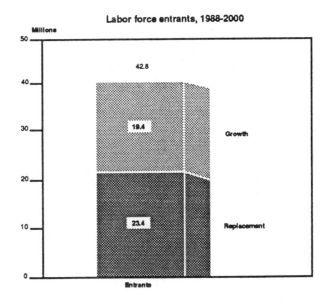

Labor force entrants, 1988-2000

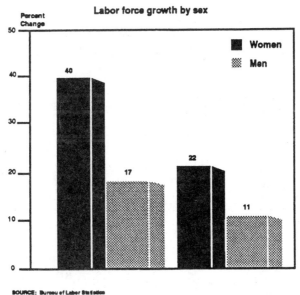

Labor force growth by sex

Figure 5.1

Career information and occupational information is synthesized labor market information. Most published sources of career and labor market information can be characterized as containing numbers, words, graphs and/or pictures. It also can be described as existing on a continuum from primary data, to synthesized information, to knowledge.

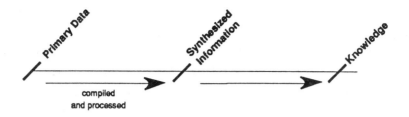

A Continuum from Primary Data to Knowledge

Figure 5.2

As analysis and synthesis are added to primary data, it becomes easier to understand and integrate into the process of career decision making.

How Can Career and Labor Market Information Be Accessed? How Can It Be Used?

When we talk about "access" we are talking about information delivery systems. When we talk about "using" information, we are referring to the process of integrating information into career decision making.

To be effective, the career decision making process must be client centered. A client's interest in labor market information frequently begins with personal interests, experience and aptitudes. The goal is to help a student or client achieve a better understanding of his/her abilities, experiences and interests as they relate to occupations. Following a better understanding of self, the client can begin the process of occupational and job exploration.

There are three key decision areas that use information in the career development process. They represent ports of entry into a wide variety of information resources. The decision areas are:

- Choice of an occupation
- Choice of a work setting (business or industry)
- Choice of a geographic area

Decision Area: An Occupation

Career and labor market information helps people explore a variety of occupational opportunities. The information is used to:

- analyze the tasks completed by people in the occupation;
- examine projected employment opportunities;

- learn about job openings;
- become informed about preparation and training requirements;
- discover advancement opportunities and career ladders;
- determine wage levels within an occupation; and
- find out where and how to locate more information.

Resources for occupational information include:

- Career Information Delivery Systems (CIDS)
- *Occupational Outlook Handbook* (OOH)
- *Dictionary of Occupational Titles* (DOT)
- *Guide to Occupational Exploration* (GOE)
- *Military Career Guide*, and
- *Standard Occupational Classification System* (SOC)

Career Information Delivery Systems (CIDS)

CIDS are systems that provide individuals with current, accurate and locally relevant occupational and educational information. CIDS use computer programs, print materials and videos that allow individuals to search for and access information about themselves and career options. Figure 5.3 and 5.4 illustrate the type of information found in CIDS.

CIDS Files and File Cross References
(Example)

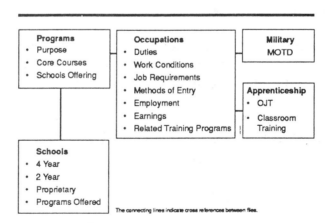

The connecting lines indicate cross references between files.

This chart illustrates the type of information found in CIDS programs.

Figure 5.3

3620.2

Ultrasound Technologists

Work Description

Ultrasound technologists use special kinds of sound waves to help people who are ill. They are also known as diagnostic medical sonographers. They use machines known as ultrasound scanners to find medical problems in patients.

A technologist carefully places a patient against the machine. Only the area of the body that must be tested is put against the machine. A technologist then starts the scanner. This points high frequency sound waves at the correct part of the patient's body. Sound waves go through the outside of the body and bounce off the patient's body organs and tissues. Shadowy pictures, called images, can be recorded on a screen or film. The images show the shape and position of body parts such as the heart, kidneys, or muscle and tissue masses. These images can show places where liquids, called fluids, are building up in the body. They can also show the rate of growth of a baby while it is inside of its mother. Then doctors study these images to find out what kind of treatment the patient needs.

An ultrasound technologist must first study the results of other medical tests, called diagnostic tests, that have been done on the patient. They look for information that will help them choose the right ultrasound equipment. This information also helps them find which area of the patient's body to treat. Technologists explain to patients how each test works and what it is for. They make sure that the images the machine makes can be read and understood clearly. Only then do they record the test results.

Some ultrasound technologists specialize in brain testing, heart testing, eye testing or testing how babies develop in the womb. To become certified to give a special type of test, an individual must pass a national exam in each specialty area.

Working Conditions

Ultrasound technologists generally work 40 hours per week. Some work rotating shifts. Others must be ready to go to work at any time.

Work Places

Ultrasound technologists work in hospitals and clinics. They may also work in some doctor's offices.

Workers' Comments

Ultrasound technologists like working with patients. They like giving ultrasound tests because the tests are painless and do not expose patients or themselves to any harmful effects. Ultrasound technologists like being members of health care teams. They think doctors respect them and the work that they do.

Getting the Job

Some hospitals have training programs in ultrasound technology. Training programs generally last one year. To get into one of these programs, ultrasound technicians must finish two years of college or a two-year vocational school program in allied health. After finishing the one-year training program, an ultrasound technologist may become certified by taking an exam. The American Registry of Diagnostic Medical Sonographers gives this exam. Technicians may be certified in one or more specialties and are then known as registered diagnostic medical sonographers.

Applicants must have good grades in math, physics, biology, zoology, and English. Some understanding of how to use computers may be valuable in the future.

Pay and Employment

Typical salaries range from about $19,700 to $32,900 per year.

Salaries vary a great deal from hospital to hospital. Ultrasound technologists are often paid on the same salary scale as X-ray technicians.

The national outlook for this occupation is good. Job openings may exceed the number of qualified applicants throughout the 1980's.

Moving Up

Ultrasound technologists may be promoted by becoming certified to give more than one kind of ultrasound test. With more work experience, a technologist may be promoted to a supervisor or educational coordinator. Some technologists earn college degrees so they can teach ultrasound technology to others.

Where to Write

You may be able to get more information about this occupation by writing to:
American Soc of Radiologic Technicians
15000 Central Avenue, S.E.
Albuquerque, NM 87123

Figure 5.4

A typical CIDS describes 250 or more occupations. They are designed to digest a multitude of local, state and national career and labor market information. Each state has its own program of collection, analysis, synthesis, organization and linkage of data. The following types of information are included in a CIDS.

- Occupational Descriptions
- Wages, Hours, and Fringe Benefits
    Local
    State
    National
- Employment Trends and Outlook
    Local
    State
    National
- Method of Entry, Qualifications
- Advancement Opportunities
- Educational/Training Programs
- Military Training and Employment
- Type of Industry or Business
- Educational Program
- Financial Aid Packages
- Occupational Classification Systems Based on Similarities in Work Performed Interests
- Occupational Characteristics
    Aptitudes
    Industry Designation
    Environmental Conditions
    General Educational Development (GED)
    Reasoning
    Mathematics
    Language
    Physical Demands
    Specific Vocational Preparation (SVP)
    Temperaments
    Work Fields (Work Methods)
    Worker Functions (Data-People-Things)

Many CIDS also have developed print, computer and video materials to supplement the occupational and educational data files. These might include computer programs that teach the user how to write a resume, career tabloids, and videotapes on subjects such as career exploration, career planning and decision making.

CIDS implements a significant number of the competencies in the National Career Development Guidelines (See Figure 1.4). Each state has its own plan for adopting the Guidelines and using the CIDS to interface with the Guidelines. Some materials have been developed for classroom use that are keyed directly to the national guidelines and can be used in any state. Examples are include in Figures 5.5 and 5.6

INTERVIEW A WORKER

OBJECTIVE
Students will obtain information about careers they are interested in.

MATERIALS
• chalkboard
• chalk

ACTIVITY
1. Ask each student to identify a career that they would like to know more about. Record their answers on the chalkboard.
2. Ask the class if they know anyone who works in any of these careers.
3. Have students interview someone who is in the career that they are interested in.
   a. What do they do on their job?
   b. What education/training is needed?
   c. How did they find this job?
   d. Other questions suggested by class
4. Have students report the results of their interview back to the class.
5. Discuss with the class, "Are you more or less interested in this career as a result of this interview?"

COMMENTS
This exercise may be repeated a number of times throughout the year.

PERFORMANCE INDICATORS
The middle/junior high school student will be able to:
12.4: Describe skills needed in a variety of occupations, including self-employment.

EVALUATION
Each student has personally interviewed someone engaged in a career of interest to the student.

RESOURCES
Career Exploration Workbook. (VSC)

Schrank, Louise. *Lifeplan: A Practical Guide to Successful Career Planning.* (Workbook)

Grade					
7	8	9	10	11	12

Curriculum Area	
Lang. Arts	●
Math	
Health/Science	
Social Studies	●
Family/Cons. Sci.	
Art/Music	
Tech/Voc. Education	●

Self-Knowledge	
Positive Self-Concept	●
Interaction Skills	●
Growth and Change	

Exploration	
Achievement	●
Work and Learning	
Career Information	●
Job-Seeking Skills	
Needs of Society	

Career Planning	
Decision Making	
Life Roles	
Occupational Roles	
Career Planning	●

DG Activity 35

Figure 5.5

NATIONAL CAREER DEVELOPMENT GUIDELINES COMPETENCIES AND STUDENT PERFORMANCE INDICATORS

Each competency is broken down into its corresponding student performance indicators. The number(s) in parentheses following each performance indicator denote the activities in this book (for grades 7-9) that address that specific performance indicator. Note: while each activity addresses several performance indicators only the key indicators are listed on the activity page under "Performance Indicators."

NATIONAL STUDENT PERFORMANCE INDICATORS FOR MIDDLE/JUNIOR HIGH SCHOOL

Self-Knowledge

1. Knowledge of the influence of a positive self-concept.
   1.1 Describe personal likes and dislikes.
   (5, 6, 8, 15, 16, 17, 18, 22, 30, 34, 35, 44, 45, 53, 54, 58, 60, 66, 69, 70, 71, 72, 79, 83, 86, 87, 90, 93, 95, 100, 108, 109, 114, 115, 117, 120, 121, 132, 134, 137, 139, 141)

   1.2 Describe individual skills required to fulfill different life roles.
   (6, 13, 19, 22, 27, 30, 38, 54, 56, 58, 60, 61, 62, 64, 65, 66, 67, 68, 69, 71, 75, 82, 83, 85, 86, 91, 93, 94, 97, 100, 103, 105, 108, 109, 110, 114, 115, 116, 117, 118, 120, 121, 123, 124, 125, 126, 127, 128, 129, 130, 134, 135, 138, 140)

   1.3 Describe how one's behavior influences the feelings and actions of others.
   (9, 23, 24, 50, 54, 55, 61, 62, 79, 80, 84, 85, 86, 87, 89, 90, 91, 94, 97, 98, 101, 103, 105, 108, 111, 114, 115, 116, 117, 120, 122, 124, 126, 128, 129, 130)

   1.4 Identify environmental influences on attitudes, behaviors, and aptitudes.
   (18, 38, 57, 78, 80, 81, 82, 84, 90, 92, 94, 96, 97, 99, 101, 102, 103, 106, 107, 108, 110, 112, 114, 118, 119, 122, 123, 125, 127, 133, 134)

2. Skills to interact with others.
   2.1 Demonstrate respect for the feelings and beliefs of others.
   (14, 17, 29, 41, 54, 59, 62, 63, 70, 72, 79, 80, 84, 85, 86, 87, 91, 93, 96, 97, 99, 100, 101, 102, 103, 105, 111, 112, 114, 115, 117, 120, 122, 123, 124, 125, 126, 127, 128, 137, 139)

   2.2 Demonstrate an appreciation for the similarities and differences among people.
   (17, 23, 24, 54, 61, 62, 63, 71, 79, 86, 87, 88, 93, 95, 97, 99, 100, 101, 103, 109, 110, 112, 113, 114, 117, 121, 123, 127, 139)

   2.3 Demonstrate tolerance and flexibility in interpersonal and group situations.
   (9, 14, 23, 29, 38, 39, 41, 61, 62, 63, 69, 71, 72, 79, 85, 87, 91, 92, 93, 95, 99, 102, 103, 105, 108, 110, 111, 112, 113, 114, 115, 117, 120, 122, 125, 126, 127, 128, 130, 131, 137, 139)

   2.4 Demonstrate skills in responding to criticism.
   (69, 80, 84, 91, 100, 103, 111, 122, 131, 134)

   2.5 Demonstrate effective group membership skills.
   (9, 14, 23, 27, 36, 39, 41, 50, 51, 54, 56, 59, 61, 62, 63, 69, 70, 71, 72, 74, 76, 79, 83, 84, 85, 86, 88, 89, 91, 92, 93, 95, 96, 97, 98, 99, 101, 102, 103, 104, 105, 106, 107, 108, 114, 115, 116, 117, 119, 120, 122, 122, 124, 126, 127, 128, 129, 130, 134, 137, 138, 139, 140)

   2.6 Demonstrate effective social skills.
   (9, 21, 35, 36, 44, 54, 62, 72, 84, 88, 89, 93, 97, 98, 103, 113, 114, 115, 116, 117, 120, 123, 124, 126, 129, 137, 139)

   2.7 Demonstrate understanding of different cultures, lifestyles, attitudes, and abilities.
   (2, 18, 38, 39, 54, 70, 72, 74, 79, 86, 93, 95, 100, 103, 109, 110, 112, 115, 119, 123, 127, 132, 133, 139, 141)

Figure 5.6

Occupational Outlook Handbook (OOH)

The *Occupational Outlook Handbook* is an affordable reference on current and future occupational prospects. It gives greatest attention to those occupations that are projected to grow the most rapidly or require lengthy training and/or education. In addition, a major section discusses employment trends and projections. The remainder of the book describes the nature of work; working conditions; employment, training, and advancement opportunities; job outlook; earnings; and sources of additional information. The information is nontechnical, and easily accessed.

This reference will answer many general questions about occupations. It describes what workers do, the training and education they need, earnings, working conditions and expected job prospects.

Teacher Aides

(D.O.T. 099.327-010; 219.467-010; and 249.367-074, and -086)

Nature of the Work
Teacher aides help classroom teachers in a variety of ways to give them more time for teaching. They help and supervise students in the classroom, cafeteria, school yard, or on field trips. They record grades, set up equipment, or help prepare materials for instruction. They may also tutor and assist children in learning class material.

Aides' responsibilities vary greatly by school district. In some districts, teacher aides just handle routine nonteaching and clerical tasks. They grade tests and papers, check homework, keep health and attendance records, type, file, and duplicate materials. They may also stock supplies, operate audiovisual equipment, and keep classroom equipment in order. In other districts, aides also help instruct children, under the supervision and guidance of teachers. They work with students individually or in small groups—listening while students read, reviewing class work, or helping them find information for reports. Sometimes, aides take charge of special projects and prepare equipment or exhibits—for a science demonstration, for example.

Working Conditions
About half of all teacher aides work part time during the school year. Most work the traditional 9- to 10-month school year. They may work

Teacher aides help children review and understand their lessons.

outdoors supervising recess when weather allows and spend much of their time standing, walking, or kneeling. Working closely with the students can be both physically and emotionally tiring.

Employment
Teacher aides held about 682,000 jobs in 1988. About 8 out of 10 worked in elementary and secondary schools, with many concentrated in the lower grades. Some assisted special education teachers with physically, mentally, or emotionally handicapped children. Most of the others worked in child daycare centers. Employment was distributed geographically much the same as the population.

Training, Other Qualifications, and Advancement
Educational requirements for teacher aides range from less than a high school diploma to some college training. Districts that give aides some teaching responsibilities usually require more training than those that don't assign teaching tasks.

A number of 2-year and community colleges offer associate degree programs that prepare graduates to work as teacher aides. However, most teacher aides receive on-the-job training. Aides are taught how to operate audiovisual equipment, keep records, and prepare instructional materials. In addition, they are made familiar with the organization and operation of a school and with teaching methods.

Teacher aides should enjoy working with children and be able to handle classroom situations with fairness and patience. Preference in hiring may be given to those with previous experience in working with children. Aides also must demonstrate initiative and a willingness to follow a teacher's directions. They must have good oral and writing skills and be able to communicate effectively with students and teachers. Clerical skills may also be necessary.

Some States have voluntary certification for general teacher aides. To qualify, an individual may need a high school diploma or general equivalency degree (G.E.D.), or even some college training. Kansas, Louisiana, Texas, and Wisconsin grant permits for paraprofessionals, as some aides are called, in special education.

Advancement for teacher aides, usually in the form of higher earnings or increased responsibility, comes primarily with experience or additional education. Some school districts provide release time so that aides may take college courses. Aides who earn bachelor's degrees may become certified teachers.

Job Outlook
Employment of teacher aides is expected to increase faster than the average for all occupations through the year 2000, primarily reflecting rising enrollments and increases in the ratio of teacher aides to teachers. Enrollment growth will not occur at the same rate in all parts of the country. Largely because of migration to the South and West, enrollment increases are expected to be greater in those regions than in the Northeast and Midwest.

Teacher aide employment is sensitive to changes in State and local expenditures for education. Pressures on education budgets are greater in some States and localities than in others. A number of teacher aide positions are financed through Federal programs. For example, a 1986 law requires that public schools provide special education services to all children between the ages of 3 and 6 who need it. This will stimulate the demand for teacher aides who work with special education teachers.

Because of a relatively high turnover in the occupation, most openings for teacher aides are expected to occur as a result of the need to replace workers who transfer to other occupations or who leave the labor force to assume full-time housekeeping responsibilities, return to school, or for other reasons.

Earnings
In 1988-89, aides involved in teaching activities earned an average of $7.05 an hour; those performing only nonteaching activities averaged $6.14 an hour. Earnings varied by region and also by work experience and academic qualifications. Many aides are covered by collective bargaining agreements and have health and pension benefits similar to those of the teachers in their schools.

Related Occupations
The educational support activities that teacher aides perform demand organizational skills, cooperativeness, recordkeeping ability, and a talent for getting along with people. Other occupations requiring some or all of these skills include childcare workers, career guidance technicians, home health aides, library attendants, medical record technicians, nursing aides, receptionists, and retail sales clerks.

Sources of Additional Information
Information on teacher aides as well as on a wide range of education-related subjects, including teacher aide unionization, can be obtained from:
➛American Federation of Teachers, 555 New Jersey Ave. NW., Washington, DC 20001.

School superintendents and State departments of education can provide details about employment requirements.

Figure 5.7

The *Dictionary of Occupational Titles* (DOT)

The *Dictionary of Occupational Titles* (DOT) is the most comprehensive document containing occupational information. It not only contains descriptions of over 20,000 occupations, but also has a unique coding number that is indexed, or cross classified, with many other frequently used sources, such as the *Standard Occupational Classification*, the *Guide for Occupational Exploration* (GOE) and the Military Career Guide.

The DOT provides information on the structure of work, particularly the data-people-things functions of an occupation. It describes the relationships among occupations and gives a summary of what particular workers do. A companion publication, *Selected Characteristics of Occupations Defined in the Dictionary of Occupational Titles*, provides detailed supplementary information about occupations in the DOT. It describes physical demands, environmental working conditions, and the amount of training time required. Many find the DOT overwhelming and difficult to manage.

Because of the technical style used to describe occupations, the voluminous amounts of information, and the complexity of accessing the information, the DOT is not used as frequently as the OOH.

The DOT enables the user to learn facts about occupations to incorporate into the decision making process. It can be used most effectively to determine the following:

- specific tasks and skills required of occupations;
- purpose of the occupation;
- the machine, tools, equipment or work aids used;
- service, products, materials and academic subject matter included;
- industries with which the occupation is typically identified;
- worker/function requirements; and
- location of work for each occupation.

The following are examples of key questions about the occupation, Recording Engineer.

Question	Answer
What are the typical work activities performed?	Operates recording machine Listens for imperfections Keeps record of recordings Services and repairs machines
What skills are needed to perform the required work?	Listening, recording, observing, manipulating equipment, repairing and servicing
What is the typical industry where the job is performed?	Radio and TV Broadcast
What are the work aids typically used?	Recording machines, microphones, earphone machines to adjust volume, log book

Example from the DOT

526.685-014

526.685-014 COOK, FRY, DEEP FAT (can. & preserv.; hotel & rest.)
Tends deep-fat cookers to fry meats, vegetables, or fish in cooking oil: Empties containers or opens valves to fill cookers with oil. Sets thermostat to heat oil to specified temperature. Empties containers of meat, vegetable, or fish into metal basket and immerses basket into vat manually or by hoist. Sets timer. Observes color at end of frying time to determine conformity to standards and extends frying time accordingly. Removes basket from cooker, drains it, and dumps contents onto tray. May dip foods into batter or dye before frying. May specialize in a particular food product for canning or freezing or may fry variety of foods for immediate consumption.

526.685-018 COOK, VACUUM KETTLE (can. & preserv.)
Tends vacuum cooker and open kettle to cook fruit and berries preparatory to making jams and jellies: Observes thermometer, turns rheostat and steam valve, or pushes switch or lights burner to heat vacuum cooker and open kettle to specified temperature. Turns valve to transfer contents of kettle into vacuum cooker. Observes *refractometer* on vacuum cooker to determine sugar content and adds ingredients according to formula. Places container under discharge outlet of distillation jacket of cooker to reclaim esters. Opens valve or starts pump to transfer contents of vacuum cooker to holding tank or filling machine.

526.685-022 COOKER (cereal)
Tends steam-heated pressure cookers to cook cracked and tempered grain for further processing into cereal products: Presses button to load first cooker with measured amount of grain and liquid flavor. Clamps lid of cooker in place, using wrench. Moves dials and turns valves to attain specified temperature and pressure in cooker. Removes lid of cooker and dumps cooked grain onto conveyor after determining that grain has reached specified color and consistency. Records cooking time and number of batches prepared. May start automatic equipment that admits steam, rotates cooker, and stops cooker after specified time.

Figure 5.8

The *Guide for Occupational Exploration* (GOE)

The *Guide for Occupational Exploration* (GOE) is designed to assist job seekers find occupations that are in accord with their interests, skills, values and abilities. Information is presented to assist users in evaluating their own interests and potential.

The GOE is a rich source of material for career exploration and decision making. The authors identify a five step process for using the GOE. The first step directs the individual to relate their interests to job titles. In the second step, one or more work groups are chosen to explore and investigate. Step three focuses attention and information on the most interesting work group. Step four involves exploring subgroups in specific occupations. Step five involves the process of integrating the information into the decision making process. Details on the most effective way of using the GOE are included in the preface of the book.

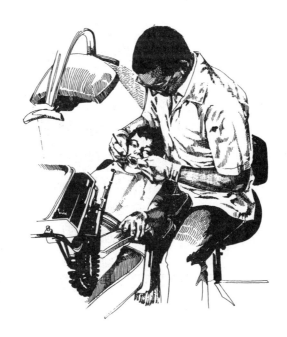

Example from the GOE

04.01 Safety and Law Enforcement

Workers in this group are in charge of enforcing laws and regulations. Some investigate crimes, while others supervise workers who stop or arrest lawbreakers. Others make inspections to be sure that the laws are not broken. Most jobs are found in the Federal, State, or local governments, such as the Police and Fire Departments. Some are found in private businesses, such as factories, stores, and similar places.

What kind of work would you do?

Your work activities would depend upon your specific job. For example, you might
- set procedures, prepare work schedules, and assign duties for jailers.
- direct and coordinate daily activities of a police force.
- direct and coordinate activities of a fire department.
- hire, assign, and supervise store detectives.
- investigate and arrest persons suspected of the illegal sale or use of drugs.
- patrol an assigned area in a vehicle or on foot and issue tickets, investigate disturbances, render first aid, and arrest suspects.
- patrol an assigned area to observe hunting and fishing activities and warn or arrest persons violating fish and game laws.

What skills and abilities do you need for this kind of work?

To do this kind of work you must be able to:
- work with laws and regulations, sometimes written in legal language.
- use practical thinking to conduct or supervise investigations.
- supervise other workers.
- plan the work of a department or activity.
- deal with various kinds of people.
- work under pressure or in the face of danger.
- patrol an assigned area to observe hunting and fishing activities and warn or arrest persons violating fish and game laws.
- keep physically fit.
- use guns, fire-fighting equipment, and other safety devices.

How do you know if you would like or could learn to do this kind of work?

The following questions may give you clues about yourself as you consider this group of jobs.
- Have you had courses in government, civics, or criminology? Did you find these subjects interesting?
- Have you been a member of a volunteer fire department or emergency rescue squad? Were you given training for this work?

- Have you watched detective television shows? Do you read detective stories? Do you try to solve mysteries?
- Have you been an officer of a school safety patrol? Do you like being responsible for the work of others?
- Have you used a gun for hunting or in target practice? Are you a good shot?
- Have you spoken at a civic or community organization? Do you like work that requires frequent public speaking?
- Have you been a military officer?

How can you prepare for and enter this kind of work?

Occupations in this group usually require education and/or training extending from one to over ten years, depending upon the specific kind of work. Local civil service regulations usually control the selection of police officers. People who want to do this kind of work must meet certain requirements. They must be U. S. citizens and be within certain height and weight ranges. In addition, they may be required to take written, oral, and physical examinations. The physical examinations often include tests of physical strength and the ability to move quickly and easily. To work in these jobs, persons should

Figure 5.9

Example from the GOE continued

04.01

have the physical condition to use firearms or work on dangerous missions. Personal investigations are made of all applicants.

Most police departments prefer to hire people who have a high school education or its equal. However, some departments hire people if they have worked in related activities, such as guarding or volunteer police work.

Jobs with federal law enforcement agencies usually require a college degree. For example, to be hired as customs enforcement officer, a degree or three years of related work experience is required. FBI Special Agents are required to have a degree in law or accounting. Accounting degrees should be coupled with at least one year of related work experience.

Most management or supervisory jobs in this group are filled from within the ranks. Promotions are usually based on written examinations and job performance and are usually subject to civil service laws.

What else should you consider about these jobs?

Most workers in these jobs are on call any time their services are needed. They may work overtime during emergencies. Many of these jobs expose workers to great physical danger.

If you think you would like to do this kind of work, look at the job titles listed on the following pages. Select those that interest you and read their definitions in the Dictionary of Occupational Titles.

Safety and Law Enforcement

04.01.01 Managing
Fire Marshal (any ind.) 373.167-018
Guard, Chief (any ind.) 372.167-014

Manager, Internal Security (bus. ser.) 376.137-010

Battalion Chief (gov. ser.) 373.167-010
Captain, Fire-Prevention Bureau (gov. ser.) 373.167-014
Commanding Officer, Homicide Squad (gov. ser.) 375.167-010
Commanding Officer, Investigation Division (gov. ser.) 375.167-014
Commanding Officer, Motorized Squad (gov. ser.) 375.163-010
Correction Officer, Head (gov. ser.) 372.137-010
Deputy, Court (gov. ser.) 377.137-018
Deputy Sheriff, Chief (gov. ser.) 377.167-010
Deputy Sheriff, Commander, Civil Division (gov. ser.) 377.137-010
Deputy Sheriff, Commander, Criminal and Patrol Division (gov. ser.) 377.137-014
Desk Officer (gov. ser.) 375.137-014
Detective Chief (gov. ser.) 375.167-022
Fire Assistant (gov. ser.) 169.167-022
Fire Captain (gov. ser.) 373.134-010
Fire Chief (gov. ser.) 373.117-010
Harbor Master (gov. ser.) 375.167-026
Jailer, Chief (gov. ser.) 372.167-018
Launch Commander, Harbor Police (gov. ser.) 375.167-030
Park Superintendent (gov. ser.) 188.167-062
Police-Academy Instructor (gov. ser.) 375.227-010
Police Captain, Precinct (gov. ser.) 375.167-034
Police Chief (gov. ser.) 375.117-010

Police Commissioner (gov. ser.) I 188.117-118
Police Inspector (gov. ser.) I 375.267-026
Police Lieutenant, Patrol (gov. ser.) 375.167-038
Police Sergeant, Precinct (gov. ser.) I 375.133-010
Sheriff, Deputy, Chief (gov. ser.) 377.117-010
Traffic Lieutenant (gov. ser.) 375.167-046
Traffic Sergeant (gov. ser.) 375.137-026

Special Agent-in-Charge (r.r. trans.) 376.167-010

04.01.02 Investigating
Investigator, Private (bus. ser.) 376.267-018

Fire Warden (forestry) 452.167-010

Accident-Prevention-Squad Police Officer (gov. ser.) 375.263-010
Customs Patrol Officer (gov. ser.) 168.167-010
Deputy Sheriff, Civil Division (gov. ser.) 377.667-018
Detective (gov. ser.) 375.267-010
Detective, Narcotics and Vice (gov. ser.) 375.267-014
Fire Marshal (gov. ser.) 373.267-014
Fish and Game Warden (gov. ser.) 379.167-010
Investigator, Narcotics (gov. ser.) 375.267-018
Investigator, Vice (gov. ser.) 375.267-022
Pilot, Highway Patrol (gov. ser.) 375.163-014
Police Inspector (gov. ser.) II 375.267-030
Police Officer (gov. ser.) I 375.263-014
Sheriff, Deputy (gov. ser.) 377.263-010
Special Agent (gov. ser.) 375.167-042
Special Agent, Customs (gov. ser.) 188.167-090
State-Highway Police Officer (gov. ser.) 375.263-018
Wildlife Agent, Regional (gov. ser.) 379.137-018

Investigator (light, heat, & power) 376.367-022

Figure 5.9 continued

The *Military Career Guide*

The *Military Career Guide* provides descriptive information on various military jobs. It is a compendium of military occupational and training information. It is a single reference source for the diverse employment and training opportunities in the Army, Navy, Air Force, Marine Corps and Coast Guard. It contains descriptions of 134 enlisted and officer military occupations arranged in 12 broad career groups.

This resource cross references occupations with DOT codes so information on related civilian occupations in the DOT can be accessed. Also, if a student has taken the Armed Services Vocational Aptitude Battery (ASVAB), they can identify military careers related to the highest composite scores.

Example from the *Military Career Guide*

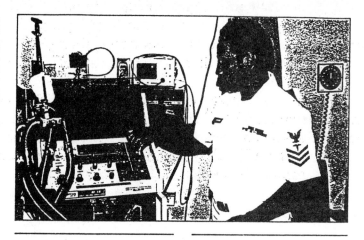

RESPIRATORY THERAPISTS

Army
Navy
Air Force

Asthma and emphysema (lung disease) patients suffer from breathing difficulties. Victims of heart failure, stroke, or near drowning may also have long-term breathing problems. Respiratory therapy is provided to patients with breathing problems. Respiratory therapists help patients regain breathing functions through therapy, exercise, and medication.

What They Do

Respiratory therapists in the military perform some or all of the following duties:

- Assist in reviving patients who are no longer breathing or whose hearts have stopped
- Operate and monitor respiratory therapy equipment during treatment
- Observe and record patient response to respiratory therapy
- Clean, sterilize, and maintain respiratory therapy equipment
- Instruct patients in breathing exercises to help clear lungs of fluids
- Instruct patients on how to operate home respiratory therapy equipment

Physical Demands

Respiratory therapists may have to lift and position patients for treatment.

Helpful Attributes

.Helpful school subjects include general science, chemistry, and biology. Helpful attributes include:

- Ability to deal with stressful situations
- Ability to respond quickly to emergencies
- Interest in helping others

Work Environment

Respiratory therapists usually work in hospitals or clinics. In combat situations, they may work in mobile field hospitals.

Training Provided

Job training consists of between 32 and 41 weeks of classroom instruction, including practice in providing respiratory therapy. Course content typically includes:

- Procedures for operating respiratory therapy equipment
- Methods for providing emergency care
- Techniques of respiratory therapy

Further training occurs on the job and through advanced courses.

Civilian Counterparts

Civilian respiratory therapists work in hospitals and clinics and for ambulance services. Their duties are similar to those of military respiratory therapists. Civilian respiratory therapists may be called inhalation therapists or pulmonary therapists.

Opportunities

The military has about 310 respiratory therapists. On average, the services need about 30 new therapists each year. After job training, therapists provide treatment under the direction of a supervisor. With experience, they advance from caring for patients with minor respiratory problems to caring for patients with more serious problems. They may also supervise and direct the work of other respiratory therapists.

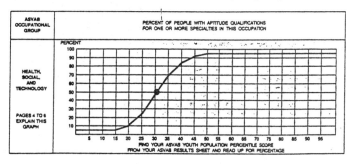

Military Career Guide

75

Figure 5.10

Standard Occupational Classification (SOC)

Since 1982, many federal government occupational publications have been organized and cross referenced by the *Standard Occupational Classification* (SOC) codes. Aside from the SOC's value as a classification system, the SOC groups occupations on the basis of the type of work performed. Therefore, it is a valuable reference for identifying occupations related to each other.

If a client is interested in a particular occupation, but finds the industry or work setting in that locale is undesirable, he or she can identify occupations that are similar in nature, but may cross into other industry settings through the SOC. The SOC has been particularly useful for research and classification purposes but its value in practical applications is unclear.

5233 Health Aides, Except Nursing

This unit group includes occupations involving performing various duties under the direction of trained medical practitioners, such as mixing pharmaceutical preparations, issuing medicines, labeling and storing supplies; assisting during physical examination of patients, giving specified office treatments, and keeping patients' records; preparing treatment room, inventory of supplies and instruments; preparing, bottling and sterilizing infant formulas. May also assist in physical and other therapy treatment.

Pharmacy helper	573	074387010
Physical therapist assistant	573	076224010
Occupational therapy assistant	573	076364010
Laboratory assistant, blood and plasma	323-573	078687010
Chiropractor assistant	573	079364010
Medical assistant	573	079367010
Podiatric assistant	573	079374018
Physical therapy aide	573	355354010
Ambulance attendant	573	355374010
Occupational therapy aide	573	355377010
Morgue attendant	573	355667010
Graves registration specialist	574	355687014
Formula-room worker	313-573	520487014
Ambulance driver	573	913683010

Note: See page 9 for explanation of job title codes.

Figure 5.11

Decision Area: A Work Setting (Business or Industry)

Information about a work setting is commonly referred to as information about an industry. It is another dimension of career decision making. Clients and students need some understanding of the environment in which occupations exist. Each type of industry or business has a different working environment even though they may employ persons in similar occupations. For example, a truck driver who works for a moving and storage company will usually have to load and unload the trucks by hand whereas an over-the-road driver may not touch the freight. Likewise, the skills and work of a plumber will vary considerably between residential and industrial work settings. The type of industry or business is a major influence on the specific job conditions, pay, benefits and numerous other conditions of employment.

Students or clients making career decisions who have seriously considered a specific occupational area may be more interested in certain industrial sectors. They may be interested in working at a particular local firm, such as a health care facility or a local bank. To assist, the career development facilitator needs to identify the industry and help research its occupational staffing pattern. This process will reveal the types of occupations employed in that industry, giving the client a choice of occupations to investigate.

Two references can be used to collect this information: The *Standard Industrial Classification* (SIC) Manual and Occupational Information Systems (OIS).

Standard Industrial Classification (SIC)

The SIC can help identify industries and places of employment. It is a system by which an industry, or work setting, is classified. It gives a detailed description of the industrial division and major groups classified within each industrial division.

The manual does not list specific companies by name but it is an excellent resource for understanding the industrial makeup of a city, community or state. Similar industries are listed together, which makes it helpful when determining which firms might employ people with skills or work experiences obtained from a similar industry.

Major Group 54.—FOOD STORES

The Major Group as a Whole

This major group includes retail stores primarily engaged in selling food for home preparation and consumption. Establishments primarily engaged in selling prepared foods and drinks for consumption on the premises are classified in Major Group 58, and stores primarily engaged in selling packaged beers and liquors are classified in Industry 5921.

Industry Group No.	Industry No.	

541   **GROCERY STORES**

    5411   **Grocery Stores**

      Stores, commonly known as supermarkets, food stores, and grocery stores, primarily engaged in the retail sale of all sorts of canned foods and dry goods, such as tea, coffee, spices, sugar, and flour; fresh fruits and vegetables; and fresh and prepared meats, fish, and poultry.

Convenience food stores—retail	Grocery stores, with or without fresh
Food markets—retail	meat—retail
Frozen food and freezer plans, except	Supermarkets, grocery—retail
meat—retail	

542   **MEAT AND FISH (SEAFOOD) MARKETS, INCLUDING FREEZER PROVISIONERS**

    5421   **Meat and Fish (Seafood) Markets, Including Freezer Provisioners**

      Establishments primarily engaged in the retail sale of fresh, frozen, or cured meats, fish, shellfish, and other seafoods. This industry includes establishments primarily engaged in the retail sale, on a bulk basis, of meat for freezer storage and in providing home freezer plans. Meat markets may butcher animals on their own account, or they may buy from others. Food locker plants primarily engaged in renting locker space for the storage of food products for individual households are classified in Industry 4222. Establishments primarily engaged in the retail sale of poultry are classified in Industry 5499.

Fish markets—retail	Meat markets—retail
Freezer food plans, meat—retail	Seafood markets—retail
Freezer provisioners, meat—retail	
Frozen food and freezer plans, meat—	
retail	

543   **FRUIT AND VEGETABLE MARKETS**

    5431   **Fruit and Vegetable Markets**

      Establishments primarily engaged in the retail sale of fresh fruits and vegetables. They are frequently found in public or municipal markets or as roadside stands. However, establishments which grow fruits and vegetables and sell them at roadside stands are classified in Agriculture, Major Group 01.

Fruit markets and stands—retail	Vegetable markets and stands—retail
Produce markets and stands—retail	

Figure 5.12

Occupational Information Systems (OIS)

The OIS can help identify the industries that employ a given occupation and will identify the occupations employed within a given industry (the staffing patterns) and their demand/supply outlook.

Some State Occupation Information Coordinating Committees (SOICCs) have created computerized Occupational Information Systems (OIS) programs which use data from the Occupational Employment Statistics Program (OES). These databases may provide information on the industries that employ a specified occupation, as well as the occupations employed by a specific industry.

Industry/Occupational Relationships Route

<Chart 3>

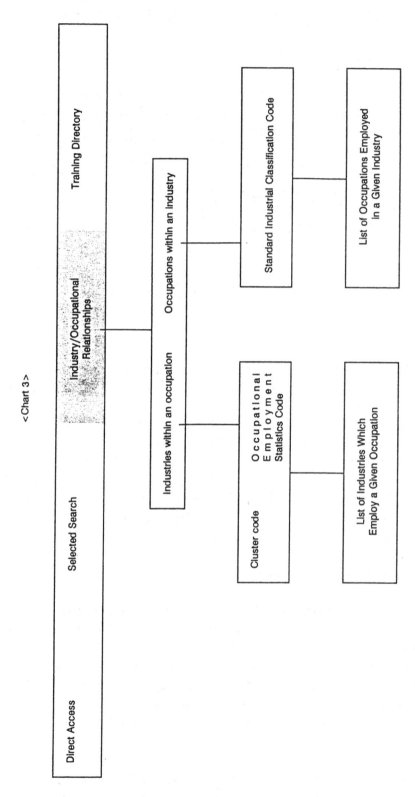

Figure 5.13

For example, Figure 5.14 illustrates where the occupations Bookkeeping and Accounting Clerks are employed in North Dakota industries.

```
                                                          Press Return
                  NORTH DAKOTA OCCUPATIONAL INFORMATION SYSTEM
NORTH DAKOTA            M A T R I X   R E P O R T
CLUSTER TITLE: BOOKKEEPING & ACCOUNTING CLERKS    NORTH DAKOTA CLUSTER # 0050

         >>> OES OCCUPATION: [553383051] -- BOOKKEEPING & ACCOUNTING CLERKS
                                          (Employment Level = 6111)
  SIC -  -- STANDARD INDUSTRIAL CLASSIFICATION (SIC) TITLE -     PERCENT OF
  CODE                                                          OES EMPLOYMENT

   581   EATING AND DRINKING PLACES, TOTAL                        2.89 %
   517   PETROLEUM AND PETROLEUM PRODUCTS                         3.02 %
   508   MACHINERY, EQUIPMENT, AND SUPPLIES                       3.06 %
   515   FARM-PRODUCT RAW MATERIALS                               4.37 %
   903   LOCAL GOVERNMENT, EXC. EDUCATION                         4.57 %
   602   COMMERCIAL AND STOCK SAVINGS BANKS                       4.89 %
   882   SELF EMPLOYED AND UNPAID FAMILY WORKERS                  8.90 %
```

[FIGURE 27] INDUSTRIES WITHIN AN OCCUPATION REPORT {sample}

Figure 5.14

The codes and titles on the left are *Standard Industrial Codes* (SIC) and select groupings of businesses by common activity or product. The percent of employment shown in the right column is a percent of the total employment, which is listed in the heading of the report, "Employment Level." To determine the number of Accounting and Bookkeeping Clerks within a given industry, multiply the percent times the Employment Level. For example, Eating and Drinking places employ 177 (2.8% of 6111) bookkeeping and accounting clerks in North Dakota. Farm Products and Raw Materials employ 267 Accounting and Bookkeeping Clerks (4.37% of 6111).

Decision Area: A Geographic Area

This decision area allows the student or client to explore career options based on a preference for a particular geographic area. For those who are undecided or unenthusiastic about any particular occupational or industrial sector, the most important starting point may be geography. Where would the person prefer to live? Sometimes people begin to explore options by considering family ties, or the weather, and maybe the unemployment rate. In other cases, the attraction may be family or friends.

To illustrate the importance of geographic location, consider the following. McKee and Froeschle (1985) found that two metropolitan areas of roughly the same population, Pittsburgh and Dallas-Fort Worth, differed significantly in their opportunities for clerical workers. Pittsburgh anticipated that 195,303 clerical workers would be employed in 1985, while Dallas-Fort Worth anticipated 362,100. This discrepancy was accounted for by the industrial structure of the areas. Dallas-Fort Worth is a regional service center and financial hub. Therefore, it has a greater need for clerical support positions. Conversely, Pittsburgh has more of a manufacturing economy and has a lower demand for clerical positions.

When looking for information by geographic area, many have noted that in contrast to the abundance of national and state information, local information is often the most difficult to find. There are several sources that provide details on the local economy and industrial structure. Two of these sources, CIDS and OIS provide local data that is easily accessed. *County Business Patterns* is another example that identifies the number of business establishments in each industry and the distribution of business establishments by employee size.

Example of Local Information

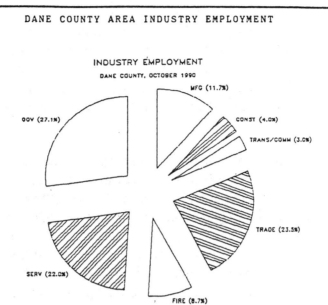

DANE COUNTY AREA INDUSTRY EMPLOYMENT

INDUSTRY EMPLOYMENT
DANE COUNTY, OCTOBER 1990

Preliminary figures indicate GOVERNMENT (Gov), Dane County's largest employing sector, increased 400 in October for a total of 60,700. State government increased by 100 to 41,900, and local government increased by 300 for a total of 15,500. Federal government lost 100 positions for a total of 3,300. There were 1,500 more public sector jobs this October than last year.

TRADE (Trade) increased by 800 to 52,700 positions in October. Wholesale trade remained the same at 9,000 ,but retail trade increased by 800, for a total of 43,700. Area retail locations are adding new positions for the holiday trade. This is the second month in a row that retail trade has added 800 positions.

SERVICES (Serv) increased by 200 from 49,000 in September to 49,200 in October, 1990. There were 1,000 more jobs in the service sector this October than last.

MANUFACTURING (Mfg) decreased 300, for a preliminary October total of 26,300. Durable goods remained the same at 13,800, while nondurables fell by 300 to a preliminary 12,400. There were 1,300 more manufacturing jobs this October than in October of last year.

FINANCE, INSURANCE & REAL ESTATE (FIRE) reported in with 19,400 jobs. This was the same as last month, September. However, there were still 500 more FIRE industry positions this October than last year.

TRANSPORTATION, COMMUNICATION & UTILITIES (Trans/Comm) also remained unchanged at 6,700, but was down 100 from last year.

CONSTRUCTION (Const) was down by 100 from September to October at 8,900. Employment in this sector was up 800 from last year.

Data produced in cooperation with the Bureau of Labor Statistics—USDOL.

Figure 5.15

The State Employment Security Agency (SESA) also publishes industrial employment data for individual counties.

Another source, often overlooked, is the Yellow Pages in the local telephone directory. With this resource, one can determine the number of industries in the local area and can easily find employer names, addresses and telephone numbers.

Using Crosswalks to Ease the Process

Accessing the most useful information can be complicated for the novice because there are many data collection programs that provide career and labor market information. In addition, there are many different ways to classify and organize that information.

Within the descriptions of various resources, it was pointed out that one could move from one system to another, such as from the *Military Career Guide* to the DOT. This movement is called "crosswalking." It enables the user to move back and forth across the various classification systems in order to analyze and compare occupations. To maximize our use of information, these bridges, or crosswalks, between the various information systems are actually conversion tables between the different systems. Crosswalks are similar to a dictionary, which moves us from an English word to its Spanish equivalent; they allow the user to translate one information system to another. An example of a crosswalk can be found in a CIDS. The system links occupational information with related educational and training requirements "behind the scenes." These two pieces of information are linked in the system and presented in a single profile so the user has a more complete picture of the occupation.

For more information on crosswalks, contact the National Crosswalk Service Center at the Iowa SOICC office (515/242-4890).

Labor Force, Industry and Occupational Projections

The following is an example of career and labor market information that can be used to enhance career decision making. These labor force, industry and occupational projections can provide insight into how the nation's work force and economy are likely to grow, e.g., which occupations will grow the fastest, which will decline, which will provide the greatest number of new jobs, and which occupations have the highest and lowest turnover rates.

It is relatively easy to describe the demographics of the labor supply, but projecting which way the economy will go and which industries and occupations will grow and decline is not as predictable. A combination of statistical techniques and human judgment is required.

The major goal of this section in Module 5 is to present information that describes and analyzes significant trends in the labor force, economy, industries and occupations that will have an impact on the effectiveness of career decision making. The results of the Bureau of Labor Statistics (BLS) projections from 1990-2005 are included. Much of the information is available at the state and local levels through offices of labor market information and SOICCs.

Several trends need to be noted as the projections are discussed:

- the rate of economic growth will be much slower;
- women's share of the labor force will continue to increase;
- the work force will age;
- employment will be concentrated in a few industries, namely the services and retail trade industries;
- workers with the most education and training will have the best opportunities; and
- technology will continue to change the structure of employment and how work is done.

These trends have far reaching implications for how we direct our clients and students to make educational and career choices.

These projections were made given the following assumptions about general economic or social conditions:

- Work patterns will not change significantly over the projections period, meaning that the average workweek will not change markedly.
- Broad social and educational trends will continue. For example, women will continue to be a large portion of the labor force.
- There will be no major war.
- There will be no significant change in the size of the Armed Forces.
- Fluctuations in economic activity due to the business cycle will continue to occur.

These projections cover the period 1990-2005. An expanded version of the projections can be found in the November 1991 issue of the *Monthly Labor Review* or in *Outlook 1990-2005*, published by the Bureau of Labor Statistics.

OUTLOOK 1990 - 2005

Bureau of Labor Statistics
Office of Employment Projections

- The BLS projections program is carried out in the Office of Employment Projections.

- The program began with the development of career guidance information to assist returning veterans from World War II.

- Projections for a 10- to 15-year period have been developed every other year since the mid-1960's.

- The latest set of projections, which covers the 1990 - 2005 period, is the subject of this slide presentation.

Figure 5.16

A four step analysis leads to the projections. Components analyzed are:

- Labor Force
- Economy
- Industry
- Occupations

Sequence of Projection Procedures
to Determine Occupational Demand

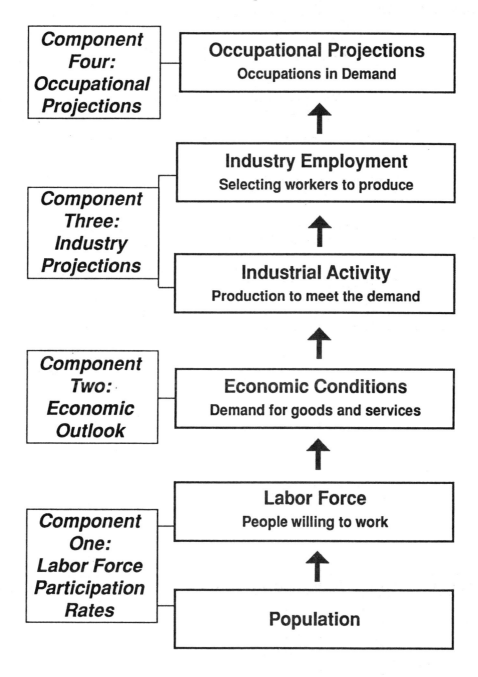

Component Four: Occupational Projections

Occupational Projections
Occupations in Demand

Component Three: Industry Projections

Industry Employment
Selecting workers to produce

Industrial Activity
Production to meet the demand

Component Two: Economic Outlook

Economic Conditions
Demand for goods and services

Component One: Labor Force Participation Rates

Labor Force
People willing to work

Population

Figure 5.17

OUTLOOK: 1990-2005

- ***Labor force***

- Economic outlook

- Industry employment

- Occupational employment

Figure 5.18

The labor force is expected to expand but at a slower pace than in 1975-90.

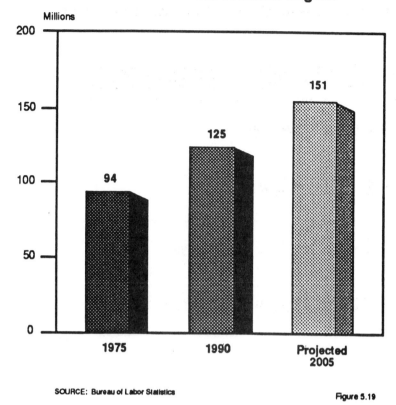

Labor force will continue to grow

Millions

SOURCE: Bureau of Labor Statistics

Figure 5.19

The declining birthrate contributes to this slowing of the growth rate.

Labor force grows faster than population

Percent change

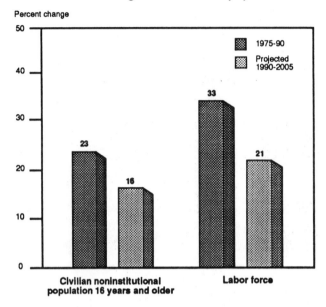

SOURCE: Bureau of Labor Statistics

Figure 5.20

Labor force growth by age

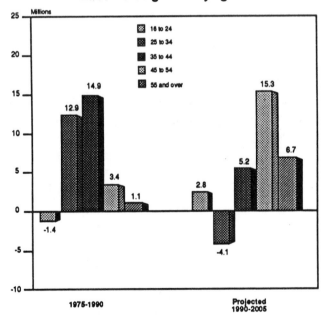

SOURCE: Bureau of Labor Statistics

Figure 5.21

The baby boom, declining birth rates in the 1960s, and children of the baby boom cohort will continue to have an impact on the labor force.

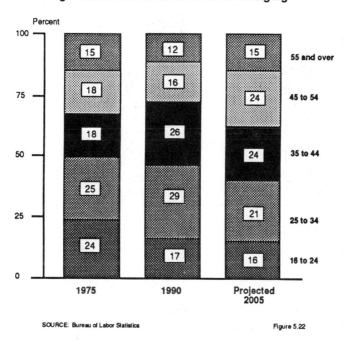

Age distribution of labor force is changing

SOURCE: Bureau of Labor Statistics   Figure 5.22

Although rates of labor force growth are projected to drop for both men and women, labor force growth for women will be greater, reflecting their increasing labor force participation.

Women's share of labor force is growing

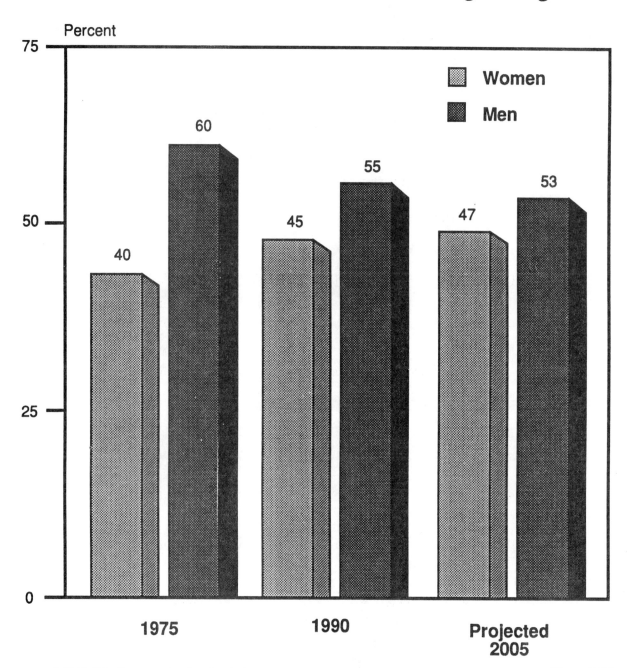

SOURCE: Bureau of Labor Statistics

Figure 5.23

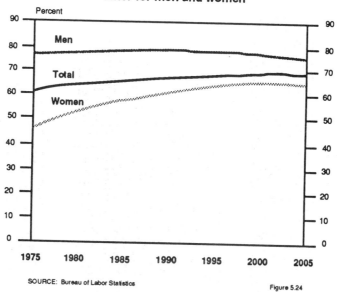

Labor force participation rate trends differ for men and women

SOURCE: Bureau of Labor Statistics

Figure 5.24

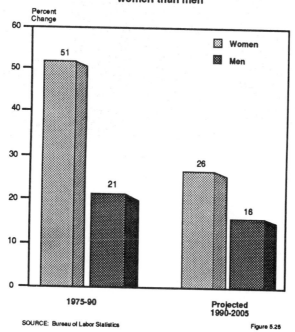

Labor force growth slows more for women than men

SOURCE: Bureau of Labor Statistics

Figure 5.25

Minorities' share of the labor force will continue to grow. Some of the entrants into the labor market will be needed to replace those leaving the labor force. The others represent a net growth of 26 million workers. Despite these increases, the majority of the entrants will continue to be white, non-Hispanic, men and women.

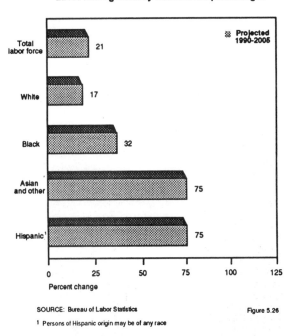

Labor force growth by race and Hispanic origin

SOURCE: Bureau of Labor Statistics

Figure 5.26

1 Persons of Hispanic origin may be of any race

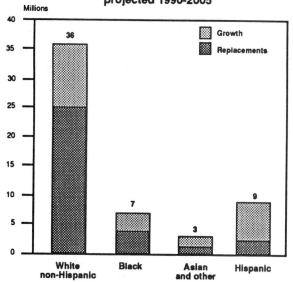

Labor force entrants by race and Hispanic origin, projected 1990-2005

SOURCE: Bureau of Labor Statistics

Figure 5.27

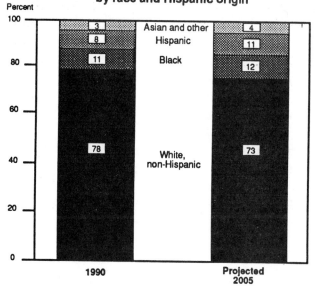

Distribution of the labor force by race and Hispanic origin

SOURCE: Bureau of Labor Statistics

Figure 5.28

ICDM

OUTLOOK: 1990-2005

* Labor force

* *Economic outlook*

* Industry employment

* Occupational employment

Figure 5.29

After the labor force participation rates are projected, the second stage is to determine the sum total of all economic activity in the United States, also known as the aggregate economic activity. This includes real gross national product (GNP), and the distribution of GNP across five major demand and income categories:

1. personal consumption expenditures (buying a car);
2. gross private domestic investment (business investment in equipment);
3. exports (e.g., selling wheat to Russia);
4. imports (buying oil from OPEC); and
5. government (spending on Medicaid).

Through this analysis, the relative wealth of the nation is determined. Estimates of demand are then made by industry, both public and private.

Summary results from recent analyses show:

* Goods and services purchased by individuals will grow at about the same rate as total GNP and will continue to be the largest component of demand.
* Investment will continue to grow faster than total GNP.
* Exports will grow faster than imports.

- Federal government expenditures will continue to decline due to cuts in defense expenditures.
- State and local government expenditures are the only major category that will increase faster during this period than it did from 1975 to 1990.

According to a moderate growth scenario, the unemployment rate is assumed to remain unchanged and the rate of GNP growth is expected to grow. This is attributable to the slowing labor force growth.

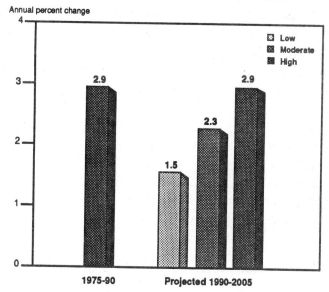

GNP growth and projected alternatives

SOURCE: Bureau of Labor Statistics

Figure 5.30

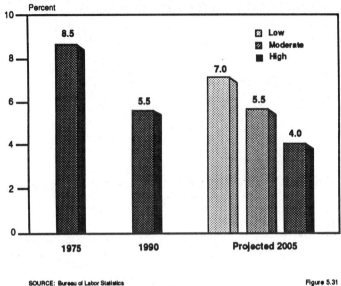

Unemployment rates and projected alternatives

Percent

Legend:
- ⊠ Low
- ▨ Moderate
- ■ High

1975: 8.5
1990: 5.5
Projected 2005: 7.0, 5.5, 4.0

SOURCE: Bureau of Labor Statistics

Figure 5.31

Component Three: Industry Projections

This component analyzes the trends in employment by industry.

OUTLOOK: 1990-2005

- ❋ Labor force

- ❋ Economic outlook

- • *Industry employment*

- ❋ Occupational employment

Figure 5.32

It is projected that of the 26 million new jobs by the year 2005, the service-producing sector will dominate and the goods-producing sector will remain stable. Total employment is projected to increase but at a slower rate. This slowdown reflects the slower growth of the labor force.

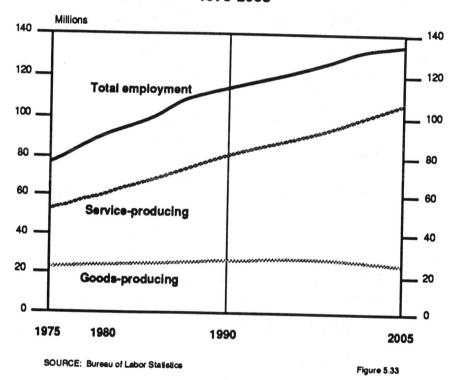

Employment growth by major economic sectors, 1975-2005

SOURCE: Bureau of Labor Statistics

Figure 5.33

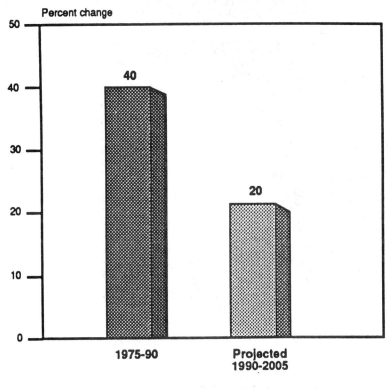

Employment growth, 1975-90 and projected 1990-2005

Percent change

1975-90	**40**
Projected 1990-2005	**20**

SOURCE: Bureau of Labor Statistics

Figure 5.34

Employment gains will continue to be in service producing industries.

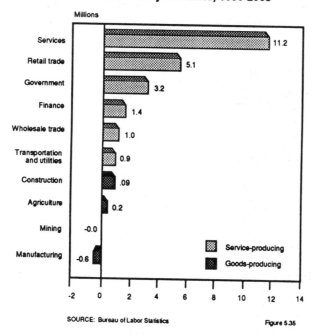

Job growth in services outpaces other industry divisions, 1990-2005

Millions

Services	11.2
Retail trade	5.1
Government	3.2
Finance	1.4
Wholesale trade	1.0
Transportation and utilities	0.9
Construction	.09
Agriculture	0.2
Mining	-0.0
Manufacturing	-0.6

Service-producing
Goods-producing

-2   0   2   4   6   8   10   12   14

SOURCE: Bureau of Labor Statistics

Figure 5.35

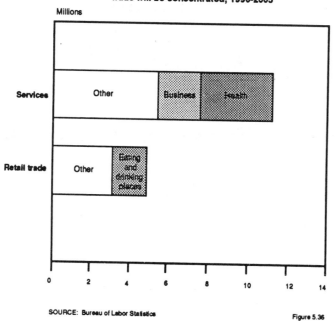

Employment growth within services and retail trade will be concentrated, 1990-2005

Millions

Services: Other | Business | Health

Retail trade: Other | Eating and drinking places

0   2   4   6   8   10   12   14

SOURCE: Bureau of Labor Statistics

Figure 5.36

Industries adding the most jobs, 1990-2005

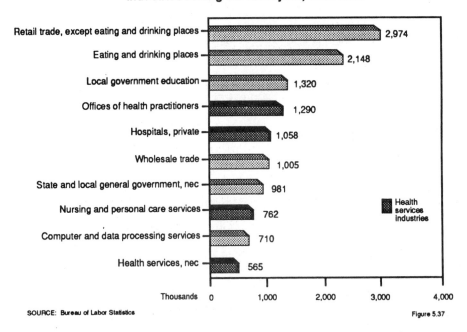

Retail trade, except eating and drinking places	2,974
Eating and drinking places	2,148
Local government education	1,320
Offices of health practitioners	1,290
Hospitals, private	1,058
Wholesale trade	1,005
State and local general government, nec	981
Nursing and personal care services	762
Computer and data processing services	710
Health services, nec	565

■ Health services industries

Thousands

SOURCE: Bureau of Labor Statistics

Figure 5.37

Industries with the fastest job growth, 1990-2005

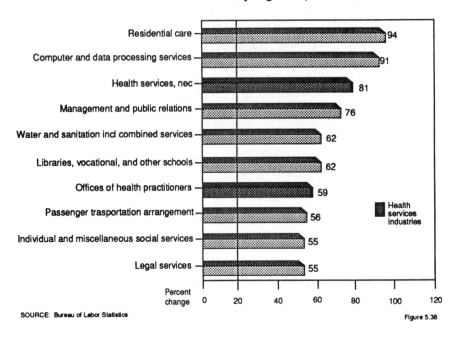

Residential care	94
Computer and data processing services	91
Health services, nec	81
Management and public relations	76
Water and sanitation incl combined services	62
Libraries, vocational, and other schools	62
Offices of health practitioners	59
Passenger trasportation arrangement	56
Individual and miscellaneous social services	55
Legal services	55

■ Health services industries

Percent change

SOURCE: Bureau of Labor Statistics

Figure 5.38

ICDM

The majority of the most rapidly declining industries, in terms of employment, will be in manufacturing.

Industries with the most rapid job declines, 1990-2005

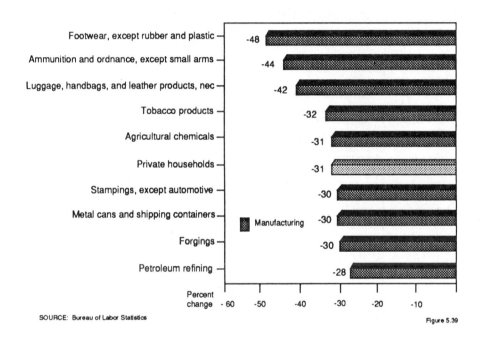

SOURCE: Bureau of Labor Statistics

Figure 5.39

Another way to talk about industries is to look at their output. High technology manufacturing industries will be among the fastest growing in terms of output.

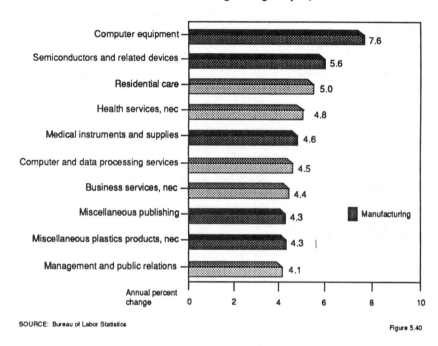

Industries with the fastest growing output, 1990-2005

Industry	Annual percent change
Computer equipment	7.6
Semiconductors and related devices	5.6
Residential care	5.0
Health services, nec	4.8
Medical instruments and supplies	4.6
Computer and data processing services	4.5
Business services, nec	4.4
Miscellaneous publishing	4.3
Miscellaneous plastics products, nec	4.3
Management and public relations	4.1

■ Manufacturing

SOURCE: Bureau of Labor Statistics

Figure 5.40

Even though total manufacturing employment will decline slightly, a handful of manufacturing industries are projected to experience some employment growth.

Fastest growing and declining manufacturing industries, 1990-2005

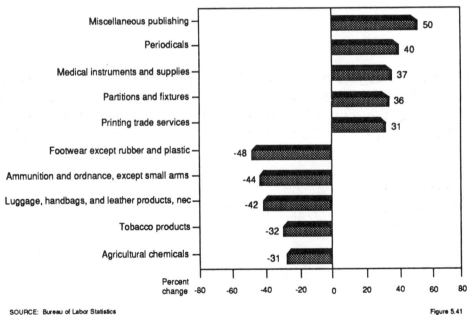

Industry	Percent change
Miscellaneous publishing	50
Periodicals	40
Medical instruments and supplies	37
Partitions and fixtures	36
Printing trade services	31
Footwear except rubber and plastic	-48
Ammunition and ordnance, except small arms	-44
Luggage, handbags, and leather products, nec	-42
Tobacco products	-32
Agricultural chemicals	-31

SOURCE: Bureau of Labor Statistics

Figure 5.41

Component Four: Occupational Projections

The fourth major phase of the projections process is to develop employment projections for approximately 500 occupations. An industry-occupation matrix is used to project employment in these occupations for over 200 industries.

OUTLOOK: 1990-2005

* Labor force

* Economic outlook

* Industry employment

* *Occupational employment*

Figure 5.42

It is projected that jobs will be available for workers at all educational levels, but those with the most education and training will enjoy the best opportunities. The occupational groups with the highest levels of educational attainment will experience faster than average growth. They are:

- technicians,
- professional specialty occupations, and
- managers.

Employment growth by major occupational group, 1990-2005

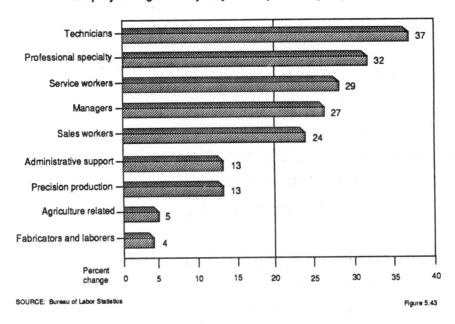

SOURCE: Bureau of Labor Statistics

Figure 5.43

In contrast, precision production operators and agriculture related occupations have the lowest proportion of workers with college training, and these occupations are projected to have the slowest employment growth.

Job openings for replacement and growth, 1990-2005

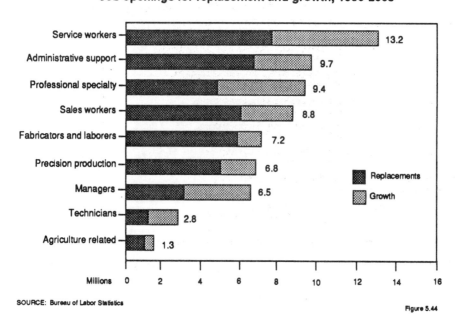

SOURCE: Bureau of Labor Statistics

Figure 5.44

Due to rapid growth in the health services industry, many growing occupations are health-related.

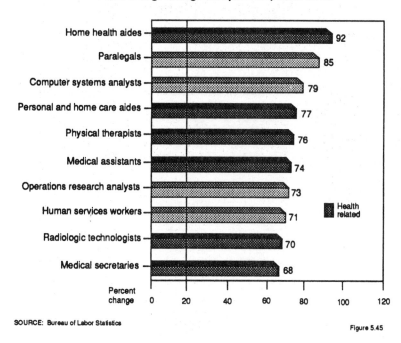

Fastest growing occupations, 1990-2005

Home health aides — 92
Paralegals — 85
Computer systems analysts — 79
Personal and home care aides — 77
Physical therapists — 76
Medical assistants — 74
Operations research analysts — 73
Human services workers — 71
Radiologic technologists — 70
Medical secretaries — 68

■ Health related

Percent change

0 20 40 60 80 100 120

SOURCE: Bureau of Labor Statistics

Figure 5.45

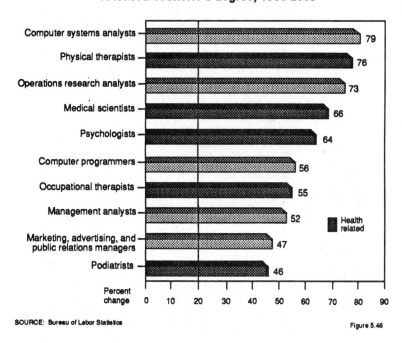

Fastest growing occupations generally requiring at least a bachelor's degree, 1990-2005

Computer systems analysts — 79
Physical therapists — 76
Operations research analysts — 73
Medical scientists — 66
Psychologists — 64
Computer programmers — 56
Occupational therapists — 55
Management analysts — 52
Marketing, advertising, and public relations managers — 47
Podiatrists — 46

■ Health related

Percent change

0 10 20 30 40 50 60 70 80 90

SOURCE: Bureau of Labor Statistics

Figure 5.46

ICDM

Fastest growing occupations generally requiring post-secondary training but less than a college degree, 1990-2005

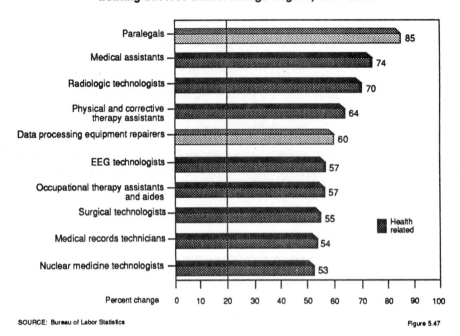

Paralegals — 85
Medical assistants — 74
Radiologic technologists — 70
Physical and corrective therapy assistants — 64
Data processing equipment repairers — 60
EEG technologists — 57
Occupational therapy assistants and aides — 57
Surgical technologists — 55
Medical records technicians — 54
Nuclear medicine technologists — 53

■ Health related

Percent change   0 10 20 30 40 50 60 70 80 90 100

SOURCE: Bureau of Labor Statistics

Figure 5.47

Fastest growing occupations generally requiring no more than a high school diploma, 1990-2005

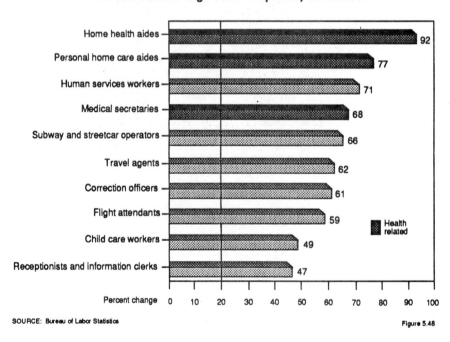

Home health aides — 92
Personal home care aides — 77
Human services workers — 71
Medical secretaries — 68
Subway and streetcar operators — 66
Travel agents — 62
Correction officers — 61
Flight attendants — 59
Child care workers — 49
Receptionists and information clerks — 47

■ Health related

Percent change   0 10 20 30 40 50 60 70 80 90 100

SOURCE: Bureau of Labor Statistics

Figure 5.48

ICDM

Do not always assume that occupations with the fastest growth rate provide the most new jobs. Remember, "growth" refers to the percentage of already existing jobs, not the actual number of jobs.

Job growth may be viewed in two ways:
Changes, 1990-2005

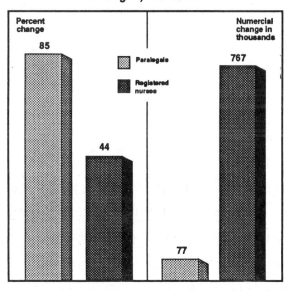

SOURCE: Bureau of Labor Statistics

Figure 5.49

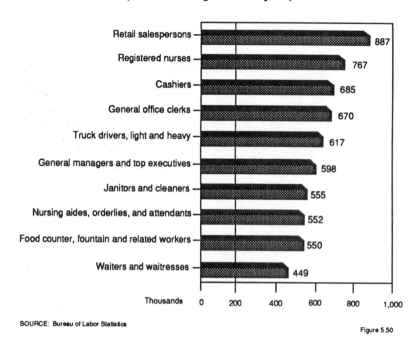

Occupations adding the most jobs, 1990-2005

Occupation	Thousands
Retail salespersons	887
Registered nurses	767
Cashiers	685
General office clerks	670
Truck drivers, light and heavy	617
General managers and top executives	598
Janitors and cleaners	555
Nursing aides, orderlies, and attendants	552
Food counter, fountain and related workers	550
Waiters and waitresses	449

SOURCE: Bureau of Labor Statistics

Figure 5.50

Workers who might experience layoffs include those in occupations within declining industries and those whose occupations are changing due to technological innovations. Even though the demand for a particular occupation may be declining, there will still be a need for new workers to replace people leaving these occupations.

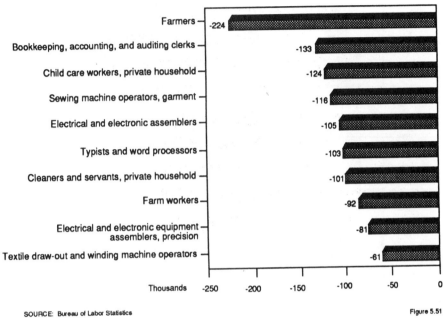

Employment change in declining occupations, 1990-2005

Occupation	Change (Thousands)
Farmers	-224
Bookkeeping, accounting, and auditing clerks	-133
Child care workers, private household	-124
Sewing machine operators, garment	-116
Electrical and electronic assemblers	-105
Typists and word processors	-103
Cleaners and servants, private household	-101
Farm workers	-92
Electrical and electronic equipment assemblers, precision	-81
Textile draw-out and winding machine operators	-61

SOURCE: Bureau of Labor Statistics

Figure 5.51

Combining Projections with Other Information

Another way to use labor market information is to combine it with other indicators such as educational attainment.

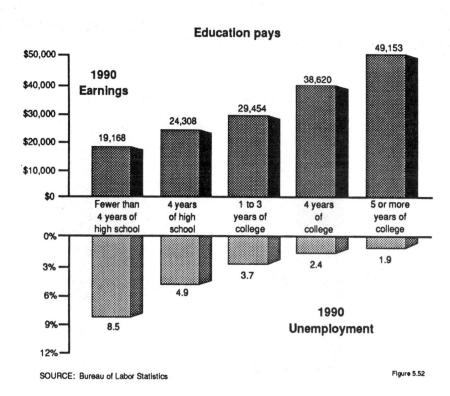

Figure 5.52

SOURCE: Bureau of Labor Statistics

Not only is education important in getting higher paying jobs, but people with more education have higher earnings within virtually all occupations.

Annual earnings of workers by highest level of educational attainment, 1987					
Occupational group	Total	Less than high school	High School	1 to 3 years of college	4 years of college or more
Average, all occupations	$21,543	$15,249	$18,902	$21,975	$31,029
Managerial	30,264	22,306	23,286	27,255	37,252
Professional speciality	30,116	19,177	23,233	27,458	31,311
Technicians	24,489	16,207	21,358	23,830	28,004
Marketing and sales	22,220	13,746	17,654	22,546	32,747
Administrative support	17,120	15,535	16,554	17,491	20,823
Service	13,443	10,764	13,093	16,937	21,381
Precision production	24,856	20,465	25,140	27,042	30,938
Operators	18,132	15,365	19,303	21,627	22,114
Agriculture-related	11,781	10,571	12,730	16,331	17,130

SOURCE: Bureau of Labor Statistics

Figure 5.53

Blacks and Hispanic workers have lower educational attainment than whites. As a result, blacks and Hispanics are underrepresented in the fast growing and higher paying occupations.

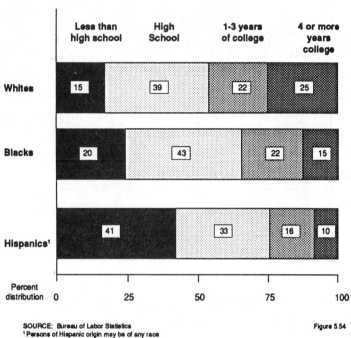

Educational attainment of workers by race and Hispanic origin, 1990

	Less than high school	High School	1-3 years of college	4 or more years college
Whites	15	39	22	25
Blacks	20	43	22	15
Hispanics¹	41	33	16	10

Percent distribution 0   25   50   75   100

SOURCE: Bureau of Labor Statistics
¹ Persons of Hispanic origin may be of any race

Figure 5.54

Concentration of blacks and Hispanics by major occupation group, 1990

Occupation	Percent of total employment		Projected growth rate	Earnings	Unemployment rate
	Black	Hispanic			
Total	10.1	7.5			
Managers	6.2	3.6	H	H	L
Professional specialty	6.7	3.4	H	H	L
Technicians	9.1	4.3	H	High	L
Sales workers	6.4	5.3	H	Average	A
Administrative support	11.4	6.5	L	Low	L
Service workers	17.3	11.2	H	L	H
Precision production	7.8	8.5	L	H	A
Fabricators and laborers	15.0	12.2	L	L	H
Agriculture related	6.1	14.2	L	L	H

SOURCE: Bureau of Labor Statistics

Figure 5.55

ICDM

Women continue to increase their participation rate although average earnings are still short of men's earnings.

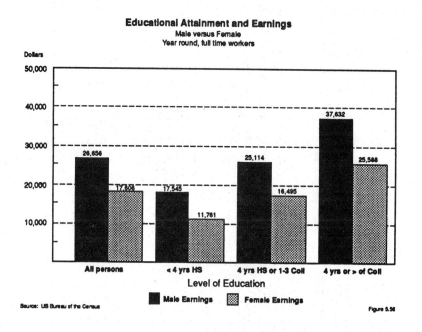

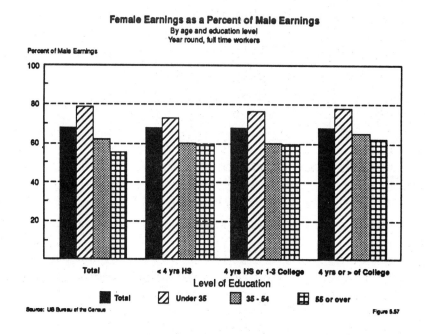

In conclusion, despite changes in individual occupations, the overall structure of occupations will remain relatively stable. However, it is important to note that those without some education beyond high school will be at a serious disadvantage in the labor market. They will face low wages, dislocation and disruption throughout their working lives.

Issues and Implications

Given these projections, we need to consider a number of challenges.

- Productivity: Development of world markets would provide an impetus to focus on high technology goods and services.
- Education: The potential imbalance between the educational preparation of those entering the labor force and the skill requirements of industry, requires attention.
- Labor Shortage: Those employers looking for 16-24 year old workers will feel increasing competition in recruitment. Tightened immigration laws will also effect the numbers of entry level workers.
- Minorities: All minority groups are projected to increase their share of the labor force. Specific outreach programs will be needed to educate and train all minority groups to compete effectively.
- Women: Women will continue to exert their influence on the work world.
- Industrial Shift: Closer collaboration with public training institutions can help industries maintain a skilled work force.
- Occupational Shift: Shifting skills within occupations requires a flexible work force.

Conclusion

All of these issues are interrelated. Understanding the dynamics of the labor force and the specific projections for the economy, industries and occupations can guide career development professionals to assist clients and students in making good career choices. The slowing rate of growth in productivity is linked to the need for our economy to remain competitive. Remaining competitive requires an available pool of highly skilled, educated and adaptable workers. The increasing sophistication of jobs in the future challenges all of us to meet the educational needs of all those who will enter the labor force.

Other Uses of Information

Career and labor market information also describes the specific populations in our country. It can be used to break down sexist and stereotypical preconceptions about people in the labor force. The following example illustrates how educators have used labor market statistics to promote self-awareness and sex equity in the classroom. The boxed statements indicate those built upon labor market information.

Sample of How Labor Market Information is Used

- When elementary school girls are asked to describe what they want to do when they grow up, they frequently identify only a few career options, and even these fit stereotypic patterns. The majority identify only two careers, teaching and nursing. Boys, on the other hand, are able to identify many more potential occupations.

- Many girls enter college without completing four years of high school mathematics. This lack of preparation in math serves as a "critical filter," inhibiting or preventing girls from many science, math, and technologically related careers.

- The preparation and counseling girls receive in school contributes to the economic penalties that they encounter in the workplace. Although *over 90 percent of the girls in our classrooms will work in the paid labor force for all or part of their lives*, the following statistics reveal the cost of the bias that they encounter.

Using Labor Market Information to Promote Self-Awareness and Sex Equity

- More than a third of families headed by women live below the poverty level.

- A woman with a college degree will typically earn approximately the same amount as a male who is a high school graduate.

- The typical working woman will earn 59 cents for every dollar earned by a male worker.

- Minority women earn even less, averaging only 50 percent of the wages earned by white males.

- Women are 79 percent of all clerical workers, but only 5 percent of all craft workers.

- Women must work nine days to earn what men get paid for five days of work.

- In contrast to the popular belief that things are getting better for female workers, since 1954 the gap between the wages earned by men and women has not gotten smaller.

- A majority of women work not for "extra" cash but because of economic necessity. Nearly two-thirds of all women in the labor force are single, widowed, divorced, or separated, or are married to spouse earning less than $10,000 a year.

Developed by Myra and David Sadker
Mid-Atlantic Center for Sex Equity

Distributed by the Department of Public Instruction,
P.O. Box 7841, Madison, Wisconsin 53707

Barbara Bitters-Vocational Equity
Melissa Keyes-Sex Equity

Figure 5.58

Limitations of Career and Labor Market Information

An understanding of the limitations is helpful in understanding and using various sources.

- Complete versus Sample. Most surveys are answered by a sample of the population and then inflated to represent the entire country.
- National versus State versus Local Data. Given the limitations of sample surveys, it is not always easy to find current, local data.
- Timeliness. Not all data are updated monthly or even annually. Another problem is the length of processing time for the larger data collection programs.
- Institutional Bias. Remember that those who have an argument to present will select the data necessary to make a point.

Networks as Sources

The old maxim "It is not what you know, but who you know" also applies to finding people to help you access and interpret labor market information. If the long list of published sources seems more like a maze, remember that there are people in the community or state who can help you find the information you need. Most of these human resources are more than willing to help you answer the occasional question or direct you to resources that you can use with clients or students.

There are many people in the community or state who can help you locate the information you need. One of the closest resources is the local library. Other resources include:

- **The State Occupational Information Coordinating Committees** also offer another point of access to the wide range of LMI. (See Appendix B for a list of the SOICCs.)
- **Regional planning agencies** frequently have staff skilled at analyzing labor market statistics.
- Each state has a **State Data Center** affiliated with the Bureau of the Census, which prepares reports and helps people use data produced by the Bureau. (See Appendix O for a list of the State Data Centers.)
- **Employment Security Offices** in each state have labor market analysts, sometimes at both state and local levels, who collect, analyze and disseminate labor market statistics.
- **Government Printing Office Bookstores** are located in

several major cities. They serve as retail outlets for publications of the federal government. They usually have copies of the major reference works as well as copies of the most recent releases. They frequently concentrate on reports with information about the state and region in which they are located. (See Appendix J for a list of the Government Printing Office Bookstores.)

- State and local **Chambers of Commerce** are another possible source of labor market information, especially information about local geographical areas.

Notes

Module 6
Developing An Awareness of Multicultural Issues

National Career Development Guidelines-Counselor Competencies

Knowledge of different cultures to interact effectively with all populations.

Skills to assist individuals in changing biased attitudes that stereotype others by gender, race, age, and culture.

Knowledge of basic concepts related to career counseling, such as career development, career progressions, and career patterns.

Knowledge of differing cultural values and their relationship to work values.

Knowledge of unique career planning needs of minorities, women, persons with disabilities, and older persons.

Knowledge of alternative approaches to career planning needs for individuals with specific needs.

Developing An Awareness
of Multicultural Issues
Module 6

Introduction

Self-knowledge is essential in forming one's identity. Part of this self-knowledge comes from the values and beliefs derived from one's cultural and ethnic background. These values and beliefs often form the core of one's identity. Likewise, one's cultural and ethnic background is often the basis for how one evaluates the relative status among careers and concomitantly how decisions are made about careers.

To be effective, career development facilitators are encouraged to adopt counseling goals and strategies that are consistent with the client's cultural and ethnic orientation. To do that it is important to develop an awareness of one's own cultural background and that of other cultures.

This module will seek to develop an awareness of cultural and ethnic influences which are central to each individual's development.

Definitions

First, a few key terms and definitions will be presented.

Ethnic Minority
A person who identifies with a common and distinctive culture or language that is not of the majority population in a country. (Rifenbary, 1991)

Ethnocentrism
A tendency to view cultures other than one's own with disfavor, which results in a sense of inherent cultural superiority. (Rifenbary, 1991)

Multiculturalism
Recognizing, understanding and appreciating cultures other than one's own. It stresses an appreciation of the impact of differences--race, class, age, sex, physical attributes, sexual/affectional orientation and religion. A multicultural philosophy is one that promotes the acknowledgement, appreciation and usage of cultural differences as

a critical factor in the development and implementation of any system, institution, program or curriculum. (Rifenbary, 1991)

Multicultural Counseling

An intervention process that places equal emphasis on the ethnic and cultural impressions of both counselor and client. The goal in multicultural counseling is to help clients empower themselves for environmental mastery and competence. (Lee, 1991)

Why Multicultural Career Counseling?

According to the 1990 Census, people of color and ethnic minorities will be a growing share of the work force. Blacks remain the largest minority but the dramatic increase in Hispanics and Asians indicate an increasingly diversified racial, ethnic and cultural mix in this country. In fact, between 1985 and 2000, people of color will comprise 29% of the net additions to the work force and will make up more than 15% of the work force in the year 2000.

NON-WHITES ARE A GROWING SHARE OF THE WORKFORCE
(numbers in millions)

	1970	1985	2000
Working Age Population (16+)	137.1	184.1	213.7
Non-White Share	10.9%	13.6%	15.7%
Labor Force	82.8	115.5	140.4
Non-White Share	11.1%	13.1%	15.5%
Labor Force Increase (Over Previous Period)	X	32.7	25.0
Non-White Share	X	18.4%	29.0%

Source: Workforce 2000, 1987

Figure 6.1

**Concentration of Blacks and Hispanics
by Major Occupational Group, 1988**

Occupation	Percent of total employment		Projected growth rate	Earnings	Unemployment rate
	Black	Hispanic			
Total	10.1	7.2			
Managers	5.6	4.0	H	H	L
Professional specialty	6.7	4.0	H	H	L
Technicians	9.4	4.3	H	High	L
Sales workers	6.1	5.3	H	Average	L
Administrative support	11.3	6.5	L	Low	A
Service workers	17.6	10.2	H	L	L
Precision production	7.5	8.2	L	A	H
Fabricators and laborers	15.0	11.1	L	L	A
Agriculture related	6.6	13.0	L	L	H

Source: Bureau of Labor Statistics

Figure 6.2

In conjunction with these statistics, the authors of *Workforce 2000* (1987) note that:

- relative rates of unemployment and earnings among minorities have not improved during the past decade and may become worse;
- blacks and Hispanics are overrepresented among declining occupations; and
- blacks, Hispanics and other minority groups frequently are concentrated in a small number of central cities beset by severe economic and social problems.

Traditionally, our educational efforts have focused on the average student and have tended to overlook the special needs of students who are at a disadvantage in the white, middle class, physically able society. Also, we have frequently overlooked the needs of minority populations.

If we are to do our job effectively as career development facilitators, it is essential that the educational and career needs of these individuals be addressed. Given the state of the labor market and the declining birth rate, we are witnessing a rare opportunity to present better job prospects for historically disadvantaged people, many of whom are cultural and ethnic minority groups.

Some ethnic and cultural minorities see the counseling process as contrary to their own life experiences and inappropriate or insufficient for their needs. In particular, many career development theories are inherently ineffective because they do not account for the effects of racism, sexism, and classism on career development. The traditional theories frequently focus on the role of personality and neglect the influence of sociocultural, environmental and economic forces on individual choice, assuming people of all cultures have the same array of choices open to them.

Cultural Awareness Questionnaire

In order to become aware of your multicultural experiences, take a few minutes to think about the following questions.

1. Think back to your childhood days.

   Did you have much contact with people of cultures different from your own? If yes, at what age? If no, when did you finally experience people of other cultures?

   Did you benefit from your contact (i.e., spending time with families that had configurations different than your own or enjoying the experience of a friend's Bar Mitzvah celebration)? If yes, what were the benefits?

   Were there customs or behaviors in the culture that you did not understand? Where there reaction from your parents or friends that you did not understand?

   Did you react or interact with people from another culture the way you wanted to at the time, or the way others (peers, parents) wanted you to act? Why?

   What messages did your family and friends give you about people from other cultures?

2. Think about the present.

Do you have much contact with students or peers of cultures unlike your own?

If yes, have you benefitted in some way from your contact with them? (i.e., learning about a different perspective on a political issue or hearning about a country unknown to you.) If no, why has there been little contact in your life with other cultures?

Do you feel that you interact with people from other cultures the way you want to, or the way others want you to act? Why?

How does the media affect your views of people from other cultures?

What is different about your attitude and beliefs regarding cultural differences now, that did not exist when you were a child? Why?

(Adapted from: *An Introduction to Multicultural Issues in Career Development*)

Dynamics in Culturally Responsive Counseling

Lee and Richardson (1991) have identified dynamics that are especially important in culturally responsive counseling. They are built on the assumption that culturally responsive counselors must work with the understanding of culture. The challenge of client diversity can be addressed by considering the following:

The Client's Level of Ethnic Identity and Acculturation. These stages of personal development can range from little or no identification with the dominant culture and complete identification with the group of origin to complete identification with the dominant culture and little identification with the ethnic group of origin. The status of ethnic identity and acculturation may be influenced by a variety of factors such as age, length of residence in the United States, level of education attained, extent of experience with racism and socioeconomic status.

Sue (1978) developed a framework for understanding clients who are culturally different than the counselor. Sue's framework responds to this challenge to understand the level of ethnic identity and acculturation that Lee and Richardson discuss. Sue's model incorporates the concepts of locus of control and locus of responsibility in a person's ethnic identity. First, a few definitions:

- Internally controlled people are those who believe that reinforcement is primarily a product of their own actions.
- Externally controlled people are those who believe that reinforcement is not entirely self-related, but can also result from luck, chance, fate or others.
- Internal locus of responsibility means that a person's success or failure can be attributed to personal qualities or skills.
- External locus of responsibility means that a person's environment is more powerful than personal qualities or skills.

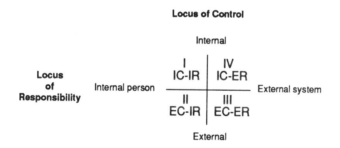

Source: Sue, D.W. (1978). World view and counseling. *Personnel and Guidance Journal.* 56, 428-462.

Figure 6.3

As seen in Figure 6.3, these two concepts are put together to provide four different ways in which to view how individuals interact with their environment. Please note that there are differences within race and ethnic groups based on factors such as gender and class. Sue believes that Quadrant I typifies the American middle class culture. People in this quadrant believe they are responsible for what happens to them and have the power to change their fate. Sue believes that more minorities fit into one of the other quadrants. Members of minority groups frequently feel as though they have less power to change themselves or their environment. Counselors need to understand their own world view, as it exists on these interacting continuums, but also that of their clients. Most importantly, they need to accept the legitimacy of the other's point of view.

There are other factors to be considered by career development facilitators in multicultural counseling. These factors can either serve to limit or enhance career development. They are:

Family Influences. Understanding and appreciation of how the family of origin and current partner and/or children play a critical role as one's support system in the career decision making process.

Sex-Role Socialization. Different perceptions of the roles of men and women effect career development and should be considered in culturally responsive counseling.

Religious and Spiritual Influences. Religious institutions are important sources of psychological support. Religious leadership is an important support system during decision making and problem resolution.

Immigration Experience. In addition to cultural beliefs and practices, immigrants bring with them the trauma and history of separation from their homelands. Some have been lured by the promise of economic opportunity and others have fled political unrest, wars, starvation, etc. The major challenge is often reconciling their wishes to maintain cultural customs while adapting to a new culture and new expectations.

The Role of Schools

Schools have often been seen as the support for all individuals in their educational and career pursuits. The school can play a major role in linking the many cultures within it and outside it. Some schools do an outstanding job of establishing these liaisons and celebrating cultural diversity; others do not. According to Axelson (1985), serious problems will arise in educational and training systems under the following conditions (Note: Although the following discussion focuses on the school, many of these concepts can be transferred to the work place):

- When formal segregation, isolation and alienation are present, this can lead to divisiveness and racial conflicts. The vicious and ugly race riots over enforced school busing to achieve a racial balance in Boston's public schools are an illustration of the effects of school segregation.
- When there is informal segregation, i.e., castelike social separation, such as educational tracking systems that separate students according to past achievement records, situations that

hinder cross cultural understanding and communication will continue to occur.
- When cultural diversity goes unrecognized and acceptance is left to chance, an enriched educational climate will be wasted.

In addition, there will be communication problems for people when the following conditions exist:

- **When cultural differences are viewed only as deficiencies** people will not be valued for their individual differences and their special heritages.
- **When subcultures are viewed as a group,** we tend to lump all minority groups together and depict them as having identical attributes and problems.
- **When language differences are viewed only as deficits,** bilingualism is not longer seen as an asset.
- **When presumptions of intellectual inferiority are based on cultural group identity or membership** we can fall into the mental trap of thinking, for example, that all members of a particular racial group do poorly in particular disciplines.
- **When individual potential goes undiscovered and unrecognized,** every persons's unique abilities and personal talents are not awakened and expanded.
- **When individual personality traits are over generalized according to cultural group identity or membership,** we see a person only as a member of a group rather than as an individual.
 (Axelson, 1985)

The Role of Career and Labor Market Information

Along with stress, language, class bound, and cultural barriers, the lack of career and labor market information and the limited knowledge that many ethnic and cultural minorities have about the world of work presents additional challenges to their career development. An individual's knowledge of the world of work partially depends upon past work experiences and the degree of exposure to people who work in a wide range of occupations (Martin, 1991).

In addition to the lack of information that all students have about careers, some students also have to face cultural barriers, such as prejudice, language differences, cultural differences and isolation.

Those providing educational and career planning services also need to:

- learn to recognize and appreciate differences between themselves and the clients they serve;
- examine their own ethnocentric values and the language associated with these values;
- understand the importance of and need for positive role models who represent the client's racial and ethnic backgrounds;
- create a multicultural environment for clients and value the backgrounds from which they come;
- consider issues surrounding racism when they arise by addressing them directly and talking about them;
- read and research information about the historical, social, economic and political factors affecting clients, including statistics related to work force participation rates;
- identify and promote full development of a client's potential;
- respect and value ethnic and racial diversity;
- recognize when cultural differences are affecting communication and make appropriate adjustments;
- promote responsible, critical thinking in clients to empower them to be their own advocates;
- awaken and expand each client's desire to strive for his/her full potential; and
- be open and accepting.
  (Brown and Brooks, 1984)

Actions to Be Taken

There are specific actions that can be taken by career development facilitators to achieve these personal and professional goals:

- Career development facilitators need to recognize and eliminate the educational and career voids in disadvantaged clients.
- Career development facilitators need to get out of their offices and become change agents and facilitators who modify the effects of discriminatory political, social and economic forces on minority groups.
- Career development facilitators need to work toward increasing the participation rate of ethnic minorities in nontraditional careers and to develop strategies that encourage achievement in academic courses that are prerequisites for entering those careers.
- Techniques that broaden career options for clients should be

mastered. This awareness of opportunity is critical.
- Strategies to strengthen self-concept must be included.

Summary

In order to serve the many cultures in this country, career development facilitators have a responsibility to meet multicultural needs as they assist their clients in career planning and development. In addressing the need to reach out to one another across cultures, the late Jawaharlal Nehru, the leader of India, advised:

"If we seek to understand a people, we have to try to put ourselves, as far as we can, in that particular historical background...If we wish to convince them, we have to use their language as far as we can, not language in the narrow sense of the word, but the language of the mind."

Developing An Awareness of Multicultural Issues
Module 6
References

Atkinson, D. R., Marten, G. and Sue, D. W. (1979). *Counseling American minorities: Across cultural perspective.* Dubuque, IA: William C. Brown.

Axelson, J. A. (1985). *Counseling and development in a multicultural society.* Monterey, CA: Brooks/Cole.

Brown, D., & Brooks, L. (1984). *Career choice and development.* San Francisco: Jossey-Bass.

Cheatham, H. E. (1990, June). Africentricity and Career Development of African Americans. *The Career Development Quarterly, 38,* pp. 334-344.

Johnston, W. B., & Packer, A. H. (1987). *Workforce 2000.* Indianapolis, IN: Husdson Institute.

Lee, C. (1991, January/February). Empowerment in counseling: A multicultural perspective. *Journal of Counseling and Development, 69*(3), 229-230.

Lee, C. C., & Richardson, B. L. (eds.). (1991). *Multicultural issues in counseling: New approaches to diversity.* Alexandria, VA: American Association for Counseling and Development.

Martin, W. E., (1991, March). Career development and American Indians living on reservations: Cross-cultural factors to consider. *Career Development Quarterly, 39*(3), 273-283.

Rifenbary, D. (1991, Spring). *An introduction to multicultural issues in career development.* Available from the New Mexico Career Information System, University of New Mexico, College of Education, Department of Educational Administration.

Sue, D. W., (1978). World views and counseling. *Personnel and Guidance Journal, 56,* 428-462.

Alderfer, C. P. (1982). Problems of changing white males' behavior and beliefs concerning race relations. In P. Goodman (ed.). *Change in Organizations* (pp. 122-165). San Francisco: Jossey-Bass.

Arbona, C. (1989). Hispanic employment and the Holland typology of work. *Career Development Quarterly, 37,* 257-268.

Arbona, C. (1990). Career counseling research and Hispanics: A review of the literature. *The Counseling Psychologist, 18,* 300-323.

Atkinson, D. R., Morten, G., & Sue, D. W. (1983). *Counseling American Minorities,* Dubuque, IA: Wm. C. Brown.

Attneave, C. L. (1985). Practical counseling with American Indian and Alaska Native clients. In P. Pedersen (ed.) (1985). *Handbook of Cross-Cultural Counseling and Therapy* (pp. 135-140). Westport, CT: Greenwood Press.

Campbell, R. E. (1975). Special groups and career behavior: Implications for guidance. In J. Picou, & R. E. Campbell (eds.) *Career Behavior of Special Groups* (pp. 424-444). Columbus, OH: Merrill.

Carney, C. G., & Kahn, K. B. (1984). Building competencies for effective cross-cultural counseling: A developmental view. *The Counseling Psychologist, 12*(1), 111-119.

Carter, R. T., & Helms, J. E. (1987). Relationship of black value orientations to racial identity attitudes. *Measurement and Evaluation in Counseling and Development, 19,* 185-195.

Casas, J. M., & Atkinson, D. R. (1981). The Mexican American in higher education: An example of subtle stereotyping. *Personal and Guidance Journal, 59,* 473-476.

Christensen, E. W. (1983). Counseling Puerto Ricans: Some cultural considerations. In D. R. Atkinson, G. Morten, & D. W. Sue. *Counseling American Minorities* (pp. 204-212). Dubuque, IA: Wm. C. Brown.

Chun, K. T. (1980). The myth of Asian Americans; success and its educational ramifications. *IRCD Bulletin, 15,* 1-2.

Decker, W. H. (1986). Occupations and impressions: Stereotypes of males and females in three professions. *Social Behavior and Personality, 14,* 69-75.

Dillard, J. M. (1985). *Multicultural Counseling,* Chicago: Nelson-Hall.

Doughtie, E. B., Chang, W. N., Alston, H. L., Wakefield, J. A., Jr., and Yom, B. L. (1976). Black-white differences on the Vocational Preferences Inventory. *Journal of Vocational Behavior,* 8:41-44.

England, P. (1981). Assessing trends in occupational sex segregation, 1900-1976. In I. Berg (Ed.), *Sociological perspectives on Labor Market* (pp. 273-295). New York: Academic Press.

Fukuyama, M. A. (January 1990). Career Development and Asian-Americans: A response to the Gallup Survey. Paper presented at the National Conference of the National Career Development Association, Scottsdale, AZ.

Garcia, F., Jr., & Ybarra-Garcia, M. (1988). Strategies for Counseling Hispanics: Effects of racial and cultural stereotypes. (Revised). ERIC reports, ED #300-687., U.S. Department of Education.

Gettys, L. D., & Cann, A. (1981). Children's perceptions of occupational sex stereotypes. *Sex Roles, 7,* 301-308.

Gottfredson, L. S. (1978). Providing black youth more access to enterprising work. *Vocational Guidance Quarterly, 27,* 114-123.

Griffith, A. R. (1980). Justification for a black career development. *Counselor Education and Supervision, 19,* 301-309.

Hageman, M. B., & Gladding, S. T. (1983). The art of career exploration: Occupational sex-role stereotyping among elementary school children. *Elementary School Guidance & Counseling, 17,* 280-287.

Harmon, L. W. (1977). Career counseling for women. In E. Rawlings & D. Carter (eds.), *Psychotherapy for women* (pp. 197-206). Springfield, IL: Thomas.

Helms, J. E. (1984). Toward a theoretical explanation of the effects of race on counseling: A black and white model. *The Counseling Psychologist, 12*(4), 153-165.

Henton, W. A. (1985). Toward counseling the Japanese in America: A cross-cultural primer. *Journal of Counseling and Development, 63,* 500-503.

Ibrahim, F. A. (1985). Effective cross-cultural counseling and psychotherapy: A framework. *The Counseling Psychologist, 13,* 625-638.

Jackson, S. M. (1982). *Career Planning for Minority Women.* Washington, DC: Women's Educational Equity Act Program, U.S. Department of Education.

Jones, A., & Seagull, A. A. (1983). Dimensions of the relationship between the Black client and the White therapist: A theoretical overview. In D. R. Atkinson, G. Morten, & D. W. Sue, *Counseling American Minorities* (pp. 156-166). Dubuque, IA: Wm. C. Brown.

Kitano, H. H. L., & Matsushima, N. (1981). Counseling Asian Americans. In P.D. Pedersen, et al. (eds.) *Counseling Across Cultures* (pp. 163-230). Honolulu: University Press of Hawaii.

La Fromboise, T. D. (1982). *Assertion Training with American Indians: Cultural Behavioral Issues for Trainers.* Las Cruces, NM: ERIC Clearinghouse on Rural Education and Small Schools.

Lee, C. C. (1982). The school counselor and the black child: Critical roles and functions. *Journal of Non-White Concerns in Personnel and Guidance, 10,* 94-101.

Leong, F. T. L. (1985). Career development of Asian Americans. *Journal of College Student Personnel 26,* 539-546.

Leong, F. T. L., & Hayes, T. J. (1990). Occupational Stereotyping of Asian Americans. *The Career Development Quarterly, 39*(2), 143-154.

Lewis, R. G., & Ho, M. K. (1983). Social work with Native Americans. In D. R. Atkinson, G. Morten, & D. W. Sue. *Counseling American Minorities* (pp. 65-72). Dubuque, IA: Wm. C. Brown.

Lonner, W. J. (1985). Issues in testing and assessment in cross-cultural counseling. *The Counseling Psychologist, 13,* 599-614.

McDavis, R. J., & Parker, W. M. (1981). Strategies for helping ethnic minorities with career development. *Journal of Non-White Concerns in Personnel and Guidance, 9,* 130-136.

O'Leary, V. E. (1974). Some attitudinal barriers to occupational aspirations in women. *Psychological Bulletin, 81,* 809-826.

Oppenheimer, K. C., & Miller, M. D. (1988). Stereotypic views of medical educators toward students with a history of psychological counseling. *Journal of Counseling Psychology, 35,* 311-314.

Osipow, S. H. (1975). The relevance of theories of career development to special groups: Problems, needed data, and implications. In J.S. Picou, & R.E. Campbell (eds.). *Career Behavior of Special Groups* (pp. 9-22). Columbus, OH: Merrill.

Padilla, A. M., Ruiz, R. A., & Alvarez, R. (1983). Community mental health services for Spanish-speaking/surnamed population. In D. R. Atkinson, G. Morten, & D. W. Sue. *Counseling American Minorities* (pp. 181-203). Dubuque, IA: Wm. C. Brown.

Paneck, P. E., Rush, C. R., & Greenawalt, J. P. (1977). Current gender stereotypes of 25 occupations. *Psychological Reports, 40,* 212-214.

Parham, T. A. (1989). Cycles of psychological nigrescence. The *Counseling Psychologist, 17,* 187-226.

Parham, T. A., & Helms, J. E. (1981). The influence of Black students' racial identity attitudes on preference for counselor's race. *Journal of Counseling Psychology, 28,* 250-257.

Parham, T. A., & Helms, J. E. (1985a). Relation of racial identity attitudes to self-actualization and affective states of Black students. *Journal of Counseling Psychology, 32,* 431-440.

Parham, T. A., & Helms, J. E. (1985b). Attitudes of racial identity and self-esteem of Black students: An exploratory investigation. *Journal of College Student Personnel, 26,* 143-46.

Pedersen, P. D., Draguns, J. G., Lonner, W. J., & Trimble, J. E. (1981). *Counseling Across Cultures.* Honolulu, University Press of Hawaii.

Pomales, J., Claiborn, C. D., & La Fromboise, T. D. (1980). Effects of black students' racial identity on perceptions of white counselors varying in cultural sensitivity. *Journal of Counseling Psychology, 33,* 57-61.

Ponterotto, J. G. (1987). Counseling Mexican Americans: A multimodal approach. *Journal of Counseling and Development, 65,* 308-312.

Richardson, E. H. (1981). Cultural and historical perspectives in counseling American Indians. In D. W. Sue. *Counseling the Culturally Different* (pp. 216-255). New York: John Wiley.

Rosenthal, R., & Jacobson, L. (1968). *Pygmalion in the classroom: Teacher expectations and pupils' intellectual development.* New York: Holt, Rinehart, and Winston.

Ruiz, R. A. (1981). Cultural and historical perspectives in counseling Hispanics. In D.W. Sue. *Counseling the Culturally Different* (pp. 186-215). New York: John Wiley.

Ruiz, R. A., & Casas, M. M. (1981). Culturally relevant and behavioristic counseling for Chicano college students. In P. D. Pedersen et al. *Counseling Across Cultures* (pp. 181-202). Honolulu: University Press of Hawaii.

Ruiz, R. A., & Padilla, A. M. (1983). Counseling Latinos. In D. R. Atkinson, G. Morten, & D. W. Sue, *Counseling American Minorities* 213-231. Dubuque, IA: Wm. C. Brown.

Shipp, P. L. (1983). Counseling blacks: A group approach. *Personnel and Guidance Journal, 62,* 108-111.

Smith, E. J. (1975). Profile of the black individual in vocational literature. *Journal of Vocational Behavior, 6,* 41-59.

Smith, E. J. (1980). Career development of minorities in nontraditional fields. *Journal of Non-White Concerns in Personnel and Guidance, 8,* 141-156.

Smith, E. J. (1983). Cultural and historical perspectives in counseling Blacks. In D. W. Sue (1981). *Counseling the Culturally Different* (pp. 141-185). New York: John Wiley.

Smith, E. J. (1983). Issues in racial minorities' career behavior. In W. B. Walsh, & S. H., Osipow (eds.). *Handbook of Vocational Psychology, 1,* 161-222. Hillsdale, NJ: Lawrence Erlbaum.

Smith, E. J. (1985). Ethnic minorities: Life stress, social support, and mental health issues. *The Counseling Psychologist, 13*(4), 537-580.

Spencer, B. G., Windham, G. O., Peterson, J. H., Jr. (1975). Occupational orientations of an American Indian group. In J. S. Picou, & R. E. Campbell (eds.), *Career Behavior of Special Groups* (pp. 199-223). Columbus, OH: Merrill.

Stewart, E. C. (1981). Cultural sensitivities in counseling. In P. Pedersen et al (eds.), *Counseling Across Cultures* (pp. 61-86). Honolulu, HI: The University Press of Hawaii.

Sue, D. W. (1975). Asian-Americans: Social psychological forces affecting their life styles. In J. S. Picou & R. E. Campbell (eds.), *Career Behavior of Special Groups: Theory, research and practice.* (pp. 97-121). Columbus, OH: Merrill.

Sue, D. W. (1981). *Counseling the Culturally Different.* New York: John Wiley.

Sue, D. W., Bernier, J. E., Feinberg, L., Pedersen, P., Smith, E. J., Vasquez-Nuttall, E. (1982). Position paper: Cross-cultural counseling competencies. *The Counseling Psychologist* 10(2): 45-52.

Sue, D. W., & Kirk, B. A. (1972). Psychological characteristics of Chinese American students. *Journal of Counseling Psychology, 19,* 471-478.

Sue, D. W., & Kirk, B. A. (1973). Differential characteristics of Japanese and Chinese American college students. *Journal of Counseling Psychology, 20* 142-148.

Sue, D. W., & Sue, S. (1977). Barriers to effective cross-cultural counseling. *Journal of Counseling Psychology, 24,* 420-429.

Sue, D. W., & Sue, D. (1985). Asian-Americans and Pacific Islanders. In P. Pedersen (ed.) *Handbook of Cross-cultural Counseling and Therapy* (pp. 141-146). Westport, CT: Greenwood Press.

Sue, S., & Zane, N. (1987). The role of culture and cultural techniques in psychotherapy: A critique and reformulation. *American Psychologist, 42,* 37-45.

Suinn, R. M., Rickard-Figueroa, K., Lew, S., & Vigil, P. (1987). The Suinn-Lew Asian Self-Identity Acculturation Scale: An initial report. *Educational and Psychological Measurement* 47: 401-07.

Szapocznik, J., Scopetta, M. H., Kurtines, W., & Arnalde, M. A. (1978). Theory and measurement of acculturation. *Interamerican Journal of Psychology, 12,* 113-120.

Toldson, I. L., & Pasteur, A. B. (1976). Therapeutic dimensions of the Black aesthetic. *Journal of Non-White Concerns in Personnel and Guidance, 4,* 105-117.

Trimble, J. E. (1976). Value differences among American Indians: Concerns for the concerned counselor. In P. Pedersen, W. L. Conner, & J. G. Draguns (eds.). *Counseling Across Cultures,* 65-81. Honolulu: The University Press of Hawaii.

Trimble, J. E., & La Fromboise, T. (1985). American Indians and the counseling process: Culture, adaptation, and style. In P. Pedersen (ed.) *Handbook of Cross-Cultural Counseling and Therapy,* 127-133. Westport, CT: Greenwood Press.

Tucker, S. J. (1973). Action counseling: An accountability procedure for counseling the oppressed. *Journal of Non-White Concerns in Personnel and Guidance, 2,* 34-41.

Tucker, C. M., Chemault, S. A., & Mulkerne, D. J. (1981). Barriers to effective counseling with blacks and therapeutic strategies for overcoming them. *Journal of Non-White Concerns in Personnel and Guidance,* 68-76.

Vontress, C. E. (1981). Racial and ethnic barriers in counseling. In P. Pedersen, et al. (eds.). *Counseling Across Cultures* (pp. 87-107). Honolulu: University Press of Hawaii.

Wood, P. S., & Mallinckrodt, B. (1990). Culturally sensitive assertiveness training for ethnic minority clients. *Professional Psychology: Research and Practice, 21,* 5-11.

Yanico, B. J. (1978). Sex bias in career information: Effects of language on attitudes. *Journal of Vocational Behavior, 13,* 26-34.

Youngman, G., & Sandongei, M. (1983). Counseling the American Indian child. In D. R. Atkinson, G. Morten, & D. W. Sue. *Counseling American Minorities* (pp. 73-80). Dubuque, IA: Wm. C. Brown.

Notes

Module 7
Specific Needs of Adults

National Career Development Guidelines-Counselor Competencies

Knowledge of developmental issues individuals address throughout the life span.

Knowledge of decision making and transition models.

Skills to assist individuals in changing biased attitudes that stereotype others by gender, race, age, and culture.

Knowledge of basic concepts related to career counseling, such as career development, career progressions, and career patterns.

Skills to use career development resources and techniques designed for specific groups.

Knowledge of unique career planning needs of minorities, women, persons with disabilities, and older persons.

Specific Needs of Adults
Module 7

Introduction

There are many issues that distinguish the needs of an adult in career transition from those of a younger person. This module examines the issues facing those in adult life stages who are making career changes. Of special merit are the adult's experiences in their work, leisure time, family and overall lifestyle. Another factor to consider is the need for reassurance that career changes are not unusual but instead can be healthy moves for an individual to undertake.

According to Zunker (1990) particular issues of concern for adults in career transition are:

- they are generally unaware of potential occupations and lack direction;
- they have not kept pace with changing job technologies, procedures and practices;
- many have a single career orientation and do not understand the benefits and problems which accompany a career change; and
- they are unfulfilled in their present career and are searching for challenge and meaning.

Assumptions

Assumption 1. Career development is a continuous process over the life span.

Assumption 2. Career development involves both choice and adjustment issues.

Assumption 3. Both career choice and adjustment involve content and process variables.
(Minor 1985)

A Theoretical Framework

Based on these assumptions, Minor (1985) developed a theoretical basis for adult career counseling programs:

- Individuals seldom regard their careers in the same way throughout their lives and they behave differently at various times in their lives.

- Choices of occupational fields and specific jobs at certain times are influenced by, and can be predicted from, certain individual characteristics, such as intelligence and achievement; special skills and talents; the ability to relate to people; individual needs, values and goals; and personality type.

- Choices of occupational fields and specific jobs also are influenced by factors external to the individual. These include the reinforcement received from parental and career related activities; community influences; family requirements and values; the economic and social conditions of the family and society; opportunities for learning; the availability of information; and historical events.

- The process of making choices about occupational fields or specific jobs follows a general pattern of exploration, crystallization, choice, and clarification.

- The process of making adjustments to new choices follows a pattern of induction and integration, or balance, between the needs of the individual and the needs of those around him/her, such as the family. For example, a person may aspire to a career as a concert pianist, but, as a result of personal abilities and environmental factors, he/she may become a piano teacher.

- Adjustment to the consequences of occupational or specific job choices depends on factors in the work environment and on the characteristics of the individual. The most difficult adjustment is related to the magnitude of the discrepancy between what the individual expects to find, in terms of requirements and rewards, and what the environment provides in those areas. In short, people do not always get what they hoped to get from a particular job.

- Satisfaction and success depends on how people fit into their work environment. Individuals must be able to express their values and interests, play roles, and perform activities that they feel are appropriate.

- Satisfaction in a specific job comes from receiving positive feedback on a successful performance and/or meeting an internally defined challenge and accomplishment.

- An individual's career is very much a part of one's life activities. The interaction of occupational and family life cycles, life style, leisure and other issues cannot be separated. They must be considered together in career planning.

- Individuals can be assisted in making choices and planning their careers by

    - helping them understand their own characteristics, making them aware of the work environment and other external forces;
    - providing access to information and appropriate training; and
    - considering the impact of occupational and job choices on other aspects of their lives.

Subgroups of Adults with Career Development Needs

Goodman, Hoppin and Kent (1990) have identified the following groups:

Midlife Career Changers. Midlife career change can take many forms. The change can be voluntary or involuntary. It can result from external circumstances, such as a company moving from one part of the country to another. Other changes are due to circumstances such as the incongruence between an individual's values or skills and the work that he/she is expected to complete.

The following questions should be considered when working with midlife career changers:

- How is midlife career change a part of the larger process of change and growth during adulthood?
- How is career change related to re-establishing self-definitions during middle life?
- How is career change related to satisfaction, or distress, in other adult roles?
- What is the meaning of work beyond providing a livelihood?
- When does your "career" reflect continued growth and development, and when might it minimize opportunities for personal self-actualization?
    (Abrego and Brammer, 1985)

Displaced Workers. Employees who have lost their jobs through the actions of others are likely to experience anger, denial and depression towards the "system." One of the major goals when working with displaced workers is to help them express their anger and then re-enter the career decision making process to explore new options and opportunities.

The Underemployed. These workers are adults who work part-time and wish to work full-time, or those employed at a job for which they are over qualified. It is usually necessary to help them gather more information in order to broaden their horizons so that they are aware of all the options outside their current work environment.

Adults Entering the Job Market for the First Time. These adults have no work history, so they are often viewed by employers with some skepticism. In addition, they often lack firsthand knowledge of the labor market, have minimal employability skills and little experience coping with employer expectations.

Women Entering or Reentering the Labor Market. (See Module 8 - Specific Needs of Women)

Older Workers. These workers not only need to update their knowledge about the world of work but also need to learn how to counter age-related stereotypes and express their advantages in terms of life experiences and maturity.

Adults with Limited English Proficiency (LEP). Many of these adults are immigrants. As a result of being newcomers, both to the culture and the world of work, they face many barriers to employment despite the fact that they may have marketable skills. Their primary need frequently is English as a Second Language instruction and counseling to understand culturally appropriate behavior.

Adults with Disabilities. (See Module 9 - Specific Needs of Persons with Disabilities)

Adults Who Live in Rural Areas. Inaccessibility, a lack of support services, and a lack of knowledge about the world of work, outside of opportunities in rural areas, often prevent these adults from fully participating in the labor market.

Components of a Successful Program

There are differences and similarities among these adults. Their career development needs are numerous and complex. Career development facilitators who work with adults can best serve them by including components of successful programs in their support services. Zunker (1990) includes seven components for adults in career transition:

Component 1: Identification of Key Experiences

Work and life experiences are evaluated to determine how they can contribute to a career. This can be accomplished through an interview, autobiography, collection of background information or a work and leisure analysis. Some skills are easy to identify through work and life experiences, and others, such as communication, social, organizational and leadership skills, are only implied.

The goal of these activities is to identify specific work tasks, leisure experiences, family concerns associated with work, lifestyle needs and potential reasons for change. Using this information, it is possible to identify a partial list of "career satisfaction" variables.

Component 2: Interest Identification

Measured interests often are used to predict job satisfaction. Interest identification can serve to broaden and stimulate career options for adults. One way to broaden options is to identify interesting components of uninteresting jobs. This finding should lead to the building of "interest clusters," or patterns, as well as specific interest indicators.

Component 3: Skills Identification

The focus of this program component is on identifying skills mastered from previous work experiences, hobbies, leisure interests, social activities and community volunteer work. Many adults not only have trouble recognizing their skills, but they also do not know how to relate them to occupational requirements. Adults often underestimate the value of their life experiences. They need to learn how to translate terms they use to describe their transferable skills into the language of the market place(s) they seek to enter.

Skills identification can be completed by understanding the adult's functional/transferable skills. This can be accomplished by a self-analysis of marketable skills, estimates of developed skills, or by the more traditional method of standardized testing. The critical factor in identification is to encourage the adult to consider skills mastered in a variety of experiences. The next step would be to cluster the identified skills in adaptive, functional and occupational categories so that a more precise relationship to occupational requirements is completed at the same time.

Component 4: Lifestyle Identification

It is important to focus on the adult's total lifestyle, not just their work. This concentration should include their values and needs in relation to work, their leisure time, peer relationships and family ties. The goal is not only to identify these values and needs, but also to communicate that life is indeed multifaceted and that the process for making a satisfactory career choice should not be oversimplified.

Component 5: Education and Training

Once an area of interest is identified, adults frequently need assistance to find sources of information that will direct them to appropriate educational and training resources. These resources might include printed materials, a computerized career delivery system that is both interactive and information oriented, local information resources and/or a microfiche system. Publications such as *The Wall Street Journal* and *USA Today* routinely present career focused information. Various sections of local newspapers and files of local resource persons can be extremely valuable. Adults need to be shown how to systematically make effective use of this information.

Tasks to complete include:

- identify sources of information;
- identify continuing education programs;
- understand admission requirements;
- investigate how to obtain credit for past work experiences and completed training programs;
- evaluate accessibility and feasibility;
- identify and communicate with support systems such as financial aid offices; and
- relate skills needed and careers of interest to education training programs to evaluate the best use of one's time and money.

Component 6: Occupational Planning

This component also focuses on the need for career and labor market information in terms of access and effective integration into a plan of action. This information can be accessed at the same time as education and training information. Adults need a variety of information about job tasks, work availability, the training needed to enter the field and salary estimates. They must then reflect upon how their abilities and needs match with that information. They need the opportunity to access and evaluate all the variables that will affect their lifestyle. This can be accomplished with published materials, computer-based systems, microfiche and gathering of information from workers, organizations and personal contacts. The information gathered should be more than simply work tasks. It should be processed so that lifestyle needs and values become integrated with the occupational information. Tasks to complete might include:

- identify sources of occupational information;
- access and assess the information;
- relate skills, values and goals to specific careers;
- evaluate how needs will be met;
- relate family needs to career; and
- identify education and training needs for entry and advancement.

Component 7: Toward a Life Learning Plan

Throughout many career moves, it is important to use life planning and decision making skills. Because of rapid change, we all need periodic information updates and we must strive to upgrade our skills, thus minimizing the chances of becoming obsolete. We need to remain flexible. For this reason, life learning plans are cyclical and can be revised as changes are needed.

Summary

The average worker can expect to change jobs approximately seven times during his/her adult life. These movements are sometimes voluntary, but often they are not. The adults who make these changes often are in a state of personal crisis or transition. Many of them, such as the displaced workers or homemakers, have specific needs due to their circumstances or position in life. They need career counseling services to:

- help them reassess their work records and life experiences;
- provide information about the occupations and opportunities available to them; and lastly,
- reassure them of their potential not only to cope with change, but to grow as a result of it.

Career and labor market information can help accomplish these goals.

Abrego, P. & Brammer, L. (1985). Counseling adults for career change. In Z. Leibowitz & D. Lea (Eds.), *Adult Career Development* (pp. 17-39). Alexandria, VA: American Association for Counseling and Development.

Bradley, L. (1990). *Counseling midlife career changers*. Washington DC: National Career Development Association.

Brown, D. & Brooks, L. (1984). *Career choice and development*. San Francisco: Jossey-Bass.

Goodman, J., Hoppin, J., & Kent, R. (1990). *A practical guide for job hunting*. Rochester, MI: Oakland University.

Miller, J. V. (1982, June). Lifelong career development for disadvantaged youth and Adults. *The Vocational Guidance Quarterly*, 359-366.

Minor, C. W. (1985). Career development theories and issues. In Z. Leibowitz & D. Lea (Eds.), *Adult career development* (pp. 17-39). Alexandria, VA: American Association for Counseling and Development.

Morris, L. (1985). Adult learning: A brief overview. In Z. Leibowitz & D. Lea (Eds.), *Adult Career Development* (pp. 40-48). Alexandria, VA: American Association for Counseling and Development.

Perrone, P. A., Wolleat, P. L., Lee, J. L., & Davis, S. A. (1977). Counseling needs of adult students. *Vocational Guidance Quarterly, 28*(1), 27-36.

Schlossberg, N. K. (1985). Adult development theories: Ways to illuminate the adult experience. In Z. Leibowitz & D. Lea (Eds.), *Adult career development* (pp. 2-16). Alexandria, VA: American Association for Counseling and Development.

Zunker, V. G. (1990). *Career counseling: Applied concepts of life planning*. Pacific Grove, CA: Brooks/Cole.

Notes

Module 8
Specific Needs of Women and Teen Parents

National Career Development Guidelines-Counselor Competencies

Skills to assist individuals in changing biased attitudes that stereotype others by gender, race, age, and culture.

Knowledge of changes taking place in the economy, society, and job market.

Knowledge of education, training, employment trends, labor market, and career resources.

Knowledge of basic concepts related to career counseling, such as career development, career progressions, and career patterns.

Knowledge of changing gender roles and how these impact on work, family, and leisure.

Knowledge of unique career planning needs of minorities, women, persons with disabilities, and older persons.

Specific Needs of Women and Teen Parents
Module 8

Issues Facing Women in the Work Place

Women have become and will continue to be full participants in the work force. This participation opens up new horizons for women but at the same time presents many new challenges. Legislation and regulations have opened up new opportunities for women that enable them to develop their talents and abilities in the work force but at the same time, women are also being faced with new challenges. We need to help girls and women overcome these barriers by providing information and strategies that will promote freedom of choice in both their personal and professional lives.

Recognizing The Uniqueness of Women's Career Patterns

The realities of women's career development are quite different from those of men. Critical issues to consider are:

- their career patterns are often interrupted because of family responsibilities;
- career development facilitators need to become aware of all the stereotypes and myths that have influenced previous decisions and will continue to influence future decisions; and
- women's choices are complicated by others' expectations.

The barriers and challenges are real but they are also surmountable. Some can be overcome with information during career decision making. Women need information not only to make a career choice but also to understand the networking, role models and supports can help them function to their fullest in the work place.

What is the Status of Women in the Work Force?

- Women's participation has increased. Not only are more women working, but they also represent an increasing share of the labor force.

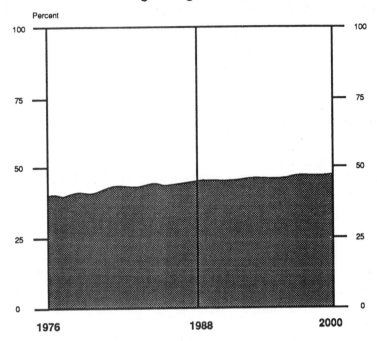

**Women's share of labor force
is growing in the U.S.**

Figure 8.1

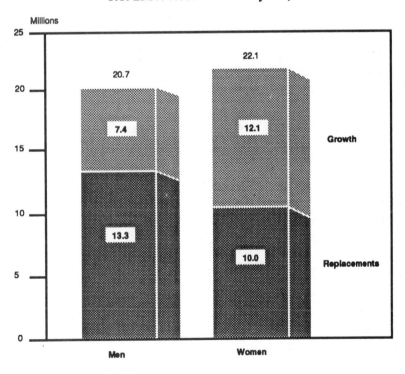

U.S. Labor force entrants by sex, 1988-2000

SOURCE: Bureau of Labor Statistics

Figure 8.2

- There is a myth that women are in the work force not out of necessity but for pleasure. Women need to be cognizant of the critical nature of their economic contributions whether they are single, heads of households or married.
- Educated women experience more success in the world of work. The more education, the higher the median earnings for both men and women. Women who do not have advanced degrees also work but often in low paying jobs.

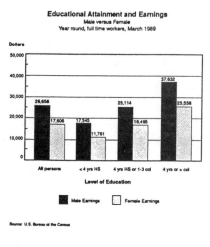

Educational Attainment and Earnings
Male versus Female
Year round, full time workers, March 1989

Figure 8.3

- Women are heavily concentrated in low paying jobs and they receive less pay than men for equal work.

Percent Distribution and Median Earnings
of Males and Females aged 35-54 by Occupation
Year round Full time Workers in the U.S.

Occupational Category	Percent Male	Percent Female	Median Earnings Male	Median Earnings Female
Total	46.6	46.3	31,435	19,599
Exec., Managerial and Professional Specialty	16.2	16.0	41,321	26,601
Technical, Sales, and Administrative Support	9.1	19.1	31,021	17,990
Service	3.1	5.1	21,612	11,524
Precision, Production, Craft, and Repair	9.2	1.4	29,896	18,742
Operators, Assemblers, Inspectors, Transportation, and Material Moving	7.7	4.5	25.031	13,906
Farm, Forestry, and Fisheries	1.2	.2	17,112	7,188

U.S. Bureau of the Census, "Money Income and Poverty in the US: 1988;
(Advanced data from Mar. 89) CPR Series P. 60 No. 166.

Figure 8.4

• A critical barrier in the career development of women is their continued occupational segregation. Does this occupational segregation really hurt? In terms of wages, the answer is an unequivocal yes.

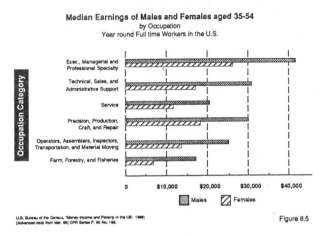

Figure 8.5

• Women in the work force, especially mothers, experience many conflicts between their career and family responsibilities. This problem is growing; the number of families with children at home in which both spouses work outside the house continues to increase.

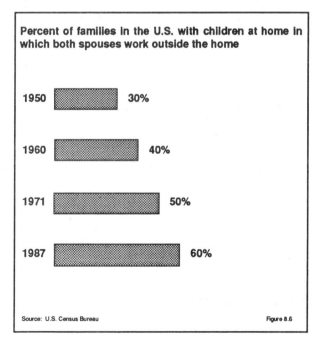

Figure 8.6

- The lack of basic literacy skills has stifled women's work force participation. An estimated 23% of all adult females have severely limited skills. The feminization of poverty is one result of these barriers.

Teen Parents

One group of women who need special attention are teen parents. Without appropriate intervention such as career development programs, their educational and employment opportunities will remain very limited. In addition to the social and economic problems they face, there are other factors that impact on their education and training including:

- low self-concept and self-esteem;
- lack of information about academic planning and occupational choices;
- lack of role models;
- lack of educational skills;
- lack of self-awareness;
- lack of assertiveness;
- low aspirations, motivation and expectations of themselves;
- low level of trust in others;
- poor communication and decision making skills;
- unrealistic goals and ambitions;
- defensive attitudes
- limited emotional resources for support and maintenance;
- immature behavior;
- need for immediate gratification; and
- Low socio-economic status

Programs for teen parents need to also include life skills such as

- parenting and nutrition;
- learning how to give and receive emotional support;
- learning how to access available child care, transportation services and other support services necessary to one's survival;
- self-concept building;
- learning how to meet the challenge of combining work and family roles;
- building support systems;
- networking for work opportunities and connections;
- enhancing interpersonal communication and relationships;
- avoiding the role of a victim .

How Can Access to Information Lead to Women's Full Participation in the Work Force?

One way to help girls and women make choices that will lead to a career that not only values their contribution but also provides them with a wage that is commensurate with their contribution, is to provide information about higher wage occupations.

An important component of addressing that need is to expand our services to women who do not have easy access to information. An example is the void of information directed to women on apprenticeships.

Occupational segregation is also holding women back. As noted, three out of four adult women work full time but they are employed in low paying jobs in areas such as retail sales and service. Once again, we can combat this problem by providing appropriate information that recognizes, communicates, and challenges inequities and stereotypes and at the same time raises expectations and monitors choices.

Specific Needs of Women and Teen Parents
Module 8
References

Brown, D., & Brooks, L. (1991). *Career counseling techniques.* Needham Heights, MA: Allyn and Bacon.

Hansen, L. S. (1978). Promoting female growth through a career development curriculum. In L. S. Hansen and R. S. Ropoza (eds.). *Career development and counseling women.* Springfield, IL: Charles C. Thomas.

Lindner, F. *Career survival kit for teen educational employment.*

Nash, M. A. (1991). *The changing roles of men and women: Educating for equity in the work place.* Available from the Vocational Studies Center, 1025 West Johnson Street, Madison, WI 53706.

American Psychological Association. (1985). Report of the task force on sex bias and sex-role stereotyping in psychotherapeutic practice. *American Psychologist, 30,* 1169-1175.

Astin, H. S. (1984). The meaning of work in women's lives: A sociopsychological model of career choice and work behavior. *The Counseling Psychologist, 12,* 117-126.

Bem, S. L. (1977). Beyond androgyny: Some presumptuous prescriptions for a liberated sexual identity. In C. G. Carney & S. L. McMahon (eds.), *Exploring Contemporary Male/Female Roles: A Facilitator's Guide,* 209-29. San Diego:" University Associates.

Berger, M., & Wright, L. (1980). Divided allegiance: Men, work, and family life. In T.M. Skovholt, P.G. Schauble, & R. Davis (eds.). *Counseling Men,* 157-63. Monterey, CA: Brooks/Cole.

Betz, N. E., & Fitzgerald, L. F. (1987). *The Career Psychology of Women.* Orlando, FL: Academic Press.

Birk, J. M., Tanney, M. F., & Cooper, J. F. (1979). A case of blurred vision: Stereotyping in career information illustrations. *Journal of Vocational Behavior, 15,* 247-57.

Brooks, L. (1988). Encouraging women's motivation for non-traditional career and lifestyle options: A model for assessment and intervention. *Journal of Career Development, 4,* 223-41.

Brooks, L. & Haring-Hidore, M. (1988). Career interventions with women. *Journal of Career Development, 14*(4): (entire issue).

Broverman, I. K., Broverman, D. M., Clarkson, F. E., Rosenkrantz, P. S., & Vogel, S. R. (1970). Sex-role stereotypes and clinical judgments of mental health. *Journal of Consulting and Clinical Psychology, 34,* 1-7.

Brown, L. S. (1990). Taking account of gender in the clinical assessment interview. *Professional Psychology: Research and Practice, 21,* 12-17.

Carter, B. (1989). Gender sensitive therapy: Moving from theory to practice. *Family Therapy Networker, 13,* 57-60.

Coombs, L. C. (1979). The measurement of commitment to work. *Journal of Population, 2,* 203-23.

Diamond, E. E. (ed.) (1975). *Issues of sex bias and sex fairness in career interest measurement.* Washington, DC: National Institute of Education.

DiBenedetto, B., & Tittle, C. K. (1990). Gender and adult roles: Role commitment of women and men in a job family trade-off context. *Journal of Counseling Psychology, 37,* 41-8.

Fitzgerald, L. F. (1986). Career counseling women: Principles, procedure, and problems. In Z.B. Leibowitz & H. D. Lea (eds.) *Adult Career Development: Concepts, Issues and Practices,* 116-31. Washington, DC: National Career Development Association.

Fitzgerald, L. F. (1980). Nontraditional occupations: Not for women only. *Journal of Counseling Psychology, 27,* 252-59.

Gilbert, L. H. (1987). Dual-career families in perspective. *The Counseling Psychologist, 15,* (1): (entire issue).

Good, G. E., Gilbert, L. A., & Scher, M. (1990). Gender aware therapy: A synthesis of feminist therapy and knowledge about gender. *Journal of Counseling and Development, 68,* 376-80.

Hansen, L. S. (1984). Interrelationships of gender and career. In N.C. Gysbers and Associates, *Designing Careers,* 216-47. San Francisco: Jossey-Bass.

Mintz, L. B., & O'Neill, J. M. (1990). Gender roles, sex, and the process of psychotherapy: Many questions and few answers. *Journal of Counseling and Development, 67,* 381-87.

Osipow, S. H. (1982). Research in career counseling: An analysis of issues and problems. *The Counseling Psychologist, 282,* 77-90.

Thomas, A. H., & Stewart, N. R. (1971). Counselor response to female clients with deviate and conforming career goals. *Journal of Counseling Psychology, 18,* 352-57.

Tittle, C. K., & Zytowski, D. G. (eds.) (1978). *Sex-fair Interest Measurement: Research and Implications.* Washington, DC: National Institute of Education.

Module 9
Specific Needs of Persons with Disabilities

National Career Development Guidelines-Counselor Competencies

Knowledge of decision making and transition models.

Skills to assist individuals in setting goals and identifying strategies for reaching goals.

Knowledge of basic concepts related to career counseling, such as career development, career progressions, and career patterns.

Skills to use career development resources and techniques designed for specific groups.

Knowledge of unique career planning needs of minorities, women, persons with disabilities, and older persons.

Knowledge of alternative approaches to career planning needs for individuals with specific needs.

Specific Needs of Persons with Disabilities
Module 9

Introduction

The process of enabling persons with disabilities to enter the mainstream of life may be a long and sometimes arduous task, but the rewards to our society are enormous. This module will discuss the career counseling needs of persons with disabilities, review some of the federal legislation that supports their career development, and describe the components of a school to work transition program. The career development facilitator has a key role to play in helping persons with disabilities enter the mainstream of life. Serving students and clients with disabilities needs to be a concern of all career development facilitators.

What Is a Disability?

It is important to remember that the term "disability" has a broad interpretation. Title I of the Americans with Disabilities Act defines "disability" to mean a physical or mental impairment that substantially limits one or more of the major life activities of an individual. What is critical when working with persons with disabilities is to emphasize their abilities, not their limitations.

Career Counseling Persons with Disabilities

Is saving students with disabilities a concern for educators and career counselors? The answer is a resounding "yes." Today, students with disabilities comprise approximately 10% of our school age population.

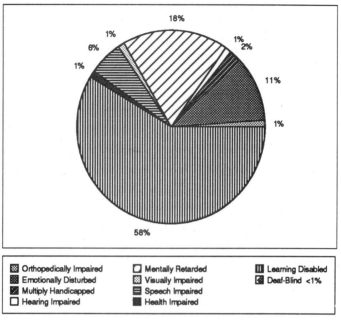

National Longitudinal Transition Study of Special Education Students, 1987
SRI International, Menlo Park, CA.

Figure 9.1

Persons with disabilities often have been isolated from society. Therefore, they have a greater need for information to become aware of all options. There are many barriers to better paying jobs for persons with disabilities but providing labor market information can be part of the solution. The barriers are numerous. Many persons with disabilities do not have an employment history, nor have they participated in work experience programs. Therefore, they may not only lack marketable skills, but they also lack information about the work place. In many cases, they are not aware of the careers that are open to them. Because some individuals have been socially isolated, they have not been exposed to successful role models with similar conditions. In addition, due to a lack of information, many individuals with disabilities are unaware of the physical modifications that are available to them that could enhance their performance in the work place.

The directions for career development facilitators are quite clear. Students with disabilities need:

- an assessment of their abilities and limitations;
- an individualized educational program to develop their strengths;
- career information, education and exploration;
- work study programs or on-the-job training;

- independent living skills;
- a knowledge of the federal and state legislation affecting them; and
- effective school to work transition services.

Special Counseling Considerations

Research states that there are four major areas that should be included in the career development plans of persons with disabilities:

- career information, such as an understanding of the roles, responsibilities and the realities of the work place;
- learning strategies to enable individuals to master the information they need to know;
- prevocational skills such as responsibility, initiative, punctuality, care of materials and task completion; and
- social skills, with an emphasis on job interviewing, accepting and providing criticism, and relating to authority figures.

Making the School to Work Transition

Career counseling is also one of the ways to bridge the gap between school and the work place. Transition periods can occur between high school, postsecondary education or training and the first years of employment.

The Individuals with Disabilities Education Act of 1990 (IDEA) defines transition services as:

"a coordinated set of activities for a student, designed within an outcome-oriented process, which promotes movement from school to postschool activities, including postsecondary education, vocational training, integrated employment (including supported employment), continuing and adult education, adult services, independent living, or community participation. The coordinated set of activities shall be based upon the individual student's needs, taking into account the student's preferences and interests, and shall include instruction, community experiences, the development of employment and other postschool adult living objectives, and when appropriate, acquisition of daily living skills and functional vocational evaluation." Sec. 602(a)(19).

Career development facilitators are part of the network that assists students in making the transition. Recent literature to help counselors with transition planning for students with disabilities has illustrated the following points to consider:

- Due to a lack of information, persons with disabilities do not always perceive the same possibilities or obstacles that others may see for them. Therefore, their goals may need to be established and clarified. Labor market information will enhance this process.
- Adolescence is a difficult period of life when children want to be accepted by their peers. It can be further complicated by a disability that may set them apart from others.
- Transition involves preparation for a change in environment, from school to work, and a change in roles, from student to employee.
- Transition services must focus on enabling self-determination, independence, and participation in society.
  (Humes, Szymanski & Hohenshil, 1989)

What are the ingredients of a successful school-to-work transition program? The following components have been suggested by Stern (1991):

- Career information and career guidance programs are consolidated.
- Counselors have established systems for career information, delivery, placement and a method of teacher/business exchange.
- An effective school that has a strong leader, clear goals and a safe climate for learning is critical.
- A vocational and academic secondary to postsecondary program, with no tracking, that includes science and technology courses with hands-on experiences and on-the-job training must be included.
- The school needs to maintain extensive business and community involvement.
- The school operates with performance standards.

Many schools throughout the United States have adopted the Life Centered Career Education Curriculum, which was first published by the Council for Exceptional Children in 1978, to prepare students to make the transition from school to the work place (Brolin and Gysbers, 1989). Its career areas and competencies are as follows:

Curriculum Areas: Occupational Guidance and Preparation Competencies:

- knowing and exploring occupational possibilities;
- selecting and planning occupational choices;
- exhibiting appropriate work habits and behavior;
- seeking, securing and maintaining employment;
- exhibiting sufficient physical-manual skills; and
- obtaining specific occupational skills.

Life-Centered Career Education (LCCE) Curriculum

	Competency:	Subcompetency: The student will be able to:						
Curriculum Area: Occupational Guidance and Preparation	Knowing & Exploring Occupational Possibilities	Identify wage/salary aspects of work	Locate sources of occupational & training information	Identify personal values met through work	Identify societal values met through work	Classify jobs into occupational categories	Investigate local occupational & training opportunities	
	Selecting & Planning Occupational Choices	Make realistic occupational choices	Identify requirements of appropriate & available jobs	Identify occupation aptitudes	Identify major occupational interests	Identify major occupational needs		
	Exhibiting Appropriate Work Habits & Behavior	Follow directions & observe regulations	Recognize importance of attendance & punctuality	Respect importance of supervision	Demonstrate knowledge of occupational safety	Work with others	Meet demands for quality work	Work at satisfactory rate
	Seeking, Securing & Maintaining Employment	Search for a job	Apply for a job	Interview for a job	Maintain postschool occupational adjustment	Demonstrate knowledge of competitive standards	Know how to adjust to changes in employment	
	Exhibiting Sufficient Physical-Manual Skills	Demonstrate stamina & endurance	Demonstrate satisfactory balance & coordination	Demonstrate manual dexterity	Demonstrate sensory discrimination			
	Obtaining Specific Occupational Skills		There are no specific subcompetencies as they depend on skill being taught					

Source: Brolin, Donn. (1978,1983,1989). Reston, VA: The Council for Exceptional Children.

Figure 9.2

All of these skills, for both students and counselors, should be achieved with the use of current and accurate labor market information. According to Brolin and Gysbers (1989), the following counselor competencies are necessary to carry out this curriculum:

- counsel students with disabilities;
- counsel with parents regarding the career development of their children;
- conduct or arrange for a career assessment for students with disabilities;
- consult with other educators concerning the development of self-awareness and decision making competencies in students with disabilities;

- contribute to the development and monitoring of individual learning programs in cooperation with other educators and parents;
- work with students with disabilities in the selection of training opportunities and the selection of job possibilities;
- develop and use community resources, particularly for referral purposes; and
- become an advocate for students with disabilities.

The Impact of Federal Legislation

The legislation has greatly enhanced the outlook for persons with disabilities. The counseling needs of persons with disabilities have become more urgent since recent legislation has enabled them to take their rightful place in our schools and the work force. Students need to be equipped with the skills they will need to find work. Local labor market information can help direct them.

Federal legislation includes:

- Rehabilitation Act of 1973;
- Education for All Handicapped Children Act of 1975;
- Job Training Partnership Act of 1982 (JTPA);
- Carl D. Perkins Vocational Education Act of 1984;
- Amendments to the Perkins Act, 1990; and
- Individuals with Disabilities Education Act (IDEA).

The Train-Place-Train Transition Process

Programs such as the Train-Place-Train Transition process have been developed to help career counselors provide services required under these laws.

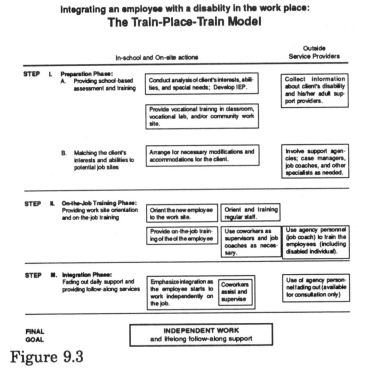

Figure 9.3

The Americans with Disabilities Act of 1990

The outlook for persons with disabilities in the work place was greatly enhanced by the Americans with Disabilities Act of 1990 (ADA). Some of the key provisions follow:

Employment

- By 1994, employers with 15 or more employees may not refuse to hire or promote qualified persons with disabilities.
- By 1992, employers with 25 employees or more must make reasonable accommodations for persons with disabilities to perform the functions of the job.
- Employers must modify the job requirements to enable persons with disabilities to do the work, unless the changes impose undue hardships upon the employers.

Transportation

- All new vehicles for public transportation must be made accessible for persons with disabilities.
- Paratransit services for persons with disabilities who cannot use the mainline system must be provided, unless this service is an undue financial burden.
- All new buses ordered by private carriers, such as Greyhound, must be accessible after 1990.

Public Accommodations

- New buildings must be accessible; barriers must be removed in older facilities if economically possible.
- Auxiliary aids and services, such as large print materials and tape recordings, are to be provided to enable persons with disabilities to enjoy the goods and services offered to the general public.
- Hotels that offer transportation generally must also provide services to persons with disabilities.

Telecommunications

- Telephone companies must offer telephone relay services to individuals who use telecommunications devices for the deaf (TTDs) at regular rates.

In short, the ADA will make the work place, public accommodations and services more accessible to persons with disabilities. In terms of career counseling, this means that many of the barriers to the employment of persons with disabilities will come down, such as the lack of job opportunities, discrimination in hiring practices, the physical demands of the work place and limited public transportation services.

Accommodations for Persons with Learning Disabilities

According to the Americans with Disabilities Act (ADA), firms that hire persons with disabilities must expect to make accommodations for them. In some cases, tax credits may be available to small businesses for expenses incurred in complying with the ADA. The Internal Revenue Service (IRS) should be contacted for information regarding tax credits. Some of the more common adaptations that have been made are as follows (Gugerty, Phelps and Tindall, 1991):

- Make fewer demands for paperwork.
- Allow for flexible scheduling and additional time to accomplish tasks.
- Provide supervision designed to reduce stress.
- Have staff and coworkers help the employee in scheduling his or her time.
- Have staff and coworkers provide guidance, instruction, and repeated directions for retention.
- Supervisors should spend more time explaining rules and procedures.

Accommodations for Persons with Mental Disabilities

- Provide closer supervision during initial training period.
- Provide employee with drawings of correct techniques and examples of finished products.
- Have supervisors demonstrate procedures instead of giving verbal instructions.
- Provide minimal constant supervision to avoid quality and quantity problems.
- Use photographs to show correct items to process, e.g., shelving.

Accommodations for Persons with Emotional Disabilities

- Provide postemployment follow-up by job placement personnel.
- Monitor work more closely.
- Provide postemployment support by an individual or a group of coworkers.
- Supply written work schedules of tasks to be accomplished.
- Have supervisors provide support to overcome or control job stress.

Accommodations for Persons with Visual Disabilities

- Use taxis or a driver to help the employee attend meetings.
- Provide a speech synthesizer, Braille or tape recorders.
- Have the job placement agency provide postemployment counseling as needed.
- Modify the work schedule to accommodate public. transportation schedules, e.g., reduced schedules at night and on weekends.
- Assign the employee to physical facilities that accommodate communication devices and Braille storage.
- Restructure the job to have coworkers do proofreading, typing of forms, etc.

Accommodations for Persons with Hearing Disabilities

- Adjust work tasks to decrease the employee's need to communicate by hearing.
- Use interpreters for meetings, for communication with supervisors, coworkers or the general public.
- Add volume controls to the telephone.
- Install communication devices where needed.
- Have employees carry notebooks and pencils.
- Assign employee to work with a coworker who knows sign language.

Accommodations for Persons with Physical Disabilities

- Raise the employee's desk to accommodate a wheelchair.
- Make facilities accessible including,

  - office facilities,
  - bathrooms,
  - meeting and eating area,
  - entrance ramps,
  - parking areas, and
  - electric door openers.

- Provide assistance in moving supplies and equipment.
- Modify building evacuation procedures.
- Provide accessible transportation, e.g., vans, cars, chairlifts, etc.
- Provide accessible equipment, e.g., computers, calculators, and telephones.

In short, there are many physical changes that can be made in the work place to accommodate persons with disabilities in order to provide them with jobs that can help them achieve independence.

Summary

Due to the impact of federal legislation supporting their civil rights, persons with disabilities will be entering the work force in much greater numbers. Under the mandates of the Americans with Disabilities Act of 1990, employers will be required to make accommodations in work places to provide employment opportunities for persons with disabilities.

Therefore, serving the academic needs of students with disabilities to prepare them to take their rightful places in the work force is of great concern to career development facilitators and educators. It is critical that students with disabilities receive education, training and career counseling to enable them to make a smooth transition from school to work or postsecondary education or training.

The career development facilitator plays an important role in working with students with disabilities, their families and other school and community personnel to ensure that career development is a vital and realistic component of students' Individualized Educational Programs (IEPs). It is critical that the IEPs be based on accurate labor market information to ensure that students with disabilities truly are competitive in today's work force.

Brolin, D. E., & Gysbers, N. C. (1989, November/December). Career education for students with disabilities. *Journal of Counseling & Development, 68.*

Council for Exceptional Children. (1990, October/November). Americans with Disabilities Act of 1990: What should you know? *Exceptional Children, 57*(2), (Suppl.).

Dougherty, B., Novak, J., & Reschke, L. (1986, September). *Ready, set... go!, Volume 1: Planning and developing a program.* Madison, WI: The Vocational Studies Center, School of Education, University of Wisconsin.

Dunn, L. M. (Ed.). (1973). *Exceptional children in the schools: Special education in transition.* New York: Holt, Rinehart and Winston.

Ehrsten, M. E., & Izzo, M. V. (1988). Special needs youth and adults need a helping hand. *Journal of Career Development, 15*(1), 53-63.

Fagan, T. K., & Jenkins, W. M. (1989, November/December). People with disabilities: An update. *Journal of Counseling & Development, 68,* 140-159.

Gugerty, J., Phelps, L. A., & Tindall, L. W. (1991, February). Implementing The Americans With Disabilities Act. *WorkAmerica, 8*(2), (4-6).

Gugerty, J. J., Tindall, L. W., & Heffron, T. J. (1988, May). *Profiles of success: Serving secondary special education students through the Carl D. Perkins Vocational Education Act.* Madison, WI: The Vocational Studies Center, School of Education, University of Wisconsin-Madison.

Harrington, T. F. (1982). *Handbook of career planning for special needs students.* Rockville, MD: Aspen Systems.

Humes, C. W., Szymanski, E. M., & Hohenshil T. H. (1989, November/December). Roles of counseling in enabling persons with disabilities. *Journal of Counseling & Development, 68,* 145-149.

Levine, M. (1984). *Summary of report: Survey of employer needs.* Washington, DC: Committee for Economic Development.

Louis Harris and Associates, Inc. (1989). *The ICD survey III: A report card on special education.* New York: International Center Disabled.

Louis Harris and Associates, Inc. (1987). *The ICD survey II: Employing disabled Americans.* New York: International Center for the Disabled.

Louis Harris and Associates, Inc. (1986). *The ICD survey of disabled Americans: Bringing disabled Americans into the mainstream.* New York: International Center for the Disabled.

Vocational Education Weekly, 3(34), 4. (1991, January 7).

Research & Training Center on Independent Living. (1990). *Guidelines for reporting and writing About people with disabilities* (3rd ed.). Lawrence, KS: author.

SRI International (1987). *National longitudinal transition study of special education students.* (Available from SRI International, The National Longitudinal Transition Study, Room BS136, 333 Ravenswood Avenue, Menlo Park, CA 94025).

Tindall, L. W., Gugerty, J. J., Heffron, T. J., & Godar, P. G. (1988, March). *Replicating jobs in business and industry for persons with disabilities, 3.* Madison, WI: The Vocational Studies Center, School of Education, University of Wisconsin.

Wilcox, J. (1991, February). The new perkins act at a glance. *The Vocational Education Journal, 66*(2).

Will, M. (1984). *OSERS programming for the transition of youth with disabilities: Bridges from school to working life.* Washington, DC: Office of Special Education and Rehabilitative Services, U.S. Department of Education.

Worklife, 3(3). (1990, Fall). P.L. 101-336 Americans with Disabilities Act of 1990.

WorkAmerica, 7(9), (2, 4). (1990, September). Equal to the task.

WorkAmerica, 8(6), (5). (1991, June). The benefits of accommodation.

Notes

Module 10

Specific Needs of Children At-Risk

National Career Development Guidelines-Counselor Competencies

Skills to assist individuals in setting goals and identifying strategies for reaching goals.

Knowledge of education, training, employment trends, labor market and career resources.

Skills to use career development resources and techniques designed for specific groups.

Knowledge of alternative approaches to career planning needs for individuals with specific needs.

Specific Needs of Children At-Risk
Module 10

Introduction

Keeping children in school through high school graduation is an effective deterrent to a life of poverty. Evidence continues to show that an education can make a difference in one's quality of life.

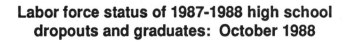

Labor force status of 1987-1988 high school dropouts and graduates: October 1988

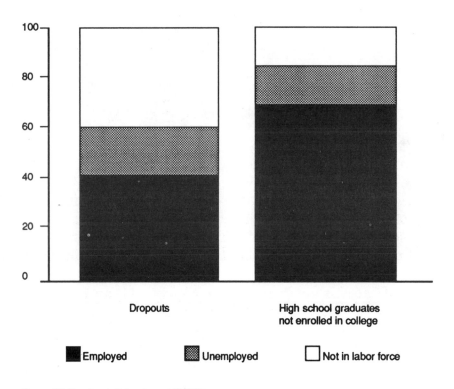

Source: U.S. Department of Labor, Bureau of Statistics

Figure 10.1

Only one in six jobs is suitable for a high school dropout. The critical nature of the relationship between income and education is illustrated in Figure 10.2.

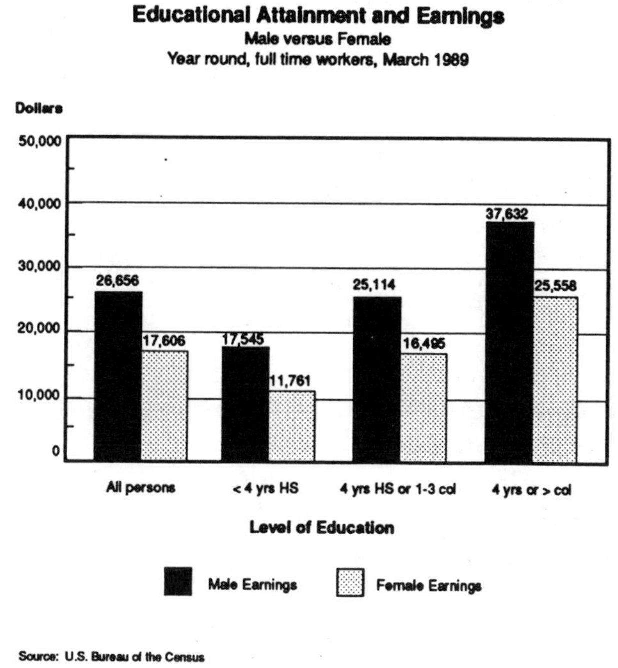
Educational Attainment and Earnings
Male versus Female
Year round, full time workers, March 1989
Dollars
50,000
40,000
30,000
20,000
10,000
0
26,656
17,606
17,545
11,761
25,114
16,495
37,632
25,558
All persons
< 4 yrs HS
4 yrs HS or 1-3 col
4 yrs or > col
Level of Education
Male Earnings
Female Earnings
Source: U.S. Bureau of the Census

Figure 10.2

Despite the importance of education, many students fail to complete high school. In an attempt to forestall our nation's alarming dropout rate, many schools have identified those students who are most at-risk of leaving school prematurely. They have then developed special educational programs to better meet the needs of these children at-risk.

The concept of "at-risk" is broad and complex. Many factors place a student at-risk. They may be environmental, emotional, social, psychological, physical and/or academic in nature.

To respond effectively to the needs of these students, our initiatives must be directed by the following assumptions:

- all children can learn;
- we know how to teach children at-risk;
- what we teach must be challenging; and
- we must produce, outcomes count.

(CCSSO, 1988)

Meeting the Needs of Children At-Risk

The literature suggests that successful strategies include the following components:

- base children at-risk policies and programs on the premise that all children can succeed;
- provide a safe and orderly environment by setting high standards for discipline and attendance; enforce them fairly, consistently and firmly;
- ensure that educational reforms positively affect children at-risk;
- provide a challenging academic curriculum to all students, including children at-risk;
- use instructional strategies that meet the educational needs of children at-risk;
- address children's needs at an early age to increase their chances for success;
- carefully plan parent involvement so that it meets the needs of the family, students, and school personnel;
- provide a multifaceted program that contains a plan of coordinated services and mobilizes all existing community resources;
- include a supervised work experience component that clearly demonstrates the relationship between school and work;
- have a staff development plan that leads to increased understanding, sensitivity and effectiveness in educating children at-risk;
- include a component that helps enhance students' perceptions of their own self-worth;
- coordinate standards for effective and appropriate education of children at-risk at the state level; endorse and implement them at the local level to meet community needs; and
- include policies, guidelines, and programs on drug and alcohol abuse in a comprehensive children at-risk program.
  (Rodenstein, 1990)

A Strategy That Works: Career Development Programs

Although this list does not include the words "career development," an underlying theme in many of these components is an attempt to help students overcome their sense of isolation from school and the world of work through career development.

A component of career development programs that appears to be successful with at-risk high school students, seeks to enhance the transition from school to work by providing access to career and labor market information delivered through a Career Information Delivery System (CIDS). According to Bloch (1988), a CIDS can establish links between school and work. The connections between what a student learns in school and the world of work becomes more obvious. Bloch believes there are four critical components of all at-risk career education programs. She refers to them as the four C's.

Cash

This means that students need to see the link between making money and the subjects they are studying in school. Students need to understand how classroom instruction fits into their career aspirations and in turn, their paycheck.

Care

Caring means that students must get the concern they need from teachers and other adults. Career education programs should be intensive and focused. There needs to be personalized, individualized attention to student needs. Students can receive immediate feedback and rewards when they interact with a CIDS.

Coalition

Coalitions of schools, businesses and local education foundations are needed, especially for those students who have trouble understanding the linkages between the classroom and the world of work. Parents and the community become resources as the students begins to understand the relationship between school and work.

Computers

The final "C" is for computers. One of the more powerful career planning tools is a Career Information Delivery System (CIDS). By using the computer to retrieve personally relevant occupational and educational information, students can relate school and learning to the world of work. CIDS also helps students feel more in charge of their own lives and gives them a sense of control. Immediate feedback is also built into the system. A CIDS has proven to be a motivator, user-friendly and a reliable source for labor market information.

Summary

In conclusion, career development programs are a tool that can motivate students to discover their likes, dislikes and career interests. Delivery of career information through a CIDS results in a wealth of easy-to-read, up-to-date and individualized information for career decision making. It helps students create a future for themselves.

Specific Needs of Children At-Risk
Module 10
References

American Association of School Administrators. (1989). *Problems and solutions.* Arlington, VA: author. (Paper no. 021-00213).

Bloch, D. P. (1988). *Reducing the risk: Using career information with at-risk youth.* Eugene, OR: Career Information System.

Council of Chief State School Officers. (1988). *School success for students at-risk: Analysis and recommendations of the council of chief state school officers.* Washington DC: CCSSO.

Mertens, D., Seitz, P., & Cox, S. (1982). *Vocational education and the high school dropout.* Columbus: The National Center for Research in Vocational Education, The Ohio State University. (ERIC Document Reproduction Service No. ED 228 397).

Miller, J. V., & Imel, S. (1987). Some Current Issues in Adult Career and Vocational Education. In E. Flaxman (Ed.), *Trends and issues in education.* Washington, DC: Council of ERIC Directors, Educational Resources Information Center, Office of Educational Research and Improvement, U. S. Department of Education.

Nash, M. A. (1990). *Improving their chances: A handbook for designing & implementing programs for at-risk youth.* Madison, WI: Vocational Studies Center, University of Wisconsin-Madison.

National School Boards Association. (1989). *An equal chance: Educating at-risk children to succeed.* Alexandria, VA: National School Board Association.

Rodenstein, J. (1990). *Children at-risk.* Madison, WI: Wisconsin Department of Public Instruction.

Author Unknown. (1988, October 19). Study urges dropout-prevention efforts in middle grades. *Education Week, 7, 7.*

Bishop, J. (1989, May). Making vocational education more effective for at-risk youth. *Vocational Education Journal*, pp. 14-19.

Bloch, D. P. (1988). *Reducing the risk: Using career information with at-risk youth.* Eugene, OR: Career Information System.

Bowman, B. (1988, July 31-August 5). *Early intervention and the public schools.* Paper prepared for the Council of Chief State School Officers Summer Institute, Boston.

Business Advisory Commission, Education Commission of the States. (1985). *Reconnecting youth: The next stage of reform.* Denver, CO: ECS. (Paper No. AR85-1).

Business Week Special Report. (1988). Human capitol: The decline of America's work force. Highstown, NJ: author.

California State Department of Education. (1990). *Toward a state of esteem: Report of the California task force to promote self-esteem and personal and social responsibility.* Sacramento: author.

Charles Stewart Mott Foundation. *Youth in crisis: Living on the jagged edge.* Flint, MI: Charles author.

Children's Defense Fund. (1989). *Key facts about children in Wisconsin.* Washington, DC: author.

Children's Defense Fund. (1989). *A vision for America's future.* Washington, DC: author.

Comer, J. P. (1988). Effective schools: Why they rarely exist for at-risk elementary school and adolescent students. In *School success for students at risk.* Washington, DC: Council of Chief State School Officers.

Council of Chief State School Officers. (1987). *Elements of a model state statute to provide educational entitlements for at-risk students.* Washington, DC: author.

Council of Chief State School Officers. (1987). *Early childhood and family education.* Washington, DC: author.

Council of Chief State School Officers. (1988). *School success for students at risk: Analysis and recommendations of the council of chief state school officers.* Washington, DC: author.

DeLone, R.H. (1989). *Mobilizing state level systems to better serve children at-risk.* Summarized by J. Rodenstein. Madison, WI: Wisconsin Department of Public Instruction.

Eastman, G. (1988). *Family involvement in education.* Paper prepared for the Wisconsin Department of Public Instruction, Madison, WI.

Fine, M. (1988). De-institutionalizing education inequity: Contests that constrict the lives and minds of public school adolescents. In *School success for students at risk.* Washington, DC: Council of Chief State School Officers.

Ford Foundation. (1989). *The common good: Social welfare and the american future.* New York: author.

Graham, P. A. (1988). Achievement for at-risk students. In *School success for students at risk.* Washington, DC: Council of Chief State School Officers.

Green Bay Area School District. (1987). *The children at-risk task force report.* Green Bay, WI: author.

Heleen, O., & Miller F. T. (1989). *Mobilizing local coalitions and collaborations to better serve children at-risk.* Madison, WI: Wisconsin Department of Public Instruction.

Hilliard, A. G. (1988). Public support for successful instructional practices for at-risk students. In *School success for students at risk.* Washington, DC: Council of Chief State School Officers.

Hispanic Policy Development Project. (1986). 1980 high school sophomores: Whites, blacks, Hispanics-- where are they now? *Research Bulletin, 1.1, 1.*

Johnston, M. E. & Williams, P. B. (n.d.). *Building a community business/education partnership: A tool kit.* Salem: Oregon Student Retention Initiative.

Joyner, E. T. (1989). *Mobilizing resources within the schools to serve children at-risk.* Mobilizing resources to better serve children at-risk series (Paper No. 1). Madison: Wisconsin Department of Public Instruction.

Levin, H. M. (1988). *Accelerated schools for children at-risk students.* (Research Report Series RR-010). New Brunswick, NJ: Rutgers University Center for Policy Research in Education.

Levin, H. M. (1988). Accelerating elementary education for disadvantaged students. In *School success for students at risk.* Washington, DC: Council of Chief State School Officers.

Lowry, C. M. (1990). *Helping at-risk youth make the school-to-work transition.* Contract No. RI88062005). Columbus, OH: Ohio State University, Center on Education and Employment. (ERIC Document No. EDO-CE-90-101)

Maeroff, G. I. (1988, May). Withered hopes, stillborn dreams: The dismal panorama of urban schools. *Phi Delta Kappan, 69*(2), 632-638.

✓ Martin, D. (1988, February) Wake up: The american dream is fading and our future is at risk. *The American School Board Journal, 175*(2), 21-24.

Massachusetts Advocacy Center and the Center for Early Adolescence. (1988). *Before it's too late: Dropout prevention in the middle grades.* Boston: Massachusetts Advocacy Center.

National Association of Social Workers.(1985). *The human factor: A key to excellence in education.* Silver Springs, MD: author.

Naylor, M. (1987). *Reducing the dropout rate through career and vocational education.* (Contract No. 800-84-0011). Columbus, OH: Ohio State University, Center on Education and Training for Employment. (ERIC Digest No. 63)

Naylor, M. (1989). *Retaining at-risk students in career and vocational education.* (Contract No. RI88062005). Columbus, OH: Ohio State University, Center on Education and Training for Employment. (ERIC Document No. EDO-CE-89-87)

Ohio Department of Education. (1988). *Ohio's formula for education success.* Columbus: author.

Olson, L. (1988, September 21). Despite years of rhetoric, most still see little understanding, inadequate efforts. *Education Week, 3,* 1 & 14-16.

Olson, L. (1988, November 2). You've got to demonstrate that there's another way. *Education Week, 3, 9.*

Orfield, G. (1988). Race, income and education inequality: Students and schools at risk in the 1980's. In *School success for students at risk.* Washington, DC: Council of Chief State School Officers.

Patterson, J. H. (1989, March). Impact of higher academic standards on youth at risk of academic failure. Paper presented at the American Educational Research Association conference in San Francisco, CA.

Rumberger, R. W. (1987). High school dropouts: A review of issues and evidence. *Review of Educational Research, 57*(2), 101-121.

Sagor, R. (1988). Teetering on the edge of failure. *Learning, 18*(8), 28-34.

Sandoval, G. T. (1988). *A compendium of what works for vocational educators in dropout prevention.* Columbus, OH: The National Center for Research in Vocational Education.

Schorr, L. B.; with D. Schorr. (1988). *Within our reach: Breaking the cycle of disadvantage.* New York: Anchor Press, Doubleday.

Search Institute. (1989). *The Wisconsin study: Alcohol and other drug abuse.* Madison: Wisconsin Department of Public Instruction.

Smith, G. A. (1989). *Mobilizing academic resources to better serve children at-risk.* Mobilizing resources to better serve children at-risk series (paper no. 3). Madison: Wisconsin Department of Public Instruction.

United Action Council for Public Education. (1988). *Public education in Wisconsin--a long term commitment.* Monroe, WI: author.

U.S. Department of Education. (n.d.). *Schools that work: Educating disadvantaged children.* Washington, DC: author.

U.S. Department of Education. (1989). *Dropout rates in the United States: 1988.* NCES #89-609. Washington, DC: Office of Educational Research and Improvement, author.

U.S. Department of Labor, U.S. Department of Education, & U.S. Department of Commerce. (1988). *Building a quality work force.* Washington, DC: Office of Public Affairs.

University of Illinois Champaign-Urbana. (1989). *Technical assistance for special populations brief.* Champaign-Urbana: University of Illinois.

Vocational Studies Center. (1979). *Staying in.* Madison: University of Wisconsin.

Wehlage, G. G., et al. (1989). *Reducing the risk.* Philadelphia: Falmer Press.

White, B. L. (1989). *Mobilizing the public to better serve children at-risk.* Mobilizing resources to Better serve children at-risk series (paper no. 5). Madison: Wisconsin Department of Public Instruction.

Willis, M. J. (1989). *Mobilizing parents to better serve children at risk.* Mobilizing resources to better serve children at-risk series (paper no. 4). Madison: Wisconsin Department of Public Instruction.

Wisconsin Department of Public Instruction. (1988). *Final recommendations of the statewide advisory committee of the year of the family in education.* Madison: author.

Wisconsin Department of Public Instruction. (1988). *Planning for state solutions to the problems of youth at risk.* Madison: author.

Wisconsin Department of Public Instruction. (1987). *Wisconsin educational standards: A blueprint for excellence.* Madison: author.

Notes

Applications and Activities

National Career Development Guidelines-Counselor Competencies

Knowledge of counseling and career development theories and techniques.

Skills to use appropriate individual and group counseling techniques to assist individuals with career decision and career development concerns.

Skills to assist individuals in identifying influencing factors in career decision making, such as family, friends, educational opportunities, and finances.

Skills to assist individuals in changing biased attitudes that stereotype others by gender, race, age, and culture.

Knowledge of changing gender roles and how these impact on work, family, and leisure.

Knowledge of employment information and career planning materials.

Skills to use career development resources and techniques designed for specific groups.

Knowledge of unique career planning needs of minorities, women, persons with disabilities, and older persons.

Knowledge of alternative approaches to career planning needs for individuals with specific needs.

Signature Activity

Type of Activity: Icebreaker

Teaching Objective(s):

To help participants become better acquainted by illustrating the diversity of attributes, experiences and work roles among them.

Behavioral Objective(s):

Each participant will try to find persons in the group who fit given descriptions on the "Signature Activity" worksheet by conversationally asking other people direct or indirect questions.

Estimated Time to Complete: 20 minutes

Points to Introduce Activity:

1. The purpose of this activity is to acquaint you with one another by exploring some of your diverse attributes, experiences and work roles.

2. Please find the "Signature Activity. The directions at the top will instruct you to find other people in the group who fit the descriptions that are given. Please note the two columns. One is for female signatures; the other for males.

3. Please use the next 20 minutes to find as many men and women who will agree to the descriptions by signing the appropriate places on your "Signature Activity" work sheet. You may have only one signature from each participant on your work sheet.

4. You may ask others these questions either directly or indirectly as you walk around the room and engage your fellow participants in conversations.

Materials and Preparation:

1. Participants will need the "Signature Activity" worksheet.

Activity:

The participants will have a worksheet "Signature Activity," that lists approximately 20 descriptive statements about a person, such as, "Someone who is athletic." The participants will engage one another in conversation to find out if any of the descriptions match the person to whom they are speaking. If the person does match any of the descriptions on the "Signature Activity" sheet, the person should sign his/her name next to it. Women should sign the sheet on the left hand side; men on the right.

Adaptations:

The descriptions on the "Signature Activity" sheet could be changed to fit the audience.

A prize could be awarded to the person who collects the most signatures or "Autographs of Distinguished People."

Questions for Discussion:

1. As you asked questions of your fellow participants, were you aware of any of your own sex role stereotypes? Why/why not?

2. Did you sense that others had preconceived ideas about members of the other sex? Why/why not?

3. How might some stereotypical ideas about sex roles interfere with a career development facilitator's effectiveness?

4. What can career development facilitators do to overcome their sex role stereotypes?

Trainer's Notes:

Signature Activity

The purpose of this activity is for you to explore the diverse attitudes and work roles that exist in our society. You will use the time allotted to you by your trainer to find as many women and men as you can who will agree to a description of themselves on the lines below. You can do this by asking people directly or indirectly about themselves in a conversational style.

Women		Men
_____	A person who strives to outdo others, never admitting defeat	_____
_____	A person who thinks men should not show affection for other men	_____
_____	Someone who is a gourmet cook	_____
_____	Someone who is athletic	_____
_____	Someone who likes to take bubble baths	_____
_____	Someone who has chopped wood for a fire	_____
_____	Someone who shows emotions freely	_____
_____	Someone who is not ashamed to cry in front of others	_____
_____	Someone who feels men and women are equal in all respects	_____
_____	Someone who feels men and women have different roles in life	_____
_____	Someone who likes to garden	_____
_____	Someone who feels their own behavior is appropriate for their gender	_____
_____	Someone who feels the other sex has it made	_____
_____	Someone who found their career by chance	_____
_____	Someone who has used a Career Information Delivery System	_____

Women		Men
_____	Someone who would like to change their career	_____
_____	Someone who follows the stock market	_____
_____	Someone who has held or holds a nontraditional work position	_____
_____	Someone who feels that women should be protected by men	_____
_____	Someone who feels that you are a failure if you do not marry	_____
_____	Someone who likes to clean house	_____
_____	Someone who thinks the nurturing instinct belongs only to women	_____
_____	Someone who would like to be the other gender	_____
_____	Someone who is a single parent	_____
_____	Someone who supervisors others in the work place	_____
_____	Someone who works or has worked in a service industry	_____
_____	Someone who works or has worked in a highly technical area	_____
_____	Someone who has been unemployed in the past two years	_____
_____	Someone who has changed their career within the past five years	_____
_____	Someone who is politically active within the community	_____
_____	Someone who started a business	_____
_____	Someone who is mechanical	_____
_____	Someone who can create a computer program	_____

Career Keno

Type of Activity: Icebreaker

Teaching Objective(s):

The purpose of this activity is to introduce participants to one another and to identify those who have special fields of interest or expertise. It will also help the participants begin to think about the types and uses of labor market information that are covered during this training.

Behavioral Objective(s):

The participants will look for persons in the room who fill the career-related descriptions on their list and ask them to sign the appropriate squares. The objective is to meet the other participants and get to know something about their backgrounds by getting as many squares signed as possible during the time period allotted.

Estimated Time to Complete: 20 minutes

Points to Introduce Activity:

1. This is a get acquainted activity called "Career Keno" that can be found on page--of your Participant's Guide. The purpose of this activity is to acquaint you with others and find out more about their interests and experiences.

2. The object of this activity is to find people who match the 25 descriptions given in the squares on your Keno sheet. For example, when you have found a person who regularly uses the *DOT*, please have him/her sign that square. Only one signature is needed in each square, do not get more than one. (If there are at least 30 participants, there should be 30 different signatures on each sheet. If there are less than 30, each person can sign two squares.) Trainers may participate, if they wish.

Materials and Preparation:

1. Each participant needs a "Career Keno" sheet from the Participant's Guide on page----.

2. Participants need pencils and adequate space to move around the room.

3.   A board or flip chart on which to list certain interest groups, if desired.

Activity:

Participants will have a worksheet of 25 squares, each with a description on it that is related to careers. The participants will look for persons in the room who fit the descriptions on their sheet and ask them to sign the appropriate squares. The participants should not sign more than one square on anyone's list. The objective is to get as many squares signed as possible during the time period allotted (15 minutes).

Adaptations:

1.   Items listed in the squares may be changed to fit the backgrounds/work settings of the participants.

2.   A prize may be offered, such as play money, for the first participant to fill all 20 squares.

3.   A completed "Career Keno" sheet could be posted in the room for future reference during the workshop, or, copies could be made for all the participants.

Questions for Discussion:

1.   What were some of the interesting things that you found out about your fellow participants?

2.   Did you meet anyone who holds a position similar to yours?

3.   Who has experience or information that you would like to hear more about? Why?

Trainer's Notes:

Career Keno

Your Name: _____

Below are 25 squares, each with a description. At the signal to begin, please move around the room, find individuals who meet each of the descriptions, and ask them to sign their names in the appropriate squares. You should have 25 different signatures on your sheet.

Someone who:

does placement	works with youth under age 21	regularly uses labor market information	assists special needs clients	has worked in a non-traditional occupation
uses creative career counseling techniques	regularly reads local business news	has worked with at-risk youth	has held a full-time job in the private sector	has provided school to work transition services to clients
has created a Career Center	has collected unemployment benefits	helps clients acquire career development competencies	has been a member of a labor union	has developed partnerships with local businesses or industries
regularly uses the *Dictionary of Occupational Titles*	follows local economic development activities	hopes to have new occupation within the next two years	uses a classification system to organize labor market information	works with retired adults
uses a computerized career information system	has participated in a job orientation program in industry	does career counseling from a theoretical framework	has had more than 3 occupations in the last 5 years	is a baby boomer

Dyadic Encounter

Type of Activity: Icebreaker

Teaching Objective(s):

To have participants feel more at ease in the training session by giving them the opportunity to interact in an informal discussion of their own careers.

To illustrate how our personal characteristics may be related to job satisfaction.

To illustrate the differences between a job and a career.

To help participants begin thinking about goal setting and a final action plan.

Behavioral Objective(s):

Participants will discuss their personality traits and their jobs with one another; they will share their job related frustrations, concerns and goals.

Estimated Time to Complete: 30 minutes

Points to Introduce Activity:

1. The purpose of this activity is to get to know another person by discussing your career.

2. You will be assigned a partner and given a list of questions to ask one another. Follow the numbered list of questions, with first one person responding to a question and then the other.

3. Do not write your responses.

Materials and Preparation:

1. Be prepared to assign or randomly select pairs of participants.

2. Direct participants to the list of questions titled Dyadic Encounter in their Guide.

Activity:

Participants will discuss a list of 20 career-related questions in pairs.

Adaptations:

Some of the discussion questions could be changed to focus on specific career issues or groups of people.

Questions for Discussion:

1. What are we best at on the job?

2. What do we dislike the most in our work?

3. What are some of the characteristics of the best supervisors?

4. What are some of the things that we hope to accomplish in our jobs?

5. What barriers do we anticipate?

6. Who/what can help us to overcome these barriers?

7. As you answered these questions, what did you note about the differences between a job and a career?

Trainer's Notes:

Dyadic Encounter

Complete the following sentences with your partner.

1.   My name is

2.   Basically, my job is

3.   The reason I am here is to

4.   Usually I am the kind of a person who

5.   I'm happiest when

6.   The thing I dislike the most is

7.   On the job, I'm best at

8.   My greatest limitation on the job is

9.   Characteristics of the best supervisor I ever had:

10. Characteristics of the worst supervisor I ever had:

11. I like people who

12. I began working at this job because

13. The next thing I am going to try to accomplish in my career is

14. The barriers I anticipate are

15. I would look to _____ for some support.

16. When I am chalenged to overcome barriers what has worked best for me in the past is

17. The kinds of clients who are the most difficult for me to work with are

18. The kinds of coworkers who are the most difficult for me to work with are

19. To work better with them, I have tried to

20. The thing that worries me about my job is

21. The thing that worries me about my career is

22. Briefly discuss your reactions to this conversation. Time permitting, you may wish to discuss other topics of your own choosing. Several possibilities are: projects at work, leadership practices, employee needs and the future.

Source: Based on the work of John E. Jones and Johanna J. Jones.

Icebreaker Interviews

Type of Activity: Icebreaker

Teaching Objective(s):

The participants will get to know one another and feel more comfortable as they begin the inservice program.

The participants will verbalize their expectations of the inservice program to the persons who interview them. In so doing, they will clarify their goals and provide the instructor with an overview of the participants' needs.

Behavioral Objective(s):

Participants will get to know one another by meeting in pairs to interview one another about their jobs and peak career experiences for five minutes in order to introduce one another to the class.

The participants will tell one another what they expect from the class.

Estimated Time to Complete: 25-45 minutes, depending on class size.

Points to Introduce Activity:

1. One of the most pleasurable aspects of taking a class such as this is meeting other professionals who share some of your challenges and concerns on the job.

2. For the next 10 minutes you will be divided into pairs. One person will interview the other for five minutes about his/her job, a peak experience in his/her career and what might be different or interesting about his/her expectations of the inservice program. After five minutes, please change roles.

3. Encourage participants to be clever and creative in the interviews. Their goal is to come up with a fresh and lively introduction of their partner to the other members of the class.

Materials and Preparation:

1. Be prepared to divide participants in pairs; avoid placing people together who already know each other.

2. Model the activity by introducing yourself to the class in a creative/humorous way, and discussing a peak experience in your

career and your expectations of the inservice, or, have a member of the class do the honors and introduce you according to your planned script.

3.   Names of the participants, their jobs, and their class expectations as they are introduced to the class should be written on a flip chart and kept in a visible location during the workshop.

Activity:

Each participant will be interviewed by a classmate who, in turn, will interview him/her. Each participant will then creatively introduce his/her partner to the class by telling what work the person does, a peak experience in his/her career, and what he/she expects from the inservice program.

Adaptations:

1.   Other items could be included in the introduction, such as how the participants made their career choices, what influenced them to make their choices, what obstacles did they have to overcome, etc.

2.   For interviews of greater depth, allow longer time periods.

Questions for Discussion:

1.   Are there similar training needs that were expressed by the class?

2.   Is there a common thread or theme to these needs? Why? Why not?

3.   Have you met any potential networking resources as a result of the introductions?

Trainer's Notes:

Career and I·MI Continuum

Type of Activity: Large group

Teaching Objective(s):

To display some of the career and LMI resources available to the participants and their comfort/discomfort level with using them.

To plan future training activities based on the participants' use of career and LMI resources.

Behavioral Objective(s):

Participants will place themselves at strategic points around the room to indicate their levels of comfort or discomfort in using resources such as the DOT, SOC, SIC, etc.

The participants will become more aware of the career and LMI resources available to them.

Estimated Time to Complete: 20 minutes

Points to Introduce Activity:

1. Some commonly used sources of career and LMI (name them) are displayed around the room. The purpose of this activity is to express your feelings about using the resources that are displayed. You will note that there are signs placed near the resources reading: EASY TO USE, SOME PARTS OK and HARD TO USE.

2. Your trainer will ask you some common questions that career counselors need to answer. After each question, please walk to the resource that you would choose to help you answer the question. If you are unsure, take an educated guess and walk to that resource.

3. When you reach the resource that you think would best answer the question that is asked, place yourself near the sign that best describes your comfort level in using the resource; EASY, SOME PARTS OK or HARD TO USE.

4. Repeat this procedure with each question that is asked.

Materials and Preparation:

1. Select five or six sources of career and LMI such as: the *Dictionary of Occupational Titles* (DOT), the *Guide for Occupational Exploration* (GOE), the *Standard Industrial Classification Manual* (SIC), the *Occupational Outlook Handbook* (OOH), and state information from the State Employment Security Agency (SESA). Set these volumes on tables around the room. Place signs

next to each resource reading: EASY TO USE, SOME PARTS OK and HARD TO USE.

2. Have a set of questions ready to read, for example:

   a. I've never really given much thought to what I want to do when I finish high school. What choices do I have?

   b. My mom works for Sarah Lee and she's always liked it there--what jobs might I find in a big company like Sarah Lee?

   c. I really like living in Vermont and I don't want to leave. What jobs are available in this area?

   d. I've always been fascinated by electronics, but I'm not sure exactly what I'd like to do--any ideas?

   e. I've always wanted to be a carpenter, but I'm worried about being able to make enough money--do you think I can?

   f. I've worked as a tool and die maker for 15 years and liked my job very much. I was recently in a car accident and I've lost the use of my left arm. I need a good paying job. What can I do?

   g. I work with black male teenagers in a group home who have had little exposure to positive career role models in the community. How can I help them?

Activity:

Participants will listen to several questions relating to common career counseling concerns. Upon hearing the questions read by the instructor, the participants will choose a resource that is displayed in the room to answer the question. They will walk over to the resource and position themselves according to their comfort/discomfort level using the resource.

Adaptations:

The continuum could be constructed to reveal the participants' attitudes, values or feelings on any issue.

Additional questions could be developed, depending upon the resources available.

Questions for Discussion:

1. What kinds of career and LMI do you most frequently need in your work? Is it readily available? Why/why not?

2. What specific difficulties do you have locating or using career and LMI?

Trainer's Notes:

Future Metaphors

Type of Activity: Large Group

Teaching Objective(s):

To illustrate how a person's view of the future may affect their decision making and the career counseling process.

Behavioral Objective(s):

After hearing the trainer read a description of four metaphors to describe the future, each participant will choose one that best describes his/her own view. The metaphors of the future will be discussed in a large group. In conclusion, the participants will verbalize their own metaphors of the future.

Estimated Time to Complete: 20 minutes

Points to Introduce Activity:

1. While there is no "right way" to do career counseling, there are a number of strategies and techniques that can help clients personalize and internalize labor market information. Using metaphors, developing images of the future, examining thinking and information processing styles, and checking out client belief systems are all examples of techniques effective career counselors should develop.

2. The purpose of this exercise is to examine our images of the future. Think about how you see the future. What best describes your vision or image of the future? I am going to ask you to listen to four metaphors of the future. A metaphor is a figure of speech in which a word or phrase that denotes one object or idea is used in place of another to suggest a likeness between them. As you listen to the metaphors that I read, pick the one that best describes your view of the future. Consider this a forced choice. There are no right or wrong answers. A particular metaphor may not be the best one for you, but pick the one that comes the closest. You will have the opportunity to develop your own metaphor later on.

3. Read "Four Metaphors for the Future."

Materials and Preparation:

1. Description of "Four Metaphors for the Future."

2. A board or flip chart on which to list the four metaphors, participant comments and the concluding metaphors developed by the participants.

Activity:

The trainer will read "Four Metaphors for the Future." Each participant will choose one metaphor that best describes his/her view of the future. The choices of the participants will be discussed in a large group. In conclusion, the participants will offer their own metaphors of the future.

Adaptations:

Other metaphors to describe the future could be written by the trainer.

The metaphors created by the participants could be written individually or in pairs. This could be a five minute contest to write the best metaphor as judged by all the participants.

Questions for Discussion:

1. Why are a person's beliefs about the future important considerations in career counseling? What part do these beliefs have in determining a client's future?

2. Why might a person who has a "Roller Coaster" view of life be a challenging client?

3. Is it important for a client to examine his/her views of the future? Why/why not? Should a counselor be aware of a client's views? Why/why not?

4. What role, if any, does culture play in a person's views of the future? Should counselors be aware of cultural differences? Why/why not?

5. Is it possible that career development facilitators have stereotypes about what kind of counseling certain client populations "need?" Why/why not?

6. Can a person's view of the future change? How? Should career development facilitators attempt to change a client's view of the future? Why/why not?

Trainer's Notes:

Source: ICDM Training Materials developed by the Washington SOICC

Four Metaphors for the Future

Roller Coaster

The future is a great roller coaster on a moonless night. It exists, twisting ahead of us in the dark, although we can only see each part as we come to it. We can make estimates about where we are headed, and sometimes see around a bend to another section of track, but it doesn't do us any real good because the future is fixed and determined. We are locked in our seats and nothing we may know or do will change the course that is laid out for us.

Mighty River

The future is a mighty river. The great force of history flows inexorably along, carrying us with it. Most of our attempts to change its course are mere pebbles thrown into the river; they cause a momentary splash and a few ripples, but they make no difference. The river's course CAN be changed, but only by natural disasters like earthquakes or landslides, or by massive concerted human efforts on a similar scale. On the other hand, we are free as individuals to adapt to the course of history, either well or poorly. By looking ahead, we can avoid sandbars and whirlpools and pick the best path through any rapids.

Great Ocean

The future is a great ocean. There are many possible destinations, and many different paths to each destination. Good navigators take advantage of the main currents of change, adapt their courses to the capricious winds of chance, keeps a sharp lookout posted, and move carefully in fog or uncharted waters. If they do these things, they will get safely to the destination (barring a typhoon or other natural disaster that they can neither predict nor avoid).

Colossal Dice Game

The future is entirely random, a colossal dice game. Every second, millions of things happen that could have happened another way and produced a different future. A bullet is deflected by a twig and kills one person instead of another. A scientist checks a spoiled culture and throws it away, or looks more closely at it and discovers penicillin. A spy at Watergate removes a piece of tape from a door and gets away safely, or he forgets to remove the tape and changes American political history. Since everything is chance, all we can do is play the game, pray to the gods of fortune and enjoy what good luck comes our way.

Source: ICDM Training Materials developed by the Washington SOICC

Career Planning Metaphors

Type of Activity: Individual

Teaching Objective(s):

To illustrate the various steps in the career planning process by comparing it to other accomplishments in our lives. This exercise follows the Future Metaphors activity. Both activities also can be used with clients.

Behavioral Objective(s):

Participants will mentally clarify the career planning process by writing five metaphors comparing the process to another experience, accomplishment or skill that they have developed. By becoming familiar with this technique, counselors can use it to encourage their clients to discuss career planning.

Estimated Time to Complete: 30 minutes

Points to Introduce Activity:

1. Research has shown that we are more likely to internalize, learn and remember something if it can be linked to our direct experiences. The purpose of this exercise is to show how career planning and decision making are much like many other activities in our lives.

2. Recall the Future Metaphors activity when we compared our vision of the future with other images, such as a mighty river, etc.

3. Think of an accomplishment, hobby or interest in your life. It could be playing a musical instrument; or a sport, such as golf; or an interest, such as stamp collecting; or a work place activity, such as a leadership role. Visualize all the steps, elements, practice, or components surrounding the topic you have chosen. Using your topic, create a metaphor for career planning. For example, a soccer player might choose the following metaphors:

   Career planning is like soccer because you must be alert and stay in shape.

   Career planning is like soccer because you must understand the rules.

   Career planning is like soccer because you are competing with others.

4. Using the "Career Planning Metaphors" worksheet, write down the topic you have selected and create five metaphors to describe it within the next ten minutes. Be prepared to present your metaphors in a large group discussion to follow.

Materials and Preparation:

1. Participants will need the "Career Planning Metaphors" worksheet.

2. A board or flip chart on which to list some of the most expressive metaphors.

Activity:

After the metaphor concept is reviewed by the trainer, the participants will think of a personal accomplishment, interest, hobby, or work place activity in their own lives. When the participants have chosen a topic, e.g., playing golf, they will compare it to career planning and write five metaphors describing it, which will be discussed in a large group.

Adaptations:

Other subjects could be selected for metaphorical comparisons, e.g., decision making, changing careers, finding a nontraditional job, etc.

Questions for Discussion:

1. What similarities did you find between your topic and planning a career? What contrasts?

2. How did you feel as you wrote your metaphors? Did the experience make you feel more or less confident of planning your career? Why/why not?

3. How could you use this exercise with clients? How might it help them? What groups, if any, would find this exercise especially valuable and why?

Trainer's Notes:

Source: ICDM Training Materials developed by the Washington SOICC

Career Planning Metaphors

Directions: Think of something that is important or meaningful to you that you would be willing to discuss in a large group. It can be a hobby, pastime, a work place activity, a skill, a relationship, a major accomplishment, or anything else of significance in your life. Visualize all the elements, steps, or components surrounding this topic. How is the topic that you have chosen like planning a career? List five metaphors to describe comparisons that can be made.

Example: Playing golf is like planning a career because you must keep your eyes on the ball and keep moving ahead toward your goals.

1. _____
   _____
   _____

2. _____
   _____
   _____

3. _____
   _____
   _____

4. _____
   _____
   _____

5. _____
   _____
   _____

Source: ICDM Training Materials developed by the Washington SOICC

Career and LMI Visualization

Type of Activity: Small or large group

Teaching Objective(s):

To make the participants more aware of the sources of career and LMI that are part of their daily lives.

To illustrate how participants can use this exercise with their clients.

Behavioral Objective(s):

By taking an imaginary walk through one of their typical days, the participants will become more aware of the various sources of career and LMI that are readily available to them and their clients.

Estimated Time to Complete: 15 minutes

Points to Introduce Activity:

Close your eyes, get comfortable and walk with me through your day. Imagine your typical routine. Think of awakening and looking around the room, getting up and dressing for the day. Be aware of all of the products surrounding you or that you are using. What information do these items give you about the labor market? Now imagine yourself having breakfast or doing whatever you do before you leave home. When you leave, where do you go and how do you get there? As you travel to your destination, what do you see? What information does that give you about the labor market in your community? Nationally?

Now you are at your destination. If you are at your work place, what kind of work do you do and what do you use to get it done? If you are somewhere else, what kinds of work are people doing and what are you doing there? If you are at work, what are others doing and how are they accomplishing their jobs? Think for a moment about all the information you are gathering about the work place.

It's lunchtime and you meet a friend at a local restaurant. What can you notice about the labor market while you are having lunch? The afternoon goes on, and soon it's time to go home. On the way you might stop to get gas or groceries, or at your health club. You might go shopping at a local mall, or be a chauffeur to some youngsters. Eventually you reach home, read the newspaper before dinner and perhaps watch some TV afterwards, or read the most recent news magazine. Maybe it's play time and you go out to a movie or nightclub. Do you pick up any other information about your labor market?

What have you learned about the marketplace, the world of work, your labor market? Think about the economy, job descriptions, industries, people eating out, the problems you see while working or going to work, shopping, your own purchases, your salary, etc. This is all useful information about the labor market.

Now, imagine yourself in your client's shoes and walk through a day in his/her role. Imagine getting up, leaving the house, coming to see you (how do you get there?). How might the information your client sees be different from your own? What kinds of labor market information might your client collect that is different from your own? How can you and your client use that information in career counseling?

Materials and Preparation:

1. Trainer should be prepared to read the above statement to the participants.

Activity:

While hearing the trainer's introduction, the participants will imagine that they are walking through their typical day and will recall the sources of career and LMI that they encounter. Secondly, they will imagine that they are walking through a day in a client's shoes and compare the career and labor market information collected by themselves and their clients.

Adaptations:

Have the participants go through the visualization exercise as members of special populations. For example, "You are a minority male looking for work." "You are a person with a disability trying to choose a career." "You are a displaced homemaker seeking to reenter the labor market after a 20 year absence."

Questions for Discussion:

1. As you walked through your day, what sources of career and LMI did you find?

2. As you imagined yourself in the shoes of one of your clients, what sources of career and LMI were available to you? What sources were not available to you? Why not?

3. How was the information to which you were exposed different from that to which your client might be exposed?

4. Might these informational differences affect your counseling and your client's decision making process? If so, how? If not, why?

5. What might be the effects of your exposure to labor market information that is different from your client's?

Trainer's Notes:

Earning Power

Type of Activity: Small Group

Teaching Objective(s):

To show participants how to find the average earnings of specific occupational groups by using the *Occupational Outlook Handbook* (OOH).

Behavioral Objective(s):

Working in pairs, the participants will research information in the OOH.

Estimated Time to Complete: 20 minutes

Points to Introduce Activity:

1. Clients are often concerned about how much money they might earn in a particular occupation.

2. One of the best sources for this information is the OOH. This exercise helps to familiarize us with the OOH.

3. For each of the groups listed, see if you can "guess" which occupations have the highest earnings. When you have finished, use the OOH to check your answers. Please keep in mind that the earnings depend on a number of factors; they are not absolute. Look upon the earnings as a clue to the attractiveness of certain occupations and their potential for long-term monetary rewards.

Materials and Preparation:

1. *Occupational Outlook Handbook* for each small group.

2. "Who Earns the Most?" work sheet.

    (Answers: 1-b, 2-c, 3-a, 4-c, 5-b, 6-a, 7-c, 8-a.)

Activity:

Using the "Who Earns the Most?" work sheet, the participants will: 1) make guesses from the list of occupational groups and 2) check their answers in the *OOH*.

Adaptations:

More occupations could be added to the list to make the activity longer; occupations can be deleted to make the activity shorter.

Additional information from the *OOH* could be researched.

Different resources, such as CIDs, and state and local wage information could be used. A comparison could be made of the resources.

Questions for Discussion:

1. What factors influence the amount of salary that is paid for a given occupation?

2. Do you think some occupations are overpaid or underpaid? Why?

3. Is salary the most important consideration when choosing a career? Why/why not?

4. What are the most important considerations in making a career choice?

5. Where are the high-paying jobs of the future?

6. How can career development facitilities use this information to help their clients?

Trainer's Notes:

Who Earns the Most?

For each of the groups listed below, see if you can "guess" which occupations have the highest earnings.

1. A file clerk, fire fighter or licensed practical nurse.

2. An aircraft pilot, TV announcer or veterinarian.

3. An urban planner, architect or lawyer.

4. A bartender, mail carrier or secondary school teacher.

5. A physical therapist, physician's assistant or dental hygienist.

6. A statistician, forester or meteorologist.

7. A building inspector, middle school principal or hospital administrator.

8. A hotel manager, insurance underwriter or retail buyer.

Lost Job

Type of Activity: Individual

Teaching Objective(s):

By simulating the career decision making process, the participants will become more aware of how personal interests, values and the availability of information influence the process.

The participants will gain some practice in using both formal and informal sources of career and LMI in their decision making process.

Behavioral Objective(s):

Imagining that they have lost their jobs, the participants will be given the names of three available jobs by the trainer. The participants will research the jobs, gathering as much information as possible about each one. They will then choose one of the three jobs, based on their interests and values. They will be prepared to share their decisions and the rationale behind them with the large group.

Estimated Time to Complete: 40 minutes

Points to Introduce Activity:

1. Imagine you have lost your job and that you are now a part of the nation's unemployment statistics. You see an employment counselor at Job Service who gives you titles of three positions that are presently available in your community. They are: TRAINING REPRESENTATIVE, VOCATIONAL REHABILITATION COUNSELOR and PERSONNEL RECRUITER.

2. Gather as much information as possible about these three positions within the next 20 minutes, using any and all resources available to you in this room. Don't forget to include the other participants in the room as resources.

3. Be prepared to communicate your career choice to the class, explaining the rationale behind your decision; include considerations such as personal interests, values and family considerations.

4. After 20 minutes, we will meet in a large group to discuss your career choices and the role "information" played in making them.

Materials and Preparation:

1. Have federal sources of career and LMI available in the classroom, such as the *Dictionary of Occupational Titles* (DOT), the *Standard Industrial Classification* (SIC) Manual, the *Standard Occupational Classification* (SOC) Manual, a

CIDS, occupational projections, wage surveys, and state and local information. Be sure to have enough resources for all the participants to research the jobs. Some informal sources of information would also be highly desirable, such as professional journals, newspapers and current periodicals related to the occupational areas.

2. Be prepared to list the career choices on a board for discussion purposes.

3. Make sure participants have comfortable work areas for research purposes.

Activity:

Participants will imagine that they have lost their jobs and research three possible a career choice with the resource materials in the room for 20 minutes. Participants will make a career choice based on their interests, values, and the information available. They will be prepared to discuss their choices and the rationale behind them in a large group discussion for approximately 15 minutes.

Adaptations:

Different or additional careers could be selected for research, depending on the audience, the time allowed and the resources available.

Questions for Discussion:

1. What were the most important factors in making your career choice? What were the least important?

2. Why is this particular career (whatever career is named) a popular choice? Why is this career (whatever career) the least popular choice?

3. Was information easy to find on these careers? Why/why not? Was the information understandable once you found it? Why/why not? Do you believe it is reliable?

4. Would your clients be able to locate and understand the information you have used today? Why/why not? What could you do to help make this information more accessible to your clients?

5. What have you learned from this activity that you could use in your work with clients?

Trainer's Notes:

Carousel of Careers

Type of Activity: Small group/Roundtables

Teaching Objective(s):

Participants will be able to select certain topics of interest and participate in small group discussions led by resource persons who can address their specific concerns.

Behavioral Objective(s):

Participants will develop skills to describe and locate a variety of labor market information.

Estimated Time to Complete: One and a half hours (three 20 minute sessions with a five minute break between discussions and a wrap-up). Sample schedule:

2:00 - 2:20 p.m.	Session One
2:20 - 2:25 p.m.	Rotate
2:25 - 2:45 p.m.	Session Two
2:45 - 2:50 p.m.	Break
2:50 - 3:10 p.m.	Session Three
3:10 - 3:20 p.m.	Wrap-up

Points to Introduce Activity:

1. This activity will allow you to select three career and LMI topics of interest from the six tables that are located around the room. You will have 20 minutes at each table with a resource person. After 20 minutes, please move to the second table. Please repeat the procedure for a third 20 minute session.

2. When we conclude the carousel, you will have the opportunity to ask any final questions you may have.

3. Trainers: Give a lively and informative introduction of the resource persons to stimulate participant interest.

Materials and Preparation:

1. Six tables that are clearly marked by Career and LMI topics and chairs for all participants.

2. Six articulate and well prepared resource persons to lead discussions at each table.

3. Ask resource persons if any materials are necessary for their presentations.

4. A listing of all the topics and resource persons on a board or flip chart to introduce the activity.

5. An introduction of all the resource persons, with a background sketch of their qualifications.

Activity:

The participants will move three times from one 20 minute discussion to another, allowing them to select specific topics of interest. There will be six discussion tables headed by resource persons on topics such as:

What Can CIDs Do for Us? What Are the National Career Development Guidelines? How Can a SOICC Help Career Counselors? What Is Gender Equity? How Can We Help Students with Disabilities? What Are Some Commonly Used LMI Resources? Where Are the Jobs of the Future? How Do We Meet the Needs of Adults in Transition? Multicultural Counseling--What Does It Mean? What Careers Does the Military Offer? What Opportunities Are Available in this Community?

The activity concludes with a large group wrap-up session to address any final concerns.

Adaptations:

The Career Carousel could be made larger, with more topics and tables to choose from, and more time allowed.

Have one product available at each table. Instead of discussing an issue, demonstrate how to use a product such as the CIDS, OOH, OIS, SOC, DOT, GOE, occupational projections, wage surveys, or Unemployment Compensation (UC) data.

Questions for Discussion:

1. Are there any final questions or comments that you would like to address to our resource persons?

2. Is there any information that you found to be particularly valuable? What specific information will you use in your work place?

3. Are there any other topics that you would like to see covered in a carousel format such as this?

Trainer's Notes:

Adapted from Oklahoma ICDM Workshops

Advertising Career and LMI Resources

Type of Activity: Small groups

Teaching Objective(s):

To familiarize the participants with federal and state government sources of information: to know where to find them, what is in them and how they can be used in career counseling.

Behavioral Objective(s):

Participants will work in small groups to develop a creative advertisement to be presented to the class for some of the more widely used sources of information, such as: the *Dictionary of Occupational Titles* (DOT), the *Standard Occupational Classification* (SOC) Manual, the *Standard Industrial Classification* (SIC) Manual and the *Guide for Occupational Exploration* (GOE).

Participants will be more familiar with the use and content of the information resources that are advertised to the class.

Estimated Time to Complete: 45-60 minutes (depending on the number of small groups)

Points to Introduce Activity:

1. This is an exercise to test your advertising creativity. Imagine that you have to sell one of our source books. How can you excite others about the wealth of information in your publication? Most importantly, how can you entice them to buy it?

2. You will have the opportunity to try your hand at advertising an information resource today. You will work with a small group to develop an ad to sell the resource that you are given, such as the DOT or SIC. You will present your ad to the class. It can be in the form of a poster, a newspaper ad, a television or radio commercial, a poem, a song, or even a door-to-door sales pitch. Be clever and creative!

3. In your ad, please try to be as informative as possible; your objective is to sell your classmates on the value of your LMI resource.

Materials and Preparation:

1. An information resource for each small group, such as the DOT, SIC, SOC, CIDS, etc.

2. Materials to create ads, such as paper, markers, tape recorders, etc.

Activity:

Participants will work in small groups to create an ad for an information resource.

Adaptations:

With video taping equipment, each group could make a 30 second commercial for their resource.

An "Addy Award" (a humorous certificate, small statue, bag of jelly beans, etc.) could be given for the best advertisement by having participants vote for their choices.

Questions for Discussion:

1. What information did your team try to project about your resource?

2. If you had more time and materials, what additional information would you present to the class about your resource?

3. What questions do you have about any of these resources?

4. Which of these resources have you used? Does the resource provide you with the information that you need? Why? Why not?

5. What resources have you not used? Why not?

6. Have you been enticed to use any new products as a result of the ads you have seen today? How will you use them?

Trainer's Notes:

Career and LMI Scavenger Hunt

Type of Activity: Individual

Teaching Objective(s):

To demonstrate that we are surrounded by career and labor market information in our everyday lives.

To evaluate the validity or reliability of certain kinds of career and labor market information.

To illustrate the various categories of career and LMI.

Behavioral Objective(s):

During their lunch break, participants will gather one piece of career and labor market information from the environment that they can share with the group.

The participants will cite the sources of their information when it is presented.

The participants will evaluate the information that is presented to the group.

The participants will categorize the kinds of information they have reported.

Estimated Time to Complete: 30 minutes

Points to Introduce Activity:

1. As we move through a typical day, we unconsciously absorb a great deal of career and labor market information in various forms from different sources.

2. When you return from lunch, we will ask each of you to share with the class one piece of information that you picked up during your break, along with the source of your information.

3. You cannot use any of the materials in this room as a source.

4. You may write your information and source on a piece of paper, if you wish.

5. Give an example of career and LMI that might be found, such as the HELP WANTED sign in the restaurant window. What kind of help is needed? What are the wages, hours and conditions of employment? Are benefits offered? Any special training needed?

Materials and Preparation:

1. A board to summarize the career and LMI that is found, and a rating scale for the information, such as QUESTIONABLE, PROBABLY RELIABLE, WELL DOCUMENTED.

2. (Optional) A list of categories that could be discussed as outlined below in Adaptations.

Activity:

The participants will find one piece of career and labor market information during their lunch break to bring back to class. The information will be summarized on a board and evaluated for its reliability.

Adaptations:

The information could be broken into categories, such as occupational, demographic and labor force information. The information could be divided into federal, state and local information.

The participants could work in teams in a contest to see which team could collect the most information over the lunch hour.

Working in competitive teams in the classroom for a period of 20 minutes, participants could be given copies of the daily newspaper to scan and hunt for career and LMI to report back to the large group.

Questions for Discussion:

1. Were you surprised by the amount and availability of the information?

2. What forms of career and LMI did you find--any labor force information? Demographic? Occupational? Federal? State? Local?

3. How would you rate the reliability of each of these pieces of information?

4. What conclusion can we come to about career and LMI in general?

5. How can you use this in career counseling?

6. How might your clients use this information?

7. What career and LMI did you look for, but could not find?

Trainer's Notes:

Adapted from Florida ICDM Workshops

Classification Systems and Resources

Type of Activity: Small group

Teaching Objective(s):

To show participants how career and labor market information is classified to make it manageable, accessible and useable.

Behavioral Objective(s):

Working in small groups, the participants will look at copies of the *Dictionary of Occupational Titles* (DOT) on their tables. They will list all of the occupations that made it possible for the DOT to be here at the training session.

Estimated Time to Complete: 30 minutes

Points to Introduce Activity:

1. Career and labor market information comes in an assortment of configurations and formats. Before it can be used effectively by either counselors or clients, it must be organized or classified in some way, so it becomes manageable. The purpose of this activity is to illustrate how classification systems work.

2. In small groups of five or six, look at a *Dictionary of Occupational Titles* (DOT) which is placed on the tables around the room. Working as a group, as quickly as possible, write down all the occupations you can think of that made it possible for the DOTs to be here at the training session today.

3. After you have completed your list of occupations, divide your list into at least three, but no more than five, categories of occupations.

4. You will have approximately 20 minutes to develop your list and occupational categories. Be prepared to share your work with the large group when you are asked to do so.

Materials and Preparation:

1. A DOT for each small group, a comfortable seating arrangement for group work, paper and pencils.

2. A board or flip chart on which to list the categories reported by each group.

3. Be prepared to discuss other LMI classification systems, such as the SIC, SOC, GOE, etc.

Activity:

Working in small groups and using the DOT as their resource, the participants will list all the occupations that made it possible for the DOT to be used in the training session. After listing the occupations, the participants will classify them into categories of not less than three and not more than five.

Adaptations:

Other books could be used as resources, such as telephone books or a city directory, a university timetable, encyclopedias, etc.

Have each small group use a different resource such as the SOC, SIC, GOE, etc., and share the results of their research with others. Why are the classification systems different? How can we relate the various systems to one another?

Questions for Discussion:

1. How many occupations did your group have on the first list?

2. How many categories did your group develop?

3. What similarities are found between the categories listed by each group?

4. How are occupations classified in other LMI sources, such as the SIC, SOC, GOE, etc.?

5. How can an understanding of classification systems help you in your work? How can it help your clients?

Trainer's Notes:

Implications Wheel

Type of Activity: Small group

Teaching Objective(s):

To illustrate ways in which the change from a manufacturing economy to a service economy has had a ripple effect on the U.S. labor market.

Behavioral Objective(s):

Participants will have a greater awareness of the declining work opportunities in manufacturing industries and the growing number of positions in the service industries. They will incorporate this knowledge into their career counseling.

Estimated Time to Complete: 45 minutes

Points to Introduce Activity:

1. Change does not occur in a vacuum; each cause has an effect that produces a chain reaction.

2. The change from a manufacturing to a service economy has many effects, or implications, especially for career counselors.

3. Let's begin with the premise that most new jobs will be in the services; make this statement in the large center circle, or hub, of your wheel.

4. There are many implications, or effects, of this economic trend; write them in the medium-sized circles that are attached to the center.

5. Add new circles to the diagram as you consider the implications (for counselors and their clients) to each circle that you add; the objective is to widen the circle by generating as many ideas as possible.

6. Be specific when you list your implications. For example, "more computers" is not as helpful as "computers will play a greater role in the work place and in the career counseling process."

Materials and Preparation:

1. Illustration of large wheel on blackboard or flip chart to introduce wheel concept.

2. Large sheets of paper and markers for each group to construct their own wheels.

3. Board or flip chart to summarize the outcomes of the activity.

Activity:

The participants will brainstorm to consider the many implications of the economic forecast that most new jobs will be in the service industries.

The participants will break up into small groups of three or four to discuss and design "Implication Wheels" that will portray the many effects of this economic change from a manufacturing to a service economy.

Adaptations:

The implications wheels can be constructed around any change in the labor market, such as: more women in the work force, more technical skills needed, more minority participation, an older work force, a plant closing, a large business relocation, etc.

This can also be done as an individual or large group activity.

Questions for Discussion:

1. What are some of the most important implications on your wheel?

2. At what points on your wheel might career development facilitators or their clients exert some influence or control?

3. What implications on your wheel are controlled by outside influences? What are they? Why?

4. What are some of the more desirable implications on your wheel? What can be done to implement them?

5. What are some of the undesirable implications? What can be done to diminish them?

6. How could you use this activity with your clients?

Trainer's Notes:

Adapted from the ICDM Materials developed by the Washington SOICC

State and Local Resources

Type of Activity: Individual

Teaching Objective(s):

To demonstrate the importance of state and local career and labor market information for clients who plan to remain and find work in their home towns.

To point out some of the sources of state, county and local career and labor market information.

Behavioral Objective(s):

Participants will imagine that they are taking a walk around the communities in which they are presently living. As they do so, they will make a list of: the occupations they encounter; what career and labor market information was necessary for people to work in those occupations; and where one might find that information.

Estimated Time to Complete: 30 minutes

Points to Introduce Activity:

1. Many of your clients plan to find work and remain in the areas in which they have grown up. You may find that career and labor market information describing the national scene is of limited use to them. They need information about the local labor markets.

2. The purpose of this activity is to stimulate your thinking about some of the occupations in your communities and the sources of labor market information about these occupations. (Give an example of an occupation from your community and describe how people would find information about work within it.)

3. Please find the "State and Local Resources" work sheet and complete it according to the directions. You will have 20 minutes. Be prepared to discuss your responses in a large group.

Materials and Preparation:

1. "State and Local Resources" work sheet.

2. Examples of state and local sources of LMI.

3. A board or flip chart on which to list state and local resources.

4. A state/local resource person to answer any questions.

Activity:

After a brief introduction with some examples from the trainer, participants will complete the worksheet, "State and Local Resources."

Adaptations:

Participants could work in pairs.

If the participants come from a large and diverse work place, this activity could be applied to that environment.

Questions for Discussion:

1. What were some of the occupations you listed from your community?

2. How might people find work in these occupations?

3. What specific LMI is needed for these occupations? Where can it be found?

4. Is state and local information accessible to you and your clients? Is it readily available? Is it easy to use? Why/why not?

5. How can you use state and local resources in your work? How can your clients use state and local resources? What could be done to make these resources more available or useable in your community?

Trainer's Notes:

State and Local Resources

Think about the community in which you presently live. As you imagine yourself walking around town, pick an interesting block. As you walk that block, make a list of all the occupations that are represented within its boundaries.

_____
_____
_____
_____

Now, imagine the block in which you live. Walk that block. What kind of jobs do the people on your block have? Where do they work?

_____
_____
_____
_____

What do they do?

_____
_____
_____
_____

What kinds of career and labor market information do you suppose they needed to get their jobs?

_____
_____
_____
_____

If you were to enter any of the occupations in which these people are working, what would you need to know and where would you find it?

_____
_____
_____
_____

If someone in your block were unemployed, what must they do to find work? What resources are available to them?

_____
_____
_____
_____

Helping Anna Find Work

Type of Activity: Small group

Teaching Objective(s):

To simulate the ways in which career development facilitators can use career and labor market information to help their clients.

Behavioral Objective(s):

The participants will work in small groups of three or four on an exercise that requires them to use several sources of labor market information in a simulated job search for a client.

Estimated Time to Complete: 45 minutes

Points to Introduce Activity:

1. This activity, "Helping Anna Find Work," is completed by answering questions 1-13 on the worksheet. You will work in pairs to research the questions for approximately 30 minutes. You will need to refer to several LMI resources that are here in the room. If you are unable to locate a particular resource, someone else may be using it, so please go on the next question. When you are finished using materials, please replace them promptly for others who may need them.

Materials and Preparation:

1. The following LMI resources:

    Dictionary of Occupational Titles (DOT),
    Standard Occupational Classification Manual (SOC),
    Career Information Delivery System (CIDS),
    Occupational Projections,
    Occupational Employment Statistics (OES)
    Occupational Outlook Handbook (OOH),
    Standard Industrial Classification Manual (SIC),
    State/National Projections,
    State Employment Review,
    State Employment Picture,
    State Covered Employment by Industry and County,
    Classified Directory of State Manufacturers,
    State Service Directory,
    State/local area wage surveys, economic indicators, etc.,
    Local resources such as telephone books, etc.

Activity:

Using the LMI resources that are provided, the participants will work in small groups to assist Anna, a woman who has lost her job. This activity simulates many of the steps career development facilitators need to take in using LMI resources with their clients.

Adaptations:

The person seeking work could have special needs, such as a person with a disability, a teen parent, a displaced homemaker, a retiree or an adult with limited English proficiency.

The beginning job description could be changed from a salesperson to a computer programmer, an auto mechanic, etc.

Questions for Discussion:

1. What resources were the most valuable in helping Anna find work? Why?

2. Did you have difficulty using any of the resources? Which ones? Why?

3. Were you surprised by the amount of information you were able to find within the time period? Do you think it was time well spent? Why? Why not?

4. What resources would you be most likely to use in counseling your clients? Why? What additional resources do you recommend? Why?

Trainer's Notes:

Helping Anna Find Work

Occupation Questions	Sources	Answers
1. Anna sells electronic equipment and related supplies at Radio Shack. She has an associate degree in marketing. Select an occupational title for Anna from the following LMI publications and list its numerical code.	*Dictionary of Occupational Titles* (DOT)	DOT Title: DOT Code:
	Standard Occupational Classification Manual (SOC)	SOC Title: SOC Code:
	Guide for Occupational Exploration (GOE)	GOE Title: GOE Code:
	State Career Information Delivery System (CIDS)	CIDS Title: CIDS Code:
	Occupational Employment Statistics (OES): See State Occupational Projections for list of occupations	OES Title:
2. Anna has been laid off and is looking for other work. What are some occupations that are related to Anna's?	SOC CIDS GOE	List related occupations:

Occupation Questions

	Occupation Questions	Sources	Answers
3.	What occupational descriptions can you find of Anna's work? Please include the major tasks and skills required.	OOH DOT CIDS	Brief description, include major tasks and skills:
	List the occupational characteristics of Anna's job, the physical demands and environmental conditions.	Selected Characteristics of Occupations defined in the DOT	Physical demands: Environmental conditions:

Industry Questions

	Industry Questions	Sources	Answers
4.	Determine the industries that employ Anna's occupation. (These are places where she may find work)	SIC DOT OOH CIDS Local and state resources Use your own knowledge (be expansive and creative, take a clue from some of the variant occupational titles)	List employing industries (kinds of businesses):
5.	Identify the specific industry title(s) and numerical codes.	SIC - use alphabetical index to get into the classification scheme Look at definition and example Look at the hierarchy of the classification manual	Major industry title and SIC code: 2 digit title and code: 3 digit title and code: 4 digit title and code:

Occupation Questions	Sources	Answers
6. What are the projections for these industries?	State and National Occupational Projections, 1988-2000: (Prepublication pages) CIDS Local information resources	Projections:

Geography and Industry

Occupation Questions	Sources	Answers
7. Review the industrial base in the local labor market to assess job opportunities for Anna.	Employment Review State Employment Picture	Give industry employment:
How many businesses are in the industry?	State Covered Employment	Number of businesses:
Are they large or small?		Large or small?
8. List specific companies or businesses in your area.	Use your own knowledge. Classified Directory of State Manufacturers State Service Directory Local telephone books	List two or three business establishments:

More about the Occupation	Sources	Answers
9. Examine projections to determine employment opportunities for Anna.	State and National Occupational Projections	
10. If you identified related occupations, list the occupational preparation and training requirements for Anna, determine whether Anna will need to supplement her current education and training.	OOH CIDS DOT Selected Characteristics Occupations Defined in the DOT	List levels of education needed or specific training programs: What is the specific vocational preparation (SVP): What are requirements in Math (M) and Language (L):
11. Look for wage rates.	CIDS State Wage Survey	Occupational wage rate:

Questions	Sources	Answers
12. Examine advancement opportunities (or lack thereof) and career ladders available to Anna.	OOH CIDS	List any information found:
What are the implications for Anna's career development?	Local Resources	Implications:
13. Examine job openings in the occupations you identified.	State and National Occupational Projections CIDS State or SDA reports	Average annual openings:

Around the House

Type of Activity: Small group

Teaching Objective(s):

To demonstrate the use of the *Standard Industrial Classification* (SIC) Manual and state and national occupational projections.

To broaden the participants' awareness and understanding of the concept of an "industry."

To discuss industrial projections and the growth or decline of occupations commonly found within them by referencing state and national projections and/or the *Occupational Outlook Handbook* (OOH).

Behavioral Objective(s):

Working in small groups, the participants will brainstorm to develop a list of industries involved in the production of several common household items. After a list of industries has been developed, the participants will make some projections concerning their future growth patterns. The participants will select one industry and describe it in detail to the large group from information taken from the SIC, state and national occupational projections, the OOH and other related sources.

Estimated Time to Complete: 45 minutes

Points to Introduce Activity:

1. The production of even the most common items around our homes is often a complex process that requires the work of many people in diverse occupations in far-reaching places. Working in a small group, you will be given a household item as a topic for brainstorming about the many industries involved in its production and the future growth patterns in these industries.

2. Your group will choose one of the industries to investigate in greater detail, using the SIC and state and national occupational projections as your resources. You will discuss the projections for the industry and the occupations commonly found within it. A spokesperson should be prepared to report your findings in a large group discussion.

3. Assign one of the following items to each group:

> Your favorite pair of shoes or slippers
> A piece of cookware from your kitchen
> A towel from the bathroom
> Notepaper from your desk
> A plastic food container from your refrigerator
> The laundry soap you use

Materials and Preparation:

1. *Standard Industrial Classification* (SIC) Manuals or reprints of the classification index for each small group.

2. State and national occupational projections, industry projections and/or the *Occupational Outlook Handbook* (OOH).

3. Participant worksheets "Around the House."

4. A board, overhead or flip chart for group reporting.

Activity:

Working in small groups, the participants will brainstorm about the industries involved in the production and distribution of a common household item. Using state and national occupational projections as resources, they will make some group projections concerning future growth and occupational needs in the industries they have listed. Finally, they will select one of the industries to report on to the large group using SIC data, offering their own comments about the industry, its economic future and its occupational projections.

Adaptations:

The list of household items could be changed.

Questions for Discussion:

1. What relationships among industries can be seen in the SIC Manual?

2. How could you use the SIC with your clients? What information does it provide that you could not find in the DOT? OOH? SOC? GOE?, etc.?

3. Why would an understanding of an industrial classification system increase employment opportunities for clients?

4. Why are national and state projections an important component of career planning?

Trainer's Notes:

Around the House

Directions: Your group will be assigned a common household item to research the industries involved in its production and distribution. You also will make some industrial growth and occupational projections. The sources of information are the SIC and State and National Projections.

Take five minutes to brainstorm about the various industries that were involved in the production of your item. List them in the blanks below.

_____
_____
_____
_____
_____

Choose one of the industries from the above list to research in greater depth in the *Standard Industrial Classification* (SIC) Manual. Give the name of the industry as it appears in the SIC:_____

What is its Major Group number? (e.g., Agricultural Services is 07)_____

How is the Major Group as a whole described in the SIC (be brief)?

_____
_____

List the industries that are grouped with the one you have chosen and give their *SIC* classification numbers. In your small group, discuss the industries and occupations that you would expect to grow or decline and the reasons for your projections. Place a plus (+), minus (-) or an equal (=) next to the industries and occupations that you have listed to indicate the pattern of growth or decline. As resources, use state and national projections, common sense, etc.

_____number   _____number
_____number   _____number
_____number   _____number
_____number   _____number
_____number   _____number

List ten occupations found in these industries:

_____   _____
_____   _____
_____   _____
_____   _____
_____   _____

Choose a spokesperson to report your findings to the large group.

Public and Private Self

Type of Activity: Large group

Teaching Objective(s):

To illustrate cultural differences by demonstrating that what is considered to be a public topic in one culture may be a private topic in another.

To make participants more aware of and sensitive to cultural differences.

Behavioral Objective(s):

Given questionnaires that list a variety of topics, participants will check responses to indicate their public or private views on the subjects listed.

Estimated Time to Complete: 30 minutes

Points to Introduce Activity:

1. We often assume that topics we consider to be public information will also be considered public by others; therefore, we may unintentionally violate the privacy of others.

2. On the "Public/Private Questionnaire," check the topics that you consider to be public and those that you consider to be private. For example, the first question on the questionnaire asks you about your views on religion. If you feel your views are private, meaning that you can only discuss this topic with those close to you, mark the Private Column. If you would feel comfortable if your views on religion were made public, check the Public Column.

3. We will discuss our differences when you have completed the questionnaire.

Materials and Preparation:

1. The "Public/Private Questionnaire" from the Participant's Guide for each participant.

2. The definition of public and private written on board or flip chart.

Activity:

Participants will individually complete the Public/Private Questionnaires and discuss the results in a large group.

Adaptations:

Additional topics related to career development could be added to the questionnaire.

Questions for Discussion:

1. How many people checked public items in the six categories?

2. What categories had the fewest number of public checks? Why?

3. Were differences found between the participants' responses, or were the responses fairly uniform? Why? Why not?

4. In what situations might we find a greater variance in responses? Why?

5. What are the implications for career counseling?

6. What is the effect of learning about individual and cultural differences and respecting the privacy of others?

Trainer's Notes:

Adapted from Pedersen, P. (1988). *A Handbook For Developing Multicultrual Awareness.* Alexandria, VA, American Association for Counseling and Development.

Private/Public Questionnaire

Please mark each of the following topics as:

Private: if it is comfortable to discuss only with intimates, such as close friends or members of your immediate family.

Public: if it is comfortable to discuss with casual friends, acquaintances or strangers.

Public	Private	
		Attitudes and Opinions
		1. What I think and feel about my religion.
		2. My views on Communism.
		3. My views on racial integration.
		4. My views on sexual morality.
		5. The things I regard as desirable for a person to be.
		Tastes and Interests
		1. My favorite foods.
		2. My likes and dislikes in music.
		3. My favorite reading matter.
		4. The kinds of movies and tv programs I like best.
		5. The kind of party or social gathering I like best.
		Work or Studies
		1. What I feel are my shortcomings that prevent me from getting ahead.
		2. What I feel are my special strong points for work.
		3. My goals and ambitions.
		4. How I feel about my career.
		5. How I really feel about the people I work for or with.

Public	Private	
		Money
		1. How much money I make at work.
		2. Whether or not I owe money.
		3. My total financial worth.
		4. My most pressing need for money right now.
		5. How I budget my money.
		Personality
		1. Aspects of my personality I dislike.
		2. Feelings I have trouble expressing or controlling.
		3. Facts of my present sex life.
		4. Things I feel ashamed or guilty about.
		5. Things that make me feel proud.
		Body
		1. My feelings about my face.
		2. How I wish I looked.
		3. My feelings about parts of my body.
		4. My past illnesses and treatment.
		5. Feelings about my sexual inadequacies.

Source: Pedersen, P. (1988). *A Handbook For Developing Multicultrual Awareness.* Alexandria, VA, American Association for Counseling and Development.

Label Awareness

Type of Activity: Small group

Teaching Objective(s):

To demonstrate how each of us may wear a culturally assigned label on our forehead.

Behavioral Objective(s):

Participants will be more aware of how culturally assigned labels influence the ways in which others perceive and interact with us.

Estimated Time to Complete: 20 minutes

Points to Introduce Activity:

1. The purpose of this activity is to illustrate how others perceive us according to our cultural background or group identification.

2. Discuss the examples of labeling that you have seen in your own life or in the media.

3. Each participant will have a label placed on his/her forehead or back with a one word adjective or noun to describe him/her. He/she will not know what the label says.

4. Break into small groups of four to six and discuss an assigned topic, e.g., the impact of more women in the work force, for 10-15 minutes.

5. Interact with each participant in your group as if the label assigned to him/her were true, e.g., INTELLIGENT, HOMEMAKER, TRANSIENT, etc.

6. At the end of the activity, participants will try to guess what their labels might be.

Materials and Preparation:

1. Labels for participants to be placed on their foreheads or pinned on their backs, such as: bright, stupid, homeless, wealthy, uneducated, teacher, sneaky, at-risk, agreeable, philosophical, bus driver, school principal.

2. Select an interesting topic that will generate group discussion.

Activity:

Participants will break up into small groups and discuss an interesting topic for 15-20 minutes. Each participant will wear a label on his/her forehead; the others will treat him/her as if that label were true. The participant will not know what his/her label says. When the discussion period ends, each participant will try to guess what his/her label says. Group members will then reveal their labels to one another and discuss their feelings during this exercise.

Adaptations:

Could be done for a longer period of time.

Could repeat activity twice with a different label for each participant.

Questions for Discussion:

1. When did you first feel that you had a special label?

2. What happened to make you feel that you had a positive or negative label?

3. Did you try to do anything to overcome your label? If so, what? Did it help?

4. What were your feelings as the discussion progressed?

5. How might this be compared to real life?

6. How might you use this activity in your work?

7. What does this say about how we stereotype individuals to fit our expectations?

Trainer's Notes:

Decision Making

Type of Activity: Large group

Teaching Objective(s):

To illustrate individual differences by showing that what seems logical to one person may not seem logical to another person.

Behavioral Objective(s):

Participants will gain an understanding of individual differences in how decisions are made.

Participants will identify the decision outcomes and be aware of the rationale surrounding it.

Participants will have a better understanding of the decision making process from another cultural perspective, instead of from their own point of view.

Estimated Time to Complete: 45 minutes

Points to Introduce Activity:

1. What seems logical to one person may not seem logical to another.

2. Our resource person for this activity is (introduce speaker). Our resource person will describe a difficult decision in his/her life wherein personal values were an important factor. Our speaker will describe the background and circumstances leading up to his/her final decision.

3. After he/she has completed telling you about his/her decision making experience, you will have the opportunity to ask him/her any questions you may have.

4. Our resource person will not tell what his/her final decision was. We will ask each participant to: 1) predict the resource person's final decision, and, 2) provide the rationale that guided the decision. (The predictions of the participants can be written anonymously on a piece of paper or be given orally in a large group.

5. Our resource person will then disclose his/her decision and the rationale behind it.

Materials and Preparation:

1. A resource person who is willing to share an important decision making experience in his/her life wherein values were an important factor.

2. If participants' responses are written, paper and pencils will be needed. If responses are given orally, a board or flip chart to record them.

Activity:

A resource person who is culturally different from the majority of the participants will discuss an important decision that he/she has made wherein personal values were an important factor. The resource person will discuss the background and circumstances leading up to the decision. The final decision that the resource person made will not be revealed. The participants can ask the resource person questions to provide them with more background, but they may not ask questions related to the final decision. The participants will guess what the final decision of the resource person was and the rationale behind it. The resource person will then share his/her decision and the reasons behind it with the participants.

Adaptations:

More than one resource person could address the group.

Questions for Discussion:

1. Why did you guess that the resource person came to a particular decision?

2. How does the resource person's background relate to your guess?

3. Has your background been a factor in your decision making? To what extent?

4. Are there universally "right" or "wrong" patterns of logic leading to decision making? What evidence can you offer?

5. How can individual differences in logical decision making affect career counseling?

6. How might you use this exercise in your work?

Trainer's Notes:

Past Challenges

Type of Activity: Individual

Teaching Objective(s):

To illustrate the steps in one's decision making process.

Behavioral Objective(s):

The participants will reflect upon difficult or important decisions that have resulted in major changes in their lives. By recalling the steps in their decision making processes and the outcomes of their decisions, the participants will be better able to help their clients make career-related decisions based on their own past experiences.

Estimated Time to Complete: 20 minutes

Points to Introduce Activity:

1. At one time or another, most of us have been faced with making a difficult or important decision that had a major impact on our lives. During this activity we will review one of those decisions and the process we went through in making it. We will look for any similarities between that decision and the decisions you are currently considering about career changes.

2. Find the worksheet "Past Challenges." Please answer the 12 questions and we will discuss them when you are finished.

Materials and Preparation:

1. Participants will need the "Past Challenge" worksheet.

2. A board or flip chart on which to list common decision making steps and outcomes.

Activity:

The participants will answer 12 questions from the "Past Challenges" Worksheet about difficult or important decisions they have made that resulted in major changes in their lives. The participants will share their experiences in a large group discussion.

Adaptations:

Participants could discuss the questions in pairs.

Questions for Discussion:

1. From your own experience, what steps in the decision making process did you find to be the most difficult?

2. What helped you to reach your decision? What assistance is generally available to people who are struggling to make decisions?

3. What specific roles can career development facilitators play to assist their clients in the decision making process?

4. Does culture play a role in the decision making process? How?

5. What differences and similarities in decision making have you found in your work?

6. Is there anything that career development facilitators should avoid doing in their efforts to help their clients?

Trainer's Notes:

Past Challenges

Directions:

Take a few minutes to think about a situation in which you were faced with a difficult or important decision that involved a major change in the direction of your life. After you have identified the issue, proceed with the following 12 questions.

1. What was the decision?

2. What major change did the decision involve?

3. Did the decision represent a loss or gain for you? For another individual? Why? How?

4. What were your feelings at the time you were initially aware of your need to make the decision?

5. Did your feelings remain the same or did they change during the decision process?

6. How did you proceed in making the decision?

7. Did anyone help you in the decision making process? Who? How?

8. What was the outcome of the decision?

9. How did you feel about yourself after you made the decision? Why?

10. If you had an opportunity to remake the decision, would you make any changes? What changes, if any?

11. Do you see any similarities between the way you handled the past decision and the way you are handling your current decision about a career change?

12. What did you learn from the past decision making process that could be applied to your present situation?

Adapted from Loretta Bradley, *Counseling Midlife Career Changers*, NCDA, 1990.

Career Lifeline

Type of Activity: Individual

Teaching Objective(s):

To help participants identify their past, present and future career paths. To illustrate how this exercise can be used with clients in career counseling.

Behavioral Objective(s):

Participants will be more aware of the directions their careers have taken in the past and the risks that were involved in making certain choices. As a result of reviewing their career lifelines, participants will be better able to make future career decisions.

Estimated Time to Complete: 30 minutes

Points to Introduce Activity:

1. The purpose of this activity is to help you identify your past, present and future career paths.

2. Illustrate how to draw approximate time lines of a person's paid work life on the board with a horizontal line, using 10 year intervals up to eighty years.

0	10	20	30	40	50	60	70	80

    The trainer should use his/her own career experience as an example.

3. At the approximate point on the line, label the time when your career began with a CB. At the time when you anticipate your full-time career to end, mark a CE. Place an X on the continuum to indicate where you are now.

4. Use felt tip markers to identify and illustrate the following:

    a. Your best career decision in green
    b. Your worst career decision in red
    c. Greatest career risk ever taken in yellow
    d. Obstacle(s) that prevented you from making a career move you wanted in red
    e. Career obstacles that you overcame in green
    f. A lucky break in green
    g. A person who helped you in green
    h. Your future career goals in green
    i. A critical decision in the future in yellow
    j. Something holding you back at the present time in red.

5. All green entries should be made above the line; all red entries below the line, and all yellow entries on the line.

Materials and Preparation:

1. Large pieces of paper to make horizontal time lines.

2. Be prepared or have a horizontal time line drawn on the board as an illustration.

3. A red, green and yellow felt tip marker for each participant.

Activity:

Participants will draw career lifelines showing their past lives and future career plans, indicating both positive and negative directions that have been taken.

Participants will then break into pairs and discuss their career lines.

Adaptations:

Participants could include more or less on their career lines, such as highest salary earned, greatest responsibilities, etc.

Questions for Discussion:

1. Did you have any difficulty in deciding what items should be placed above the line in green? Below the line in red? Why?

2. Were the risks that you took in the past worthwhile--did they pay off in some way?

3. Would you consider taking risks again? Why? Why not?

4. Can you clearly see where you are headed?

5. Could you change directions if necessary? Why? Why not?

6. Does your career lifeline point out anything to you?

7. What differences do you see among yourselves in the ways in which you look at the risks you've taken and the impact of those risks on your careers?

8. How would an adult career development theorist such as Donald Super look at the career lifeline?

9. How might you use this activity with your clients?

Trainers Notes:

Sex Role Commandments

Type of Activity: Individual

Teaching Objective(s):

To illustrate how people learn their sex roles from their parents as they are growing up.

Behavioral Objective(s):

Participants will list ten commandments that their mothers, older sisters, grandmothers or significant female role models gave them about being boys/girls. They will list ten commandments that their fathers, older brothers, grandfathers or significant male role models gave them about being boys/girls.

Estimated Time to Complete: 30 minutes

Points to Introduce Activity:

1. Parents typically give a variety of commandments that influence the behavior of their children. Sharing these commandments with others can increase our understanding of ourselves, others and cultural norms.

2. Please find the "Sex Role Commandments" work sheet. You will have ten minutes to complete your list of commandments. We will discuss our responses in a large group to compare similarities and differences in sex role commandments.

Materials and Preparation:

1. "Our Mothers' and Fathers' Sex Role Commandments" work sheet.

Activity:

After a brief introduction by the trainer, the participants will have ten minutes to complete "Sex Role Commandments" work sheet. The commandments listed by the participants will then be discussed by the large group.

Adaptations:

The list could also include commandments learned in school, from peer groups or religious groups.

Questions for Discussion:

1. Was it easy or difficult for you to remember the commandments that you have listed? Why? Why not?

2. Were you surprised by these commandments in any way? In your opinion, were there too many or too few commandments? Why? Why not?

3. What commandments have you (or have you not) handed down to your children or other young people that you might influence? Why? Why not?

4. Do you feel that your life was enriched or restricted by any of the sex role commandments that you have listed? Why? Why not?

5. What commandments continue to influence your life?

6. Have you adopted any new commandments? What are they?

7. How can career development facilitators help their clients recognize sex role stereotypes and overcome the barriers they may impose in career development?

8. How are these commandments evident in the work place today?

Trainer's Notes:

Sex Role Commandments

The objective of this exercise is to help you understand how you learned sex roles as part of growing up.

Directions: List ten commandments that your mother, older sisters, grandmothers or significant female role models gave you about being a boy/girl.

1. _____
2. _____
3. _____
4. _____
5. _____
6. _____
7. _____
8. _____
9. _____
10. _____

List ten commandments that your father, older brothers, grandfathers or significant male role models gave you about being a boy/girl.

1. _____
2. _____
3. _____
4. _____
5. _____
6. _____
7. _____
8. _____
9. _____
10. _____

From *Beyond Sex Roles*, Sargent, 1985.

Sentence Completions

Type of Activity: Large Group

Teaching Objective(s):

To illustrate the sex role expectations that many of us maintain.

Behavioral Objective(s):

Participants will become more aware of their sex role stereotypes and seek to eliminate them in their career counseling.

Estimated Time to Complete: 20 minutes

Points to Introduce Activity:

1. Frequently people organize their behaviors around "shoulds" for themselves and their expectations of others. Sometimes we are not conscious of the "shoulds" we carry with us that can lock us into certain ways of thinking and behaving.

2. One way to bring out some of these expectations and feelings about others is to do some rapid verbal free associations by completing sentences that are started for us. We will do some of these free associations in the large group for approximately five minutes. We will discuss our responses after that time.

3. We will begin 15 sentences with a word or two and ask you to quickly shout out a few words to complete the verbal associations. For example, when you hear a noun such as "teachers," please complete the sentence with the first thoughts that come to your mind about teachers.

Materials and Preparation:

1. Ask for a volunteer that can write very quickly to record the verbal responses, or free associations, of the participants.

2. Ask the participants to free associate words in each of the following categories:

a. Single mothers	f. Businesswomen	k. Male bosses
b. Male nurses	g. Bachelors	l. Married women
c. Divorced women	h. Old women	m. Female basketball coaches
d. Secretaries	i. House husbands	n. Male basketball coaches
e. Truck drivers	j. Blondes	o. Businessmen

Activity:

Participants will be asked to complete sentences by free associating verbal responses to the sentence subjects that are called out by the trainer. After the sentences have had several completions offered by the participants, the large group will discuss the free associations that were called out by the participants, with attention given to the presence or lack of sex role expectations and stereotyping.

Adaptations:

Participants could write their sentence completions and discuss them afterward.

Questions for Discussion:

1. Were you surprised by some of the associations that you made? Why/why not?

2. Where do these "shoulds" and expectations of other come from?

3. Do these stereotypes of others increase or decrease with age or experience?

4. Why is it important for career counselors to be aware of stereotyping?

5. What skills must counselors develop to move beyond stereotyping when working with their clients?

6. How can a client's potential be affected by stereotyping?

Trainer's Notes:

What Do You Know About Women in the Work Force?

Type of Activity: Individual

Teaching Objective(s):

To make participants more aware of the working conditions of women.

Behavioral Objective(s):

Participants will take a quiz, "What Do You Know About Women in the Work Force?"

Estimated Time to Complete: 30 minutes

Points to Introduce Activity:

1. Many people are unaware of the role women play in today's work place. To test your knowledge, please take the quiz, "What Do You Know About Women in the Work Force?". This is a self-test; your score need not be reported. We will use the quiz for discussion purposes when you have completed it.

Materials and Preparation:

1. Participants will need pencils and "What Do You Know About Women in the Work Force?"

2. A board or flip chart on which to write the answers to the quiz.

3. Answers to quiz:

1. (d) 69%,	8. (b) $14,485,	15. (c) 62%,
2. (a) 35-44 years,	9. (a) $17,819,	16. (a) 44.7%,
3. (b) 68%,	10. (d) $25,187,	17. (d) 80%,
4. (c) 29.3 years,	11. (a) $26,045,	18. (d) 9%,
5. (d) 50%,	12. (d) $.70,	19. (b) 53%,
6. (c) 45%,	13. (c) 30%,	20. (d) 33%
7. (a) $27,228,	14. (c) 56%,	

(Source: U.S. Department of Labor Women's Bureau, No. 90-2, September, 1990)

Activity:

Participants will take a self-quiz, "What Do You Know About Women in the Work Force?" from the Participant's Guide. The answers to the quiz will be given and discussed in a large group.

Adaptations:

Questions could be added to the quiz to reflect new information or local conditions.

Questions for Discussion:

1. What facts surprised you the most from the quiz? What surprised you the least? Why? Why not?

2. What facts best describe situations that you have encountered?

3. What figures indicate the "Feminization of Poverty?"

4. What figures indicate the conditions of minority working women?

5. What statistics illustrate occupational segregation?

6. What actions could be taken to improve conditions for working women? Will these actions be taken? By whom? How? When?

7. What future do you envision for working women in the year 2000?

8. How can you use this information with your clients?

Trainer's Notes:

What Do You Know About Women in the Work Force?

Is your awareness of women in the work force increasing? Here are some questions to test your knowledge. Circle the answer that you think is correct.

1. In 1989, the percentage of all women, ages 18 to 64, who were in the labor force.

   a. 50% b. 60% c. 45% d. 69%

2. In this age group, 76% of the women are working.

   a. 35-44 b. 45-54 c. 25-34 d. 16-24

3. Although most women workers are employed full-time, what percentage of all part-time workers are women?

   a. 45% b. 68% c. 75% d. 50%

4. The average woman worker of 16 years of age between 1970-80 could expect to spend how many years of her life in the work force?

   a. 20.2 b. 24.5 c. 29.3 d. 32.5

5. Among black workers, what percentage are women?

   a. 35% b. 42% c. 30% d. 50%

6. Among white workers, what percentage are women?

   a. 37% b. 55% c. 45% d. 40%

7. In 1988, the median income for white men working year-round and full-time was:

   a. $27,228 b. $22,429 c. $19,405 d. $29,998

8. In 1988, the median income for Hispanic women working year-round and full-time was:

   a. $16,424 b. $14,485 c. $18,093 d. $12,029

9. In 1988, the median income for white women working year-round and full-time was:

   a. $17,819 b. $20,413 c. $15,423 d. $21,567

10. In 1988, the median income for women who had completed four years of college was:

   a. $21,899 b. $19,038 c. $29,765 d. $25,187

11. In 1988, the median income for men who had a high school diploma was:

   a. $26,045 b. $29,413 c. $23,788 d. $31,129

12. When 1989 median weekly earnings of full-time wage and salary workers were compared, the average woman earned how many cents compared to every dollar earned by the average man?

   a. $.65 b. $.60 c. $.75 d. $.70

13. More women are choosing to start their own businesses. Women's share of all non-farm sole proprietorships rose to what percent in 1986?

   a. 15% b. 22% c. 30% d. 39%

14. What percentage of mothers with preschoolers (children under 6 years) was in the labor force in 1988?

   a. 20% b. 45% c. 56% d. 38%

15. Of all persons over 16 years of age with poverty level incomes in 1988, what percentage were women?

   a. 34% b. 41% c. 62% 71%

16. In 1988, the poverty rate for all families maintained by women with children under the age of 18 was:

   a. 44.7% b. 36.2% c. 50.3% d. 26.3%

17. In 1989, women represented what percentage of administrative support (clerical) workers?

   a. 56.1% b. 68.9% c. 76.8% d. 80.0%

18. In 1989, women represented what percentage of precision production, craft and repair workers?

   a. 16.4% b. 21.2% c. 3.2% d. 9.0%

19. In 1988, the percentage of all poor families that were maintained by women:

   a. 35% b. 53% c. 47% d. 61%

20. The 1989 unemployment rate for black female teenagers, from 16-19 years, was:

   a. 20.7% b. 18.5% c. 26.4% d. 33.0%

Source: U.S. Department of Labor Women's Bureau, No. 90-2, Sept., 1990.

Gender Equity

Type of Activity: Individual

Teaching Objective(s):

To identify some of the trends in business, industry and society that support the need to achieve gender equity.

Behavioral Objective(s):

Participants will list at least five trends in business, industry and society that support the need to achieve gender equity.

Participants will become more aware of gender equity issues as they affect their clients.

Estimated Time to Complete: 20 minutes

Points to Introduce Activity:

1. The unequal treatment of women in the work place has become costly to business, industry and our society as a whole. Discriminatory conditions can no longer be ignored; there are many trends in business and industry today that support the need to achieve gender equity.

2. Think about the social, political and economic changes that have taken place in the last few decades; think of the changes that are ahead. What trends in business and industry support increased opportunities for women? How do these trends support gender equity in the work place?

3. Please list at least five of these trends on a piece of paper. You have ten minutes to compile your list.

4. We will list the trends on the board and discuss them as a large group.

Materials and Preparation:

1. Have a board or flip chart on which to list the trends.

2. Be prepared with your own list of trends to incorporate into the discussion in the event that they are not listed by the participants, such as: more women in the work force, more service jobs, a need for educated/skilled/trained workers, a decline in the number of workers entering the work force, the aging of the work force, more female consumers, women more politically conscious, more businesses catering to female clients, legislation to promote gender equity, more women moving into management positions, gender equity education, wider acceptance of women in the work place, women better

educated and trained, more occupations now open to women, more women supporting families, etc.

3. Be sure to bring out the changes necessary to accommodate the needs of working women, such as: work site day care for dependents, flexible scheduling, policies guaranteeing parental leave, protection from sexual harassment, equity in pay and promotional practices, and a better understanding of the different communication/management styles of men and women.

Activity:

After a brief introduction from the trainer, the participants will list the trends in business, industry and society that support the need to achieve gender equity. These trends will be summarized, written on the board and discussed in a large group.

Adaptations:

This exercise could be done by listing trends in business, industry and society that support the need for: technical education, multicultural counseling, increased opportunities for special populations such as: minorities, children at-risk, older adults, persons with disabilities, etc.

Questions for Discussion:

1. What trends in business, industry and society support the need to achieve gender equity?

2. What changes in the work place do you foresee as a result of greater gender equity?

3. What could career development facilitators do to promote gender equity?

4. What obligations do career development facilitators have to promote gender equity?

Trainer's Notes:

Walk in My Shoes

Type of Activity: Small group

Teaching Objective(s):

To make the participants more sensitive to and aware of the challenges persons with disabilities must meet in the work place.

To create an awareness of the adaptations that can be made in the work place to accommodate the needs of persons with disabilities.

Behavioral Objective(s):

The participants will place themselves in the roles of persons with different disabilities. They will list the ways in which their work places could be altered to accommodate their needs.

Estimated Time to Complete: 45 minutes

Points to Introduce Activity:

1. During this activity you will place yourself in the role of a person with a specific disability. You must imagine that your life has been suddenly changed by an automobile accident or a medical diagnosis. What effect would your disability have on your present career? What adaptations would be necessary for you to continue in your present work role? Each small group will discuss the implications of the disability that they are assigned and create a list of adaptations that would be necessary for them to do their jobs. After 20 minutes, we will discuss your findings in a large group.

2. In your discussion, please recall the mandates of the Americans with Disabilities Act of 1990.

Materials and Preparation:

1. Participants will need to be assigned a scenario from "Walk in My Shoes," worksheet.

Activity:

Working in pairs or small groups, the participants will take on the roles of persons with disabilities. They will make a list of the adaptations that would be needed in their work places to enable them to continue in their present roles.

Adaptations:

Short scenarios could be written describing different disabilities.

Participants could work individually.

Using the scenarios of disabilities, the participants could research alternative career choices using labor market information.

After the list of adaptations are made, the participants could role play their requests to their employers regarding the adaptations needed.

Questions for Discussion:

1. How did you feel as you took on the role of a person with disabilities? Would some/any/all of the disabilities affect your level of self-confidence? In what ways? Why? Why not?

2. How would the disabilities affect your social life? Would your friends remain the same or would they change?

3. What work place adaptations would be necessary? Would you anticipate any problems, such as funding or supervisory support? Why? Why not?

4. What work tasks, if any, do you feel that you would be unable to complete, despite the available modifications? How might this affect your job?

5. How has the Americans with Disabilities Act of 1990 opened doors for persons with disabilities?

6. How can you incorporate the ADA into your career counseling of persons with disabilities?

Trainer's Notes:

Walk in My Shoes

Directions: Each small group should work with a different scenario. Placing themselves in the roles of the persons with disabilities, the group should make a list of the ways their present career would be effected and the ways in which their work places would need to be adapted in order to accommodate their needs.

1. As a result of an automobile accident, you have lost the use of both legs and are now confined to a wheelchair.

2. As a result of a head trauma suffered in a bicycle fall, you are now subject to convulsive epileptic seizures.

3. Your vision has been severely impaired as a result of cataracts.

4. You have developed an asthmatic condition. You need to carry an inhaler, medication, and be alert for allergic reactions at all times.

5. Your cancerous larynx has been surgically removed. You must speak through an artificial voice box.

6. Your hearing is impaired due to a severe respiratory infection.

7. After suffering a stroke, you have poor handwriting and written work is difficult for you.

8. You have a chronic disease that makes it painful and difficult for you to move your body.

Questions for Discussion:

1. How did you feel as you took on the roles of a persons with disabilities? Would some/any/all of the disabilities affect your level of self-confidence? In what ways? Why/why not?

2. How would the disabilities affect your social life? Would your friends remain the same or would they change?

3. In what ways might you experience growth as a person with a disability?

4. What work place adaptations would be necessary? Would you anticipate any problems, such as funding, supervisory support, etc.? Why? Why not?

5. What work tasks, if any, do you feel that you would be unable to complete, despite the available modifications? How might this affect your job?

6. How has the Americans with Disabilities Act of 1990 opened doors for persons with disabilities?

7. How can you incorporate the ADA into your career counseling of persons with disabilities?

The Most That I Think I Could Handle

Type of Activity: Individual

Teaching Objective(s):

To demonstrate an activity that can be used to assess and build the self-confidence of children at-risk.

Behavioral Objective(s):

Given the worksheet, "The Most That I Think I Could Handle," the participants will take on the roles of at-risk students and answer questions that are related to their personally perceived capabilities in school, social situations and future job searches. The participants will assess levels of self-confidence of at-risk students in the situations that are described.

Estimated Time to Complete: 20 minutes

Points to Introduce Activity:

1. The purpose of this activity is to help us understand how children at-risk would assess their capabilities in certain school, social and job search situations by answering the questions, "The Most That I Think I Could Handle."

2. You will have five to ten minutes to answer the questions on the work sheet. We will discuss your answers in a large group after that time.

Materials and Preparation:

1. Participants will need "The Most That I Think I Could Handle."

2. A board or flip chart on which to list strategies for building self confidence in specific areas of concern, such as speaking in front of an audience.

Activity:

Taking on the roles of children at-risk, the participants will answer the questions from "The Most That I Think I Could Handle", a brief self-assessment of their self-confidence in school, social and job search situations. After the questions have been answered, the participants will discuss them in a large group and identify some strategies for building self-esteem.

Adaptations:

Questions could be designed for any special needs group, persons with disabilities, older adults, displaced homemakers, teen parents, etc.

Questions for Discussion:

1. How did you feel about yourself after answering the questions? Why?

2. In what areas do you have the most self-confidence? Why? In what areas do you have the least? Why?

3. Is having self-confidence an important personal quality? Why? Why not? What qualities do you think are necessary to succeed in school? In social situations? In searching for a job?

4. What can we do to improve the self-confidence of our at-risk students in school? In social situations? In searching for a job?

5. Who are some of the people who could help at-risk students? What public and private facilities or institutions might help at-risk students develop their confidence? How?

6. If you could do one thing to boost the self-confidence of at-risk students, what would it be? Can you do it? Why? Why not?

Trainer's Notes:

The Most That I Think I Could Handle

Read each phrase and fill in the blank following it to describe how much of each activity you feel is the most you can handle.

Hours of homework in a day

Parties or dates during a weekend: parties   dates

Phone calls in a day

Boyfriends or girlfriends at one time

Chores at home in a day: How many?   How much time?

People living in my house at once

Slices of pizza to eat at one sitting

Pounds I could lift

Tests to take in one day

Number of people in an audience to whom I could speak

How long I would wait patiently for anything without complaining

The number of business establishments that I could walk into on a given day to ask about employment opportunities

The number of people I could telephone in one day to inquire about employment opportunities

The number of job applications I could fill out during a job search

The amount of time I would set aside to read the Help Wanted ads in the Sunday paper

How many adults I would ask to be a reference for prospective employers

How many hours I could work during the week and still complete all my school work

How many reprimands could I take from my employer within a four hour period

Adapted from *Personal Growth and Development Workbook*, Winneconne High School, Winneconne, Wisconsin.

Case Study - Carl Young

(Developed by the New Mexico SOICC)

Carl Young is a high school dropout. You are trying to find him a job in one of the large local motels or hotels but it appears to be a stagnant industry, employment-wise. Is this true? Is there any hiring at all? What are the long-term prospects? Name some jobs found in the industry. Does he meet the educational qualifications? Who are the largest local employers?

Major Labor Market Information Topics by Reports

	Outlook		Requirements		Job Hunting			Economic Trends			Wages
	National	State	Education	Work Environment	Employers' Area	Occupation	Resume & Interview	Unemployment	Employment	Industry	
Occupational Outlook Handbook	x		x	x							x
State Occupational Outlook to 1995		x									
State Supply/Demand		x									
State Job Hunter's Guide					x		x				
Prospects	x	x			x		x				
Large Employers					x						
Industries-Companies-Occupations						x					
Employers with most hires					x						
Employers by Occupation						x					
Jobs for Graduates						x					
State Labor Market Review								x	x	x	
Regional Wage Surveys											x
Other:											

Case Study - Marie Alvarez
(Developed by the New Mexico SOICC)

Marie Alvarez is a recent high school graduate considering possible employment fields and wants your advice on the Automotive Mechanic field. What she knows about the job interests her. Previous testing indicates she has an aptitude for mechanical work. She would like a job offering favorable employment opportunities nationally, but would prefer staying in a metropolitan area and working for a local company. She wants to know if formal training or on-the-job training is preferable. Any additional school would need to be available locally. Salary levels, both beginning and experienced, are also a consideration. What can you tell her about job opportunities, employers, training and pay?

Major Labor Market Information Topics by Reports

	Outlook		Requirements		Job Hunting			Economic Trends			Wages
	National	State	Education	Work Environment	Employers' Area	Occupation	Resume & Interview	Unemployment	Employment	Industry	
Occupational Outlook Handbook	x		x	x							x
State Occupational Outlook to 1995		x									
State Supply/Demand		x									
State Job Hunter's Guide					x		x				
Prospects	x		x		x		x				
Large Employers					x						
Industries-Companies-Occupations						x					
Employers with most hires					x						
Employers by Occupation						x					
Jobs for Graduates						x					
State Labor Market Review								x	x	x	
Regional Wage Surveys											x
Other:											

Case Study - Joseph Deer
(Developed by the New Mexico SOICC)

Joseph Deer, who has just graduated, did well in several work-experience courses in high school. He does not plan to continue his education and is considering looking for work as either a typist or entry level bookkeeper in

_____ or _____
(insert metropolitan area)   (insert name of another area in your state)

What can you tell him about job prospects, employers and wages?

Major Labor Market Information Topics by Reports

	Outlook		Requirements		Job Hunting			Economic Trends			Wages
	National	State	Education	Work Environment	Employers' Area	Occupation	Resume & Interview	Unemployment	Employment	Industry	
Occupational Outlook Handbook	x		x	x							x
State Occupational Outlook to 1995		x									
State Supply/Demand		x									
State Job Hunter's Guide					x		x				
Prospects	x	x			x		x				
Large Employers					x						
Industries-Companies-Occupations						x					
Employers with most hires					x						
Employers by Occupation						x					
Jobs for Graduates						x					
State Labor Market Review								x	x	x	
Regional Wage Surveys											x
Other:											

Case Study Activity - Jane Williamson
(Developed by the Montana SOICC)

Includes:

1. The Problem and the Plan

2. Jane's high school transcript and ASVAB test scores

3. CIDS questions and answers

4. Thoughts on ASVAB interpretations

5. Occupational Profile

6. Occupational Information Resource Matrices - National and State

1. The Problem and the Plan

The Problem

You have a client that desperately needs your help. Her name is Jane Williamson. She arrived at your office this morning with a set of ASVAB scores, a CIDS questionnaire, her high school transcript, and a list of questions. She desperately wants to know what kind of careers to look into.

You were unable to see her when she was in your office. She left the information and made an appointment to see you tomorrow morning. You can only spend a few minutes getting to know her in the morning. You plan to spend tomorrow afternoon researching available resources. You also made another appointment with Jane later in the week to go over your recommendations with her.

After reviewing her questions, you decide you could use some help. You arrange for several "experts" to be available to answer your questions. You also contact several colleagues who agree to work with you.

Most importantly, you have developed a plan.

The Plan

I. Review Information Jane left at the Office.

Review the ASVAB test scores, CIDS answers and Jane's high school transcript.

Even though you have not met Jane, describe her strengths and weaknesses.

II. Interview Jane. (A volunteer from the group or the trainer) All small groups will interview Jane at the same time.

As a group, decide what you want to find out from Jane.

Select a spokesperson in your group to interview Jane.

Try to find out more about Jane than is shown by the documents. Are there any conflicts between her expectations and the results of her test scores, CIDS answers and her high school record?

All the groups will interview Jane at the same time. Jane can stay only for about 20 minutes.

III. Run a CIDS Program to Get a List of Occupations.

Contact the CIDS representative and make arrangements to run Jane's CIDS answers through the occupational search program. This will give you a list of occupations with which you can begin working. Remember that Jane is a teenager.

IV. Choose Possible Occupations.

As a group, use all the information you now have to choose three occupations to research further. You have decided to limit your research to three occupations for time's sake. You can always recommend others she should research. The possibilities should be based upon the ASVAB, CIDS results, high school record, and your interview with Jane. You realize that Jane should be doing some of this work with you, but because of time limitations, complete the tasks without her.

You also realize there are many other testing and evaluation instruments that could be helpful. However, you do not have time to give any other tests. So, you decide to use the ASVAB and CIDS in this case. If you feel other tests would be useful, you can tell Jane when you present your findings.

When choosing the occupations, try not to consider anything but Jane's skills, abilities, aptitudes and interests. You will be looking at many other factors as your research progresses.

V. Research the Occupations

Now divide your group into pairs of "researchers." Each pair will take one of the occupations chosen and complete the occupational profile for that occupation.

You can complete the parts of the profile in any order. We suggest that you do Part I, Section A first. This will give you the basic codes to access the other data.

VI. Prepare & Present Recommendations to Jane.

You need to prepare a presentation of your findings for Jane. Prepare the presentation as a group. You may do the presentation however your group chooses.

Jane will be in your office at 8:00 tomorrow morning. Your group will only have about 5 minutes to talk to her because she has several other groups working on her problem and must see them also.

PERMANENT RECORD

BETA HIGH SCHOOL

Anytown, IL

Student Name: Public, Jane Q.   M/(F)

Address: 1234 Maple Avenue

Telephone: 123-4567

Father's Name (Guardian) John Z. Public

Mother's Name (Guardian) Mary L. Public

Parents' Address (if different) _____

Grade 9: 1981-82

English I	C	1
Soc. Stu.	C-	1
P. E.	A	1/2
Alg. I	B+	1
Gen. Sci.	A-	1
Typing I	C	1

TOTAL CR: 5 1/2

Grade 10: 1982-83

English II	D+	1
Wld Hist	C-	1
Softball	A	1/2
Geometry	B+	1
Biology	B-	1
Computer Sk.	A-	1

TOTAL CR: 5 1/2

Grade 11: 1983-84

Comp. III	B-	1
U.S. Hist.	C-	1
Alg. II	B+	1
Woodwork I	A	1
Speech	B	1
Chemistry	B-	1

TOTAL CR: 6

Grade 9: 1981-82

English I	C-	1
Soc. Stud.	D+	1
P.E.	A	1/2
Alg. I	A-	1
Gen. Sci.	B	1
Typing I	C+	1

TOTAL CR: 5 1/2

Grade 10: 1982-83

English II	C	1
Wld History	C-	1
Basketball	A	1/2
Geometry	A-	1
Biology	B	1
Dr. Ed.	B-	1

TOTAL CR: 5 1/2

Grade 12:

Am. Lit	
U.S. Hist.	
Alg. II	
Drafting	
Drama	
Chemistry	

Activities: (* = letter)
Basketball 10,11
Track 10*, 11
Drama Club 11

BETA HIGH SCHOOL TERM REPORT CARD

Jane Q. Public _____ 11 _____
(Student Name)   (Grade)

1234 Maple Avenue
_____
(Address)

	1	2	Sem.		1	2	Sem.
Comp III	C	B	B-	Am. Lit.	C		
U.S. Hist.	D+	C	C-	U.S. Hist.	C		
Alg. II	A-	B	B+	Alg. II	A		
Woodwork I	A	A	A	Drafting	A-		
Speech	B-	B	B	Drama	B		
Chemistry	C	B+	B-	Chemistry	B		

ASVAB ALPHA ROSTER REPORT
STANDARD SCORES
PUBLIC JANE Q
GS 57   CS 48
AR 60   AS 66
WK 43   MK 57
PC 40   MC 53
NO 49   EI 54

Categories
of Occupational Characteristics

SCHOOL SUBJECTS

Check ✓ 1 to 3 **School Subjects** that you like.

201. **Language Arts:** literature, composition, grammar, speech, foreign language
202. **Mathematics:** general math, geometry, algebra, trigonometry, calculus ✗
203. **Chemistry**
204. **Physics**
205. **Biology**
206. **Social Studies:** history, geography, government, sociology, psychology
207. **Economics**
208. **Music/Art/Drama:** drawing, painting, sculpture, textile art, music
209. **Physical Education/Health Fitness:**
211. **Industry/Technology:** drafting, graphic arts, metalworking, mechanics, woodworking, electronics, construction, manufacturing, transportation ✗
212. **Family/Consumer Science:** foods and nutrition, clothing, housing, parenting and child development, community service, consumer education, independent living
213. **Agriculture:** agricultural production, services, mechanics
214. **Marketing:** merchandising, marketing, services, entrepreneurship
215. **Business/Accounting:** accounting, bookkeeping, business math, management and finance
216. **Office/Clerical:** typing, shorthand, wordprocessing,
217. **Health/Medical**
218. **Computers/Applications:** computer programming, systems design and analysis, electronic spreadsheets, data bases, etc.

EDUCATIONAL PROGRAMS

Check ✓ 1 to 3 **Educational Programs** you would like to pursue.

221. **Agriculture/Natural Resources**
222. **Business**
223. **Computers/Applications**
224. **Education**
225. **Engineering/Architecture**
226. **Family, Food, and Consumer Sciences** ✗
227. **Fine Arts**
228. **Health Sciences**
229. **Industry/Technology** ✗
230. **Language/Communication Arts/Interdisciplinary Studies**
231. **Mathematics**
232. **Personal and Protective Services**
233. **Sciences**
234. **Social Sciences/Services**

INDUSTRIES

Check ☑ 1 to 3 **Industries** where you want to work.

- ◯ 691. **Agriculture - Production and Services**
- ◯ 692. **Forestry, Fishing, Hunting, and Trapping**
- ◯ 693. **Mining**
- ◯ 694. **Construction**
- ◯ 695. **Manufacturing**
- ◯ 696. **Transportation**
- ◯ 697. **Communications**
- ◯ 698. **Electric, Gas, and Sanitary Services**
- ◯ 699. **Wholesale Trade**
- ☒ 700. **Retail Trade**
- ◯ 701. **Finance, Insurance, and Real Estate**
- ◯ 702. **Lodging and Personal Services**
- ☒ 703. **Business Services**
- ◯ 704. **Automotive and Other Repairs and Services**
- ◯ 705. **Motion Picture, Amusement, and Recreation Services**
- ◯ 706. **Health and Legal Services**
- ◯ 707. **Education, Social, and Membership Services**
- ◯ 708. **Professional Services**
- ◯ 709. **Public Administration**

APTITUDES

Check ☑ 1 to 3 **Skill(s)** that you want to use at work.

- ◯ 141. **Verbal:** speak well and write clearly
- ☒ 142. **Numerical:** work quickly and accurately with numbers
- ◯ 143. **Visual:** see shades of colors, important details, and relationships among shapes and objects
- ☒ 147. **Coordination:** quickly and accurately control movements with your body
- ◯ 152. **Clerical Perceptions:** understand details in spoken and written communications, proofread words and numbers, understand basic math

INTERESTS

Check ☑ 1 to 3 of the following that most interest you.

- ☒ 131. **Data:** making judgments and decisions based on facts or figures
- ◯ 132. **People:** directing, helping, or influencing people
- ☒ 133. **Objects:** operating machines, using equipment to perform tasks
- ◯ 134. **Ideas:** using information or concepts to solve problems and make decisions
- ◯ 135. **Living Things:** working with plants, animals, and living organisms

EDUCATION

Check ✅ 1 to 3 levels of **Education** that you are considering.

- ⬭ 401. **No High School Diploma**
- ⊗ 402. **High School Diploma or G.E.D.**
- ⬭ 406. **Associate degree** (2-year program)
- ⊗ 410. **Vocational or Technical Training**
- ⬭ 407. **Bachelor's degree** (4-year program)
- ⬭ 408. **Master's degree**
- ⬭ 409. **Doctoral degree** (Ph.D., M.D., etc.)
- ⬭ 411. **Four years or more of college**

WORK METHODS

Check ✅ 1 or 2 **Work Methods** that you think match your work style.

- ⬭ 121. **Structured:** Work activities are clearly defined. Specific procedures or instructions must be followed. Consistency and precision may be required. You may do similar tasks each day.
- ⬭ 122. **Creative:** Work activities involve developing new solutions to produce products or thinking up new themes or ideas. Each work day may be different, but you may work on one project for several months.
- ⊗ 123. **Problem-Solving:** Work activities require thinking about problems and choosing solutions that may affect many people. Quick decisions may be required, so you must feel comfortable making decisions with incomplete information.

TRAVEL

Check ✅ 1 or 2 styles of **Travel** that you would like.

- ⊗ 351. Work at the same place every day
- ⬭ 352. Travel to different places during the day, but come home each evening
- ⬭ 353. Travel regularly, stay overnight often

JOB LOCATION

Check ✅ one **Job Location** you prefer.

- ⊗ 551. **Urban:** big cities and suburbs
- ⬭ 552. **Rural:** small towns and country areas

WORKING CONDITIONS

Check ✅ the **Working Conditions** you prefer.

- ⬭ 361. Mostly outside
- ⬭ 362. Mostly inside
- ⊗ 363. Both inside and outside

PHYSICAL EFFORT

Check ☑ 1 to 3 amounts of **Physical Effort** you prefer.

- ☒ 301. **Lift up to 10 lbs.**
- ⬭ 302. **Lift up to 25 lbs.** or more; carry up to 10 lbs.
- ⬭ 303. **Much lifting or physical exertion**
- ⬭ 304. **Lift up to 50 lbs.** or more; carry up to 25 lbs.
- ⬭ 305. **Lift up to 100 lbs.** or more; carry up to 50 lbs.

SALARY

Check ☑ 1 to 3 levels of starting **Salary** you would like.
(If you pick higher salaries, you might not have as many occupations to choose from.)

- ⬭ 521. **Up to $8,000 per year** (to $4.00 per hour)
- ⬭ 522. **$10,000 per year** ($5.00 per hour)
- ⬭ 523. **$12,000 per year** ($6.00 per hour)
- ⬭ 524. **$14,000 per year** ($7.00 per hour)
- ⬭ 525. **$16,000 per year** ($8.00 per hour)
- ⬭ 526. **$18,000 per year** ($9.00 per hour)
- ⬭ 527. **$20,000 per year** ($10.00 per hour)
- ☒ 528. **$24,000 per year** ($12.00 per hour)
- ⬭ 529. **$28,000 per year** ($14.00 per hour)
- ⬭ 530. **$32,000 per year** ($16.00 per hour)
- ⬭ 531. **$36,000 per year** ($18.00 per hour)
- ⬭ 532. **$40,000 per year** ($20.00 per hour)
- ⬭ 533. **Above $40,000 per year** (over $20.00 per hour)

WORK FIELDS

Check ☑ 1 to 3 Work Field(s) that you might like.

- ⬭ 661. **Artistic:** Literary and visual arts, drama, music, dance, and crafts
- ⬭ 662. **Scientific:** Physical and life sciences, medicine, and laboratory technology
- ⬭ 663. **Plants and Animals:** Animal care and training, plant care, and related areas
- ⬭ 664. **Protective:** Safety and law enforcement and security services
- ☒ 665. **Mechanical:** Engineering, quality control, transportation, and related work
- ☒ 666. **Industrial:** Production work, production technology, and elemental work
- ☒ 667. **Business Detail:** Administration, math and finance related work, clerical work, etc.
- ⬭ 668. **Selling:** General sales and related work
- ⬭ 669. **Accommodating:** Hospitality services, personal care services, and passenger and customer services
- ⬭ 670. **Humanitarian:** Social services, nursing, therapy, specialized teaching services, etc.
- ⬭ 671. **Leading-Influencing:** Education, law, management and administration, communications, etc.
- ⬭ 672. **Physical Performing:** Sports and related areas

READING, WRITING, AND SPEAKING

Check ☑ 1 or 2 **Reading** levels that you want on the job.

161. **Reading level 1** - Little or no reading required. Read simple words or compare names and numbers.
162. **Reading level 2** - Read simply written material, such as recipes, invoices, charts, labels, or rules.
163. **Reading level 3** - Read specialized terms and understand concepts, such as methods of mechanical drawing, or medical terms.
164. **Reading level 4** - Read service manuals, legal documents, blueprints, instructions on care of equipment, or methods of preparing solutions.
165. **Reading level 5** - Read scientific or technical material related to specialized fields, such as medicine, chemistry, or law.

Check ☑ 1 or 2 **Writing** levels that you want on the job.

171. **Writing level 1** - Little or no writing required. Print simple words and series of names, numbers, and addresses.
172. **Writing level 2** - Write some sentences using proper style and punctuation.
173. **Writing level 3** - Write short reports and keep records using forms.
174. **Writing level 4** - Write reports or letters using a specific format. Prepare business letters, summaries, and reports.
175. **Writing level 5** - Write speeches and technical material. This level involves the ability to be able to write precisely, creatively, and clearly so that others can understand the material.

Check ☑ 1 or 2 **Speaking** levels that you want on the job.

181. **Speaking Level 1** - Speak simple sentences. Includes following simple oral instructions, and asking co-workers and supervisors simple questions.
182. **Speaking Level 2** - Speak clearly using correct English, such as conversing with customers at a restaurant, answering customer questions, and discussing work to be done with a supervisor.
183. **Speaking Level 3** - Speak confidently to a small group, such as greeting customers and answering questions, calling on new customers, talking to patients, giving orders to other workers, and presenting reports to supervisors.
184. **Speaking Level 4** - Discuss a variety of subjects in a group, such as consulting with a number of people working on different parts of a project, and participating in debates and discussions at business meetings.
185. **Speaking Level 5** - Talk effectively to a group using persuasive techniques and a well-trained voice, such as discussing technical material with supervisor and workers, speaking to community organizations, speaking before television audiences, or teaching students to speak effectively.

THOUGHTS ON ASVAB INTERPRETATIONS
by
Gene M. Harris
ASVAB Test Specialist
Butte Military Entrance Processing Center

It is useful in a school ASVAB testing situation if the counselor is able to schedule a group presentation to cover basic definitions and concerns general to the particular class. Then, a short individual session to review specific scores or developments can be scheduled with students wishing specific counseling. Group work is appropriate for explaining standard scores, percentile scores, confidence intervals, the Youth Population norming group and sub-groups, the Grade/Sex Percentile, the Grade/Opposite Sex Percentile, and the Grade Percentile. Interpretive materials that can be explained in group format include the Military Career Guide, the ASVAB Student Workbook, Department of Labor publications, and career information in computer format.

Group session could cover the following:
Standard Scores:

The ten subtests of the ASVAB are reported on the counselor's alphabetical roster in standard score format. The tests are: General Science (GS), Word Knowledge (WK), Paragraph Comprehension (PC), Arithmetic Reasoning (AR), Numerical Operations (NO), Math Knowledge (MK), Auto and Shop Information (AS), Mechanical Comprehension (MC), Electronics Information (EI), and Coding Speed (CS). These tests are combined in various ways to achieve the composite scores on the student results sheet. While the composite scores have reliability coefficients ranging from .90 to .96, utilization of individual subtests would not due to fewer items resulting in lower reliability. Counselors must keep in mind this fact when showing students subtest scores and realize potential variation from these subtest scores can occur. Also, the standard scores (T-Scores) do not measure the same as percentile scores. They must be converted with use of a normal curve format to arrive at approximate percentile equivalents. Rough approximations are:

T Score:	30	40	50	60	70
%ile:	2.5	15	50	85	97.5

Students should be encouraged to see the counselor since the only source of specific sub-test scores rests there and care must be used to not over interpret a sub-test score.

Percentile Scores:

A percentile score tells not how a student scored on a test, but rather how many people in a particular group, out of one hundred, the student's score has beaten. Thus, a Youth Population percentile score of 72 indicates that 72 out of 100 people aged 18-23 were beaten by the individual student's score. The Grade/Sex, Grade/Opposite Sex, and Grade Percentile scores usually differ due to the fact that different groups of people are used as a comparison or standard for the student's score. As a group, the sophomore norm group will not do as well on the ASVAB as the junior norm group, therefore, the same score will beat more shphomores than juniors.

It should be noted that percentile scores should be used to indicate probable levels of competitiveness in the measured areas rather than trying to judge whether a students will be successful in a program. The various percentile scores are listed on the Counselor's Portion of the Student Results Sheet. In parentheses, the abbreviations for the sub-tests included in the composites scores are listed. Please note the parentheses within parentheses as these scores are added together and divided by 2 to weigh verbal tests accurately.

Academic Ability	((WK + PC) + AR)
Verbal	(GS + WK + PC)
Math	(AR + MK)
Mechanical-Crafts	(AR + AS + MC + EI)
Business-Clerical	((WK + PC) + MK + CS)
Electronics-Electrical	(GS + AR + MK + EI)
Health, Social, & Technology	((WK + PC) + AR + MC)

Use of sub-test scores with composite scores will show students which skills were measured for each composite, and they might indicate what skills were tested higher or lower within a composite. Care must be used here, however, as the reliability of a subtest is less than a composite. Questions might be raised, but other information should be used to verify potential answers.

It is sometimes informative for students to see how the academic tests are used within the Occupational Composites. Thus, they can see the importance of academics and realize that high school courses offer advantages for later employment in chosen fields.

Youth Population Norm Group:
This group is aged 18-23 and represents the beginning work force in America. It is a compilation of people from a Department of Labor study which set out to define parameters of America's entering labor force. The Department of Defense sampled the group with the ASVAB and developed the ASVAB-14 norms. Students can see how they compare with these people early and plan accordingly.

Grade/Sex Percentile and Grade/Opposite Sex Percentiles:
These percentile scores are used to show students how they compete with people of their grade and sex or opposite sex. As students choose possible careers or training programs, they should be aware that many are still dominated by one sex or the other. While this is in flux, the dominance still remains, and students might want to see how they compare in areas with either the same sex if entering traditional employment or opposite sex if entering a non-traditional career. These scores are not to be construed as limiting options. They are used to help indicate truer comparisons of scores with people actually in the work fields.

Individual sessions could cover the following:
Students who might wonder how individual test scores might reflect their abilities should receive additional counseling. Other sources of information available to counselors such as school grades could be consulted to see if sub-test scores seem to reflect actual performance. With verification from other information, counselors might be able to suggest specific courses that will help the student achieve skills and

abilities most beneficial to the future.

At either a general or individual session, students should be acquainted with
the Military Career Guide, at least briefly. The chart of scores for the enlisted
programs halps give guidance to how scores relate to training programs in the
military. Of course, like everything else, this must be taken with a grain of
salt. The Military Career Guide is three years old now, and that is quite old
for career information. The newest edition will contain updated information on
enlisted programs along with a section of several officer programs. Instead of
a chart indicating probability of being accepted into a training program, the
officer section will list collegiate coursework appropriate for the particular
program in question.

The charts for the enlisted programs help counselors who are uncomfortable
with predicting success in non-academic training programs. Since counseling is
an academic area, counselors often are more comfortable discussing this type of
preparation. Thus, the charts for enlisted training is a start to approximate
difficulty of various programs students might consider. Of course, other material
regarding each program should serve as a beginning to help narrow the search for
additional material regarding specific civilian or military careers and programs.

Of course, much more than academic or skill ability should be considered in
a career choice. At this point, the ASVAB Student Workbook could be used to let
students explore their values, interests and skills, "must avoid" areas, and education
level after high school. These topics have been related to over one hundred careers
in the civilian job market by Educational Testing Service through their SIGI Plus
program. Students are encouraged to pick three values, three interests and skills,
and a level of education that they aspire to. They are not encouraged to take
any of the "must avoid" areas, however, in extreme cases, they should pick one to
avoid careers that contain public speaking, sitting still, or heavy labor if these
are impossible or dreadful for them. The major advantage of the workbook is that
all of this information is presented in one place so the student can do some
comparison shopping in his/her own time and pace. Decisions made with this
information can later be discussed with counselors, parents, or teachers if
desired. This material will also help limit the huge variety of careers so the
students can better pinpoint the careers apparently best suited for them.

After use of the ASVAB materials, students can go to the counselor to use
Department of Labor information, computer based information, or other sources
the school has available. The materials are intended to help students find a
list of suitable careers and learn the proper process of gathering information
for informed choice making. Future classes in school and future programs that
are available after high school can then be studied in a context of informed
choice.

Occupational Profile
Outline of Contents

(Developed by the Montana SOICC. Substitute local information where appropriate.)

PART I - OCCUPATIONAL DESCRIPTION

    A. Occupation name and related occupations.
    B. Duties of the occupation.
    C. Aptitudes and skills needed for the occupation.
    D. Earnings in the occupation.
    E. Health hazards related to the occupation.
    F. Employee organizations for workers in the occupation.

PART II - EDUCATION AND TRAINING REQUIREMENTS

    A. Recommended high school or postsecondary preparatory courses.
    B. Educational and experience requirements
    C. Schools that offer training for this occupation.
    D. Schools outside the state that offer training for this occupation.

PART III - INDUSTRIES AND BUSINESSES THAT EMPLOY THIS OCCUPATION

    A. Industry employment and trends.
    B. Projected employment in this occupation.
    C. Current events affecting the outlook for this occupation.
    D. Supply of workers for this occupation.

OCCUPATIONAL PROFILE

GROUP_____   DATE_____

PARTICIPANT NAMES _____

Complete the blanks or check either **Yes** or **No**. Use additional pages if necessary.

SUGGESTED RESOURCES are listed at the end of each question. A space is also provided for additional resources that contain the information. Some other resources can be found by using the Occupation Information Resource Matrix. Sources of information for a local area or town could be the local Job Service office, the local Chamber of Commerce, the local newspaper, and others suggested by your trainers.

PART I - OCCUPATIONAL DESCRIPTION

I.A.   OCCUPATION NAME AND RELATED OCCUPATIONS:

Occupation Name: _____

Code Numbers: DOT_____   OES_____
                SOC_____   Other_____

Related Occupations and/or specialties (for further study if desired):

Name _____   Number_____
Name _____   Number_____
Name _____   Number_____
Name _____   Number_____

Source/s used to answer section I.A.:

OCCUPATIONAL OUTLOOK HANDBOOK (OOH)
STANDARD OCCUPATIONAL CLASSIFICATION MANUAL (SOC)
DICTIONARY OF OCCUPATIONAL TITLES (DOT)
INDUSTRY/OCCUPATIONS PROJECTIONS
STATE CAREER INFORMATION SYSTEM (CIS)
OTHER CAREER INFORMATION SYSTEMS (CIS)
FILL IN OTHER SOURCES:

_____
_____

I.B.   DUTIES OF THE OCCUPATION:

Duties of the job (list minimum of five duties):

1. _____
2. _____
3. _____
4. _____
5. _____
6. _____
7. _____

Source/s used to answer section I.B.:

DICTIONARY OF OCCUPATIONAL TITLES (DOT)
STANDARD OCCUPATIONAL CLASSIFICATION MANUAL (SOC)
OCCUPATIONAL OUTLOOK HANDBOOK (OOH)
STATE CAREER INFORMATION SYSTEM (CIS)
OTHER CAREER INFORMATION SYSTEMS (CIS)
FILL IN OTHER SOURCES:

_____
_____

I.C.   APTITUDES AND SKILLS NEEDED FOR THE OCCUPATION:

List at least six.

   1. _____
   2. _____
   3. _____
   4. _____
   5. _____
   6. _____
   7. _____
   8. _____
   9. _____
   10. _____

Source/s used to answer section I.C.:

OCCUPATIONAL OUTLOOK HANDBOOK (OOH)
STATE CAREER INFORMATION SYSTEM (CIS)
OTHER CAREER INFORMATION SYSTEMS (CIS)
FILL IN OTHER SOURCES:

_____
_____

I.D.   EARNINGS AND HOURS WORKED BY THIS OCCUPATION:

Earnings:

National Wages   _____
State Wages   _____
                 (indicate per hour, week, or year)

Other benefits:

   1. _____
   2. _____
   3. _____

Hours of Work:

On the average, how many hours would one work at this job?

   1. Hours Worked Daily _____

2. Hours Worked Weekly _____
   Are there seasonal layoffs? ____ Yes ____ No

Source/s used to answer section I.D.:

OCCUPATIONAL OUTLOOK HANDBOOK (OOH)
OCCUPATIONAL OUTLOOK QUARTERLY (OOQ)
CAREER INFORMATION SYSTEM (CIS)
STATE OCCUPATIONAL INFORMATION SYSTEM (OIS)
STATE SUPPLY DEMAND REPORT
STATE FRINGE BENEFIT AND WAGE INFORMATION
ECONOMIC CONDITIONS IN STATE
OTHER CAREER INFORMATION SYSTEM (CIS)
FILL IN OTHER SOURCES:

_____
_____

I.E.   HEALTH HAZARDS RELATED TO THE OCCUPATION:

Are there health hazards involved? ____ Yes ____ No
If so, what kinds?_____
_____

Source/s used to answer section I.E.:

SELECTED CHARACTERISTICS OF THE DOT
CAREER INFORMATION SYSTEM
OTHER CAREER INFORMATION SYSTEMS (CIS)
FILL IN OTHER SOURCES:

_____
_____

I.F.   EMPLOYEE ORGANIZATIONS IN THE OCCUPATION:

Employee organizations for full-time workers:

Would you be expected to join a union or other employee organizations?
____ Yes ____ No

Source/s used to answer section I.F.:

OCCUPATIONAL OUTLOOK HANDBOOK (OOH)
OTHER CAREER INFORMATION SYSTEMS (CIS)
CAREER INFORMATION SYSTEM (CIS)
UNION REPRESENTATIVES
FILL IN OTHER SOURCES:

_____
_____

PART II - EDUCATION AND TRAINING INFORMATION

II.A   RECOMMENDED HIGH SCHOOL AND POSTSECONDARY PREP COURSES:

What general high school or post secondary courses would help to prepare the client for this job?

_____   _____
_____   _____
_____   _____
_____   _____

Source/s used to answer section II.A.:

GUIDE FOR OCCUPATIONAL EXPLORATION (GOE)
OCCUPATIONAL OUTLOOK HANDBOOK (OOH)
CAREER INFORMATION SYSTEM (CIS)
OTHER CAREER INFORMATION SYSTEMS (CIS)
FILL IN OTHER SOURCES:

_____
_____

If this client has deficiencies in basic courses needed for this occupation, what courses would you recommend to overcome those deficiencies?

_____   _____
_____   _____
_____   _____

II.B.   EDUCATION AND EXPERIENCE REQUIREMENTS:

Number of years of education required _____
Type (high school, college, Vo-Tech, etc) _____

Is this occupation apprenticeable? _____ Yes _____ No
Length of apprenticeship _____
Name of address of organization to contact to find out more about apprenticeships:
_____
_____

Source/s used to answer section II.B.:

GUIDE FOR OCCUPATIONAL EXPLORATION (GOE)
OCCUPATIONAL OUTLOOK HANDBOOK (OOH)
STATE APPRENTICEABLE OCCUPATIONS
STATE CAREER INFORMATION SYSTEMS (CIS)
OTHER CAREER INFORMATION SYSTEMS (CIS)
STATE OCCUPATIONAL INFORMATION SYSTEM (OIS)
FILL IN OTHER SOURCES:

_____
_____

II.C.   STATE SCHOOLS THAT OFFER TRAINING FOR THIS OCCUPATION:

What schools in the state offer training for this job?

1. _____
2. _____
3. _____

Source/s used to answer section II.C.:

STATE CAREER INFORMATION SYSTEM (CIS)
OTHER CAREER INFORMATION SYSTEMS (CIS)
FILL IN OTHER SOURCES:

_____
_____

II.D.   OUT OF STATE SCHOOLS THAT OFFER TRAINING FOR THIS OCCUPATION:

What schools outside your state offer training for this job?

1. _____
2. _____
3. _____

Source/s used to answer section II.D.:

STATE CAREER INFORMATION SYSTEM (CIS)
OTHER CAREER INFORMATION SYSTEMS (CIS)
FILL IN OTHER SOURCES:

_____
_____

PART III - INDUSTRIES & BUSINESSES THAT EMPLOY THIS OCCUPATION

III.A.   INDUSTRY EMPLOYMENT AND TRENDS:

1. List FOUR industries that would probably employ this occupation. Use the two digit SIC level.

Industry Name   SIC code

_____   _____
_____   _____
_____   _____
_____   _____

2. Using THE INDUSTRY/EMPLOYMENT OUTLOOK 1984/1990 complete the table below for the FOUR industries identified in 1 above.

SIC CODE	1984 ANNUAL AVG EMPL	1990 ANNUAL CHANGE AVG EMPL	PERCENT IN EMPL	TOTAL PERCENT CHANGE	ANNUAL PERCENT CHANGE

Sources used to answer section III.A.:

STATE INDUSTRY/OCCUPATION EMPLOYMENT OUTLOOK
OCCUPATIONAL EMPLOYMENT STATISTICS
STATE OCCUPATIONAL INFORMATION SYSTEM (OIS)
STANDARD INDUSTRIAL CLASSIFICATION MANUAL (SIC)
FILL IN OTHER SOURCES:

_____

_____

III.B.   INDUSTRIES WITH BEST OPPORTUNITY FOR EMPLOYMENT IN THIS OCCUPATION:

Using the information from the tables above, list the two or three industries that you feel would offer the best opportunities for employment in this occupation.

_____

_____

III.C.   LOCAL EMPLOYMENT IN THE INDUSTRIES:

For the county where the inservice is being held, list the Annual Average employment for each industry you listed in Part III.B.

INDUSTRY	COUNTY	AVG EMP
_____	_____	_____
_____	_____	_____
_____	_____	_____

Source/s used to answer section III.A & B.:

STATE EMPLOYMENT WAGES AND CONTRIBUTIONS
STANDARD INDUSTRIAL CLASSIFICATION MANUAL (SIC)
FILL IN OTHER SOURCES:

_____

_____

III.D.   BUSINESSES TO CONTACT:

For each industry in Part III.C. that shows employment, list a business that could be contacted to find out more about this occupation. If none of the industries show employment in this area, skip Part III.D.1. and complete Part III.D.2.

    1.   INDUSTRY NAME: _____
        BUSINESS: _____
        NAME: _____
        ADDRESS:_____

        _____
        PHONE: _____

        BUSINESS: _____
        NAME: _____
        ADDRESS: _____

        _____
        PHONE: _____

Source/s used to answer section III.A & B.:

TELEPHONE BOOK
LOCAL JOB SERVICE
CITY DIRECTORY
CHAMBER OF COMMERCE
FILL IN OTHER SOURCES:

_____
_____

    2.   If there are no businesses employing the occupation in the area what would you advise the client?

_____
_____

PART IV - OUTLOOK FOR THIS OCCUPATION

IV.A.   CURRENT EMPLOYMENT IN THIS OCCUPATION:

What is the recent state employment in this occupation?

Date of data _____ Employment_____
   (Use most recent data you can find.)

What is the recent U.S. employment in this occupation?

Date of data _____ Employment_____
   (Use most recent data you can find.)

Source/s used to answer section IV.A.:

STATE INDUSTRY/OCCUPATION OUTLOOK
STATE CAREER INFORMATION SYSTEM (CIS)
OCCUPATIONAL OUTLOOK HANDBOOK (OOH)
OTHER CAREER INFORMATION SYSTEMS (CIS)

FILL IN OTHER SOURCES:

_____

_____

IV.B.   PROJECTED EMPLOYMENT

What is the projected state employment for this occupation to 2000?

2000 Employment _____

What is the projected number of average annual openings in the state for this job to 2000?

Average Annual Openings _____

Source/s used to answer section IV.B.:

STATE INDUSTRY/OCCUPATION OUTLOOK
STATE CAREER INFORMATION SYSTEM (CIS)
OCCUPATIONAL OUTLOOK HANDBOOK (OOH)
OTHER CAREER INFORMATION SYSTEMS (CIS)
FILL IN OTHER SOURCES:

_____

_____

IV.C.   CURRENT EVENTS AFFECTING THE OUTLOOK FOR THIS OCCUPATION:

What current factors are affecting the outlook for this occupation in the state? in the nation?

_____

_____

Source/s used to answer section IV.C.:

NEWSPAPERS
OTHER MEDIA
JOB SERVICE OFFICES
LOCAL CAREER PROFESSIONALS
CHAMBER OF COMMERCE
FILL IN OTHER SOURCES:

_____

_____

IV.D.   SUPPLY OF WORKERS FOR THIS OCCUPATION:

Occupational supply is information on workers who have completed training or are job ready in this occupation.

Occupations are grouped into "clusters" based on their relationships to each other. For example: File clerk and typist would be in the "clerical office practice" cluster, number OF2.

Write the name of the occupation you are researching:_____

What is the supply for this occupation? _____

What source(s) provided training for this occupation?_____

What is the name and number of the cluster that includes this occupation?

    NAME _____ NUMBER _____

What is the cluster total or all related supply total for the cluster including this occupation?_____

During the past year how many people have applied for work in this occupation through the Job Service?_____

Source/s used to answer section IV.D.:

    SOICC
    STATE SUPPLY DEMAND REPORT
    STATE OCCUPATIONAL INFORMATION SYSTEM (OIS)
    FILL IN OTHER SOURCES:

    _____

    _____

Occupational Information Resource Matrix

Categories of Information

State Information Sources	Occupation Activities	Occupational Characteristics	Preparation for Work	Advancement	Related Occupations	Industry	Employment Outlook	Earnings	Places of Employment	Resource People
County Business Patterns						x	x			
State Employment and Labor Force						x	x			
Statistics in Brief						x	x			
Industry/Occupation Projections						x	x			
Career Information System	x	x	x	x	x	x	x	x	x	
State Apprenticeable Occupations	x	x	x	x			x	x		
Occup. Employment Statistics Publications					x	x	x		x	
State Occup. Information System (OIS)					x		x	x	x	
State Supply/Demand Report					x		x	x	x	
State Fringe Benefit & Wage Information								x		
Economic Conditions in the State						x		x		

Resource People: (enter names of presenters here)

1.

2.

3.

4.

5.

6.

Occupational Information Resource Matrix

Categories of Information

National Information Sources	Occupation Activities	Occupational Characteristics	Preparation for Work	Advancement	Related Occupations	Industry	Employment Outlook	Earnings	Places of Employment	Resource People
Dictionary of Occupational Titles (DOT)	x				x	x				
Standard Industrial Classification (SIC)						x				
Standard Occupational Classification (SOC)	x				x					
Occupational Outlook Handbook (OOH)	x	x	x	x	x	x	x	x	x	
Occupational Outlook Quarterly (OOQ)	x	x	x	x	x	x	x	x		
Guide for Occupational Exploration (GOE)			x		x					
Exploring Careers	x	x								
U.S. Industrial Outlook						x	x			
Occupational Projections and Training Data			x				x			
Selected Characteristics of Occupations-DOT		x								
Career Information System	x	x	x	x	x	x	x	x	x	

Resource People: (enter names of presenters here)

1.

2.

3.

4.

5.

6.

Case Study - Bernie Maas
(Developed by the Maine SOICC)

My name is Bernie Maas. Since leaving the military a year ago, I have been living in
_____. I married my high school sweetheart, and now we have two little girls.
I never was afraid of anything when I was in the Army, but I am now. I'm afraid that
I won't be able to make enough money to provide for my family.

I never liked school much. Oh, I loved playing sports. I was the second best swimmer
on the school team. I even taught a swim class for young kids in the summer. I really
liked Automotive Shop, too. I spent a lot of time tinkering with cars. But I just
couldn't seem to pass English. I dropped out of school in December of my senior year
and joined the Army. After basic training I was assigned to the motor pool. I learned
to drive and fix just about everything the Army had on wheels or tracks. Eventually,
I became the personal driver for the CO (Commanding Officer), because he knew I
could fix the jeep if it broke down out in the boonies.

When I got out of the Service, I got a truck driving job for a construction company. I
ran the dozer sometimes, too. The company helped me convert my military operator
licenses to civilian licenses. But work got real slack so they had to lay me off. I've
tried working with other construction companies, and I have worked on specific jobs,
but they haven't paid enough for a family to live on.

I've thought about getting a different job, or moving to an area that might have more
jobs. But everywhere I look either the employer wants a high school graduate or the
job doesn't pay enough. I just don't know what to do.

Reprinted with permission from:

Kenneth Bridges, Senior Economic Analyst
Division of Economic Analysis and Research
Bureau of Employment Security

and

Maine SOICC
State House Station 71
Augusta, ME 04333

1. Where would you begin with Bernie? List the first three steps you would take:

    a.
    b.
    c.

2. What are three job titles that match Bernie's skills or interests?

    a.
    b.
    c.

3. What is the outlook for these occupations in your state?

    a.
    b.
    c.

4. How much can Bernie earn in each of these occupations?

    a.
    b.
    c.

5. How many people are employed in each of these occupations in one of your local counties?

    a.
    b.
    c.

6. In what counties are the highest numbers employed for each of these occupations?

    a.
    b.
    c.

7. What are the overall economic conditions like in the county you selected compared to the state in terms of employment, and the unemployment rate?

8. Who can Bernie contact for more labor market information about the local and statewide labor market area?

Trainer's Answer Sheet - Bernie Maas

(Answers are given for the state of Maine. Determine answers for your particular state and enter the data on your answer sheet. Provide state, local and national resources that contain answers to these questions.)

1. Where would you begin with Bernie?

Review interests, work history
Get GED or Equivalency Diploma
Explore options

2. What are three job titles that match Bernie's skills or interests?

a. *Automative Mechanic*
b. *Delivery/Route Worker*
c. *Tractor-Trailer-Truck Driver*
d. *Heavy Equipment Operator*

3. What is the outlook for these occupations in your state?
(Resources used - Occupational Outlook to 1995, Occupational Matrices)

a. *Faster than average, annual openings 292, Growth 24.5%*
b. *About as fast, annual openings 130, Growth 15.1%*
c. *About as fast, annual openings 294, Growth 16.2%*
d. *About as fast, annual openings 103, Growth 18.4%*

4. How much can Bernie earn in each of these occupations? (Reported as hourly wage)

	Occ. Matrices	Manf. Wage Surv.	Nmfg. Wage Surv.
a.	*$8.47*	*$8.57*	*$8.46-8.97-9.97*
b.	*7.47*		*6.58*
c.	*8.94*	*6.90-8.40*	*7.17-8.54*
d.	*7.66*	*7.66*	

5. How many people are employed in each of these occupations in one of your local counties?

	County 1	County 2	County 3
a.	*131*	*131*	*51008*
b.	*94*	*94*	*55A87*
c.	*65*	*65 All Truck 271*	*54003 54000*
d.		*80*	*54B52*

6. In what counties are the highest numbers employed for each of these occupations?

a. *Cumb. 1352* *Pen. 848* *Ken. 622*
b. *Cumb. 1687* *Pen. 672* *Ken. 533*
c. *Cumb. 661*   *Pen. 430* *Aroos. 238*
d. *Cumb. 551*   *Pen. 246* *York 190*

What are overall economic conditions like in the county you selected compared to the state in terms of employment, unemployment, and the unemployment rate?

Resource - Labor Market Digest and local information resources

Who can Bernie contact for more labor market information about the local and statewide Labor Market Area?

LMI Directory, CIDS and local information resources

Case Study Activity--Thomas Lee

Your client, Thomas Lee, has been referred to you by a social service agency. Tom is a minority male, age 26, who is out of work. Tom dropped out of school in the tenth grade; he claims that he could not read well and no one seemed to care about kids like him. Tom has done odd jobs since that time. As you question Tom about his work history, the information that you get is sketchy and he appears reluctant to offer details. He tells you that he has worked in service stations, restaurants and work for a landscaping service. The job he liked the best was laying sod, because he likes doing physical work out-of-doors. Despite his many jobs, he can provide only one employment reference from three years ago, when he worked in a fast-food restaurant. Upon questioning, Tom admits to personality conflicts with supervisors on several jobs. Tom claims that the conflicts were largely due to his drug and alcohol abuse on those occasions. Tom has been in trouble with the law and has recently completed a court ordered drug and alcohol rehabilitation program. His social worker is encouraging Tom to enroll in a community sponsored reading program. As you try to get to know Tom, he appears to be withdrawn and angry. When you question him about his apparent hostility toward you, he says that he does not trust persons from your culture.

Tom has multiple barriers to employment and he is working with personnel from several agencies to help him address his problems. Your responsibility as a career development facilitator is to help Tom explore his career options.

1. As a career development facilitator, where would you begin with Tom?

2. With what other individuals or agencies would you need to work to help Tom become ready for employment?

3. Using the following resources: CIDS, OOH, SOC, DOT, and GOE, see if you can identify three job titles that might be of interest to Tom.

    a.
    b.
    c.

4. How much can Tom earn in each of these occupations?

    a.
    b.
    c.

5. Will these earnings be sufficient to cover his basic needs and allow him to live independently?

6. How many people are employed in each of these occupations in your county?

7. In what counties are the highest numbers employed in each of these occupations?

8. What are the overall economic conditions like in your county compared to the rest of the state in terms of employment and the unemployment rate?

9. Who can Tom contact for more labor market information about the local and statewide Labor Market Area?

Activity Evaluation
(Developed by the Montana SOICC)

Name of Activity:

We would appreciate your thoughts on the activity you have just completed. Please answer the questions below. More importantly, use the rest of the sheet for your comments, positive and negative. We are constantly searching for ways to improve. Tell us what you think.

Although optional, your name and phone number would be appreciated. Then we can contact you if we need clarification on your ideas. We promise not to send anyone with a violin case to see you.

NAME_____ PHONE_____

1. Which part of the activity did you like the best?

2. Which part did you like the least?

3. Did you have enough time to complete the activity?

4. Were the instructions clear?

5. Were the trainers available when you needed them?

6. Did you have sufficient resource materials? If no, please explain.

7. Can you use this activity in your work?

8. On a scale of one to ten, how would you rate this activity? (Ten is the highest rating.)

9. Comments and suggestions for improvement:

Appendices

Appendix A: NCDA Career Counseling Competencies

Appendix B: SOICC Offices

Appendix C: NOICC Staff

Appendix D: Directory of State-Based Career Information Delivery Systems

Appendix E: National Career Development Guidelines

Appendix F: State Guidance Supervisors

Appendix G: Guidelines for the Use of Computer-Based Career Information and Guidance Systems

Appendix H: Career Software Review Guidelines

Appendix I: Guidelines for the Preparation and Evaluation of Career and Occupational Information Literature

Appendix J: Government Printing Offices

Appendix K: Sources of State and Local Job Outlook

Appendix L: Annotated List of Selected Printed References

Appendix M: Overview of Equal Opportunity Legislation

Appendix N: Labor Market Information Directors

Appendix O: State Data Center Program Coordinating Organizations

Appendix P: Acronyms

Appendix A

NCDA Career Counseling Competencies

Appendix A
Introduction to Competency Statements

The following statements were considered as the attached standards were being constructed:

1. **Definition of career counseling.** Career counseling consists of vocational counseling and those activities performed or coordinated by individuals who have the professional credentials to work with and counsel other individuals or groups of individuals about occupations, careers, life/career roles and responsibilities, career decision making, career planning, leisure planning, career pathing, and other career development activities, e.g., resume preparation, interviewing and job search techniques, and issues or conflicts associated with the preceding items. (This definition is a slight revision of the definition found on page 3 of NCDA's **The Professional Practice of Career Counseling and Consultation: A Resource Document**, and it includes additional revisions, noted by brackets, by a board member.)

2. The statements provide guidance for those professionals at or above the master's degree level. Specifically, they are for those counseling individuals who are completing or have completed at least a master's in counseling and desire a career counseling concentration or advanced certificate in career counseling.

3. The statements are revised with regard to the following specialties (taken from NCDA's **The Professional Practice of Career Counseling and Consultation: A Resource Document**): Career Counselors (Private and Public Settings); Human Resources/Career Development Specialist (Organizational Setting); and Job Placement Specialists (Public Setting).

4. The statements do not reflect competency guidelines for the following specialties (because professionals in these areas should not be counseling): Career/Employment Search consultant (Private Setting); Employment Agent (Private Setting); Cooperative Education Instructors (Educational Setting). These specialties, along with NEW job titles such as Career Aides, Career Librarian, or Career Resource Specialist (in industry), Career Librarian, or Career Resource Specialist (in industry), should have a separate set of competency statements that would include some of the career counseling statements, but also include a stronger emphasis on the administrative, planning, guidance, and resource aspects of career development.

    With the above information in mind, Larry Burlew, Ed.D., selected 3 career counseling professionals to work on a subcommittee to the Standards Committee to revise the NCDA competency statements. The subcommittee members included: Dr. James Benshoff, a university professor who teaches career counseling; Dr. Linda Gast, a practitioner who directs a university career counseling center; and Dr. Janet Treichel, a practitioner working for the Federal government who helped construct the NOICC standards for career counseling. Once this group was formed, the following procedures were followed:

    A. Each member was requested to be part of the subcommittee and told what their responsibilities would be.

B.   The following competency statements/standards were forwarded to each member: NCDA, NBCC, NOICC, CAS Standards and Guidelines for Services/Development Programs, and NECA.

C.   Members were asked to review the career counseling literature and suggest competency categories that were not presently part of the NCDA standards. Although other categories were suggested, the following were new categories mutually agreed upon: career development theory, special populations, supervision, ethical/legal issues, and research/evaluation.

D.   Each member was then assigned 2-3 competency categories with the following goals in mind: 1) review all current standards and revise NCDA's to reflect the most complete requirements in each category and 2) review the current career counseling literature and add new terminology and theory as necessary.

E.   The subcommittee met in mid-May of 1989 and carefully reviewed/critiqued the work of each member. Final statements were agreed upon.

F.   Dr. Burlew had the statements rewritten and forwarded to each subcommittee member for final approval.

G.   Once approved, the statements were forwarded to Dr. Edwin Herr, Chair of the NCDA Standards Committee.

The committee still feels that a clear introduction statement related to professional issues (e.g., training and practicums) must be included in a final document.

In the attached document, the competency statements have not been placed in any particular order. However, the original six competency areas (i.e., Individual and Group Counseling Skills, Information /Resources, Individual and Group Assessment, Program Management and Implementation, Consultation) are grouped together and first; the new categories (i.e., Career Development Theory, Special Populations, Ethical/Legal Issues, Research/Evaluation) follow.

Introduction to Career Counseling Competency Statements

The competency statements are for those professionals interested and trained in the field of career counseling. For the purpose of these statements, career counseling is defined as counseling individuals or groups of individuals about occupations, careers, life/career roles and responsibilities, career decision making, career planning, leisure planning, career pathing, and other career development activities (e.g., resume preparation, interviewing and job search techniques), together with the issues or conflicts that individuals confront regarding their careers.

These statements are a revised version of the "Vocational/Career Counseling Competencies" of 1982. They were revised by counselor educators and career counseling practitioners, then reviewed and approved by the Board of Directors of the National Career Development Association (NCDA). Career development competency statements developed by other groups, such as the National Occupational Information Coordinating Committee (NOICC), the National Board for Certified Counselors (NBCC), the Council for the Advancement of Standards for Student Services/Development Programs (CAS), and the Council for Accreditation of Counseling and

Related Educational Programs (CACREP), were reviewed prior to the NCDA competency statements being revised. The NCDA Standards Committee responsible for this review and revision was led by Dr. Edwin Herr, Dr. James Sampson and Dr. Larry Burlew. Other committee members were Dr. Linda Gast, Dr. James Benshoff, and Dr. Janet Treichel.

The "Career Counseling Competencies" are intended to represent minimum competencies for those professionals at or above the master's degree level of education. They can also serve as guidelines for any professional or paraprofessional working in a career development setting. However, for those practitioners without a master's degree in counseling, additional competency statements may be required (e.g., a career librarian may need competency in cataloging); in addition, basic educational requirements for other competencies (e.g., counseling-related statements) may be lacking.

Purpose

Professional competency statements provide guidance for the minimum competencies necessary to effectively perform a particular occupation or job within a particular occupation. Professional career counselors (a master's degree or higher), or persons in career development positions, must demonstrate the knowledge and skills for a specialty in career counseling that the generalist counselor might not possess. These skills and knowledge are represented by designated competency areas which have been developed by professional career counselors and counselor educators. The Career Counseling Competency Statements can serve as a guide for career counseling training programs or as a checklist for persons wanting to acquire or to enhance their skills in career counseling.

Minimum Competencies

In order to work as a professional engaged in Career Counseling, the individual must demonstrate minimum competencies in ten designated areas. These ten areas are: Career Development Theory, Individual and Group Counseling Skills, Individual/Group Assessment, Information/Resources, Program Management and Implementation, Consultation, Special Populations, Supervision, Ethical/Legal Issues, Research/Evaluation.

Career Development Theory: Theory base and knowledge considered essential for professionals engaging in career counseling and development.

Individual and Group Counseling Skills: Individual and group counseling competencies considered essential to effective career counseling.

Individual/Group Assessment: Individual/group assessment skills considered essential for professionals engaging in career counseling.

Information/Resources: Information/resource base and knowledge essential for professionals engaging in career counseling.

Program Management and Implementation: Skills necessary to develop, plan, implement, and manage comprehensive career development programs in a variety of settings.

Consultation: Knowledge and skills considered essential in enabling individuals and organizations to effectively impact upon the career counseling and development process.

Special Populations: Knowledge and skills considered essential in providing career counseling and development processes to special populations.

Supervision: Knowledge and skills considered essential in critically evaluating counselor performance, maintaining and improving professional skills, and seeking assistance from others when needed in career counseling.

Ethical/Legal Issues: Information base and knowledge essential for the ethical and legal practice of career counseling.

Research/Evaluation: Knowledge and skills considered essential in understanding and conducting research and evaluation in career counseling and development.

Professional Preparation

The competency statements were developed to serve as guidelines for persons interested in career development occupations. They are intended for persons training at the master's level or higher with a specialty in career counseling. However, this does not prevent other types of career development professionals from using them as guidelines for their own training. The competency statements provide counselor educators, supervisors, and other interested groups with guidelines for the minimum training required for counselors interested in a career counseling specialty.

The statements might also serve as guidelines for those professional counselors who seek in-service training to qualify as career counselors.

Ethical Responsibilities

Career development professionals must only perform the job for which they "possess or have access to the necessary skills and resources for giving the kind of help that is needed" (see AACD Ethical Standards). If a professional does not have the appropriate training or resources for the type of career problem presented, then an appropriate referral must be made. No person should attempt to use skills within these competency statements for which he/she has not been trained. For additional ethical guidelines, refer to NCDA Ethical Standards for career counselors.

Career Counseling Competencies

Individual and Group Counseling Skills

Individual and group counseling competencies considered essential to effective career counseling.

Demonstration of:

1. Ability to establish and maintain productive personal relationships with individuals.

2. Ability to establish and maintain a productive group climate.

3. Ability to collaborate with clients in identifying personal goals.

4. Ability to identify and select techniques appropriate to client or group goals and client needs, psychological states, and developmental tasks.

5. Ability to plan, implement and evaluate counseling techniques designed to assist clients to achieve the following:

   a. Identify and understand clients' personal characteristics related to career.
   b. Identify and understand social contextual conditions affecting clients' careers.
   c. Identify and understand familial, subcultural and cultural structures and functions as they are related to clients' careers.

      d.   Identify and understand clients' career decision making processes.

      e.   Identify and understand clients' attitudes toward work and workers.

      f.   Identify and understand clients' biases toward work and workers based on gender, race and cultural stereotypes.

6.   Ability to challenge and encourage clients to take action to prepare for and initiate role transitions by:

      a.   Locating sources of relevant information and experience.

      b.   Obtaining and interpreting information and experiences.

      c.   Acquiring skills needed to make role transitions.

7.   Ability to support and challenge clients to examine the balance of work, leisure, family and community roles in their careers.

Individual/Group Assessment

Individuals/Group assessment skills considered essential for professionals engaging in career counseling.

Demonstration of:

1.   Knowledge about instruments and techniques to assess personal characteristics (such as aptitude, achievement, interests, values and other personality traits).

2.   Knowledge about instruments and techniques to assess leisure interests, learning style, life roles, self-concept, career maturity, vocational identity, career indecision, work environment preference (e.g., work satisfaction), and other related life style/development issues.

3.   Knowledge about instruments and techniques to assess conditions of the work environment (such as tasks, expectations, norms and qualities of the physical and social settings).

4.   Ability to evaluate and select instruments appropriate to the client's physical capacities, psychological states, social roles and cultural background.

5.   Knowledge about variables such as ethnicity, gender culture, learning style, personal development, and physical/mental disability which affect the assessment process.

6.   Knowledge of and ability to effectively and appropriately use computer-assisted assessment measures and techniques.

7.   Ability to identify assessment (procedures) appropriate for specified situations and populations.

8.   Ability to evaluate assessment (procedures) in terms of their validity, reliability, and relationships to race, gender, age, and ethnicity.

9.   Ability to select assessment techniques appropriate for group administration and those appropriate for individual administration.

10.   Ability to administer, score and report findings from career assessment instruments.

11. Ability to interpret data from assessment instruments and present the results to client and to others designated by client.

12. Ability to assist client and others designated by the client to interpret data from assessment instruments.

13. Ability to write a thorough and substantiated report of assessment results.

Program Management and Implementation

Management/Implementation skills necessary to develop, plan, implement, and manage comprehensive career development programs in a variety of settings.

Demonstration of:

1. Knowledge of designs that can be used in the organization of career development programs.

2. Knowledge of needs assessment and evaluation techniques and practices.

3. Knowledge of organizational theories, including diagnosis, behavior, planning, organizational communication, and management, useful in implementing and administering career development programs.

4. Knowledge of leadership theories, evaluation and feedback approaches, organizational change, decision-making and conflict resolution approaches.

5. Knowledge of professional standards for accreditation and program development purposes.

6. Knowledge of personal and environmental barriers affecting the implementation of career development programs.

7. Knowledge of using computers for forecasting, budgeting, planning, communicating, and policy analysis and resource allocation.

8. Knowledge of educational trends and state and federal legislation that may influence the development and implementation of career development programs.

9. Ability to implement individual and group programs in career development for specified populations.

10. Ability to train and/or inform teachers and others about the use and application of computer-based systems for career information.

11. Ability to plan, organize, and manage a comprehensive career resource center.

12. Ability to work as a lead person in developing and implementing career development programs involving collaborative arrangements with teachers and other professionals or paraprofessionals.

13. Ability to prepare budgets and time lines for career development programs.

14. Ability to identify staff competencies needed to remain current in the field of career counseling and development.

15. Ability to identify, develop, and use record keeping methods.

16. Ability to implement a public relations effort in behalf of career development activities and services.

Consultation

Knowledge and skills considered essential in relating to individuals and organizations that impact the career counseling and development process.

Demonstration of:

1. Knowledge of and ability to use consultation theories, strategies, and models.

2. Ability to establish and maintain a productive consultation relationship with people in roles who can influence the client's career such as the following: parents, teachers, employers, business and professional groups, community groups, and the general public.

3. Ability to convey career counseling goals and achievements to business and professional groups, employers, community groups, the general public, and key personnel in positions of authority, such as legislators, executives, and others.

4. Ability to provide data on the cost effectiveness of career counseling and development intervention.

Information/Resources

Information/resource base and knowledge essential for professionals engaging in career counseling.

Demonstration of:

1. Knowledge of employment information and career planning resources for client use.

2. Knowledge of education, training, and employment trends; labor market information and resources that provide information about job tasks, functions, salaries, requirements and future outlooks related to broad occupational fields and individual occupations.

3. Knowledge of the changing roles of women and men and the implications for work, education, family and leisure.

4. Knowledge of and the ability to use computer-based career information delivery systems (CIDS) and computer-assisted career guidance systems (CACGS) to store, retrieve and disseminate career and occupational information.

5. Knowledge of community/professional resources to assist clients in career/life planning, including job search.

Career Development Theory

Theory base and knowledge considered essential for professionals engaging in career counseling and development.

Demonstration of:

1. Knowledge about counseling theories and associated techniques.

2. Knowledge about theories and models of careers and career development.

3. Knowledge about differences in knowledge and values about work and productive roles associated with gender, age, ethnic and race groups, cultures and capacities.

4. Knowledge about career counseling theoretical models, associated counseling and information techniques, and sources to learn more about them.

5. Knowledge about developmental issues individuals address throughout the lifespan.

6. Knowledge of the role relationships to facilitate personal, family, and career development.

7. Knowledge of information, techniques, and models related to computer-assisted career guidance systems and career information delivery systems and career counseling.

8. Knowledge of the information, techniques, and models related to career planning and placement.

9. Knowledge of career counseling theories and models that apply specifically to women or are inclusive of variables that are important to women's career development.

Special Populations

Knowledge and skills considered essential in relating to special populations that impact career counseling and development processes.

Demonstration of:

1. Knowledge of the intrapersonal dynamics of special population clients while understanding resistances and defenses that may occur naturally during the counseling process.

2. Sensitivity toward the developmental issues and needs unique to minority populations.

3. Sensitivity toward and knowledge of various disabling conditions and necessary assistance and requirements.

4. Ability to define the structure of the career counseling process to accommodate individual cultural frames of reference and ethnic and racial issues.

5. Ability to distinguish between the special needs of the culturally different, immigrants, the disabled, the elderly, persons with the AIDS virus, and minority populations.

6. Ability to find appropriate methods or resources to communicate with limited-English proficient individuals.

7. Ability to identify alternative approaches to career planning needs for individuals with specific needs.

8. Ability to identify community resources and establish linkages to assist clients with specific needs.

9. Ability to assist other staff members, professionals and community members in understanding the unique needs/characteristics of special populations with regard to career exploration, employment expectations and economic/social issues.

10. Ability to advocate for the career development and employment of special populations.

11. Ability to deliver and design career development programs and materials to hard-to-reach special populations.

Supervision

Knowledge and skills considered essential in critically evaluating counselor performance, maintaining and improving professional skills, and seeking assistance from others when needed.

Demonstration of:

1. Knowledge of supervision models and theories.

2. Ability to provide effective supervision to career counselors at different levels of experience.

3. Ability to utilize supervision on a regular basis to maintain and improve counselor skills.

4. Ability to consult with supervisors and colleagues regarding client and counseling issues and issues related to one's own professional development as a career counselor.

5. Ability to recognize own limitations as a career counselor and to seek supervision or refer clients when appropriate.

Ethical/Legal Issues

Information base and knowledge essential for the ethical and legal practice of career counseling.

Demonstration of:

1. Knowledge about the code of ethical standards of the American Association for Counseling and Development, the National Career Development Association, NBCC, CACREP, and other relevant professional organizations.

2. Knowledge about current ethical and legal issues which affect the practice of career counseling.

3. Knowledge about ethical issues related to career counseling with women, cultural minorities, immigrants, the disabled, the elderly, and persons with the AIDS virus.

4. Knowledge about current ethical/legal issues with regard to the use of computer-assisted career guidance.

5. Ability to apply ethical standards to career counseling and consulting situations, issues, and practices.

6. Ability to recognize situations involving interpretation of ethical standards and to consult with supervisors and colleagues to determine an appropriate and ethical course of action.

7. Knowledge of state and federal statutes relating to client confidentiality.

Research/Evaluation

Knowledge and skills considered essential in understanding and conducting research and evaluation in career counseling and development.

Demonstration of:

1. Knowledge about and ability to apply basic statistics and statistical procedures appropriate to research related to career counseling and development.

2. Knowledge about and ability to use types of research and research designs appropriate to career counseling and development research.

3. Knowledge about and ability to convey major research findings related to career counseling and development processes and effectiveness.

4. Knowledge about and ability to apply principles of proposal writing.

5. Knowledge about major evaluation models and methods.

6. Ability to design, conduct, and use the results of evaluation programs.

7. Ability to design evaluation programs which take into account the needs of special populations, minorities, the elderly, persons with the AIDS virus, and women.

Appendix B

SOICC Offices

SOICC ADDRESSES

Dr. Mary Louise Simms, Director
Alabama OICC
Bell Building, Suite 400
207 Montgomery Street
Montgomery, AL 36130
TEL: 205/242-2990

Ms. Brynn Keith, Executive Director
Alaska Department of Labor
Research and Analysis Section
P. O. Box 25501
Juneau, AK 99802
TEL: 907/465-4518

Mr. Patolo Mageo, Program Director
American Samoa State OICC
Office of Manpower Resources
American Samoa Government
Pago Pago, AS 96799
TEL: 684/633-4485

Mr. Stan Butterworth, Executive Director
Arizona State OICC
P. O. Box 6123, Site Code 897J
1789 W. Jefferson St., 1st Floor N.
Phoenix, AZ 85005
TEL: 602/542-3680
FAX: 602/542-6474

Mr. C. Coy Cozart, Executive Director
Arkansas OICC
Arkansas Employment Security Division
Employment and Training Services
P. O. Box 2981
Little Rock, AR 72203
TEL: 501/682-3159
FAX: 501/682-3713

Mr. Sigurd Brivkains, Executive Director
California OICC
1116 - 9th Street, Lower Level
Sacramento, CA 94244-2220
TEL: 916/323-6544

Mr. James L. Harris, Director
Colorado OICC
State Board Community College
1391 Speer Boulevard, Suite 600
Denver, CO 80204-2554
TEL: 303/866-4488

Dr. Prudence Brown Holton
Executive Director
Connecticut OICC
Connecticut Department of Education
25 Industrial Park Road
Middletown, CT 06457
TEL: 203/638-4042

Mr. James K. McFadden, Executive Director
Office of Occupational and LMI/DOL
University Office Plaza
P. O. Box 9029
Newark, DE 19714-9029
TEL: 302/368-6963
FAX: 302/368-6748

Ms. Etta Williams, Executive Director
District of Columbia OICC
Department of Employment Services
500 C Street, NW, Room 215
Washington, DC 20001
TEL: 202/639-1090
FAX: 202/639-1765

Mr. Garry L. Breedlove, Manager
Bureau of LMI/DOL and ES
Suite 200, Hartman Building
2012 Capitol Circle, SE
Tallahassee, FL 32399-0673
TEL: 904/488-7397
FAX: 904/488-2558

Mr. Clifford L. Granger, Executive Director
Georgia OICC/Department of Labor
148 International Boulevard-Sussex Place
Atlanta, GA 30303
TEL: 404/656-9639
FAX: 404/651-9568

Mr. Jose S. Mantanona, Executive Director
Guam OICC
Human Resource Development Agency
Jay Ease Building, 3rd Floor
P. O. Box 2817
Agana, GU 96910
TEL: 671/646-9341 thru 9344

Mr. Patrick A. Stanley, Executive Director
Hawaii State OICC
830 Punchbowl Street, Room 315
Honolulu, HI 96813
TEL: 808/586-8750
FAX: 808/586-9099

Mr. Charles R. Mollerup, Director
Idaho OICC
Len B. Jordan Building, Room 301
650 West State Street
Boise, ID 83720
TEL: 208/334-3705
fax: 208/334-2365

Mr. Jan Staggs, Executive Director
Illinois OICC
217 East Monroe, Suite 203
Springfield, IL 62706
TEL: 217/785-0789
FAX: 217/785-6184

Ms. Linda Piper, Executive Director
Indiana OICC
309 W. Washington St., Room 309
Indianapolis, IN 46204
TEL: 317/232-8528
FAX: 317/232-1815

Penelope Shenk, Acting Executive Director
Iowa OICC
Iowa Department of Economic Development
200 East Grand Avenue
Des Moines, IA 50309
TEL: 515/242-4890
FAX: 515/242-4859

Mr. Randall Williams, Director
Kansas OICC
401 Topeka Avenue
Topeka, KS 66603
TEL: 913/296-2387
FAX: 913/296-2119

Mr. Don Sullivan, Information Liaison
Kentucky OICC
275 E. Main Street - 1 East
Frankfort, KY 40621-0001
TEL: 502/564-4258 or 5331

Mr. George Glass, Coordinator
Louisiana OICC
P. O. Box 94094
Baton Rouge, LA 70804-9094
TEL: 504/342-5149
FAX: 504/342-5115

Ms. Susan Brown, Executive Director
Maine OICC
State House Station 71
Augusta, ME 04333
TEL: 207/289-2331

Ms. Jasmin M. Duckett, Coordinator
Maryland SOICC
State Department of Employment & Training
1100 N. Eutaw Street, Room 600
Baltimore, MD 21201
TEL: 301/333-5478
FAX: 301/333-5304

Mr. Robert Vinson, Director
Massachusetts OICC
MA Division of Employment Security
C.F. Hurley Building, 2nd Floor
Government Center
Boston, MA 02114
TEL: 617/727-6718
FAX: 617/727-8014

Mr. Robert Sherer, Executive Coordinator
Michigan OICC
Victor Office Center, Third Floor, Box 30015
201 N. Washington Square
Lansing, MI 48909
TEL: 517/373-0363
FAX: 517/335-5822

Mr. John Cosgrove, Director
Minnesota OICC
Department of Jobs & Training
390 N. Robert Street
St. Paul, MN 55101
TEL: 612/296-2072
FAX: 612/297-5820

Ms. Liz Barnett, Acting Executive Director
Dept. of Economic & Community Dev.
SOICC Office
301 West Pearl Street
Jackson, MS 39203
TEL: 601/949-2002
FAX: 601/359-3605

Ms. Kay Raithel, Director
Missouri OICC
421 E. Dunklin Street
Jefferson City, MO 65101
TEL: 314/751-3800
FAX: 314/751-7973

Mr. Robert N. Arnold, Program Manager
Montana OICC
1327 Lockey Street, 2nd Floor
P. O. Box 1728
Helena, MT 59624
TEL: 406/444-2741
FAX: 406/444-2638

Mr. Phil Baker, Administrator
Nebraska OICC
P. O. Box 94600
State House Station
Lincoln, NE 68509-4600
TEL: 402/471-4845

Ms. Valerie Hopkins, Director
Nevada OICC
1923 N. Carson Street, Suite 211
Carson City, NV 89710
TEL: 702/687-4577
FAX: 702/883-9158

Dr. Victor P. Racicot, Director
New Hampshire State OICC
64B Old Suncook Road
Concord, NH 03301
TEL: 603/228-3349
FAX: 603/228-8557

Mr. Laurence H. Seidel, Staff Director
New Jersey OICC
1008 Labor & Industry Building
CN 056
Trenton, NJ 08625-0056
TEL: 609/292-2682
FAX: 609/292-6692

Mr. Charles Lehman, Director
New Mexico OICC
401 Broadway, NE-Tiwa Building
P. O. Box 1928
Albuquerque, NM 87103
TEL: 505/841-8455

Mr. David Nyhan, Executive Director
New York State OICC/DOL
Research & Statistics Division
State Campus, Building 12 - Room 400
Albany, NY 12240
TEL: 518/457-6182
FAX: 518/457-0620

Ms. Nancy H. MacCormac, Executive Director
North Carolina OICC
1311 St. Mary's Street, Suite 250
P. O. Box 27625
Raleigh, NC 27611
TEL: 919/733-6700

Dr. Dan Marrs, Coordinator
North Dakota SOICC
1720 Burnt Boat Drive
P. O. Box 1537
Bismarck, ND 58502-1537
TEL: 701/224-2733

Mr. Konrad Reyes, Executive Director
Northern Mariana Islands OICC
Northern Mariana College
Room 12, Building A
P. O. Box 149
Saipan, CM 96950
TEL: 671/234-7394

Mr. Mark Schaff, Director
Ohio OICC/Division of LMI
Ohio Bureau of Employment Services
1160 Dublin Road, Building A
Columbus, OH 43215
TEL: 614/644-2689
FAX: 614/481-8543

Mr. Curtis Schumaker, Executive Director
Oklahoma OICC
Department of Voc/Tech Education
1500 W. Seventh Avenue
Stillwater, OK 74074
TEL: 405/743-5198
FAX: 405/743-5142

Ms. Virlena Crosley, Asst. Administrator for
Research & Statistics
Employment Division
875 Union Street, NE
Salem, OR 97311
TEL: 503/378-5490
FAX: 503/373-7515

Mr. Fritz J. Fichtner, Jr., Director
Pennsylvania OICC
Pennsylvania Dept. of Labor and Industry
1224 Labor and Industry Building
Harrisburg, PA 17120
TEL: 717/787-8646 or 8647
FAX: 717/772-2168

Mr. Jesus Hernandez Rios, Executive Director
Puerto Rico OICC
202 Del Cristo Street
P. O. Box 6212
San Juan, PR 00936-6212
TEL: 809/723-7110
FAX: 809/724-6374

Ms. Mildred Nichols, Director
Rhode Island OICC
22 Hayes Street - Room 133
Providence, RI 02908
TEL: 401/272-0830

Ms. Carol Kososki, Director
South Carolina OICC
1550 Gadsden Street
P. O. Box 995
Columbia, SC 29202
TEL: 803/737-2733
FAX: 803/737-2642

Mr. Phillip George, Director
South Dakota OICC
South Dakota Department of Labor
420 S. Roosevelt Street
P. O. Box 4730
Aberdeen, SD 57402-4730
TEL: 605/622-2314

Dr. Chrystal Partridge, Executive Director
Tennessee OICC
11th Floor Volunteer Plaza
500 James Robertson Parkway
Nashville, TN 37219
TEL: 615/741-6451
FAX: 615/741-3203

Mr. Richard Froeschle, Director
Texas OICC
Texas Employment Commission Building
12th and Trinity, Room 526T
Austin, TX 78778
TEL: 512/463-2399

Ms. Tammy Stewart, Director
Utah OICC
c/o Utah Department of Employment Security
P. O. Box 11249
140 East 300 South
Salt Lake City, UT 84147
TEL: 801/536-7806 or 7861
FAX: 801/533-2466

Mr. Tom Douse, Director
Vermont OICC
Green Mountain Drive
P. O. Box 488
Montpelier, VT 05601-0488
TEL: 802/229-0311

Ms. Dolores A. Esser, Executive Director
Virginia OICC/VA Employment Commission
703 E. Main Street
P. O. Box 1358
Richmond, VA 23211
TEL: 804/786-7496
FAX: 804/786-7844

Mr. Lee W. Eisenhauer, Coordinator
Virgin Islands OICC
P. O. Box 3359
St. Thomas, US VI 00801
TEL: 809/776-3700

Mr. A. T. Woodhouse, Director
Washington OICC
c/o Employment Security Dept.
P.O. Box 9046
Olympia, WA 98507-9046
TEL: 206/438-4803
FAX: 206/438-3215

Dr. George McGuire, Executive Director
West Virginia OICC
One Dunbar Plaza, Suite E
Dunbar, WV 25064
TEL: 304/293-5314
FAX: 304/766-7846

Ms. Janet Pugh, Acting Director
The Wisconsin OICC/Division of E&T Policy
201 East Washington Avenue
P. O. Box 7972
Madison, WI 53707
TEL: 608/266-8012
FAX: 608/267-0330

Mr. Michael E. Paris, Executive Director
Wyoming OICC
P. O. Box 2760
100 West Midwest
Casper, WY 82602
TEL: 307/235-3642

Appendix C

NOICC Staff

THE NOICC STAFF
2100 M Street, NW - Suite 156
Washington, DC 20037
202/653-2123

Juliette Lester, Executive Director
653-5665

Mary Alston, Management Services Assistant
653-5665

James Woods, Coordinator
Occupational Information Systems
653-5665

*Pamela Frugoli, OIS Specialist
653-5665

Harvey Ollis, OIS Specialist
653-5671

Rodney Slack, OIS Specialist
653-7680

Robert Rittle, IPA
653-7680

Billye Armstrong, Secretary
653-5665

Walton Webb, Coordinator
State & Interagency Network
653-5671

Kay Brawley, IPA
653-7680

Burton Carlson, OIS Specialist
653-5671

Betty Nicholson, Program Analyst
653-5671

Mary Sue Vickers, OIS Specialist
653-7680

Mary Williams, Secretary
653-5665

Mary Margaret Walker, Contractor
(301) 422-0466 {(301) 422-1160}

*Part-time - Tuesdays through Fridays

Numbers in { } brackets represent fax numbers

Appendix D

Directory of State-Based Career Information Delivery Systems

Alabama SOICC
Bell Building, Suite 400
207 Montgomery Street
Montgomery, AL 36130
TEL: 205/242-2990

Alaska Career Information System (AKCIS)
Department of Education
Office of Adult and Vocational Education
(OAVE)
Box F
Juneau, AK 99811
TEL: 907/465-4685
FAX: 907/465-3436

Occupational Information System of Arizona
P.O. Box 6123
Site Code 897J
Phoenix, AZ 85005
TEL: 602/542-3680
FAX: 602/542-6474

Arkansas Occupational and Educational
Information System
P.O. Box 2981
Little Rock, AR 72203
TEL: 501/682-1543
FAX: 501/682-2209

EUREKA
The California Career Information System
P.O. Box 647
Richmond, CA 94808-0647
TEL: 415/235-3883

Colorado Career Information system
3800 York Street, Unit B
Denver, CO 80205
TEL: 303/837-1000, Ext. 2136
FAX: 303/837-1000, Ext. 2135

Connecticut Information System (COIS)
ACES Computer Services
205 Skiff Street
Hamden, CT 06517
TEL: 203/288-1883
FAX: 203/287-8081

Delaware GIS
Educational Computing Services Division
Department of Public Instruction
Townsend Building, Federal and Lockerman
Streets
P.O. Box 1402
Dover, DE 19903
TEL: 302/739-3721

DC Guidance Information System
DC Occupational Information Coordinating
Committee
500 C Street, NW, Room 215
Washington, DC 20001
TEL: 202/639-1090
FAX: 202/639-1765

CHOICES
Bureau of Career Development
Department of Education
Florida Education Center
Tallahassee, FL 32399-0400
TEL: 904/488-0400
FAX: 904/487-3601

Georgia Career Information System
Georgia State University
Box 1028, University Plaza
Atlanta, GA 30303-3083
TEL: 404/651-3100

Career Kokua: The Hawaii Career
Information Delivery System
615 Piikoi Street, Suite 100
Honolulu, HI 96815
TEL: 808/548-5330
FAX: 808/5866-8633

Idaho Career Information System
Room 301, Len B. Jordan Building
650 W State Street
Boise, ID 83720
TEL: 208/334-3705
FAX: 208/334-5315

Illinois Career Information Delivery System
HORIZONS
217 East Monroe Street, Suite 203
Springfield, IL 62706
TEL: 217/785-0789
FAX: 217/785-6184

Career Information System of Iowa
Iowa Department of Education
Grimes State Office Building
Des Moines, IA 50319-0146
TEL: 515/281-5501

Kansas Careers
Room 304, Fairchild Hall
Kansas State University
Manhattan, KS 66506
TEL: 913/532-6540
FAX: 913/532-7304

Kentucky Career Information System (KCIS)
KOICC
275 E Main Street - 2 Center
Frankfort, KY 40621-0001
TEL: 502/564-4258

Louisiana CHOICES
Louisiana State Occupational Information
Coordinating
P.O. Box 94094
Baton Rouge, LA 70804
TEL: 504/342-5151

Maine Career Information Delivery System
Maine Occupational Information
Coordinating Committee
State house Station #71
Augusta, ME 04333
TEL: 207/289-2331

VISIONS
The Maryland Career Information Delivery
System
1100 North Eutaw Street, Room 205
Baltimore, MD 21201
TEL: 301/333-5478

Michigan Occupational Information System
(MOIS)
Michigan Department of Education
Vocational-Technical Education Service
P.O. Box 30009
Lansing, MI 48909
TEL: 517/373-0815
FAX: 517/373-2537

Minnesota Career Information System
522 Capitol Square Building
550 Cedar Street
St. Paul, MN 55101
TEL: 612/296-3653
FAX: 612/296-3272

Mississippi CHOICES
P.O. Box 849, Suite 1005
Jackson, MS 39205
TEL: 601/359-3412
FAX: 601/359-2832

Missouri CHOICES
MOICC
421 E Dunklin Street
Jefferson City, MO 65101
TEL: 314/751-3800

Missouri VIEW Program
15875 New Halls Ferry
Florisant, MO 63031
TEL: 314/831-7100

Montana Career Information System
1412 1/2 Eighth Avenue
Helena, MT 59620
TEL: 406/444-1444

Nebraska Career Information System
421 Nebraska Hall
University of Nebraska
Lincoln, NE 68588-0552
TEL: 402/472-2570
FAX: 402/472-5907

Nevada Career Information System
1923 N Carson St, Suite 211
Carson City, NV 89710
TEL: 702/885-4577

New Jersey Career Information Delivery
System
Department of Labor Building
CN 056, Room 1008
Trenton, NJ 08625
TEL: 609/292-2626
FAX: 609/292-6692

New Mexico Career Information System
College of Education, Room 111
University of New Mexico
Albuquerque, NM 87131
TEL: 505/277-5137

MetroGuide
The New York City Career Information
System
New York City Board of Education
347 Baltic Street
Brooklyn, NY 11201
TEL: 718/935-4155
FAX: 718/935-4178

North Carolina Careers
P.O. Box 27625
1311 St. Mary's Street
Raleigh, NC 27611
TEL: 919/733-6700
FAX: 919/733-2310

North Dakota CHOICES
P.O. Box 1537
Bismarck, ND 58502-1537
TEL: 701/224-2733

Ohio Career Information System
Ohio Departments Building, Room 908
65 S Front Street
Columbus, OH 43266-0308
TEL: 614/644-6771
FAX: 614/644-5702

Oklahoma Career Search
1500 West Seventh Avenue
Stillwater, OK 74074
TEL: 405/377-2000, Ext. 159
FAX: 405/377-9861

Oregon Career Information System
18787 Agate Street
Eugene, OR 97403-5214
TEL: 503/346-3872
FAX: 503/346-5890

Pennsylvania Careers
1224 Labor and Industry Building
Seventh and Forster Streets
Harrisburg, PA 17120
TEL: 717/787-8646
FAX: 717/772-2168

OPCIONES
P.O. Box 366212
San Juan, Puerto Rico
00936-6212
TEL: 809/723-7110

Rhode Island Career Information Delivery
System
(RICIDS)
22 Hayes Street
Providence, RI 02908
TEL: 401/272-0830

South Carolina Occupational Information
System (SCOIS)
1550 Gadsden Street - P.O. Box 995
Columbia, SC 29202
TEL: 803/7377=2733
FAX: 803/737-2642

South Dakota Career Information Delivery
System
South Dakota Department of Labor
Labor Market Information Center
Box 4730
Aberdeen, SD 57402-4730
TEL: 605/622-2314
FAX: 605/622-2322

INFOE
(Information Needed For Occupational Entry)
University of Tennessee
438 Claxton Addition
Knoxville, TN 37996-3400
TEL: 615/974-2574
FAX: 615/974-2725

Texas CIDS
Texas SOICC
TEC Building, Room 526T
15th and Congress Avenue
Austin, TX 78778
TEL: 512/463-2399
FAX: 512/463-2220

Utah Career Information Delivery System
Utah SOICC
174 Social Hall Avenue
Salt Lake City, UT 84147
TEL: 8001/533-2028
FAX: 801/533-2466

Vermont OIS/CIDS
VOICC
P.O. Box 488
Montpelier, VT 05601
TEL: 802/229-0311
FAX: 802/223-0750

Virginia VIEW
Virginia State Career Information Delivery
System
Virginia Tech, 205 W Roanoke Street
Blacksburg, VA 24061-0527
TEL: 703/231-7571

WOIS/The Career Information System
1415 Harrison Avenue NW, Suite 201
Olympia, WA 98502
TEL: 206/754-8222

West Virginia CIDS
One Dunbar Plaza, Suite E
Dunbar, WV 25064
TEL: 304/348-0061
FAX: 304/293-6661

Wisconsin Career Information System
University of Wisconsin - Madison
1025 West Johnson Street, Room 964
Madison, WI 53706
TEL: 608/263-2725
FAX: 608/262-9197

Wyoming Career Information System
Box 3808, University Station
University of Wyoming
Laramie, WY 82071
TEL: 307/766-6533

Appendix E

National Career Development Guidelines

Career Development Competencies by Area and Level

	Elementary	Middle/Junior High School	High School	Adult
Self- Knowledge				
	Knowledge of the importance of self-concept.	Knowledge of the influence of a positive self-concept.	Understanding the influence of a positive self-concept.	Skills to maintain a positive self-concept.
	Skills to interact with others.	Skills to interact with others.	Skills to interact positively with others.	Skills to maintain effective behaviors.
	Awareness of the importance of growth and change.	Knowledge of the importance of growth and change.	Understanding the impact of growth and development.	Understanding developmental changes and transitions.
Educational and Occupational Exploration				
	Awareness of the benefits of educational achievement.	Knowledge of the benefits of educational achievement to career opportunities.	Understanding the relationship between educational achievement and career planning.	Skills to enter and participate in education and training.
	Awareness of the relationship between work and learning.	Understanding the relationship between work and learning.	Understanding the need for positive attitudes toward work and learning.	Skills to participate in work and life-long learning.
	Skills to understand, and use career information.	Skills to locate, understand, and use career information.	Skills to locate, evaluate, and interpret career information.	Skills to locate, evaluate, and interpret career information.
	Awareness of the importance of personal responsibility and good work habits.	Knowledge of skills necessary to seek and obtain jobs.	Skills to prepare to seek, obtain, maintain, and change jobs.	Skills to prepare to seek, obtain, maintain, and change jobs.
	Awareness of how work relates to the needs and functions of society.	Understanding how work relates to the needs and functions of the economy and society.	Understanding how societal needs and functions influence the nature and structure of work.	Understanding how the needs and functions of society influence the nature and structure of work.
Career Planning				
	Understanding how to make decisions.	Skills to make decisions.	Skills to make decisions.	Skills to make decisions.
	Awareness of the interrelationship of life roles.	Knowledge of the interrelationship of life roles.	Understanding the interrelationship of life roles.	Understanding the impact of work on individual and family life.
	Awareness of different occupations and changing male/female roles.	Knowledge of different occupations and changing male/female roles.	Understanding the continuous changes in male/female roles.	Understanding the continuing changes in male/female roles.
	Awareness of the career planning process.	Understanding the process of career planning.	Skills in career planning.	Skills to make career transitions.

National Occupational Information Coordinating Committee • Suite 156, 2100 M Street, N.W., Washington, D.C. 20037 • (202) 653-5665

National Career Development Guidelines

Counseling

Knowledge of developmental issues individuals address throughout the life span.
Knowledge of counseling and career development theories and techniques.
Knowledge of decision-making and transition models.
Knowledge of role relationships to facilitate personal, family, and career development.
Knowledge of different cultures to interact effectively with all populations.
Skills to build productive relationships with counselees.
Skills to use appropriate individual and group counseling techniques to assist individuals with career decisions and career development concerns.
Skills to assist individuals in identifying influencing factors in career decision making, such as family, friends, educational opportunities, and finances.
Skills to assist individuals in changing biased attitudes that stereotype others by gender, race, age, and culture.
Skills to assist individuals in understanding the relationship between interpersonal skills and success in the workplace.
Skills to assist individuals in setting goals and identifying strategies for reaching goals.
Skills to assist individuals in continually reassessing their goals, values, interests, and career decisions.
Skills to assist individuals in preparing for multiple roles throughout their lives.

Information

Knowledge of changes taking place in the economy, society, and job market.
Knowledge of education, training, employment trends, labor market, and career resources.
Knowledge of basic concepts related to career counseling such as career development, career progression, and career patterns.
Knowledge of the changing gender roles and how these impact on work, family, and leisure.
Knowledge of employment information and career planning materials.
Knowledge of employment-related requirements such as labor laws, licensing, credentialing, and certification.
Knowledge of state and local referral services or agencies for job, financial, social, and personal service.
Knowledge of federal and state legislation that may influence career development programs.
Skills to use career development resources and techniques designed for specific groups.
Skills to use computer-based career information systems.

Individual and Group Assessment

Knowledge of assessment techniques and measures of skills, abilities, aptitudes, interests, values, and personalities.
Skills to identify assessment resources appropriate for specific situations and populations.
Skills to evaluate assessment resources and techniques related so that their validity, reliability, and relationships to race, gender, age, and ethnicity can be determined.
Skills to administer, interpret, and personalize assessment data in relation to the career development needs of the individual.

Management and Administration

Knowledge of program designs that can be used in organizing career development programs.

Knowledge of needs assessment techniques and practices.

Knowledge of management concepts, leadership styles, and techniques to implement change.

Skills to assess the effectiveness of career development programs.

Skills to identify staff competencies for effective career development programs.

Skills to prepare proposals, budgets, and timelines for career development programs.

Skills to identify, develop, and use record keeping methods.

Skills to design, conduct, analyze, and report the assessment of individual and program outcomes.

Implementation

Knowledge of program adoption and planned change strategies.

Knowledge of barriers affecting the implementation of career development programs.

Skills to implement individual and group programs in a variety of areas such as assessment decision making, job seeking, career information and career counseling.

Skills to implement public relations efforts which promote career development activities and services.

Skills to establish linkages with community-based organizations.

Consultation

Knowledge of consulting strategies and consulting models.

Skills to assist staff in understanding how to incorporate career development concepts into their offerings to program participants.

Skills to consult with influential parties such as employers, community groups and the general public.

Skills to convey program goals and achievements to legislators, professional groups, and other key leaders.

Specific Populations

Knowledge of differing cultural values and their relationship to work values.

Knowledge of unique career planning needs of minorities, women, the handicapped, and older persons.

Knowledge of alternative approaches to career planning needs for individuals with specific needs.

Skills to identify community resources and establish linkages to assist adults with specific needs.

Skills to find appropriate methods or resources to communicate with limited English proficient individuals.

Appendix F

State Guidance Supervisors

Mr. Jimmy Jacobs
Coordinator
Counseling & Career Guidance
State Office Bldg.
1020 Monticello Ct.
Montgomery. AL 36117

Ms. Naomi K. Stockdale
Program Manager
Adult & Vocational Education
Alaska Department of Education
P. O. Box F, Goldbelt Bldg.
Juneau. AK 99811-0500

Ms. Brenda Epati-Tanoi
Director
Guidance & Counseling
Department of Education
Pago Pago, American Samoa 96799

Ms. Emilia Sabado Le'i
Counselor/VA Coordinator
American Samoa Community College
Mapusaga Campus
P. O. Box 2609
Pago Pago, American Samoa 96799

Dr. Tina Ammon
Guidance Specialist
Arizona Department of Education
1535 W. Jefferson St.
Phoenix. AZ 85007

Dr. Lynda D. Hawkins
Coordinator
Guidance Services/Career Education
Arkansas Department of Education
#4 Capitol Mall, Room 302-B
Little Rock, AR 72201-1071

Mr. J. B. Robertson
Career Education Supervisor
Arkansas Department of Education
#4 Capitol Mall, Room 304-B
Little Rock, AR 72201-1071

Dr. Bill Anderson
Director. Community Colleges
Chancellor's Office
1107 9th St.
Sacramento, CA 95814

Dr. Tom Bauer
Adult Education
California Department of Education
P. O. Box 944272
Sacramento, CA 94244-2720

Mr. Paul N. Peters
Supervisor
Career Development/Guidance
California Department of Education
721 Capitol Mall
Sacramento, CA 95814

Ms. Martelle Chapital
Program Manager
Guidance, Corrections & CBOs
Occupational Education System
1391 N. Speer Blvd., Suite 600
Denver. CO 80204

Mr. Fermin Kebekol
Vocational Education Counselor
Department of Education
Marianas High School
CNMI, Saipan CM 96950

Mr. Joaquin Manglona
Vocational Education Counselor
Department of Education
Rota High School
CNMI. Rota CM 96951

Mr. Richard C. Wilson
Consultant
Career Guidance & Counseling
Bureau of Vocational Education
25 Industrial Park Rd.
Middletown. CT 06457

Mr. Clifton Hutton
State Supervisor of Guidance
  & Pupil Personnel Instruction
Department of Public Instruction
Townsend Bldg., Box 1402
Dover, DE 19903

Dr. Dorothy E. Jenkins
Director, Guidance & Counseling
D.C. Public Schools
415 12th St., NW, Suite 906
Washington, DC 20004

Mr. Dale Ake
Student Services Section
Center for Career Development
Department of Education
Knott Bldg.
Tallahassee. FL 32301

Dr. Margaret Ferguson
Director, Career Development
Vocational, Adult & Community Ed.
Knott Bldg., 325 Gaines St.
Tallahassee, FL 32316

Dr. James C. Conkwright
Director of Program Development
   and Student Support
Georgia Department of Education
1766 Twin Towers East
Atlanta, GA 30334

Mr. O. C. Hill
Coordinator, Guidance & Counseling
Student Support Services
1852 Twin Towers East
Atlanta, GA 30334

Mr. Jack L. Neuber
Chairman, Counseling Dept.
Guam Community College
P. O. Box 23069
Main Postal Facility
Guam, Mariana Islands 96921

Mr. Richard P. Stoicovy
Student Services Division
Guam Community College
P. O. Box 23069
Main Postal Facility
Guam, Mariana Islands 96921

Mr. Jay Titus
Counseling Department
Student Services Division
Guam Community College
P. O. Box 23069
Main Postal Facility
Guam, Mariana Islands 96921

Guidance Specialist
Occupational Development
   & Student Services Branch
State Department of Education
941 Hind Iuka Dr.
Honolulu, HI 96821

Mr. Jim Baxter
Vocational Guidance Supervisor
Len B. Jordan Bldg.
650 W. State St.
Boise, ID 83720

Ms. Sally Keister
Coordinator
Guidance/Assessment Evaluation
Department of Education
650 W. State St.
Boise, ID 83720

Mr. Lynn Troute
Education Administrator
Vocational/Education Program
100 N. First St.
Springfield, IL 62777

Ms. Peggy O'Malley
State Coordinator of Research,
   Consultation, Coordination,
   and Articulation
Indiana Commission on Voc-Tech Ed.
325 W. Washington St.
Indianapolis, IN 46204

Mr. Edward L. Ranney
Consultant, Guidance Services
Bureau of Instruction & Curriculum
Grimes State Office Bldg.
Des Moines, IA 50319-0146

L. Craford and M. Harrison
Consultants
JTPA Services
Iowa Department of Education
Grimes State Office Bldg.
Des Moines, IA 50319

Ms. Frayna G. Scrinopskie
Guidance & Counseling Specialist
Division of Community College
   and Vocational Education
120 E. Tenth St.
Topeka, KS 66612-1103

Mr. Lou Perry
Program Manager
Student Services Branch
Office of Vocational Education
2138 Capital Plaza Tower
Frankfort, KY 40601

Mr. William Gary Steinhilber
Assistant Director
Division of Student Services
Kentucky Department of Education
1704 Capital Plaza Tower
Frankfort, KY 40601

Mr. Barry Solar
Section Administrator
Guidance and Counseling
Bureau of Student Services
P. O. Box 94064
Baton Rouge, LA 70804-9064

Ms. Thelma Hughes
Education Program Manager
Department of Education
P. O. Box 94064
Baton Rouge, LA 70804-9064

Ms. Helen Beesley
Vocational & Career Guidance
State Department of Education
  and Cultural Services
State House Station 23
Augusta, ME 04333

Ms. Nancy S. Perry
Guidance Consultant
State Department of Education
  and Cultural Services
State House Station 23
Augusta, ME 04333

Mr. Richard Scott
Specialist in Guidance
Maryland Department of Education
200 W. Baltimore St.
Baltimore, MD 21201

Dr. Joseph P. DeSantis
Specialist
Postsecondary & Adult Education
Maryland Department of Education
200 W. Baltimore St.
Baltimore, MD 21201

Mr. Charles Brovelli
Coordinator of Career Guidance
Massachusetts Department of Education
1385 Hancock St.
Quincy, MA 02169

Ms. Gertrude Bonaparte
Consultant, Career Guidance
Vocational-Technical Education
  Services
Michigan Department of Education
P. O. Box 30009
Lansing, MI 48909

Mr. Steve Frantz
Supervisor
Student Support Services
Vocational-Technical Education
550 Cedar St.
St. Paul, MN 55101

Ms. Diane Miller
Learner Support System
State Department of Education
550 Cedar St., Suite 901
St. Paul, MN 55101

Mr. Leroy Levy
State Supervisor of Guidance
State Department of Education
P. O. Box 771
Jackson, MS 39205

Mr. Robert Larivee
Director
Vocational Special Needs & Guidance
Elementary & Secondary Education
P. O. Box 480
Jefferson City, MO 65102

Mr. Marion Starr
Assistant Director
Vocational Special Needs
  & Guidance Services
Elementary & Secondary Education
P. O. Box 480
Jefferson City, MO 65102

Ms. Judy Birch
Guidance Specialist
Montana VIEW
State Capitol
Helena, MT 59620

Dr. Robert Ruthemeyer
Adult Education Specialist
Office of Public Instruction
State Capitol
Helena, MT 59620

Dr. Evelyn Lavaty
Director, Career Guidance
Department of Education
P. O. Box 94987
Lincoln, NB 68509

Dr. Carole Gribble
Occupational Guidance Consultant
Department of Education
400 W. King St.
Carson City, NV 89710

Dr. James Carr
Consultant, Vocational Guidance
State Department of Education
101 Pleasant St.
Concord, NH 03301-3860

Ms. Ann DeAngelo
Vocational Guidance & Counseling
State Department of Education
225 W. State St., CN 500
Trenton, NJ 08625

Mr. Joseph Ryczkowski
Vocational Guidance & Counseling
State Department of Education
225 W. State St., CN 500
Trenton, NJ 08625

Ms. Pat Putnam
Supervisor, Special Needs
Vocational Education
State Department of Education
Santa Fe, NM 87501

Ms. Nancy Mandell
General Guidance
Elementary & Secondary Education
Department of Education
Santa Fe, NM 87501

Dr. Richard D. Jones
Chief, Bureau of Occupational
  Education Program Development
99 Washington Ave., Room 1623
Albany, NY 12234

Ms. Lorraine M. Davis
Industry/Education Coordination
Department of Public Instruction
540 Education Bldg.
Raleigh, NC 27603-1712

Mr. J. David Edwards
Chief Consultant, Vocational Education
Department of Public Instruction
539 Education Bldg.
Raleigh, NC 27603-1712

Mr. Dennis Steele
Supervisor, Vocational Guidance
State Capitol Bldg., 15th Floor
Bismarck, ND 58505

Mr. Gaylynn L. Becker
Coordinator, Counseling & Testing
Department of Public Instruction
State Capitol Bldg., 9th Floor
600 E. Boulevard Ave.
Bismarck, ND 58505-0440

Mr. Rich Hauck
Director, Counseling Center
State School of Science
Wahpeton, ND 58075

Ms. Karen P. Heath
Assistant Director
Career Development Services
Ohio Department of Education
65 S. Front St., Room 908
Columbus, OH 43215

Dr. Edwin Whitfield
Associate Director
Guidance & Testing Section
Division of Education Services
Ohio Department of Education
65 S. Front St.
Columbus, OH 43215

Ms. Belinda McCharen
Coordinator, Vocational Guidance
Department of Vocational and
  Technical Education
1500 W. Seventh Ave.
Stillwater, OK 74074-4364

Dr. Don Perkins
Student Services Specialist
Oregon Department of Education
700 Pringle Parkway, SE
Salem, OR 97310

Dr. Joan Stoddard
Coordinator, Program Planning
Division of Vocational-Technical
  Education
Oregon Department of Education
Salem, OR 97310

Mr. Bill Lesh
Guidance Specialist
Oregon Department of Education
700 Pringle Pkwy., SE
Salem, OR 97310

Ms. Marensia E. Edward
Counselor
Micronesian Occupational College
P. O. Box 9
Koror, Palau 96940

Ms. Sarita De Carlo
Supervisor of Guidance
Division of Student Services
Department of Education
333 Market St.
Harrisburg, PA 17104

Ms. Margie Burgos
Director, Guidance Programs
Department of Education
P. O. Box 759
Hato Rey, PR 00919

Dr. Arthur Tartaglione
Career Education Coordinator
Bureau of Vocational and Adult
  Education
Department of Education
22 Hayes St.
Providence, RI 02908

Ms. Lynne Hufziger
Consultant, Guidance & Career
  Education
Department of Education
Rutledge Bldg., Room 912-E
Columbia, SC 29201

Mr. E. Jimmy Smith
Director, Adult Education
Rutledge Bldg., Room 209-A
1429 Senate St.
Columbia, SC 29201

Mr. Ken Kompelien
Vocational Guidance Coordinator
South Dakota Curriculum Center
205 W. Dakota Ave.
Pierre, SD 57501

Mr. Sam McClanahan
Director, Program Services
Vocational-Technical Education
Cordell Hull Bldg., Room 200
Nashville, TN 37217

Ms. Sylvia J. Clark
Occupational Education Specialist
Texas Education Agency
1701 N. Congress Ave.
Austin, TX 78701

Dr. Ruben Dayrit
Supervisor
State Vocational Education
Ponape State
Kolonia, Ponape 96941

Dr. Lynn Jensen
Specialist
Vocational Guidance and Counseling
250 E. South
Salt Lake City, UT 84111

Ms. Elizabeth Ducolon
Consultant, Vocational Guidance
State Department of Education
120 State St.
Montpelier, VT 05602

Ms. Ida White
State Coordinator
Student Services & Programs
44-46 Kongens Gade
St. Thomas, VI 00802

Ms. Rebecca Dedmond
Career Education Specialist
Virginia Department of Education
P. O. Box 6Q
Richmond, VA 23216

Mr. Jay Wood, Administrator
Program Development Section
Division of Vocational-Technical
  and Adult Education
Old Capitol Bldg., M/S FG-11
Olympia, WA 98504

Ms. Patricia Hindman
Coordinator, Vocational Education
State Board for Community
  College Education
319 7th Ave.
Olympia, WA 98504

Ms. Terrie Wilson
Acting Director
Office of Education Support
Department of Education
State Office Bldg.
Charleston, WV 25305

Mr. Lorran C. Celley
Consultant, Student Services
Vocational, Technical & Adult Education
310 Price Place
P. O. Box 7874
Madison, WI 53707

Supervisor
Vocational Guidance/Career Education
Department of Public Instruction
Bureau of Pupil Services
125 S. Webster St.
Madison, WI 53707

Mr. Richard Granum
Pupil Services Consultant
Guidance, Counseling & Placement
State Department of Education
Cheyenne, WY 82002

Appendix G

Guidelines for the Use of Computer-Based Career Information and Guidance Systems

Guidelines for the Use of Computer-Based Career Information and Guidance Systems

Edited by:
David Caulum, Ph.D.
Roger Lambert, Ph.D.

Association of Computer-Based Systems for Career Information

ACSCI Clearinghouse
1787 Agate Street
Eugene, OR 97403

Table of Contents

Preface

As with all tools, the effectiveness of computer-based career information and/or guidance systems depends on the quality of the product. Since adherence to professional standards offers the best assurance of quality, ACSCI has put major effort into developing, refining, and disseminating its *Handbook of Standards for Computer-Based Career Information Systems*. These standards have become the accepted guide to quality for developers and operators of such systems. The standards also help the agencies that use these systems assess their quality.

The effectiveness of these systems also depends, however, on the way they are used in a given setting. Effective use is largely a responsibility of the counselors and others who assist students and clients at a user site. The guidelines in this publication are intended to help these "mediators" achieve the best possible implementation and utilization of a computer-based career information and/or guidance system. The guidelines provide criteria for installing a system in a setting and for evaluating the operation of a facility having a system in place. Just as ACSCI's *Handbook of Standards* serves to define quality in the product of a computer-based system, the guidelines presented here help define quality in the use of the system.

ACSCI assigned development of these guidelines to its Technical Assistance and Training Committee. As co-chairs of that committee, we drew on our ten-year experience in extending the services of the Wisconsin Career Information System to more than 500 sites. Without the assistance of others, however, we could not have done the job. We wish to acknowledge with gratitude the important contributions of the following individuals:

Sally Hawker, Information Development Manager, Illinois Occupational Information Coordinating Committee, Springfield, IL

Jerry Henning, Consultant, Wisconsin Department of Public Instruction, Madison, WI

Dale Herbers, Director of Guidance, Verona High School, Verona, WI

Susan Horowitz, Director, Training & Educational Data Service, Indianapolis, IN

Helena Kennedy, Information Analyst, Washington Occupational Information System, Olympia, WA

Carol Kososki, Director, South Carolina Occupational Information System, Columbia, SC

Marilyn Maze, Director, EUREKA, The California Career Information System, Richmond, CA

Joseph McGarvey, Director, Michigan Occupational Information System, Lansing, MI

Elton Mendenhall, Director, Nebraska Career Information System, Lincoln, NE

Deborah Perlmutter, Director, MetroGuide, New York City Board of Education, Brooklyn, NY

Jan Staggs, Executive Director, Illinois Occupational Information Coordinating Committee, Springfield, IL

Patricia Waldren, Specialist, Wisconsin Career Information System, Madison, WI

Walton Webb, National Occupational Information Coordinating Committee, Washington, DC

Becki Whitaker, Specialist, Indiana Cooperative Library Services Authority, Indianapolis, IN

—David Caulum, Coordinator
—Roger Lambert, Director
 Wisconsin Career Information System
 Madison, WI

 Co-Chairs, ACSCI Technical Assistance
 and Training Committee

Introduction

Any computer-based career information and/or guidance system is most effective when its use is fully integrated with the counseling and guidance or career-development program which it serves. The guidelines presented in this publication promote such integration and foster the most effective and efficient use, in a wide variety of settings, of this important tool.

People are crucial to the good use of a computer-based system. They are essential to the total integration of the system with related activities at the site and external to the site. User site personnel, however, have need for different levels of knowledge about the system, commensurate with their roles in using it. For purposes of the guidelines presented in the following sections, user site personnel can be grouped into three categories defined by their required level of knowledge about the system:

1. Counseling and Information Staff
Level of Knowledge: Facilitation

This group includes all counselors in a school or college counseling department, all librarians in a reference department, all job service counselors in job service agencies, all rehabilitation counselors in vocational rehabilitation facilities, and any other counselors involved in direct contact with students or clients. Information assistants, such as school aides and library clerks, may be included. The "facilitation" level of knowledge includes hands-on application, search experience, and understanding the use of all aspects of the computer-based system.

In addition, at each user site there is a key staff member who coordinates the use of the system at that site. This "site coordinator" requires the same "facilitation" level of knowledge but has the added responsibility of maintaining contact with system operator personnel to provide feedback on system usage, to report any related problems, and to be aware of pending system changes.

2. Incidental Staff Users
Level of Knowledge: Orientation

This group includes teachers in a social studies department, parent volunteers, librarians in a circulation department, administrative or clerical staff in a job service agency, and others who may assist students or clients. The "orientation" level of knowledge includes hands-on experience with the use of selected aspects of the computer-based system.

3. Administrators, Students, Clients, and Others
Level of Knowledge: Awareness

Examples of this diverse group include the principal of a high school, faculty at a college, parents of student users, and users (students or clients). The "awareness" level of knowledge consists of knowing the purpose of the system, where it is located, and how to access it.

Guidelines for the Use of Computer-Based Career Information and Guidance Systems provides a voluntary means for schools and agencies using these systems to declare that they subscribe to nationally recognized standards of quality in their use. This publication also provides a model for self-assessment that can be used in periodic reviews of the delivery of service. Ultimately, such self-assessment combined with regular interaction with system operators leads to improved products.

In summary, ACSCI encourages the use of the guidelines in this publication for three purposes:

- To provide assistance in the implementation and utilization of a computer-based system, in order to maximize benefits for the students and clients who are the end users.

- To provide assistance in assessing the effectiveness of the implementation and utilization of a computer-based system.

- To assure constituencies and the general public that resources devoted to computer-based systems are invested under guidelines that insure their most efficient and effective use.

The guidelines are grouped under seven headings and numbered accordingly, from 1.1 to 7.3. The questions that follow most of the numbered statements are designed to test the extent to which those guidelines are being observed.

Theory and Practice

Computer-based career information and guidance systems reflect various career-development theories. From these theories, certain goals for the use of the systems can be derived. Goals that can be achieved through the use of a particular system should be compatible with the career-development goals of the user site. The following guidelines should apply:

GUIDELINE 1.1: **Each user site should adopt, adapt, or otherwise define its theory of career development.**

- How does the career-choice process fit into a student's or client's life?

- What are the steps in career decision-making?

- What are the characteristics of a vocationally mature student or client?

GUIDELINE 1.2: **Each user site should define a plan to facilitate the career-development process which will meet the needs of its students or clients.**

- At what point in their life/career development are most students or clients?

- At what point in the career-choice process are most students or clients when they are likely to use the systems? What are the major variations?

- What special needs do students or clients have that should be met by the user site? What is the plan to meet these special needs?

GUIDELINE 1.3: **The goals of the computer-based system should be compatible with the theory to which the user site subscribes.**

- What are the goals of the computer-based system?

- How do these system goals fit into the goals of the user site?

- Are there areas of conflict and how will they be resolved?

GUIDELINE 1.4: **The process and content of the computer-based system should fit into the career-development plan of the user site.**

- Which steps in the career-development process are satisfied by the computer-based system?

- Which steps are only partially met by the computer-based system and require further staff attention? Will this help be available?

- How will the computer-based system be integrated into the non-computer part of the career-planning process?

Process

Each user site should integrate use of the computer-based system into ongoing activities. The following guidelines should apply:

GUIDELINE 2.1: **Each user site should develop program goals for integrating use of the computer-based system into existing programs to meet student or client needs.**

- Do your goals adequately meet the needs of each student or client population?

- Are the goals realistic for your school or agency?

- Does the management support these goals? Are they consistent with the philosophy of the administrators?

- Do staff support these goals?

GUIDELINE 2.2: **Each user site should develop objectives to implement each of the goals.**

- Does each objective have a specified time frame?

- Are the objectives measurable?

- Can these objectives be achieved?

- Can expected student/client outcomes be identified?

- Are these objectives shared by staff?

GUIDELINE 2.3: **Each user site should develop a variety of activities to implement each of the objectives.**

- Do the activities carry out the objectives?

- Do the activities take into consideration the age and abilities of the target population?

- Are the activities implemented throughout the school or department?

- Are time, cost, and physical facilities provided for?

- Have all staff been appropriately trained to implement these activities?

- Is a key staff member (the site coordinator) responsible for carrying out each of these activities?

GUIDELINE 2.4: **The management team should recognize the importance of career planning in the context of the entire program and should monitor and evaluate its progress.**

- Is a key staff member responsable for this program?

- Are the funds and facilities adequate?

- Is the system readily accessible?

- Is regular maintenance provided?

GUIDELINE 2.5: **Any student or client should be oriented to the system prior to usage and should be given follow-up assistance after use.**

- Does this individual need to use the system?

- What portions of the system should be used by this individual?

- What outcomes are expected from this individual's use of the system?

- What other resources would be of help to this user? In what ways is the user directed to them?

User Needs

It is important to identify the variety of student or client needs so that staff can determine which needs can best be met by the computer-based system and which needs require other types of intervention. The following guidelines should apply:

GUIDELINE 3.1: **Agencies should identify client populations.**

- Which major groups are to be served?

- How do they differ?

GUIDELINE 3.2: **The career-planning needs of each client population should be determined.**

- What are the career-planning needs of each group?

- What personal resources do students or clients have for meeting their own needs? What do they need, and can they supply it themselves?

- What barriers do they face?

GUIDELINE 3.3: **The career-planning needs of students or clients should be met by the counseling program by using the computer-based system as an integral tool.**

- For each need, is it met by the computer-based system?

- For each need, will a counselor or aide assist to assure that the user's need is met?

- For each need, if it is not met by the computer-based system and staff, what other resources will be used to meet the need?

System Site Management

Site management of a computer-based system is critical to its effective use. A management plan for administration and staffing at the local site should be developed and reviewed annually. The management plan should cover all aspects of system use: access, long-term commitment of resources, physical environment, staff, integration into the total program, public relations, and evaluation. The plan must begin with obtaining sufficient resources to operate and maintain the system over a number of years. The following guidelines should be considered in developing the plan:

GUIDELINE 4.1: **All students or clients should have an opportunity to use the system.**

- Is the system regularly available during enough working hours to meet the needs of users?

- Are trained staff available to help individuals in making efficient use of the system?

- Have schedules been developed to facilitate efficient and equitable access to the system, based on the needs of the target population and the equipment available?

GUIDELINE 4.2: **The organization should make a long-term commitment to providing the system's service by including in the annual budget adequate funds to handle staff, system fees, hardware, and necessary supplies.**

- Are resources sufficient to cover such needs as paper, user materials, subscriber fees, and telephone lines (if required)?

- Are resources sufficient to cover purchase and maintenance of equipment, as well as acquisition and maintenance of facilities?

- Are resources sufficient to provide staff with training and in-service opportunities, including expansion and new applications?

GUIDELINE 4.3: **Site management should be involved in the evaluation of the system.**

- Is system use reviewed, using criteria such as numbers of users, value to clients, accessibility, and usefulness of information?

GUIDELINE 4.4: **Site management should be involved with promotional activities at the site and in the local community.**

- Is information on system availability shared with the general community, the professional community, the business community, labor, and specific target groups such as the handicapped and the economically disadvantaged?

- Is the system promoted through local news media?

- Is staff available to inform business groups, service clubs, and other community organizations of the system's use, functions, and availability?

- Do key staff members keep clients and colleagues informed regarding system use, functions, and availability?

GUIDELINE 4.5: **The system should be regularly updated, based on releases from the system operator.**

- Does site management keep the system operator informed of key personnel changes?

- Is there an established procedure for the site coordinator to inform the system operator of problems with the system or suggestions for changes?

- Are there procedures for users to inform the site coordinator of problems with the system or site service?

- Are outdated materials destroyed or returned to the system operator to assure that only the most up-to-date material is available to users?

GUIDELINE 4.6: **Management should insure that site coordinators receive periodic training from the system operator and that all staff receive "in-house" training in use of the system each year.**

- Are there adequate budget and release time to allow site coordinators to attend training provided by the system operator at least once per year?

- Are new staff trained in using the system within a reasonable time of being hired?

- Are continuing staff regularly updated on system changes when they occur, and are they provided training opportunities?

Physical Environment

The physical environment of the user site has an important role in the effective use of a computer-based system. Equipment must be readily accessible and available to the user, otherwise the system may not be used to the fullest extent possible. The following guidelines should apply:

GUIDELINE 5.1: **The facilities should have ample and accessible space.**

- Is the space adequate in terms of such features as comfort, temperature level, non-glare lighting, electrical outlets, telephone lines, minimal noise and distraction, privacy when needed, and unobtrusive printing capability?

- Is the space open when the client or student is available? Is the space easily identifiable, with good directions?

GUIDELINE 5.2: **The availability of computer equipment is essential to the use made of computer-based systems.**

- Is the equipment in working order, and are there annual maintenance checkups?

- Is there sufficient, workable hardware to serve the needs of clients or students, including those with special needs?

- Is the equipment easily accessible to all staff and to all potential users?

- Is the equipment accompanied by adequate instructions on use, appropriate user materials, and instructions on repair and technical assistance?

- Does the equipment complement the needs of the site—that is, does it have a permanently accessible place within the office or classroom, or does it take advantage of portable options?

- Does the microcomputer or computer terminal have printing capability?

- Does equipment acquisition, maintenance, and repair keep up with technical advances?

- Is the equipment placed in high-traffic areas such as the counseling center, library, and other areas where clients or students are served directly?

Personnel

Depending on their roles in using the system, site personnel have need for different levels of knowledge about the system (see Introduction). There is also need for at least one site coordinator who has both a "facilitation" level of knowledge and special insights derived from the system operator regarding nuances of information interpretation, idiosyncrasies of access and usage, and future system design plans. Guidelines by level of training and role are as follows:

GUIDELINE 6.1: **Staff who are regularly involved with using the system should have thorough knowledge of its operation, theoretical process, and practical interpretation (a "facilitation" level of knowledge).**

- Do staff members know how the system operates, how the system can be used to retrieve information to meet student or client needs, how to help users interpret the results, and how the system interacts with other information sources?

- Have all staff members participated in initial training sessions that include hands-on practice during the session and practice time after completion of training?

- Do staff members attend periodic follow-up sessions—whether presented in-house or by system operators—on advanced techniques, new system protocols, and updates?

GUIDELINE 6.2: **Each site should have at least one site coordinator. This person must have a special knowledge of the system through training offered by the system operator and needs to maintain a liaison contact with the system operator.**

- Has one or, in a large facility, more than one staff member been assigned the role of site coordinator?

- Does the site coordinator keep up-to-date on the system and regularly attend training sessions offered by the system operator?

- Does the site coordinator serve as an effective liaison person with the system operator, bringing any problems or concerns about the system to the operator's attention?

- Does the site coordinator keep other staff up-to-date on the system and track its usage within the site?

GUIDELINE 6.3: **Staff members should develop a process for identifying (and communicating or interacting with) related activities sponsored by other organizations. (Examples: Career Days, College Fairs, College Representative Visitations.)**

GUIDELINE 6.4: **Staff members should conduct in-house training and educational seminars for people needing "orientation" and "awareness" levels of knowledge, and for the end users of the system.**

GUIDELINE 6.5: **Incidental staff users need an "orientation" level of knowledge that can be obtained through annual updates.**

- Have incidental staff users seen a demonstration of the total system? Have they had hands-on experience with the component of the system they are most likely to use? (Training of "orientation" level groups is typically done in-house by local staff members but may be supported by the system operator.)

- Are they sufficiently aware of local system access procedures so they can access the system independently?

GUIDELINE 6.6: **Administrators, students or clients, and others should have an "awareness" level of knowledge about the system that can be obtained through a yearly demonstration.**

- Have they seen a demonstration of access and data from at least one file? (Training for the "awareness" level is usually done by local staff members but may have the support of the system operator.)

- Are they aware of local access procedures and scheduling?

- Do administrators and other staff understand what information needs they can refer to staff members and the system?

Evaluation

Continuous evaluation and systematic review of needs, goals, and achievements are important. Systems change, needs of users change, and program goals change. The following guidelines should apply:

GUIDELINE 7.1: **Objective measurement techniques should be used to provide quantitative data about use of the system. Such measurements may include number of uses of various components of the system, number and types of users, percentage of target population reached, and time-of-day usage patterns.**

GUIDELINE 7.2: **Subjective indicators of usage should be obtained at least every other year by surveys of end users and staff members.**

- Does the computer-based system meet program goals? If not, should the program goals be modified?

- Have the program objectives been met? What further actions should be taken?

- Are staff members capable of performing to the standards described in the guidelines presented in this publication?

- Are the needs of users being met?

- Is the physical environment adequate?

- Is the site management effective?

- Has the system been successfully implemented?

- Is the system—especially its content, accessing strategies, and reliability—meeting the need?

- Have the most recent improvements to the system been implemented? Have outdated materials been destroyed or deleted?

GUIDELINE 7.3: **Evaluation information should be reported to site facilitators, administrators, the system operator, and other interested parties.**

The Association of Computer-Based Systems for Career Information (ACSCI) is a professional organization for the advancement of career information. Formed in 1978, the Association and its members work to advance the development and use of career information, information technology, and services to users through standards, training, public information, and technical assistance. Full members are organizations that operate computer-based systems for career information in states and metropolitan areas. Supporting members include developers and vendors of software and hardware used in delivering career information. Individual members include researchers, administrators, counselors, and others who are interested in the field of career information. Inquiries about membership may be sent to the ACSCI Clearinghouse, 1787 Agate Street, Eugene, OR 97403.

Roger Lambert is the director of the Wisconsin Career Information System, having served in that capacity since the system's inception in 1975. He also serves as the associate director of the Vocational Studies Center at the University of Wisconsin—Madison. He has been involved in a variety of research and development activities over the past 15 years related to career development and computer-based information systems and has served as president of ACSCI.

David Caulum is the coordinator of the Wisconsin Career Information System. He was involved in the early development of the Wisconsin system and has over the years been instrumental in the development and utilization of the microcomputer for delivery of career information. He has also chaired the Research Committee and the Technical Assistance and Training Committee of ACSCI. In 1984 he was recognized by ACSCI for his outstanding contribution to the development of computerized career information systems.

Appendix H

Career Software
Review Guidelines

Copyright ©1991 National Career Development Association
5999 Stevenson Avenue
Alexandria, VA 20034
(703)823-9800

Additional copies of this publication are available from the National Career Development Association, address listed above.

Career Software Review Guidelines
National Career Development Association

Introduction

The National Career Development Association (NCDA) has a long history of evaluating career materials. The Association's career information reviews have for years helped counselors and career center coordinators select from available career information books and pamphlets.

In the last decade, several professional groups have developed evaluation criteria for career software. As computers came into use to help individuals access career information, the United States Department of Labor and then the National Occupational Information Coordinating Committee provided start-up grants so individual states could implement systems of career information. State system operators formed the Association of Computer-Based Systems for Career Information (ACSCI) and adopted standards for the operation of such systems, publishing them periodically since 1980. In 1985, ACSCI also published guidelines for the effective use of computer-based systems for career information.

Several states conducted or commissioned evaluations before adopting a system for state operation, and several individuals and research centers have published guidelines for system selection or guides to available career information delivery software. In 1988, the American Association for Counseling and Development published a comprehensive guide to counseling software.

Several educational organizations, including the International Society for Technology in Education, publish guides to instructional software and guidelines for evaluation of instructional software.

The existing standards provided ample precedence for these NCDA guidelines. All of them help clarify important issues regarding career development software while equipping professionals to choose software appropriate for their counseling practices or their school's or agency's service needs. The purpose here is not to compile all of the good guidelines or to supersede well-established software standards and evaluations, but to reinforce them with NCDA's efforts.

These NCDA guidelines apply to software that individuals use in planning their own careers. Because the computer is an information tool and its major use in career development is for information delivery, the guidelines are specific about the content, orientation, and coverage of occupational and educational information. The computer is not just an information storage and retrieval device, however, nor is career planning based solely on facts about work and schooling. Computers are also used to organize information about the individual and to aid decision making. Criteria for the evaluation of those career development programs are also included in the guidelines. By selecting the applicable criteria, a reviewer can evaluate special purpose programs as well as comprehensive career information systems.

The 1991 edition of the Career Software Review Guidelines was prepared under the direction of Bruce McKinlay, Ph.D., University of Oregon, Eugene, Oregon (chairperson of the CIRS Subcommittee on Software Resources), with the assistance of the Career Information Review Service Committee, chaired by Roger Lambert, Ph.D., University of Wisconsin-Madison. The Guidelines were approved by the NCDA Board of Directors April, 1991.

Useful software rarely consists only of computer programs and data. User guides, coordinator manuals, evaluation reports, and implementation strategies are all valuable and are covered by the guidelines.

Many career software programs have companion publications or refer users to other information sources. Similarly, software developers are beginning to add other visual and electronic media to their career programs. Therefore, these software review guidelines rely on and are designed to complement two other sets of NCDA guidelines—those for print and those for media.

These guidelines are written for use by NCDA members and others in selecting and using career software. They can also be useful to NCDA in reviewing career software and to developers in producing career planning software.

The guidelines have two parts: (a) a format for describing the software and (b) criteria for evaluating the program. These two parts can be used separately or together, depending on the purposes of the user.

References

Association of Computer-Based Systems for Career Information. (1982). *Handbook of Standards for Computer-Based Career Information Systems*. Eugene, OR: ACSCI Clearinghouse.

Association of Computer-Based Systems for Career Information. (1985). *Guidelines for the Use of Computer-Based Career Information and Guidance Systems*. Eugene, OR: ACSCI Clearinghouse.

Herlihy, B., & Golden, L. (1990). *Ethical Standards Casebook*. Alexandria, VA: American Association for Counseling and Development.

National Career Development Association Career Information Review Service. (1987). *Instructions for CIRS Committee - Career Information Review Service*. Alexandria, VA: Author.

Northwest Regional Educational Laboratory (1988). *Evaluator's Guide for Microcomputer-Based Instructional Packages*. Eugene, OR: International Society for Technology in Education (formerly International Council for Computers in Education).

Walz, G., & Bleuer, J. (1990). *Counseling Software Guide: A Resource for the Guidance and Human Development Professions*. Alexandria, VA: American Association for Counseling and Development.

Part 1: Software Description

Title: _____ Version: _____

Developer: _____

Hardware Requirements: _____

_____

Topics: _____

_____

User Materials Provided: _____

_____

Applicable to the Following Career Development Activities:

☐ Career Awareness   ☐ Career Growth

☐ Career Exploration   ☐ Career Change

☐ Skill & Knowledge Development   ☐ Other:_____

☐ Career Decision Making

Applicable in:

☐ Instruction   ☐ Job Search

☐ Counseling   ☐ Human Resource Development

Appropriate for Settings such as:

☐ Elementary Schools   ☐ Rehabilitation Agencies

☐ Middle & Junior High Schools   ☐ Counseling Agencies

☐ High Schools   ☐ Correctional Institutions

☐ Vocational Schools   ☐ Job Placement Services

☐ Community & Junior Colleges   ☐ Personnel Offices

☐ Colleges & Universities   ☐ The Work Place

☐ Job & Training Programs   ☐ Libraries & Resource Centers

Cost:

Software for: Single-User Computer $ _____

Networked or Time-Shared Computer $ _____

Consumable Materials: $ _____ per _____

Licensing provisions for multi-user installations (networks, computer labs, etc.) _____

_____

_____

Field tested data are available:
☐ On Request   ☐ With the Program   ☐ Not Available

Objectives:
☐ Stated by Developer   ☐ Inferred

_____
_____
_____
_____
_____

Prerequisites for successful use:
☐ Stated by Developer   ☐ Inferred

_____
_____
_____
_____
_____

Content and Structure:

_____
_____
_____
_____
_____

Potential Uses:

_____
_____
_____
_____
_____

Description prepared by:_____ Date: _____

Part 2: Software Evaluation Criteria

You can evaluate five aspects of a program with these criteria categories:

- information in the program,
- career development process,
- user interaction,
- technical aspects of the software and materials, and
- support services.

There are few software programs, even comprehensive career information systems, to which you would apply all 67 of the criteria listed. You will need to omit the criteria that are not appropriate to the type of program you are evaluating.

Some of the criteria are standards of quality that any career development software program should meet. These include such standards as nondiscriminatory language, current and valid information, user control of decision making, program reliability, and availability of technical assistance. Use these important standards of quality to rate every program.

Other criteria (e.g., inclusion of test results or appropriateness for small group use) are features which may not be important for a particular type of program. Do not rate items that are not applicable to the kind of product you are evaluating; cross out their rating scales instead.

If you are rating one program and doing it yourself, you can select criteria and do the rating at the same time. However, if you are comparing several programs, or if several people are doing independent ratings, you first need to make several copies of the rating form. In that case, cross out the criteria that are not applicable, then make copies of the rating form.

For each applicable criterion, rate the program:

5 = Outstanding   4 = Good   3 = Satisfactory   2 = Poor   1 = Unsatisfactory

After you have finished rating the program, you can construct a summary score for it. If you want a summary score, sum the points assigned and divide the total points by the number of items rated, omitting the items you decided were not applicable. Use the overall numeric score only as a guide. If an essential criterion is rated unsatisfactory, you may decide to reject the program even if some of its features are attractive.

Information in the Program

These information criteria cover the following aspects of the program: relevance to the audience, appropriate language, organization of the information, and information quality.

Outstanding   Unsatisfactory

1. The information is clear, concise, and informative to the intended audience 5 4 3 2 1

2. The language is nondiscriminatory. Content is free from race, ethnic, gender, age, and other stereotypes 5 4 3 2 1

3. The content is free from spelling and grammatical errors 5 4 3 2 1

4. All subjects are covered in a comprehensive manner. For example, if information about all types of occupations is presented, it covers 90% of total employment in the area where the program is being used. Or, if the information applies specifically to one field of training, it covers all relevant instructional programs 5 4 3 2 1

5. The information for each topic encourages comparisons among schools or occupations 5 4 3 2 1

6. Occupational information covers standard occupational categories, duties, abilities, skills, working conditions, equipment, earnings, employment, outlook, training, and methods of entry. It identifies related occupations..............5 4 3 2 1

7. Information about educational programs covers program objectives, specialties, degrees conferred, sample courses, and schools offering the program 5 4 3 2 1

8. Information about schools includes general information, admissions, programs of study, housing, costs, financial aid, and student service 5 4 3 2 1

9. The program lists only schools that meet basic licensing requirements. It reports accreditation by recognized organizations 5 4 3 2 1

10. The information is based on empirical data that are current and valid...................5 4 3 2 1

11. Updated information is distributed promptly, at least yearly 5 4 3 2 1

12. In a personal search questionnaire, there is a clear, empirical relationship between characteristics of the user and those of the occupations, schools, or other activities being sorted 5 4 3 2 1

13. In a program using off-line or computer-administered assessment instruments, those instruments conform to accepted standards of validity and reliability...........5 4 3 2 1

14. Advice is clearly distinguished from factual information. The sources of advice are identified 5 4 3 2 1

15. Statements made in one component are consistent with those made in other components of the program 5 4 3 2 1

16. If the program produces only lists of titles, it effectively refers users to specific sources of accurate information 5 4 3 2 1

17. Published information sources are readily available, for example, in local career information centers 5 4 3 2 1

18. To supplement objective information, the program suggests interviewing individuals about their personal career histories, including how they feel about their schools or jobs 5 4 3 2 1

Career Development Process

These criteria evaluate the compatibility of the program with important career development principles.

	Outstanding				Unsatisfactory
19. The program motivates individuals to develop their own career plans	5	4	3	2	1
20. The program fosters self-knowledge relevant to work and learning	5	4	3	2	1
21. The program helps individuals to integrate and develop their values, interests, abilities, skills, and goals	5	4	3	2	1
22. Using the program broadens an individual's awareness of current options for employment and education	5	4	3	2	1
23. If there is a search process, it broadens the outlook of individuals regardless of their race, ethnic group, gender, or age	5	4	3	2	1
24. The program supports informed decision making by helping individuals generate ideas, obtain necessary information, and evaluate alternatives in responsible and personally relevant ways	5	4	3	2	1
25. The program encourages the user to get appropriate counseling and advice in making long term decisions	5	4	3	2	1
26. Using the program integrates planning with previous experiences	5	4	3	2	1
27. The user, not the program, controls the decision making	5	4	3	2	1
28. The structure of the program demonstrates that career planning is a developmental, lifelong process	5	4	3	2	1
29. The program is appropriate for individual use	5	4	3	2	1
30. The program is appropriate for small group use	5	4	3	2	1
31. The program can be a useful resource in a counseling program	5	4	3	2	1
32. The program provides information that can be useful in instruction	5	4	3	2	1
33. The program can be a useful resource in a job search program	5	4	3	2	1
34. Using the program contributes to a person's career development	5	4	3	2	1

User Interaction

These criteria cover the user's interaction with the program, the objectives and features of the program, and your analysis of it.

	Outstanding				Unsatisfactory
35. The purpose of the program is well defined and clearly explained to the user	5	4	3	2	1
36. The organization is clear, logical, and effective, making it easy for the intended audience to understand	5	4	3	2	1
37. The language in the program and in the user's guide is clear to the intended audience	5	4	3	2	1
38. User materials are easy to use, appealing to users, and readily available	5	4	3	2	1
39. Prerequisites are identified and instruction is provided in the software or in the user guides so individuals can run the program and understand its results	5	4	3	2	1
40. The individual has the choice of going directly to desired information or using a structured search to identify relevant topics	5	4	3	2	1
41. The individual can operate the program independently, creating his or her own sequence of presentation and review	5	4	3	2	1

42. The program acknowledges input. Feedback on user responses is employed effectively 5   4   3   2   1

43. Invalid commands are handled constructively. The program tolerates variations in command formats (e.g., upper or lower case, extra spaces, etc.)........5   4   3   2   1

44. Individuals can easily start and exit the program. It is easy to back up, change answers, and give commands 5   4   3   2   1

45. If there are "help" and "hint" messages, they are easy to access...............5   4   3   2   1

46. If the program contains tests of knowledge or skill, it reports which items were missed and which were correct 5   4   3   2   1

47. The program is attractive and interesting. It motivates users to continue using the program and exploring career options......................................5   4   3   2   1

48. The program is demonstrably effective with the intended audience, including people of varying abilities and experiences 5   4   3   2   1

49. The program can be used by various cultural groups 5   4   3   2   1

50. The program achieves its purpose 5   4   3   2   1

Technical Aspects of the Software and Materials
These criteria cover aspects of the computer hardware and programs.

	Outstanding			Unsatisfactory

51. The system uses standard equipment that is reliable, widely available, and applicable to a variety of uses 5   4   3   2   1

52. Computer capabilities such as graphics, color, or sound are used for appropriate instructional reasons 5   4   3   2   1

53. If the program requires special equipment, the requirements are minimal and clearly stated by the developer...5   4   3   2   1

54. The program is reliable in normal use. Software is bug free 5   4   3   2   1

55. The program provides a copy or summary of its basic information to the user for future reference...5   4   3   2   1

56. Printouts are clear and well organized. The printouts are dated 5   4   3   2   1

57. Updates can be loaded easily into the system.......................................5   4   3   2   1

58. If any processing in the program is based on assessment scores, course grades, or other client records, the program explains to the user how the records are being used...5   4   3   2   1

59. If the program uses client records, it does not restrict an individual in exploring any of the information in the program.......................................5   4   3   2   1

60. If the program creates a permanent record for a user, that record is secure and confidential. There is provision for erasing the record when the information is no longer valuable in providing services.................................5   4   3   2   1

Support

These criteria cover aspects of support for professionals who implement the program: written materials, staff training, service, and cost.

	Outstanding			Unsatisfactory

61. The site coordinator's manual explains the content and process for updating information...5 4 3 2 1
62. Print or computer materials explain the content and effective use of the program to local site coordinators 5 4 3 2 1
63. Training on appropriate and effective use of the program is provided regularly 5 4 3 2 1
64. There is a system of communication between user sites and the system developer which may include newsletters, telephone assistance, and annual evaluations..5 4 3 2 1
65. On-site technical assistance is available for effective program use.......................5 4 3 2 1
66. Evaluations of the program's effectiveness are available to site coordinators 5 4 3 2 1
67. The cost per user makes it feasible to serve most clients who can benefit from the program 5 4 3 2 1

Summary Comments

Major Strengths:

_____
_____
_____
_____
_____

Major Weaknesses:

_____
_____
_____
_____
_____

Other Comments:

_____
_____
_____
_____

Evaluation prepared by: _____ Date: _____

Appendix I

Guidelines for the Preparation and Evaluation of Career and Occupational Information Literature

Guidelines for the Preparation and Evaluation of Career and Occupational Information Literature

National Career Development Association

These *Guidelines* are designed to be used by both the publishers and the consumers of career and occupational information literature. Because career and occupational literature is often an individual's initial (and sometimes only) exposure to a specific occupation or occupational field, it is very important that this information be accurately and comprehensively conveyed to the user. The *Guidelines* represent the National Career Development Association's (NCDA) views of what constitutes good career and occupational literature. The Association encourages the use of these *Guidelines* by publishers to ensure quality control in their publications and by those who select and use career and occupational literature to ensure maximum value from their purchases.

Helping individuals obtain, evaluate, and use career and occupational information is within the scope of NCDA's mission to facilitate the career development of individuals. The revision of these *Guidelines* is one of the services provided by NCDA to encourage the development of accurate and reliable information by publishers, and the informed use of this information by consumers and clients.

The nature of career information has changed considerably in its content and its delivery since NCDA was founded in 1913, as the National Vocational Guidance Association. However, the need for career and vocational information as an important consideration in career planning has remained constant. As recently as 1989, 65% of the adults who participated in the NCDA Gallup Survey indicated that if they could plan their work lives again, they would try to get more information about career choices and options.

In addition to their evaluative use locally, these *Guidelines* also form the basis for the ratings of current career and occupational literature by the Career Information Review Service of NCDA. These ratings appear in *The Career Development Quarterly* to assist professionals in their selection of quality career and occupational information literature.

Definition of Terms

The first step in any evaluation process is to determine that all parties concerned are using terms that communicate the same meaning to all. To address this issue of clarity, the following *Guidelines* have been designed to be used for occupational literature and for career literature. The content and purpose of these two types of literature are closely related but differ in some important aspects. Therefore, the terms occupation, occupational field, career, and career progression have been used in these *Guidelines* to refer

This 1991 edition of the Guidelines are a revision of the guidelines for career and occupational literature previously published by NCDA/NVGA. This revision was prepared under the direction of Jennifer B. Wilson, Ph.D., University of Wisconsin-La Crosse, La Crosse, Wisconsin (Chairperson of the CIRS Subcommittee on Print Materials), with the assistance of the Career Information Review Service Committee, chaired by Roger Lambert, Ph.D., University of Wisconsin-Madison. The Guidelines were approved by the NCDA Board of Directors April, 1991.

to the specific type of information being discussed. Occupation refers to a specific job, usually indicated by a job title and/or number. Occupational field refers to a group or cluster of related occupations, often but not necessarily requiring similar skills, knowledge, and abilities and sharing similar working conditions. Career is a more encompassing term that includes, but is not limited to, the series of occupations one might expect to hold in the course of his or her working history. Career progression refers to the series of occupations that might be held during one's work history, each involving increasing levels of decision making, responsibility, status, and compensation.

General Guidelines
This section discusses items related to the general preparation and presentation of career and occupational literature.

1. Dating and Revisions
The date of publication should be clearly indicated. Because of rapid changes in employment outlook and earnings, material should be revised at least every three to four years to stay current and accurate. This is particularly important in highly technical and skilled occupations and less a factor in unskilled or semi-skilled occupations.

2. Credits
Credits should include (a) publisher, (b) consultants, (c) sponsor, and (d) sources of any statistical data. Photographs and original artwork should be accompanied by the name of the photographer/artist, photographic outfit, and copyright mark (if any).

3. Accuracy of Information
Information should be accurate and free from distortion caused by self-serving bias, sex stereotyping, or dated resources. Whenever possible, resources over five years old should be avoided. Information should be secured from and/or reviewed by knowledgeable sources within the occupation, the occupational field, or career research. Reviewers should be selected to reflect different viewpoints germane to an occupation (e.g., business and labor) and be trained in the evaluation process. Reviewers must not use the literature to promote their own concerns or viewpoints. Data such as earnings and employment projections should be based on current, reliable, and comprehensive research.

4. Format
The information should be conveyed in a clear, concise, and interesting manner. Although information from the Content Guidelines should appear in all publications, publishers are encouraged to vary the manner of presentation for the sake of stimulation and appeal. A standard style and format for grammar should be adopted and utilized throughout the document.

5. Vocabulary
The vocabulary of the information should be appropriate to the target group. Career and occupational information is used by people of varying ages and abilities. Information designed for a specific age range or for any other clearly identifiable group should be clearly identified as such. Information designed for broader use should be comprehensible to younger persons but suitable in style for adults. Technical terminology or jargon should be either fully explained or avoided. The use of nonsexist language is essential.

6. Use of Information

The intended purpose, the target audience, and the potential use of the information should be clearly identified in the introduction to the material. Reviews should specify the intended audience, such as elementary schools, middle/junior high schools, high schools, vocational schools, community college, colleges/universities, employment/training programs, rehabilitation agencies, correctional agencies, libraries, or specify other audiences. Persons often do not have the opportunity to thoroughly review materials until after the materials have been purchased. The authors and publishers should help potential purchasers determine whether the materials present useful information.

7. Bias and Stereotyping

. Care should be taken in all publications to eliminate bias and stereotyping against persons with a disability, or based on gender, race, social status, ethnicity, age, or religion. Job title and information should be bias-free. Particular care should be taken to ensure the use of gender-free language. If graphics are used, people of different races, ages, sexes, and physical abilities should be portrayed at various occupational levels. Where applicable, data, information, or resources relevant to equal opportunity for women, minorities, or persons with a disability should be included.

8. Graphics

Graphic displays, when used, should enhance the value of the narrative information. Pictures should be current and portray individuals engaged in activities primary to the occupation or unique to it. Again, the importance of portraying individuals of different sexes, races, ages, and physical abilities in a variety of roles cannot be overemphasized.

Content Guidelines

This section discusses guideline items that deal with the content of information on occupations and/or occupational fields. Reviews of nonoccupational materials will rely primarily on the previously discussed criteria.

1. Duties and Nature of the Work

The career and occupational literature should describe in a clear and interesting fashion: (a) the purpose of the work, (b) the activities of the worker, (c) the skills, knowledge, interests, and abilities necessary to perform the work, and (d) any specializations commonly practiced in the occupation. Literature that describes occupational fields should also include: (a) the overall function and importance of the field, (b) the variety of occupations available, (c) the common skills, knowledge, interests, and abilities shared by members of the field or industry, and (d) contrasts among the various occupations represented in the field.

2. Work Setting and Conditions

The portrayal of the work setting and conditions should include a description of the physical and mental activities and the work environment. Where applicable, the information should include the full range of possible settings in which the work may be performed. The range of typical physical and mental activities should be described. Environmental characteristics should include the physical surroundings, the psychological environment, and the social environment. In addition to these characteristics, other conditions related to the performance of the work, such as time requirements or travel requirements, should be described.

Aspects of the work that might be regarded as undesirable are as crucial to realistic decision making as those that are generally considered desirable; therefore, care should be taken to make descriptions as comprehensive as possible. Because different individuals may view a given work condition as either positive or negative, the descriptions should be free of the author's bias and present a balanced picture. The variety and similarity of settings should be discussed. Specific geographic locations related to employment in the occupational field should be included.

3. Preparation Required

The preparation required for entrance into the occupation, or into various levels of an occupation, should be clearly stated. The length and type of training required and the skills, knowledge, abilities, and interests of successful students or trainees should be indicated. Typical methods of financial support during training should be included. Alternative means of obtaining the necessary preparation or experience should be stated where applicable. Readers should be informed of any preferred employer selection criteria over and above minimal preparation requirements. In literature that describes a range of occupations in a career progression, the various levels of preparation required for employment in each successive occupation should also be highlighted.

4. Special Requirements or Considerations

Bonafide physical requirements: Bonafide physical requirements that are necessary for entrance into a particular occupation should be included. Only bonafide occupational qualifications should be addressed. Consideration should be given to addressing job accommodations that can and are legally required to open opportunity to all the members of our society.

Licensing, certifications or membership requirements: Licenses, certifications, or memberships in unions or professional societies may also be required for some occupations. These requirements should be indicated and the process necessary for achieving any of these requirements should be described.

Personal Criteria: The listing of qualities desired of any worker (e.g., honesty, dependability) is not particularly valuable to individuals attempting to differentiate various career possibilities. On occasion it may be useful and appropriate to consider personal criteria, if available, regarding unique skills, knowledge, mental and physical abilities, and interests. The basis for the information should be clearly identified.

Social and Psychological Factors: Participation in an occupation has important effects on the lifestyle of the individual (and his or her family), and these effects should receive appropriate consideration in the presentation of information. When these factors are determined to be appropriate to the use of the material, the source of the information presented on social and psychological factors should be clearly identified.

5. Methods of Entry

The variety of means for typical entry into the occupation should be indicated, as well as any preferred avenues for entry. Alternative approaches should be described where applicable–particularly for those occupations where experience can be substituted for education and other formal preparation or where education can be substituted for work experience.

6. Earnings and Other Benefits

Current data on entry wages, average earnings and the typical range of earnings in the occupation should be presented. In addition, variations in average earnings by geographic region should be reported if available. Fringe benefits have become an increasingly important aspect of total compensation, and ample coverage of both typical benefits and those that are unique to the occupation or occupational field should be given.

7. Usual Advancement Possibilities

The typical and alternative career progressions related to the occupational field should be presented. The supplementary skills, knowledge, and abilities necessary for advancement and the alternative means for acquiring them should be indicated. Issues such as the role of job change, availability of training, and seniority should be discussed as they pertain to advancement in the particular occupational field.

8. Employment Outlook

Statements concerning the employment outlook should be realistic and include both the short-range and the long-range outlook for the occupation and occupational field. Mention of the past record of the occupation may be useful in completing its outlook picture. A broad range of factors that may have an impact on the employment outlook, including economic, demographic, technological, geographic, social, and political factors, should be considered. Current U.S. Department of Labor or other expert research should be consulted. Realism is essential, but readers should not be discouraged from entering highly competitive fields if they have the ability, interest, and motivation to succeed.

9. Opportunities for Experience and Exploration

Literature should list opportunities for part-time and summer employment; opportunities for internships, apprenticeships, and cooperative work programs; and opportunities for volunteer work. Pertinent clubs and organizations, as well as school-related activities and programs, should be described. Publishers are encouraged to give sufficient attention to this heading because these career-related possibilities can be acted on immediately and thus have high motivational value.

10. Related Occupations

Occupations that share similar requirements on aptitudes, interest patterns, or work environments with the occupation under consideration should be listed. In addition to its value in early exploration, this information is particularly useful to adults considering lateral occupational changes.

11. Sources of Additional Information

Reference should be made to additional sources of information such as professional or trade organizations and associations, specific books or pamphlets, journals or trade publications, audiovisual materials, and literature available from public agencies. For students, the assistance of school guidance counselors or college career counselors is recommended.

Career and Occupational Literature Reviewer's Rating Form—1991

Rating:_____ Type (Code Number):_____ Setting/Population:_____

GENERAL PUBLICATION DATA:
1. Title: _____
2. Author (s): _____
3. Publisher name: _____
4. Publisher address: _____
5. Year of publication: _____ 6. Number of pages: _____ 7. Price: _____

SETTING/POPULATION(s)

☐ 1. Elementary Schools
☐ 2. Middle/Junior High Schools
☐ 3. High Schools
☐ 4. Vocational Schools
☐ 5. Community Colleges

☐ 6. Colleges/Universities
☐ 7. Employment/Training Programs
☐ 8. Rehabilitation Agencies
☐ 9. Correctional Institutions
☐ 10. Libraries
☐ 11. Other: _____

TYPE OF PUBLICATION:

☐ **1. Vocational**
   ☐ a. Occupations
   ☐ b. Trends and Outlook
   ☐ c. Job Training
   ☐ d. Employment Opportunities

☐ **2. Educational**
   ☐ a. Status and Trends
   ☐ b. Schools, Colleges
   ☐ c. Scholarships, Fellowships, Grants, and Loans

☐ **3. Career/Personal**
   ☐ a. Planning (resume, how to look for a job, career planning, etc.)
   ☐ b. Adjustment
   ☐ c. Theory
   ☐ d. Assessment (Interest, Aptitude testing, etc.)

CONTENT:
5=Outstanding   4=Good   3=Satisfactory   2=Poor   1=Unsatisfactory   0=Does not apply

5	4	3	2	1	0	Date of publication is indicated on material
5	4	3	2	1	0	Appropriate credits are given in the material
5	4	3	2	1	0	Information accurate, free from distortion
5	4	3	2	1	0	Clear, concise, interesting
5	4	3	2	1	0	Vocabulary appropriate to age group and occupational level
5	4	3	2	1	0	Intended purpose/population/use is clearly identified
5	4	3	2	1	0	Free of bias (racial, sexual, age, physical ability, etc.)
5	4	3	2	1	0	Illustrations/graphic displays are current, enhance material

National Career Development Association, 1991

5	4	3	2	1	0	Duties and nature of work (purpose, activities, skills, etc.)
5	4	3	2	1	0	Conditions of work (work setting, physical activities, environment)
5	4	3	2	1	0	Preparation required (length and kind of training)
5	4	3	2	1	0	Special requirements (license, certification, degrees, memberships, personal/social criteria, etc.)
5	4	3	2	1	0	Methods of entry (typical, preferred, any alternative means)
5	4	3	2	1	0	Earnings and other benefits (figures should be current and represent range)
5	4	3	2	1	0	Usual advancement opportunities (any requirements for advancement)
5	4	3	2	1	0	Employment outlook (current, realistic, short- and long-term)
5	4	3	2	1	0	Opportunities for experience and exploration
5	4	3	2	1	0	Related occupations indicated
5	4	3	2	1	0	Sources of education and training
5	4	3	2	1	0	Sources of additional information

The following items are applicable only when the publication is a bibliography, directory, or financial assistance publication.

Bibliography
5	4	3	2	1	0	Publication date(s) listed
5	4	3	2	1	0	Price(s) available
5	4	3	2	1	0	Reference to author(s)
5	4	3	2	1	0	Annotation of materials

Financial Assistance
5	4	3	2	1	0	Sources of financial aid
5	4	3	2	1	0	Amount of aid available
5	4	3	2	1	0	Qualification requirements

Directories
5	4	3	2	1	0	Content
5	4	3	2	1	0	Format

_____ **TOTAL SCORE**

Reviewer's Overall Rating for Listing-Circle Your Choice				
5 = Outstanding	4 = Good	3=Satisfactory	2 = Poor	1 = Unsatisfactory

COMMENTS: Recommendations and suggestions for the authors/publishers (If there is an apparent discrepancy between the total score and your evaluation, please document your evaluation decision.)

Evaluation prepared by:_____ Date:_____

Appendix J

Government Printing Offices

Government Printing Offices

Alabama

O'Neill Building
2021 3rd Avenue North
Birmingham, AL 35203
205/731-1056

California

ARCO Plaza, C-Level
505 South Flower Street
Los Angeles, CA 90071
213/239-9844

Federal Building
Room 1023
450 Golden Gate Avenue
San Francisco, CA 94102
415/252-5334

Colorado

Federal Building
Room 117
1961 Stout Street
Denver, CO 80294
303/844-3964

World Savings Building
720 North Main Street
Pueblo, CO 81003
719/544-3142

District of Columbia

710 North Capitol St., NW
Washington, DC 20401
202/275-2091

1510 H Street, NW
Washington, DC 20005
202/653-5075

Florida

Federal Building
Room 158
400 West Bay Street
Jacksonville, FL 32202
904/353-0567

Georgia

Federal Building
275 Peachtree Street, NE
Room 100
P.O. Box 56445
Atlanta, GA 30343
404/331-6947

Illinois

Federal Building
Room 1365
219 South Dearborn Street
Chicago, IL 60604
312/353-5133

Massachusetts

Thomas P. O'Neill Federal Building
10 Causeway Street
Room 179
Boston, MA 02222
617/720-4180

Michigan

Federal Building
Suite 160
477 Michigan Avenue
Detroit, MI 48226
313/226-7816

Missouri

120 Bannister Mall
5600 East Bannister Road
Kansas City, MO 64137
816/767-8225

New York

Federal Building
Room 110
26 Federal Plaza
New York, NY 10278
212/264-3825

Ohio

Federal Building
Room 1653
1240 East 9th Street
Cleveland, OH 44199
216/522-4922

Federal Building
Room 207
200 North High Street
Columbus, OH 43215
614/469-6956

Oregon

1305 SW First Avenue
Portland, OR 97201
503/221-6217

Pennsylvania

Robert Morris Building
100 North 17th Street
Philadelphia, PA 19103
215/597-0677

Federal Building
Room 118
1000 Liberty Avenue
Pittsburgh, PA 15222
412/644-2721

Texas

Federal Building
Room 1C50
1100 Commerce Street
Dallas, TX 75242
214/767-0076

Texas Crude Building
801 Travis Street
Houston, TX 77002
713/228-1187

Washington

Federal Building
Room 194
915 Second Avenue
Seattle, WA 98174
206/442-4270

Wisconsin

Federal Building
Room 190
517 East Wisconsin Avenue
Milwaukee, WI 53202
414/297-1304

Warehouse Outlet

8660 Cherry Lane
Laurel, MD 20707
301/953-7974

Appendix K

Sources of State
and Local Job Outlook

Sources of State and Local Job Outlook Information

State and local job market and career information is available from State Employment Security Agencies and State Occupational Information Coordinating Committees (SOICC's). State Employment Security Agencies develop occupational employment projections and other job market information. SOICC's provide or help locate labor market and career information. The following list gives the title, address, and telephone number of State Employment Security Agency Directors of Research. SOICC Directors are listed in Appendix B.

Alabama
Chief, Research and Statistics, Alabama Department of Industrial Relations, Industrial Relations Bldg., 649 Monroe St., Room 427, Montgomery, AL 36130. Phone: 205/261-5461.

Alaska
Chief, Research and Analysis Section, Alaska Department of Labor, P.O. Box 25501, Juneau, AK 99802-5501. Phone: 907/465-4500.

Coordinator, Alaska Department of Labor, Research and Analysis Section, P.O. Box 25501, Juneau, AK 99802-5501. Phone: 907/465-4518.

American Samoa
Program Director, American Samoa State Occupational Information Coordinating Committee, Office of Manpower Resources, American Samoa Government, Pago Pago, AS 96799. Phone: 684/633-2153.

Arizona
Research Administrator, Arizona Department of Economic Security, P.O. Box 6123, Site Code 733A, Phoenix, AZ 85005. Phone: 602/255-3616.

Arkansas
Manager, Labor Market Information - UI/BLS, Employment Security Division, P.O. Box 2981, Little Rock, AR 72203. Phone: 501/371-1541.

Executive Director, Arkansas Occupational Information Coordinating Committee, Research and Analysis Section, Arkansas Employment Security Division, P.O. Box 2981, Little Rock, AR 72203. Phone: 501/682-3159.

California
Chief, Employment Data and Research Division, Employment Development Department, P.O. Box 944216, MIC-57, Sacramento, CA 94244-2160. Phone: 916/427-4675.

Colorado
Director, Labor Market Information, Colorado Division of Labor and Employment, 1330 Fox St., Suite 801, Denver, CO 80203. Phone: 303/866-6316.

Connecticut
Acting Director, Research and Information, Employment Security Division, 200 Folly Brook Blvd., Wethersfield, CT 06109. Phone: 203/566-2120.

Delaware
Chief, Office of Occupational and Labor Market Information, Delaware Department of Labor, P.O. Box 9029, Newark, DE 19714-9029. Phone: 302/368-6962.

Executive Director, Office of Occupational and Labor Market Information, Delaware Department of Labor, University Office Plaza, P.O. Box 9029, Newark, DE 19714-9029. Phone: 302/368-6963.

District of Columbia
Chief, Labor Market Information and Analysis, District of Columbia Department of Employment Services, 500 C St. NW, Room 201, Washington, DC 20001. Phone: 202/639-1642.

Florida
Chief, Bureau of Labor Market Information, Florida Department of Labor and Employment Security, 2574 Seagate Dr., Room 203, Tallahassee, FL 32399-0674. Phone: 904/488-1048.

Georgia
Director, Labor Information Systems, Georgia Department of Labor, 148 International Blvd. NE, Atlanta, GA 30303. Phone: 404/656-9639.

Guam
Administrator, Department of Labor/Bureau of Labor Statistics, Government of Guam, P.O. Box 944216 (GMF), Tamuning, GU 96911-290.

Hawaii
Chief, Research and Statistics Office, Department of Labor and Industrial Relations, 830 Punchbowl St., Room 304, Honolulu, HI 96813. Phone: 808/548-7639.

Idaho
Acting Chief, Research and Analysis, Idaho Department of Employment, P.O. Box 35, Boise, ID 83735. Phone: 208/334-2755.

Illinois
Director, Economic Information and Analysis, Illinois Department of Employment Security, 401 South State St., 2 South, Chicago, IL 60605. Phone: 312/793-2316.

Indiana
Manager, Statistical Services, Indiana Department of Employment and Training, 10 North Senate Ave., Indianapolis, IN 46204. Phone: 317/232-7701.

Iowa
Chief, Audit and Analysis, Iowa Department of Employment Services, 1000 East Grand Ave., Des Moines, IA 50319. Phone: 515/281-8181.

Kansas
Chief, Research and Analysis, Kansas Department of Human Resources, 401 Topeka Ave., Topeka, KS 66603. Phone: 913/296-5061.

Kentucky
Acting Manager, Labor Market Research and Analysis, Department for Employment Services, 275 East Main St., Frankfort, KY 40621-0001. Phone: 502/564-7976.

Louisiana
Director, Research and Statistics Section, Louisiana State Department of Labor, P.O. Box 94094, Baton Rouge, LA 70804-9094. Phone: 504/342-3141.

Maine
Director, Division of Economic Analysis and Research, Maine Department of Labor, 20 Union St., Augusta, ME 04330. Phone: 207/289-2271.

Maryland
Director, Research and Analysis Division, Maryland Department of Employment and Training, 1100 North Eutaw St., Baltimore, MD 21201. Phone: 301/383-5000.

Massachusetts
Director of Research, Massachusetts Division of Employment and Training, Charles F. Hurley Bldg., Boston, MA 02114. Phone: 617/727-6556.

Michigan
Director, Bureau of Research and Statistics, Michigan Employment Security Commission, 7310 Woodward Ave., Room 516, Detroit, MI 48202. Phone: 313/876-5445.

Minnesota
Director, Research and Statistics Office, Minnesota Department of Jobs and Training, 390 North Robert St., 5th Floor, St. Paul, MN 55101. Phone: 612/296-6545.

Mississippi
Chief, Labor Market Information Division, Mississippi Employment Security Commission, P.O. Box 1699, Jackson, MS 39215-1699. Phone: 601/961-7424.

Missouri
Chief, Research and Analysis, Missouri Division of Employment Security, P.O. Box 59, Jefferson City, MO 65104. Phone: 314/751-3591.

Montana
Chief, Research and Analysis, Department of Labor and Industry, P.O. Box 1728, Helena, MT 59624. Phone: 406/449-2430.

Nebraska
Administrator, Labor Market Information, Nebraska Department of Labor, P.O. Box 94600, Lincoln, NE 68509-4600. Phone: 402/475-8451.

Nevada
Chief, Employment Security Research, Nevada Employment Security Department, 500 East Third St., Carson City, NV 89713. Phone: 702/885-4550.

New Hampshire
Director, Economic Analysis and Reports, New Hampshire Department of Employment Security, 32 South Main St., Concord, NH 03301. Phone: 603/224-3311.

New Jersey
Director, Division of Planning and Research, New Jersey Department of Labor, P.O. Box 2765, Trenton, NJ 08625. Phone: 609/292-2643.

New Mexico
Chief, Economic Research and Analysis, (6097), Employment Security Department, P.O. Box 1928, Albuquerque, NM 87103. Phone: 505/841-8645.

New York
Director, Division of Research and Statistics, New York Department of Labor, State Campus, Bldg. 12, Room 400, Albany, NY 12240-0020. Phone: 518/457-6181.

North Carolina
Director, Labor Market Information Division, Employment Security Commission of North Carolina, P.O. Box 25903, Raleigh, NC 27611. Phone: 919/733-2936.

North Dakota
Chief, Research and Statistics, Job Service of North Dakota, P.O. Box 1537, Bismarck, ND 58502-1537. Phone: 701/224-2825.

Ohio
Acting Director, Labor Market Information Division, Ohio Bureau of Employment Services, P.O. Box 1618, Columbus, OH 43216. Phone: 614/466-8806.

Oklahoma
Director, Research and Planning Division, Oklahoma Employment Security Commission, 2401 N. Lincoln, Room 310, Oklahoma City, OK 73105. Phone: 405/557-7105.

Oregon
Assistant Administrator, Research and Statistics, Oregon Department of Human Resources, 875 Union St. NE., Room 207, Salem, OR 97311. Phone: 503/378-3220.

Pennsylvania
Chief, Research and Statistics Division, Pennsylvania Department of Labor and Industry, Seventh and Forster Sts., Room 1216, Harrisburg, PA 17121. Phone: 717/787-3265.

Puerto Rico
Director of BLS, Department of Labor and Human Resources, Research and Analysis Division, 505 Munoz Rivera Ave., 17th Floor, Hato Rey, PR 00918. Phone: 809/754-5339.

Rhode Island
Acting Supervisor, Employment Security Research, Rhode Island Department of Employment Security, 24 Mason St., Providence, RI 02903. Phone: 401/277-3704.

South Carolina
Director, Labor Market Information Division, South Carolina Employment Security Commission, P.O. Box 995, Columbia, SC 29202. Phone: 803/758-8983.

South Dakota
Director, Labor Market Information Center, Department of Labor, P.O Box 4730, Aberdeen, SD 57401. Phone: 605/622-2314.

Tennessee
Director, Research and Statistics Division, Tennessee Department of Employment Security, 500 James Robertson Pkwy., 11th Floor, Nashville, TN 37245-1000. Phone: 615/741-2284.

Texas
Chief, Economic Research and Analysis, Texas Employment Commission, Room 208-T, 1117 Trinity St., Austin, TX 78778. Phone: 512/463-2616.

Utah
Director, Labor Market Information Services, Utah Department of Employment Security, P.O. Box 11249, Salt Lake City, UT 84147-1249. Phone: 801/533-2014.

Vermont
Chief, Research and Analysis, Vermont Department of Employment and Training, P.O. Box 488, Montpelier, VT 05602-1488. Phone: 802/229-0311.

Virginia
Director, Economic Information Services, Virginia Employment Commission, P.O. Box 1358, Richmond, VA 23211. Phone: 804/786-5670.

Virgin Islands
Acting Director, Virgin Islands Department of Labor, Bureau of Labor Statistics, Research and Analysis Section, P.O. Box 3359, St. Thomas, United States VI 00801-3359. Phone: 809/776-3700.

Washington
Director, Labor Market and Economic Analysis Branch, Washington Employment Security Department, 605 Woodview Dr., Olympia, WA 98503. Phone: 206/438-4804.

West Virginia
Director, Labor and Economic Research Section, West Virginia Department of Employment Security, 112 California Ave., Charleston, WV 25305. Phone: 304/348-2660.

Wisconsin
Director, Labor Market Information Bureau, Department of Industry, Labor and Human Relations, P.O. Box 7944, Madison, WI 53707. Phone: 608/266-7034.

Wyoming
Chief Research and Analysis Section, Employment Security Commission, P.O. Box 2760, Casper, WY 82602. Phone: 307/235-3646.

Appendix L

Annotated List of
Selected Printed References

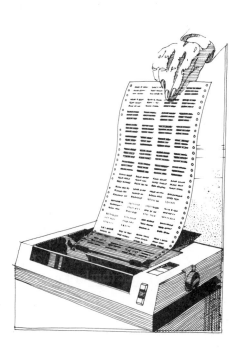

ANNOTATED LIST OF SELECTED PRINTED REFERENCES

This appendix consists of an annotated list of major printed references. The annotations include a brief description of the contents, some indications of possible uses, and ordering information. All references in this appendix have been mentioned in the modules.

These titles are by no means an exhaustive list of useful resources. They have been selected because they are basic tools available from the federal government.

Dictionary of Occupational Titles (DOT)
U.S. Department of Labor, Employment and Training Administration
4th Edition, 1977

Dictionary of Occupational Titles, 4th edition, Supplement
1986

The *Dictionary of Occupational Titles*, commonly called the DOT, defines and classifies approximately 20,000 occupations performed for pay or profit in the United States economy. It is the most comprehensive and probably the most well-known source of occupational descriptions. The DOT includes a detailed introduction and description of the organization of the book and the classification numbers.

The major portion of the DOT is the list of occupations according to DOT codes. With each entry there is a description of the most important characteristics of the job. There is also an alphabetic index, a glossary of technical terms, and an introduction to the concepts underlying the DOT classification structure. An appendix explains the job analysis concept of classifying worker's functions according to their involvement with data, people and things.

While the DOT contains a lot of important and useful information, it may be difficult for clients to use. It is more commonly used as a counselor reference. Because of the age of the DOT, it does not reflect the overwhelming technological changes of the past 20 years. However, it still is valuable for understanding the wide variety of occupations, the variations of particular occupations, and occupations related to given occupational titles.

The classification numbers in the DOT are commonly used by those who wish to identify a person's occupation in a precise way. The detail of the DOT allows better matching between an individual's experience and skill with a particular job opening. Each occupation defined in the DOT has been assigned a unique, nine-digit code. Occupations are grouped according to their similarities. Each of the nine digits signifies a particular characteristic of the occupation. The first three digits identify a particular occupational group. All occupations are clustered into one of nine broad categories, indicated by the first digit. The second and third digits represent subdivision of the broad category. The nine occupational categories are:

0/1	Professional, Technical, and Managerial
2	Clerical and Sales
3	Service
4	Agricultural, Fishery, Forestry, and Related
5	Processing
6	Machine Trade
7	Bench Work
8	Structural Work
9	Miscellaneous

The middle three digits are the worker functions ratings of the tasks performed in the occupation. Every job requires a worker to function to some degree in relation to data, people, and things. The fourth digit includes six functions related to data, the fifth digit eight functions related to people and the sixth digit, seven functions related to things. The lower numbers in each position represent more complex levels of work performance. The assignment of the middle three digits is made regardless of the occupational group involved.

It is through the combination of the first three digits with the second three digits that the full meaning of an occupation can be realized. The first three specify the occupational area in which the work is being done, and the second three digits express what the worker does. The last three digits indicate the alphabetical order of titles within six-digit code groups. They serve to differentiate a particular occupation from all others. A number of occupations may have the same first six digits; no two can have the same nine digits.

The 1986 DOT Supplement provides descriptions of additional occupations and does reflect some of the changing technology in the world of work.

Order from: Superintendent of Documents
                U.S. Government Printing Office
                Washington, DC 20402
                (202) 783-3238

                4th edition:
                        Stock number: 029-013-00079-9
                        Cost: $23.00
                4th edition supplement:
                        Stock number: unknown
                        Cost: unknown

Selected Characteristics of Occupations Defined in the Dictionary of Occupational Titles
U.S. Department of Labor, Employment and Training Administration
1981

Selected Characteristics provides an expanded interpretation of significant job characteristics for a wide range of occupations requiring similar capabilities. Supplementary information on training time (including mathematical and language development and specific vocational preparation), physical demands, and environmental (or working) conditions are listed for each job defined in the DOT. While some users may find the job characteristics in this resource outdated, it is still the only source for this kind of information.

Information presented in the supplement is arranged in two parts. Part A includes the titles arranged by the *Guide for Occupational Exploration* (GOE) work groups and physical demands. Part B is an index of titles by DOT code. The unique feature of Part A is the grouping of occupations according to similarity of physical demands requirements. For example, all jobs that are sedentary (within a work group) are listed together.

Order from: Superintendent of Documents
U.S. Government Printing Office
Washington, DC 20402
(202) 783-3238

Stock number: 1980 0-3010746
Cost: $11.50

Guide for Occupational Exploration

The **Guide for Occupational Exploration** (GOE) is designed to give job seekers information about fields of work that match their own interests and abilities. The GOE organizes occupations into 12 interest areas, 66 work groups, and 348 sub groups. The interest areas represent the broad interest requirements of occupations. They are:

01	Artistic
02	Scientific
03	Plants and Animals
04	Protective
05	Mechanical
06	Industrial
07	Business Detail
08	Selling
09	Accommodating (e.g. services)
10	Humanitarian
11	Leading-influencing
12	Physical-performing

Descriptions are provided for each of the 66 work groups. Each description contains a general overview of the occupational area and narratives related to the following questions:

What kind of work would you do?
What skills and abilities do you need for this kind of work?
How do you know if you would like or could learn to do this kind of work?
How can you prepare for and enter this kind of work?
What else should you consider about these jobs?

The final section of each work group lists the DOT codes that are covered in the description. The second half of the GOE contains several appendices. Appendix B discusses the related use of U.S. Employment Service interest and aptitude tests. Appendix C presents suggestions for using the Guide in organizing occupational information. Appendix D presents an alphabetical arrangement of the occupations, with related DOT and GOE code numbers.

The GOE also contains an explanation of how the guide might be used in career exploration.

Order from: Superintendent of Documents
               U.S. Government Printing Office
               Washington, DC 20402
               (202) 783-3238

               Stock number: 029-013-00080-2
               Cost: $12.00

Standard Occupational Classification Manual
U.S. Department of Commerce, Office of Federal Statistical Policy and Standards
1980

The *Standard Occupational Classification* (SOC) Manual was developed to standardize the list of occupations for which statistical information is collected. While the DOT may be the most complete list of occupations, it is too large for data collection purposes. The SOC Manual provides a common structure of occupations, coding all occupations in which work is performed for pay or profit, including work performed by unpaid family workers. Each title includes a list of DOT (4th edition) titles which are descriptive of the group.

The SOC is structured on a four-level system: division, major group, minor group, and unit group. There are 22 broad occupational divisions. Within the broadest classifications, there are 64 major groups, and then specific occupations. Each level represents groupings in successively finer detail.

The broad occupational divisions are:

*   Executive, Administrative and Managerial Occupations
*   Engineers, Surveyors, and Architects
*   Natural Scientists and Mathematicians
*   Social Scientists, Social Workers, Religious Workers and Lawyers
*   Teachers, Librarians, and Counselors
*   Health Diagnosing and Treating Practitioners
*   Registered Nurses, Pharmacists, Dietitians, Therapists, and Physician's Assistants
*   Writers, Artists, Entertainers, and Athletes
*   Technologists and Technicians, except Health
*   Marketing and Sales Occupations
*   Administrative Support Occupations, including Clerical
*   Service Occupations
*   Agricultural, Forestry and Fishing Occupations
*   Mechanics and Repairers
*   Construction and Extractive Occupations
*   Precision Production Occupations
*   Production Working Occupations
*   Transportation and Material Moving Occupations
*   Handlers, Equipment Cleaners, Helpers, and Laborers
*   Military Occupations
*   Miscellaneous Occupations

Since the publication of the SOC, agencies have modified the basic SOC structure to suit their own purposes. The variations of the SOC organization retain the basic division and major group structure of the SOC. Two significant variations are the occupational classification schemes used by the Bureau of the Census and the Bureau of Labor Statistics for the Occupational Employment

Statistics Program.

Order from: Superintendent of Documents
               U.S. Government Printing Office
               Washington, DC 20402
               (202) 783-3238

               Stock number: 0-332-946
               Cost: $30.00

Standard Industrial Classification Manual
U.S. Executive Office of the President
Office of Management and Budget
1987

All economic enterprises in the United States are classified by their major product of service. The ***Standard Industrial Classification*** (SIC) **Manual** contains this classification scheme. It covers the entire field of economic activities:

- Agriculture, Forestry, Fishing, Hunting, and Trapping;
- Mining;
- Construction;
- Manufacturing;
- Transportation, Communication, Electric, Gas and Sanitary Service;
- Wholesale Trade, Retail Trade;
- Finance, Insurance, and Real Estate;
- Personal, Business, Repair, and Other Services;
- and Public Administration.

This classification system was developed almost 50 years ago. Since that time, all statistical information about industries has been organized according to the SIC scheme.

The classification system includes ten major divisions, with major groups (two-digit), groups (three-digit) and particular industries (four-digit). Each level is more detailed than the previous.

The SIC Manual has been revised several times to reflect the changing nature of U.S. industry and to include the new kinds of industries appearing on the scene.

Order from: Superintendent of Documents
               U.S. Government Printing Office
               Washington, DC 20402
               (202) 783-3238

               Stock number: 041-001-00314-2
               Cost: $24.00

A Classification of Instructional Programs
U.S. Department of Education
National Center for Education Statistics
1985

In the **Classification of Instructional Programs (CIP)** instructional programs at elementary, secondary and postsecondary levels are classified into 31 programs. Within these program categories, there are 50 sub categories, and then specific instructional programs. This classification scheme is designed for collecting, reporting and interpreting data about instructional programs.

The CIP, published in 1981 and revised in 1985, attempts to address some of the problems that were found in collecting, reporting, and analyzing information about instructional programs. These problems were due mostly to the lack of a comprehensive and up-to-date classification system with definitions for describing instructional programs. There were five major design criteria used in the development of CIP:

- Distinctions among programs were made on the basis of program purposes or objectives.
- The classification applies to all instructional programs without regard to institutional types.
- The classification applies to programs at all educational levels: elementary, secondary, and postsecondary.
- For the purpose of continuity, ties to existing taxonomies are maintained as long as they do not contradict other established criteria.
- The classification reflects the historical traditions of various instructional program areas.

CIP is built on a three-level hierarchical system. It consists of six digits that permit aggregation of comparable programs at varying levels of detail, from the broad two-digit program category level through an intermediate four-digit level to the most detailed six-digit program level. CIP was designed to be exhaustive and to avoid duplication among the categories. In cases where a program has historically been classified in two places, a cross-reference has been provided from one two-digit grouping to another. However, all program titles will have a single unique code derived from a single area.

The 1985 revision to the CIP was designed to eliminate classifications for programs with relatively few completers. Consequently, the revision frequently consisted of the combination of several detailed codes into one more general program classification. A number of programs were eliminated entirely.

Order from: Superintendent of Documents
U.S. Government Printing Office
Washington, DC 20402
(202) 783-3238

Stock number: 069-000-000-88-1 (1981 edition)
Cost: unknown

1990 Census of Population and Housing
U.S. Bureau of the Census

The Decennial Census is a complete count of the population of the United States and its territories. The census is a survey of households. It has been taken every ten years since 1790. Recent censuses have collected data about characteristics such as age, sex, race, and marital status for 100% of the population. Detailed information, collected from a sample of the population includes labor force status, occupation, industry, education, income, poverty status, ancestry, primary language and numbers of children.

Data from the 1990 census will become available over a period of time from 1991 to 1993. These data will be available in several formats including published reports, CD-ROM, and computer tapes. There will also be numerous articles and reports available that describe and analyze the data in each state.

Below is a list of the planned printed reports and the projected release dates.

Occupational Outlook Handbook
U.S. Bureau of Labor Statistics
Biennial

The *Occupational Outlook Handbook* (OOH) provides an overview of about 200 occupations, clustered into 19 broader occupational groupings using the Standard Occupational Classification structure. Occupational descriptions include the nature of the work, training and other qualifications, employment outlook, earnings and working conditions, and sources of additional information. The information is based on data from a variety of sources, including business firms, trade associations, labor unions, professional societies, educational institutions, and government agencies.

An introductory chapter contains information for using and interpreting data in the OOH. Another section provides suggestions on how and where to obtain additional information about particular occupations. Another introductory section titled "Tomorrow's Jobs" describes the impact that population structure and regional differences will have on the labor force throughout the 1990s.

This is one of the best sources of information for those who are trying to make a career choice. Many occupational fields are covered and information for related occupations is clustered together, so users can easily investigate a number of occupations with similar characteristics.

Information in the OOH reflects nationwide trends, however the outlook and earnings information is likely to vary from one area to another. Users should pay particular attention to localizing the information, using wage reports from their particular state, or using the Career Information Delivery System in their state.

The OOH is published every two years in both hard cover and paper binding.

Order from: Superintendent of Documents
                U.S. Government Printing Office
                Washington, DC 20402
                (202) 783-3238

                Hard Cover
                    Cost: $22.00
                    Stock Number: 029-001-03021-5
                Paperback
                    Cost: $17.00
                    Stock Number: 029-001-03022-3

Occupational Outlook Quarterly
U.S. Bureau of Labor Statistics
Quarterly

The *Occupational Outlook Quarterly* (OOQ) helps readers keep abreast of current occupational developments between editions of the *Occupational Outlook Handbook*. It provides updated, timely information. There is a wide range of articles in the OOQ, useful for both counselors, students and clients. The articles are written in an easy to read style and graphs and illustrations help present the story.

Easy to understand summaries of national projections are included periodically. A regular article every two years, "The Job Outlook in Brief", summarizes new information in the *Occupational Outlook Handbook*.

Order from: Superintendent of Documents
                   U.S. Government Printing Office
                   Washington, DC 20402
                   (202) 783-3238
                             or
                   Regional Government Printing Office Bookstore

                   Cost: $6.50/year

Occupational Projections and Training Data
U.S. Bureau of Labor Statistics, Biennial

Occupational Projections and Training Data is published biennially as a companion to the *Occupational Outlook Handbook* (OOH). This supplement contains the statistics and technical data that underlie the occupational descriptions in the OOH. It focuses on the information needs of education planning officials, although there is data and analysis that may interest counselors, students and clients.

This report contains statistics on current and projected occupational employment and on completers of institutional education and training programs. There are also occupational data on worker characteristics: the percent who are wage and salary workers, the percent who left specific occupations, and the percent of workers who are part-time, female, black and Hispanic. Age and industry distribution are also presented.

Order from: Superintendent of Documents
                   U.S. Government Printing Office
                   Washington, DC 20402
                   (202) 783-3238
                   or
                   Regional Government Printing Office Bookstore

                   Cost: $5.00
                   Stock Number: 029-001-03053-3

Military Career Guide, 1988-89, Employment and Training Opportunities in the Military
U.S. Department of Defense
1987

The ***Military Career Guide*** is a compendium of military occupational and training information designed to explore military careers. It is a single reference source for the diverse employment and training opportunities in the Army, Navy, Air Force, Marine Corps, and Coast Guard.

The book is divided into two major sections. The first section contains descriptions of 134 enlisted military occupations and provides information regarding the aptitudes needed for each. Persons who have taken the Armed Services Vocational Aptitude Battery (ASVAB) can use their scores to determine their chances of qualifying for these military occupations. The second section contains descriptions of 71 military officer occupations. The officer information is new to the 1988-89 edition. It was added in response to requests from educators after the 1985 edition.

Over 75% of all military occupations have counterparts in the civilian world of work. For example, dental hygienist, air traffic controller, computer programmer, aircraft mechanic, and electronic technician occupations exist in both the military and civilian work forces. An index of titles also gives a code number from the *Dictionary of Occupational Titles*. The occupations in each section are grouped in broad occupational groups. The Table of Contents will help locate a specific occupational title or group of related occupations. Copies of the *Military Career Guide* are available from military recruiters, high school counselors, and local libraries.

Order from: U.S. Military Entrance Processing Command
2500 Green Bay Road
North Chicago, IL 60064
Hotline: 1-800-323-0513
Within Illinois, call collect: 708-688-4922

Military Career Paths: Career Progression Patterns for Selected Occupations from the Military Career Guide
U.S. Department of Defense, 1990

The purpose of ***Military Career Paths*** is to describe the typical duties and assignments a person could expect when advancing along the path of a 20 year military career. While the *Military Career Guide* presents an overview of the typical job duties in a military occupation, this volume presents a more comprehensive description of work performed at various stages of a military career.

In total, the career paths of 25 enlisted and 13 officer occupations are described. Each occupation contains important career information, such as requirements for career advancement, training, typical job duties, and levels of advancement. One of the most interesting features is a "career profile" that summarizes the career progression of an actual service member in the particular occupation. Each profile details the places of assignment and duties the service member performed over his/her career.

Order from: U.S. Military Entrance Processing Command
                 2500 Green Bay Road
                 North Chicago, IL 60064

                 Hotline: 1-800-323-0513
                 Within Illinois, call collect: 708-688-4922

Occupational Information Systems
State Occupational Information Coordinating Committees
Occupational Information Systems (OIS) are computerized databases of labor market and occupational information that contain mechanisms for combining data from multiple sources. The systems are designed to meet the occupational information needs of vocational education, economic development, and employment and training programs. OIS systems can also help counselors pinpoint information about particular occupations.

OIS databases in the various states contain much of the same kinds of information. Each state may, however, include additional data to meet particular needs and interests of users in that state.

OIS databases contain extensive state and locally specific labor market information, including the current and projected demand for workers by occupation and information on the current supply of graduates of related training programs. There is also information on educational requirements, average wages, percent of females in that occupation and possible employers in the area.

Information developed from the data can identify major changes and trends in local and state labor markets. A careful analysis of the data can help identify current and potential shortages and surpluses of workers in specific occupations in a given place. The data can also help identify potential trouble spots in the performance of programs and the related labor market conditions that may be causing them. The program includes information on new and emerging occupations as well.

OIS databases are designed for use on a personal computer. Many states do publish information from the system, making the data more easily available to libraries, teachers, counselors, and job placement personnel.

Order from: Contact your state's Occupational Information Coordinating Committee
                 (See Appendix B)

Outlook 2000
U.S. Bureau of Labor Statistics
1990

Outlook 2000 presents revised Bureau of Labor Statistics employment projections for the year 2000. Three alternative growth patterns provide estimates of overall and sector economic growth with consistent industry and occupational employment projections.

Part I consists of five articles reprinted from the November 1990s issues of the **Monthly Labor Review**. These articles explore the labor force of the 1990s, the structure of the economy, industry output and employment, occupational employment, emerging issues, and a summary. Part II provides a brief review of the methodology behind the projections. Part III presents the assumptions underlying the specific industry and occupational employment estimates.

These projections are the latest product of a program begun more than 25 years ago to study alternative growth combinations and their effects on employment by industry and occupation. Previous economic and employment projections in the series have been published for the years 1970, 1975, 1980, 1985, and 2000. Less comprehensive projections have been made for a somewhat longer period.

The articles in this bulletin are written so that counselors, job placement personnel, and interested clients can understand the population and employment trends in the United States economy. The statistics of occupational employment are roughly comparable with projections of occupational employment published by individual states.

Order from: Superintendent of Documents
U.S. Government Printing Office
Washington, DC 20402
(202) 783-3238
or
Regional Government Printing Office Bookstore

Cost: $7.50

Appendix M

Overview of Equal Opportunity Legislation

OVERVIEW OF EQUAL OPPORTUNITY LEGISLATION

Equal Pay Act of 1963

This act, the first piece of federal legislation forbidding sex discrimination in employment, is an extension of the Fair Labor Standards Act. It was designed to prevent sex discrimination in the payment of wages. The act essentially provides for equal pay for equal work; however, the definition of equal work is left with the courts.

Title VI of the Civil Rights Act of 1964

Title VI of the Civil Rights Act prohibits discrimination against students on the grounds of race, color or national origin in programs receiving federal funds. Title VI and related case law prohibits discrimination on the basis of race in student admissions, access to courses and programs, and student policies and their application. They also require the provision of bilingual instruction or some other method of compensating for students of limited English speaking ability. Any institution or agency receiving federal funds is covered by Title VI. Most education activities of the recipient agency or instruction are covered, even some activities or programs not in direct receipt of federal funds. Title VI is enforced by the Office of Civil Rights of the U.S. Department of Health, Education and Welfare.

Title VII of the Civil Rights Act of 1964

This act makes it illegal for private employers, labor unions, employment agencies, state and local governments, and employees of educational institutions to discriminate on the basis of race, color, religion, sex, or national origin. It is unlawful to discriminate in:

- recruitment, hiring, firing, layoff, recall
- wages, conditions or privileges of employment
- classification, assignment or promotion
- use of facilities
- apprenticeship training or retraining
- application of referral procedures
- sick leave and pay
- overtime work and pay
- insurance coverage
- retirement privileges
- printing, publishing, or circulating advertisement relating to employment
- promotion opportunities

Harassment on basis of sex is a violation of Title VII (guidelines issued, November 10, 1980)

Executive Order 11246

This order prohibits employment discrimination based on sex, as well as on race, color, religion, or national origin, by federal contractors or subcontractors. The order covers employers with a federal contract of more than $10,000 and does not exempt specific kinds of employment or employees. Unlawful practices include discrimination in recruiting or recruitment advertising; hiring, upgrading, demotion, or transfer; layoff or termination; rates of pay or other compensation; and selection for training, including apprenticeship. Regulations have been ordered which required hiring women in all construction craft jobs--3.1% of the work crews in each craft by 1979, 5% by 1980, and 6.9% by 1981. Companies and unions which run federally registered apprenticeship programs in these crafts have to enroll women at the rate equal to half their percentage of the general work force in any area--about 20% for most entering classes.

Revised Order No. 4

This order requires contractors with 50 or more employees and a contract of $50,000 or more to take affirmative action in the employment of minorities in job categories where they have been underutilized. The order requires similar goals and timetables for women as well as minorities. In brief, the order requires affirmative action programs to have the following: (1) A self-analysis of deficiencies in compliance, (2) corrective action to remedy deficiencies, (3) goals and timetables where numbers/percentages are relevant to correct situation, (4) development or reaffirmation of an equal opportunity policy, (5) dissemination of policy throughout community, (6) report system to measure program effectiveness, and (7) a procedure for getting support from local groups to improve employment opportunities for minorities and women.

Titles VII and VIII of the Public Health Services Act

These titles forbid schools and training programs in the health profession from discriminating against students on the basis of sex. The only schools and training programs affected are those receiving financial assistance under the Public Health Services Act. Teachers and employers who work with students covered by this Act are also covered.

Title VII of the Civil Rights Act of 1964

As amended by the Equal Employment Opportunity Act of 1972, this title prohibits discrimination in the employment of personnel on the basis of race, color, religion, national origin, or sex. All institutions or agencies with 15 or more employees including state and local governments and labor organizations are covered under the Act. Title VII prohibits discriminatory practices in most terms and conditions of employment.

Equal Pay Act of 1963, Amended by the Education Amendments of 1972

This amendment prohibits sex discrimination in salaries and fringe benefits. It covers all employees of educational institutions--professional, executive, and administrative positions.

Title IX

In 1972, Congress enacted Title IX of the Education Amendments Act, which prohibits discrimination on the basis of sex in any education program or activity receiving federal financial assistance. Title IX states: "No person in the United States shall on the basis of sex be excluded from participation in, be denied the benefits of or be subjected to discrimination under any education program or activity receiving Federal financial assistance. . ."

The Title IX regulations were issued after much delay on June 4, 1975. The regulations state that with certain exceptions, the law bars sex discrimination in any academic, extracurricular, research, vocational or other educational program (pre-school to post-graduate) operated by an organization or agency that receives or benefits from federal aid.

The exceptions included: U.S. military schools, although such schools began admitting women in 1976, religious schools, Girl Scouts and Boy Scouts, YMCA/YWCA, and other single-sex youth service organizations, social fraternities and sororities, Boys State/Girls State, and father-son and mother-daughter activities.

The regulations are divided into six categories: general provisions, coverage, admissions, treatment of significant implications for recruitment, facilities, financial aid, student rules, counseling programs, housing rules, health care and insurance benefits, scholarships and other recognition activities, marital and parental status of students, student employment, athletics and other extracurricular activities, course content, sexual harassment, single-sex courses, and school district provision of significant assistance to any organization, agency or individual that discriminates on the basis of sex. The regulation does not require or abridge the use of the particular textbooks or curriculum materials.

By July 21, 1976, educational institutions were to comply with the following procedural requirement of Title IX. Educational institutions were to 1) appoint a Title IX Coordinator to monitor compliance and to handle grievances; 2) adopt and publish a grievance procedure for prompt and equitable resolution of complaints; 3) annually provide notice of the districts compliance with Title IX to students, parents, employees, job applicants, unions, and other professional associations; 4) provide a public notice of compliance with Title IX in a local newspaper; 5) conduct a self-evaluation to determine where the districts' policies or practices might constitute sex discrimination and to set forth remedial steps to eliminate the affects of sex discrimination within a three-year period; and 6) to file an assurance of compliance with the U.S. Office for Civil Rights.

When Title IX was enacted, it contained employment-related protections for employees of educational institutions that were not yet covered by Title VII or state law, especially in the area of pregnancy and marital or parental status. Prior, to Title IX's passage, it was common practice to: pay female teachers less than male teachers because males were presumed to be the head of a household; to pay female coaches less than male coaches; and to require pregnant teachers to leave the classroom immediately. Title IX requires that school districts have a grievance procedure for employees to use if they have a complaint of discrimination, and requires that employees and applicants for employment be informed that the school district does not discriminate on the basis of sex in employment. Between 1979 and 1982, three separate federal district courts ruled that Title IX protected students only, not employees, from sex discrimination. During that period of time, the Office for Civil Rights did not accept or investigate complaints of employment discrimination under Title IX. In May of 1982, the Supreme Court ruled in North Haven Board of Education vs. Bell to uphold the validity of Subpart E (Employment) of the Title IX regulations.

Women's Educational Equity Act of 1974

Designed as part of the Education Amendments of 1974, this Act was passed to provide educational equity for women in the United States. Under this Act, the Commissioner is authorized to give grants to or to enter into contracts with agencies, organizations, or individuals for activities designed to carry out the purposes of the law at all levels of education--preschool, elementary/secondary, higher education, and adult education. Activities included are the development, evaluation, and dissemination of curriculum, textbooks, and other materials concerning educational equity; preservice and inservice training for personnel with special emphasis on programs to provide education equity; research and development activities designed to advance educational equity; guidance and counseling designed to assure educational equity, etc.

Nothing in this law prohibits men from participating in any programs or activities. The act establishes in the U.S. Office of Education an Advisory Council on Women's Educational Programs composed of 17 people appointed by the President--by and with the advice and consent of the Senate. The Act is administered by the Women's Program Staff, Office of the Commissioner, U.S. Office of Education.

Section 504 of the 1973 Rehabilitation Act

Section 504 prohibits discrimination on the basis of handicap in employment and programming by all recipients of federal financial assistance. Section 504 is enforced by the Office of Civil Rights.

Age Discrimination in Employment Act of 1967

The Age Discrimination in Employment Act of 1967 prohibits employment discrimination against persons between the ages of 40 and 65; on January 1, 1979, the act was extended to protect persons between the ages of 40 and 70. The Act prohibits discrimination in hiring, discharge, compensation, terms, conditions or privileges of employment. The Act prohibits mandatory retirement prior to the age of 70. The Age Discrimination in Employment Act is enforced by the EEOC.

Age Discrimination Act of 1975

The Age Discrimination Act of 1975 prohibits unreasonable discrimination on the basis of age in programs or activities receiving Federal financial assistance. This Act will protect all students in community colleges, technical schools, and universities, from discrimination on the basis of age. The Act does not define age to limit coverage to any particular group; it simply prohibits discrimination on the basis of age at any age, as long as that discrimination is "unreasonable." Employment is not covered by the Act, other than employment funded by the Comprehensive Employment Training Act (CETA).

Title VII (Section 799A) and Title VIII (Section 845) of the Public Health Service Act as Amended by the Comprehensive Health Manpower Training Act and the Nurse Training Amendment Act of 1971

Title VII and VIII of the Public Health Service Act states that institutions receiving federal funds for their health personnel training programs may not discriminate on the basis of sex in admissions or in employment practices related to employees working directly with applicants or students. Every institution receiving or benefiting from a grant, loan guarantee, or interest subsidy to its health personnel training programs or receiving a contract under Title VII or VIII is covered. Title VII and VIII are enforced by the Office of Civil Rights.

Carl D. Perkins Vocational Education Act of 1984

The Carl D. Perkins Vocational Education Act of 1984 and its predecessor the Vocational Education Act (VEA) of 1976, represent the most comprehensive effort to date to infuse sex equity into an educational program by requiring positive action to end bias and stereotyping as well as ensuring nondiscrimination. The provisions of the Vocational Education Act of 1976 required for the first time that each state hire at least one full-time staff person to coordinate and infuse sex equity throughout the vocational education system. The law required states to provide incentives to local districts to encourage nontraditional enrollments and to begin to establish programs for special target populations, such as displaced homemakers. The law required that advisory councils have a fair representation of females, males, minorities and the disabled. The Carl Perkins Act retained and expanded upon the key sex equity provisions of the 1976 Act. States are required to assign one person full time responsibility for fulfilling seven mandated functions. The Act provides two set-asides within the basic state grant; one for Single Parents and Homemakers (8.5% of the basic grant), and the other for Young Women and Sex Equity Programs (3.5% of the basic grant). Local school or vocational districts apply for these funds on an annual basis to implement programs for vocational education students. The intended long-term outcome of these programs is to provide greater economic self-sufficiency for girls and women.

Appendix N

Labor Market
Information Directors

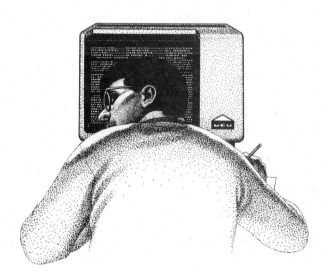

Douglas Dyer, Director
Labor Market Information
Department of Industrial Relations
649 Monroe Street, Rm. 422
Montgomery, AL 36130
205/242-8855
FAX: 205/240-3070

Chuck Caldwell, Chief
Research & Analysis
Department of Labor
P.O. Box 25501
Juneau, AK 99802-5501
907/465-4500
FAX: 907/465-2101

Dan Anderson
Research Administrator
Dept. of Economic Security
1789 West Jefferson
P.O. Box 6123, Site Code 733A
Phoenix, AZ 85005
602/542-3871
FAX: 602/542-6474

Coy Cozart
State and Labor Market Information
Employment Security Division
P.O. Box 2981
Little Rock, AR 72203
501/682-1543
FAX: 501/682-3713

Jeanne Barnett, Chief
Employment Data & Research Div.
Employment Development Dept.
P.O. Box 942880, MIC 57
Sacramento, CA 94280-0001
916/427-4675
FAX: 916/323-6674

William LaGrange, Director
Labor Market Information
Chancey Building, 8th Floor
1120 Lincoln Street
Denver, CO 80203
303/894-2589
FAX: 303/860-9167

Richard Vannuccini, Director
Research & Information
Employment Security Division
CT Labor Department
200 Folly Brook Boulevard
Wethersfield, CT 06109
203/566-2120
FAX: 203/566-1519

James McFadden, Chief
Office of Occupational & LMI
Delaware Department of Labor
University Plaza, Building D
P. O. Box 9029
Newark, DE 19702-9029
302/368-6962
FAX: 302/368-6748

Richard (Dick) Groner
Chief of Labor Market Information
Dept. of Employment Services
500 C Street, N.W., Rm. 201
Washington, D.C. 20001
202/639-1642
FAX: 202/639-1765

Rebecca Rust, Chief
Bureau of Labor Market Information
Dept. of Labor & Employment Sec.
2012 Capitol Circle, SE, Room 200
Hartman Building
Tallahassee, FL 32399-0674
904/488-1048
FAX: 904/488-2558

Milton L. Martin, Director
Labor Information Systems
Georgia Department of Labor
223 Courtland Street, N.E.
Atlanta, GA 30303
404/656-3177
FAX: 404/651-9568

Frederick Pang, Chief
Research & Statistics Office
Dept. of Labor & Industrial Rel.
830 Punchbowl St., Rm. 304
Honolulu, HI 96813
808/548-7639
FAX: 808/548-1224

Jim Adams, Chief
Research & Analysis
Department of Employment
317 Main Street
Boise, ID 83735
208/334-6169
FAX: 208/334-6427

Henry Jackson, Director
Economic Information & Analysis
Dept. of Employment Security
401 South State St., 2 South
Chicago, IL 60605
312/793-2316
FAX: 312/793-6245

Keith Kunze, Director
Labor Market Information
IN Dept. of Employ. & Training Services
10 North Senate Avenue
Indianapolis, IN 46204
317/232-8456
FAX: 317/232-6950

Stephen C. Smith, Supervisor
Audit & Analysis Department
Department of Employment Services
1000 East Grand Avenue
Des Moines, IA 50319
515/281-8181
FAX: 515/242-6301

William Layes, Chief
Labor Market Information Services
Department of Human Resources
401 Topeka Avenue
Topeka, KS 66603
913/296-5058
FAX: 913/296-0179

Ed Blackwell, Manager
Labor Market Research & Analysis
Department for Employment Services
275 E. Main Street
Frankfort, KY 40621
502/564-7976
FAX: 502/564-7452

Oliver Robinson, Director
Research & Statistics Division
Department of Employment & Training
P.O. Box 94094
Baton Rouge, LA 70804-9094
504/342-3141
FAX: 504/342-9193

Raynold A. Fongemie, Director
Div. of Econo. Analysis & Research
Bureau of Employment Security
20 Union Street
Augusta, ME 04330
207/289-2271
FAX: 207/289-5292

Pat Arnold, Director
Dept. of Economic & Employ. Develop.
Dept. of Economic & Employ. Develop.
1100 North Eutaw Street
Baltimore, MD 21201
301/333-5000
FAX: 301/333-7121

Rena Kottcamp, Director
Research
Division of Employment Security
19 Staniford Street, 2nd Floor
Boston, MA 02114
617/727-6868
FAX: 617/727-0315

Von Logan, Director
Bureau of Research & Statistics
Employment Security Commission
7310 Woodward Avenue
Detroit, MI 48202
313/876-5445
FAX: 313/876-5244

Med Chottepanda, Director
Research & Statistical Services
Department of Jobs and Training
390 N. Robert St., 5th Floor
St. Paul, MN 55101
612/296-6546
FAX: 612/296-0994

Raiford G. Crews, Chief
Labor Market Information Dept.
Employment Security Commission
P.O. Box 1699
Jackson, MS 39215-1699
601/961-7424
FAX: 601/961-7405

Tom Righthouse, Chief 314/751-3591
Research & Analysis
Division of Employment Security FAX: 314/751-7973
P.O. Box 59
Jefferson City, MO 65104

Bob Rafferty, Chief 406/444-2430
Research & Analysis
Dept. of Labor and Industry FAX: 406/444-2638
P.O. Box 1728
Helena, MT 59624

Wendell Olson 402/471-9964
Research Administrator
Labor Market Information FAX: 402/471-2318
Department of Labor
550 S. 16th Street--P.O. Box 94600
Lincoln, NE 68509-4600

James S. Hanna, Chief 702/687-4550
Employment Security Research
Employment Security Department FAX: 702/687-3424
500 East Third Street
Carson City, NV 89713

George Nazer, Director 603/228-4123
Labor Market Information
Department of Employment Security FAX: 603/228-4172
32 South Main Street
Concord, NH 03301-4587

Arthur J. O'Neal 609/292-2643
Assistant Commissioner
Policy & Planning FAX: 609/292-6692
Department of Labor
John Fitch Plaza, Rm. 1010
Trenton, NJ 08625

Larry Blackwell, Chief 505/841-8645
Economic Research & Analysis Bureau
Department of Labor FAX: 505/841-8421
P.O. Box 1928
Albuquerque, NM 87103

Jeremy P. Schrauf, Director 518/457-6181
Division of Research & Statistics
NY State Department of Labor FAX: 518/457-0620
State Campus, Bldg. 12, Rm. 400
Albany, NY 12240-0020

Gregory B. Sampson, Director 919/733-2936
Labor Market Information Div.
Employment Security Commission FAX: 919/733-8662
P.O. Box 25903
Raleigh, NC 27611

Tom Pederson, Chief 701/224-2868
Labor Market Information
Job Service North Dakota FAX: 701/224-4000
P.O. Box 1537
Bismarck, ND 58502

Keith Ewald 614/644-2689
Labor Market Information Div.
Bureau of Employment Services FAX: 614/481-8543
145 South Front Street
Columbus, OH 43215

Bernice Street, Chief 405/557-7116
Research & Planning Division
Employment Security Commission FAX: 405/557-7256
308 Will Rogers Memorial Office Bldg.
Oklahoma City, OK 73105

Virlena Crosley 503/378-3220
Assistant Administrator for
Research & Statistics FAX: 503/3737460
Oregon Employment Division
875 Union Street, N.E.
Salem, OR 97311

Carl Thomas, Director 717/787-3265
Research & Statistics Division
1216 Labor & Industry Building FAX: 717/772-2168
Harrisburg, PA 17121

Agapito Villegas, Director 809/754-5385
Research & Statistics Division
Dept. of Labor & Human Resources FAX: None
505 Munoz Rivera Ave., 15th Flr.
Hato Rey, PR 00918

Robert Langlais, Administrator 401/277-3730
Labor Market Information & Management Services
Dept. of Employment & Training FAX: 401/277-2731
101 Friendship Street
Providence, RI 02903-3740

David Laird, Director 803/737-2660
Labor Market Information
Employment Security Commission FAX: 803/737-2642
P.O. Box 995
Columbia, SC 29202

Mary Sue Vickers, Director 605/622-2314
Labor Market Information Center
Department of Labor FAX: 605/622-2322
P.O. Box 4730
Aberdeen, SD 57402-4730

Joe S. Cummings, Director 615/741-2284
Research & Statistics Division
Department of Employment Security FAX: 615/741-3203
Cordell Hull Office Bldg., Rm. 519
436 6th Avenue, North
Nashville, TN 37245-1000

Mark Hughes, Director 512/463-2616
Economic Research & Analysis
Texas Employment Commission FAX: 512/475-1241
15th & Congress Ave., Room 208T
Austin, TX 78778

Bill Horner, Director 801/533-2014
Labor Market Information
    and Research FAX: 801/533-2466
Department of Employment Security
174 Social Hall Avenue
P.O. Box 11249
Salt Lake City, UT 84147

Robert Ware, Director 802/229-0311
Policy and Information
VT Dept. of Employment & Trng. FAX: 802/223-0750
5 Green Mountain Drive
P.O. Box 488
Montpelier, VT 05602

Dolores A. Esser, Director 804/786-7496
Economic Information Services Div.
Virginia Employment Commission FAX: 804/225-3923
P.O. Box 1358
Richmond, VA 23211

Annie I. Smith, Chief 809/776-3700
Research & Analysis
Department of Labor FAX: 809/774-5908
P.O. Box 3159
St. Thomas, VI 00801

Gary Bodeutsch, Director 206/438-4804
Labor Market & Economic Analysis
Employment Security Department FAX: 206/438-4846
212 Maple Park, Mail Stop KG-11
Olympia, WA 98504-5311

Edward F. Merrifield   304/348-2660
Assistant Director
Labor & Economic Research   FAX: 304/348-0301
Bureau of Employment Programs
112 California Avenue
Charleston, WV 25305-0112

Hartley J. Jackson, Director   608/266-5843
Labor Market Information Bureau
Dept. of Industry, Labor & Human   FAX: 608/267-0330
 Relations
P.O. Box 7944
Madison, WI 53707

Tom Gallagher, Manager   307/235-3646
Research & Planning
Employment Security Commission   FAX: 307/235-3293
P.O. Box 2760
Casper, WY 82602

Appendix O

State Data Center Program
Coordinating Organizations

UNITED STATES DEPARTMENT OF COMMERCE
Bureau of the Census
Washington, D.C. 20233

State Data Center Program Coordinating Organizations

(Includes Business and Industry Data Center Initiative Components)

June 1990

Alabama

Center for Business and Economic
Research
University of Alabama
Box 870221
Tuscaloosa, AL 35487-0221
*Ms. Annette Watters
(205) 348-6191

Alabama Department of Economic
and Community Affairs
Office of State Planning
P.O. Box 250347
3465 Norman Bridge Road
Montgomery, AL 36105-0347
Mr. Parker Collins
(205) 284-8778

Alabama Public Library Service
6030 Monticello Drive
Montgomery, AL 36130
Ms. Hilda Dent
(205) 277-7330

Alaska

Alaska State Data Center
Research & Analysis
Department of Labor
P.O. Box 25504
Juneau, AK 99802-5504
*Ms. Kathryn Lizik
(907) 465-4500

Office of Management and Budget
Division of Policy
Pouch AD
Juneau, AK 99811
Mr. Jack Kreinheder
(907) 465-3568

Department of Education
Division of Libraries and Museums
Alaska State Library
Pouch G
Juneau, AK 99811-0571
Ms.Patience Frederiksen
(907) 465-2927

Department of Community &
Regional Affairs
Division of Municipal & Regional
Assistance
P.O. Box BH
Juneau, AK 99811
Mr. Paul Cunningham
(907) 465-4756

Institute for Social & Economic
Research
University of Alaska
3211 Providence Drive
Anchorage, AK 99508
Mr. Jim Kerr
(907) 786-7710

Arizona

Arizona Department of Economic
Security
1300 West Washington
P.O. Box 6123-045Z
Phoenix, AZ 85005
*Ms. Betty Jeffries
(602) 542-5984

Center for Business Research
College of Business Administration
Arizona State University
Tempe, AZ 85287
Mr. Tom Rex
(602) 965-3961

College of Business Administration
Northern Arizona University
Box 15066
Flagstaff, AZ 86011
Dr. Joseph Walka
(602) 523-3657

Federal Documents Section
Department of Library,
Archives, and Public Records
1700 West Washington
Phoenix, AZ 85007
Ms. Janet Fisher
(602) 621-4121

Division of Economic & Business
Research
College of Business & Public
Administration
University of Arizona
Tucson, AZ 85721
Ms. Holly Penix
(602) 621-2155

Arkansas

State Data Center
University of Arkansas-Little Rock
2801 South University
Little Rock, AR 72204
*Ms. Sarah Breshears
(501) 569-8530

Arkansas State Library
1 Capitol Mall
Little Rock, AR 72201
Ms. Mary Honeycutt
(501) 682-2864

Research & Analysis Section
Arkansas Employment Security
Division
P.O. Box 2981
Little Rock, AR 72203
Mr. Coy Cozart
(501) 682-3159

California

State Census Data Center
Department of Finance
915 L Street
Sacramento, CA 95814
*Ms. Linda Gage, Director
(916) 322-4651
Mr. Richard Lovelady
(916)323-2201

Sacramento Area COG
106 K Street, Suite 200
Sacramento, CA 95814
Mr. Bob Faseler
(916) 441-5930

Association of Bay Area
Governments
Metro Center
8th and Oak Streets
P.O. Box 2050
Oakland, CA 94604-2050
Ms. Patricia Perry
(415) 464-7937

Institute of Southern California
SCAG
818 West 7th Street
Los Angeles, CA 90017
Mr. Tim Douglas/Mike Schwarzmann
(213) 236-1800

San Diego Association of
Governments
First Federal Plaza
401 B Street, Suite 800
San Diego, CA 92101
Ms. Karen Lamphere
(619) 236-5353

State Data Center Program
University of California-Berkeley
2538 Channing Way
Berkeley, CA 94720
Ms. Ilona Einowski/Fred Gey
(415) 642-6571

Denotes key contact SDC
+ Denotes key contact BIDC

Colorado

Division of Local Government
Colorado Department of Local
Affairs
1,313 Sherman Street, Room 521
Denver, CO 80203
*Mr. Reid Reynolds
Ms. Rebecca Picaso
(303) 866-2156

Business Research Division
Graduate School of Business
Administration
University of Colorado-Boulder
Boulder, CO 80309
(303) 492-8227

Natural Resources & Economics
Department of Agriculture
Colorado State University
Fort Collins, CO 80523
Ms. Sue Anderson
(303) 491-5706

Documents Department
The Libraries
Colorado State University
Fort Collins, CO 80523
Ms. Suzanne Taylor
(303) 491-1101

Connecticut (BIDC)

Comprehensive Planning Division
Connecticut Office of Policy and
Management
80 Washington Street
Hartford, CT 06106
*+Mr. Theron Schnure
(203) 566-8285

Government Documents
Connecticut State Library
231 Capital Avenue
Hartford, CT 06106
Mr. Albert Palko
(203) 566-4971

Roper Center
Institute for Social Inquiry
University of Connecticut, U-164
Storrs, CT 06268
Ms. Lois Timms-Ferrara
(203) 486-4440

Connecticut Department of Economic
Development
865 Brook Street
Rocky Hill, CT 06067
Mr. Jeff Blodgett
(203) 566-4882

Employment Security Division
Connecticut Department of Labor
200 Folly Brook Boulevard
Wethersfield, CT 06109
Mr. Richard Vannuccini
(203) 566-2120

Delaware

Delaware Development Office
99 Kings Highway
P.O. Box 1401
Dover, DE 19903
*Ms. Judy McKinney-Cherry
(302) 736-4271

College of Urban Affairs and Public
Policy
University of Delaware
Graham Hall, Room 286
Academy Street
Newark, DE 19716
Mr. Ed Ratledge
(302) 451-8405

District of Columbia

Data Services Division
Mayor's Office of Planning
Room 314, Presidential Bldg.
415 12th Street, N.W.
Washington, DC 20004
*Mr. Gan Ahuja
(202) 727-6533

Metropolitan Washington Council of
Governments
777 North Capitol St., Suite 300
Washington, DC 20002-4201
Mr. Robert Griffiths
Ms. Jenean Johanningmeier
(202) 962-3200

Florida (BIDC)

Florida State Data Center
Executive Office of the Governor
Office of Planning & Budgeting
The Capitol
Tallahassee, FL 32399-0001
*Mr. Steve Kimble
(904) 487-2814

Center for the Study of Population
Institute for Social Research
654 Bellemy Building
Florida State University
Tallahassee, FL 32306-4063
Dr. Ike Eberstein
(904) 644-1762

State Library of Florida
R.A. Gray Building
Tallahassee, FL 32399-0250
Ms. Lisa Close
(904) 487-2651

Bureau of Economic Analysis
Florida Department of Commerce
107 East Gaines Street
Tallahassee, FL 32391-2000
+Ms. Sally Ramsey
(904) 487-2568

Georgia

Division of Demographic &
Statistical Services
Georgia Office of Planning and
Budget
270 Washington Street, S.W.,
Room 608
Atlanta, GA 30334
*Ms. Robin Kirkpatrick
(404) 656-0911

Documents Librarian
Georgia State University
University Plaza
Atlanta, GA 30303
Ms. Gayle Christian
(404) 651-2185

Robert W. Woodruff Library for
Advanced Studies
Emory University
Atlanta, GA 30322
Ms. Elizabeth McBride
(404)727-6880

Main Library
University of Georgia
Athens, GA 30602
Ms. Susan C. Field
(404) 542-0664

Georgia Department of Community
Affairs
Office of Coordinated Planning
100 Peachtree St, N.E. #1200
Atlanta, GA 30303
Mr. Phil Thiel
(404) 656-5526

Documents Librarian
State Data Center Program
Albany State College
504 College Drive
Albany, GA 31705
Ms. Juanita Miller
(912) 430-4799

Documents Librarian
State Data Center Program
Georgia Southern College
Statesboro, GA 30458
Ms. Lynn Walshak
(912) 681-5117

State Data Center Program
Mercer University Law Library
Mercer University
Macon, GA 31207
Ms. Jenny Rowe
(912) 744-2667

Data Services
University of Georgia Libraries
6th Floor
Athens, GA 30602
Ms. Hortense Bates
(404) 542-0727

* *Denotes key contact SDC*
+ *Denotes key contact BIDC*

Price Gilbert Memorial Library
Georgia Institute of Technology
Atlanta, GA 30332
Mr. Richard Leacy
(404) 894-4519

Guam

Guam Department of Commerce
590 South Marine Drive
Suite 601, 6th Floor GITC Building
Tamuning, Guam 96911
*Mr. Peter R. Barcinas
(671) 646-5841

Hawaii

Hawaii State Data Center
State Department of Business &
Economic Development
Kamamalu Building, Room 602A
250 S. King Street
Honolulu, HI 96813
(Mailing Address)
P.O. Box 2359
Honolulu, HI 96804
Mr. Robert Schmitt, State Statistician
*Ms. Sharon Nishi
(808) 548-3067

Information and Communication
Services Division
State Department of Budget and
Finance
Kalanimoku Building
1151 Punchbowl Street
Honolulu, HI 96813
Ms. Joy Toyama
(808) 548-6180

Idaho

Idaho Department of Commerce
700 West State Street
Boise, ID 83720
*Mr. Alan Porter
(208) 334-2470

Institutional Research
Room 319, Business Building
Boise State University
Boise, ID 83725
Mr. Don Canning
(208) 385-1613

The Idaho State Library
325 West State Street
Boise, ID 83702
Ms. Stephanie Nichols
(208) 334-2150

Center for Business Research and
Services
Campus Box 8450
Idaho State University
Pocatello, ID 83209
Dr. Paul Zelus
(208) 236-2504

Illinois

Division of Planning and Financial
Analysis
Illinois Bureau of the Budget
William Stratton Building, Rm. 605
Springfield, IL 62706
*Ms. Suzanne Ebetsch
(217) 782-1381

Census & Data Users Services
Department of Sociology,
Anthropology & Social Work
Illinois State University
604 South Main Street
Normal, IL 61761-6901
Dr. Roy Treadway
(309) 438-5946

Center for Governmental Studies
Northern Illinois University
Social Science Research Bldg.
DeKalb, IL 60115
Ms. Ruth Anne Tobias
(815) 753-1901, x221

Regional Research and Development
Service
Southern Illinois University at
Edwardsville
Box 1456
Edwardsville, IL 62026-1456
Mr. Charles Kofron
(618) 692-3500

Chicago Area Geographic
Information Study
Room 2102, Building BSB
P.O. Box 4348
University of Illinois at Chicago
Chicago, IL 60680
Mr. Jim Bash
(312) 996-6367

Indiana (BIDC)

Indiana State Library
Indiana State Data Center
140 North Senate Avenue
Indianapolis, IN 46204
Mr. Ray Ewick, Director
*Ms. Roberta Eads
(317) 232-3733

Indiana Business Research Center
Indiana University
10th and Fee Lane
Bloomington, IN 47405
Dr. Morton Marcus
(812) 855-5507

Indiana Business Research Center
801 West Michigan, B.S. 4013
Indianapolis, IN 46202-5151
+Ms. Carol Rogers
(317) 274-2205

Division of Economic Analysis
Indiana Department of Commerce
1 North Capitol, Suite 700
Indianapolis, IN 46204
Mr. Robert Lain
(317) 232-8959

Iowa

State Library of Iowa
East 12th and Grand
Des Moines, IA 50319
*Ms. Beth Henning
(515) 281-4105

Census Services
Iowa State University
320 East Hall
Ames, IA 50011
Dr. Willis Goudy
(515) 294-8337

Center for Social and Behavioral
Research
University of Northern Iowa
Cedar Falls, IA 50614
Dr. Robert Kramer
(319) 273-2105

Iowa Social Science Institute
University of Iowa
345 Shaeffer Hall
Iowa City, IA 52242
Mr. Brian Dalziel
(319) 335-2371

Census Data Center
Department of Public Instruction
Grimes State Office Building
Des Moines, IA 50319
Mr. Steve Boal
(515) 281-4730

Research Section
Iowa Department of Economic
Development
200 East Grand Avenue
Des Moines, IA 50309
(515) 281-3005

Ballou Library
Buena Vista College
Storm Lake, IA 50588
Ms. Jodi Morin
(712) 749-2203

Kansas

State Library
Room 343-N
State Capitol Building
Topeka, KS 66612
*Mr. Marc Galbraith
(913) 432-3919

Denotes key contact SDC
+ *Denotes key contact BIDC*

Division of the Budget
Room 152-E
State Capitol Building
Topeka, KS 66612
Ms. Teresa Floerchinger
(913) 296-2436

Institute for Public Policy and
Business Research
607 Blake Hall
The University of Kansas
Lawrence, KS 66045-2960
Ms. Thelma Helyar
(913) 864-3123

Center for Economic Development &
Business Research
Box 48
Wichita State University
Wichita, KS 67208
Ms. Janet Nickel
(316) 689-3225

Population and Resources Laboratory
Department of Sociology
Kansas State University
Manhattan, KS 66506
Dr. Jan L. Flora
(913) 532-5984

Kentucky (BIDC)

Urban Studies Center
College of Urban & Public Affairs
University of Louisville
Louisville, KY 40292
*+Mr. Ron Crouch
(502) 588-7990

Office of Policy & Management
State of Kentucky
Capitol Annex
Frankfort, KY 40601
Mr. Steve Rowland
(502) 564-7300

State Library Division
Department for Libraries & Archives
300 Coffeetree Road
P.O. Box 537
Frankfort, KY 40601
Ms. Brenda Fuller
(502) 875-7000

Louisiana

Office of Planning and Budget
Division of Administration
P.O. Box 94095
Baton Rouge, LA 70804
*Ms. Karen Paterson
(504) 342-7410

Division of Business and Economic
Research
University of New Orleans
Lake Front
New Orleans, La 70122
Mr. Vincent Maruggi
(504) 286-6248

Division of Business Research
Louisiana Tech University
P.O. Box 10318
Ruston, LA 71272
Dr. Edward O'Boyle
(318) 257-3701

Reference Department
Louisiana State Library
P.O. Box 131
Baton Rouge, LA 70821
Mrs. Blanche Cretini
(504) 342-4918

Center for Life Cycle and Population
Studies
Department of Sociology
Louisiana State University
Baton Rouge, LA 70803
Dr. Alan C. Acock
(504) 388-5359

Center for Business and Economic
Research
Northeast Louisiana University
Monroe, LA 71209
Dr. Jerry Wall
(318) 342-2123

Maine

Division of Economic Analysis and
Research
Maine Department of Labor
20 Union Street
Augusta, ME 04330
Mr. Raynold Fongemie, Director
*Ms. Jean Martin
(207) 289-2271

Maine State Library
State House Station 64
Augusta, ME 04333
Mr. Gary Nichols
(207) 289-3561

Maryland (BIDC)

Maryland Department of State
Planning
301 West Preston Street
Baltimore, MD 21201
*+Mr. Michel Lettre
(301) 225-4450

Computer Science Center
University of Maryland
College Park, MD 20742
Mr. John McNary
(301) 454-6030

Government Reference Service
Pratt Library
400 Cathedral Street
Baltimore, MD 21201
Mr. Wesley Wilson
(301) 396-5468

Massachusetts (BIDC)

Massachusetts Institute for Social and
Economic Research
128 Thompson Hall
University of Massachusetts
Amherst, MA 01003
+*Dr. Stephen Coelen, Director
(413) 545-3460
Ms. Nora Groves
(413) 545-0176

Massachusetts Institute for Social and
Economic Research
Box 219
The State House, Rm. 50
Boston, MA 02133
Mr. William Murray
(617) 727-3237

Michigan

Michigan Information Center
Department of Managment & Budget
Office of Revenue and Tax Analysis
P.O. Box 30026
Lansing, MI 48909
*Dr. Laurence Rosen
(517) 373-7910

MIMIC/Center for Urban Studies
Wayne State University
Faculty/Administration Bldg
656 W. Kirby
Detroit, MI 48202
Dr. Mark Neithercut
(313) 577-8350

The Library of Michigan
Government Documents Service
P.O. Box 30007
Lansing, MI 48909
Ms. F. Anne Diamond
(517) 373-1307

Minnesota (BIDC)

State Demographer's Office
Minnesota State Planning Agency
300 Centennial Office Building
658 Cedar Street
St. Paul, MN 55155
*Mr. David Birkholz
(612) 297-2360
+Mr. David Rademacher
(612) 297-3255

Interagency Resource & Information
Center
Department of Education
501 Capitol Square Building
St. Paul, MN 55101
Ms. Patricia Tupper
(612) 296-6684

* Denotes key contact SDC
+ Denotes key contact BIDC

Mississippi

Center for Population Studies
The University of Mississippi
Bondurant Bldg., Rm. 3W
University, MS 38677
Dr. Max Williams, Director
*Ms Pattie Byrd, Manager
(601) 232-7288

Governor's Office of Federal- State
Programs
Department of Community
Development
301 West Pearl Street
Jackson, MS 39203-3096
Mr. Jim Catt
(601) 949-2219

Missouri

Missouri State Library
2002 Missouri Boulevard
PO Box 387
Jefferson City, MO 65102
*Ms. Marlys Davis
(314) 751-3615

Office of Administration
124 Capitol Building
P.O. Box 809
Jefferson City, MO 65102
Mr. Ryan Burson
(314) 751-2345

Urban Information Center
University of Missouri-St. Louis
8001 Natural Bridge Road
St. Louis, MO 63121
Dr. John Blodgett
(314) 553-6014

Office of Social & Economic Data
Analysis
University of Missouri-Cloumbia
811 Clark Hall
Columbia, MO 65211
Ms. Evelyn J. Cleveland
(314) 882-7396

Montana (BIDC)

Census and Economic Information
Center
Montana Department of Commerce
1424 9th Avenue
Capitol Station
Helena, MT 59620-0401
*+Ms. Patricia Roberts
(406) 444-2896

Montana State Library
1515 East 6th Avenue
Capitol Station
Helena, MT 59620
Ms. Kathy Brown
(406) 444-3004

Bureau of Business and Economic
Research
University of Montana
Missoula, MT 59812
Mr. Jim Sylvester
(406) 243-5113

Survey Research Center
Wilson Hall, Rm. 1-108
Montana State University
Bozeman, MT 59717
Ms. Lee Faulkner
(406) 994-4481

Research & Analysis Bureau
Employment Policy Division
Montana Department of Labor &
Industry
P.O. Box 1728
Helena, MT 59624
Bob Rafferty
(406) 444-2430

Lewis & Clark Library
120 S. Last Chance Mall
Helena, MT 59601
Bruce Newell
(406) 442-2388

Nebraska

Center for Applied Urban Research
The University of Nebraska-Omaha
Peter Kiewit Conference Center
1313 Farnam-on-the-Mall
Omaha, NE 68182
*Mr. Jerome Deichert
(402) 595-2311

Policy Research Office
P.O. Box 94601
State Capitol, Rm. 1321
Lincoln, NE 68509-4601
Ms. Prem L. Bansal
(402) 471-2414

Nebraska Library Commission
1420 P Street
Lincoln, NE 68508
Mr. John L. Kopischke
(402) 471-2045

The Central Data Processing Division
Department of Administration
Services
1306 State Capitol
Lincoln, NE 68509
Mr. Skip Miller
(402) 471-2065

Nevada

Nevada State Library
Capitol Complex
401 North Carson
Carson City, NV 89710
Ms. Joan Kerschner
*Ms. Betty McNeal
(702) 885-5160

New Hampshire

Office of State Planning
2 1/2 Beacon Street
Concord, NH 03301
*Mr. Tom Duffy
(603) 271-2155

New Hampshire State Library
Park Street
Concord, NH 03301
Mr. Kendall Wiggin
(603) 271-2392

Office of Biometrics
University of New Hampshire
James Hall, 2nd Floor
Durham, NH 03824
Mr. Owen Durgin
(603) 862-1700

New Jersey (BIDC)

New Jersey Department of Labor
Division of Labor Market and
Demographic Research
CN 388-John Fitch Plaza
Trenton, NJ 08625-0388
*+Ms. Connie O. Hughes, Asst Dir
(609) 984-2593

New Jersey State Library
185 West State Street
CN 520
Trenton, NJ 08625-0520
Ms. Beverly Railsback
(609) 292-6220

Princeton-Rutgers Census Data
Project
Princeton University Computer
Center
87 Prospect Avenue
Princeton, NJ 08544
Ms. Judith S. Rowe
(609) 452-6052

Princeton-Rutgers Census Data
Project
Center for Computer & Information
Services
Rutgers University
CCIS-Hill Center, Busch Campus
P.O. Box 879
Piscataway, NJ 08854
Ms. Gertrude Lewis
(201) 932-2483

Department of Urban Planning and
Policy Development
Rutgers University
Lucy Stone Hall, B Wing
New Brunswick, NJ 08903
Dr. James Hughes, Chair and
Graduate Director
(201) 932-3822

* Denotes key contact SDC
+ Denotes key contact BIDC

New Mexico (BIDC)

Economic Development and Tourism
Department
1100 St. Francis Drive
Santa Fe, NM 87503
*Ms. Carol Selleck
(505) 827-0276

New Mexico State Library
325 Don Gaspar Avenue
P.O. Box 1629
Santa Fe, NM 87503
Ms. Norma McCallan
(505) 827-3826

Bureau of Business and Economic
Research
University of New Mexico
1920 Lomas NE
Albuquerque, NM 87131
Mr. Kevin Kargacin
+Ms. Juliana Boyle
(505) 277-2216

Department of Economics
New Mexico State University
Box 30001
Las Cruces, NM 88003
Dr. Kathleen Brook
(505) 646-4905

New York

Division of Policy & Research
Department of Economic
Development
1 Commerce Plaza, Room 905
99 Washington Avenue
Albany, NY 12245
*Mr. Robert Scardamalia
(518) 474-6005

Cornell Institute for Social and
Economic Research (CISER)
Cornell University
323 Uris Hall
Ithaca, NY 14853-7601
Ms. Ann Gray
(607) 255-1358

Law and Social Sciences Unit
New York State Library
Cultural Education Center
Empire State Plaza
Albany, NY 12230
Ms. Elaine Scheerer
(518) 474-5128
Ms. Mary Redmond
(518) 474-3940

Nelson A. Rockefeller Institute of
Government
411 State Street
Albany, NY 12203
(518) 472-1300

Division of Equalization and
Assessment
16 Sheridan Avenue
Albany, NY 12210
Mr. Wilfred B. Pauquette
(518) 474-6742

North Carolina (BIDC)

North Carolina Office of State
Budget and Management
116 West Jones Street
Raleigh, NC 27603-8005
*Ms. Francine Stephenson, Director
of State Data Center
+Mr. Alan Barwick
(919) 733-7061

State Library
North Carolina Department of
Cultural Resources
109 East Jones Street
Raleigh, NC 27611
Mr. Joel Sigmon
(919) 966-3683

Institute for Research in Social
Science
University of North Carolina
Manning Hall CB 3355
Chapel Hill, NC 27514
Mr. Glenn Deane
(919) 966-3346

Land Resources Information Service
Division of Land Resources
P.O. Box 27687
Raleigh, NC 27611
Ms. Karen Siderelis/Tim Johnson
(919) 733-2090

North Dakota

Department of Agricultural
Economics
North Dakota State University
Morrill Hall, Room 224
P.O. Box 5636
Fargo, ND 58105
*Dr. Richard Rathge
(701) 237-8621

Office of Intergovernmental
Assistance
State Capitol, 14th Floor
Bismarck, ND 58505
Mr. Jim Boyd
(701) 224-2094

Department of Geography
University of North Dakota
Grand Forks, ND 58202
Dr. Floyd Hickok
(701) 777-4246

North Dakota State Library
Liberty Memorial Building
Capitol Grounds
Bismarck, ND 58505
Ms. Susan Pahlmeyer
(701) 224-2490

Ohio

Ohio Data Users Center
Ohio Department of Development
P.O.Box 1001
Columbus, OH 43266-0101
*Mr. Barry Bennett
(614) 466-2115

Oklahoma

Oklahoma State Data Center
Oklahoma Department of Commerce
6601 Broadway Extension
(Mailing address)
P.O. Box 26980
Oklahoma City, OK 73126-0980
*Ms. Karen Selland
(405) 841-5184

Oklahoma Department of Libraries
200 N.E. 18th Street
Oklahoma City, OK 73105
Mr. Steve Beleu
(405) 521-2502

Oregon

Center for Population Research and
Census
Portland State University
P.O. Box 751
Portland, OR 97207-0751
*Mr. Ed Shafer
(503) 725-3922

Oregon State Library
State Library Building
Salem, OR 97310
Mr. Craig Smith
(503) 378-4502

Bureau of Governmental Research &
Service
University of Oregon
Hendricks Hall, Room 340
P.O. Box 97403
Eugene, OR 97403
Ms. Karen Seidel
(503) 686-5232

Oregon Housing Agency
1600 State
Salem, OR 97310-0161
Mr. Mike Murphy
(503) 378-5953

* Denotes key contact SDC
+ Denotes key contact BIDC

Pennsylvania (BIDC)

Pennsylvania State Data Center
Institute of State and Regional
Affairs
Pennsylvania State University at
Harrisburg
Middletown, PA 17057-4898
+Mr. Robert Surridge
*Mr. Michael Behney
(717) 948-6336

Pennsylvania State Library
Forum Building
Harrisburg, PA 17120
Mr. John Gerswindt
(717) 787-2327

Puerto Rico

Puerto Rico Planning Board
Minillas Government Center
North Bldg., Avenida De Diego
P. O. Box 41119
San Juan, PR 00940-9985
*Sra. Lillian Torres Aguirre
(809) 728-4430

Recinto Universitario De Mayaguez
Edificio Anexo Pineiro
Carretera Num 2
Mayaguez, PR 00708
Prfa. Grace Quinones Seda
(809) 834-4040

Biblioteca Carnegie
Ave. Ponce De Leon-Parada 1
San Juan, PR 00901
Sra. Carmen Martinez
(809) 724-1046

Rhode Island

Department of Administration
Office of Municipal Affairs
One Capitol Hill
Providence, RI 02908-5873
*Mr. Paul Egan
(401) 277-6493

Rhode Island Department of State
Library Services
300 Richmond Street
Providence, RI 02903
Mr. Frank Iacona
(401) 277-2726

Social Science Data Center
Brown University
P.O. Box 1916
Providence, RI 02912
Ms. Donna Souza
(401) 863-2550

Rhode Island Department of
Education
22 Hayes Street
Providence, RI 02908
Mr. James Karon
(401) 277-3126

Rhode Island Department of
Economic Development
7 Jackson Way
Providence, RI 02903
Mr. Vincent Harrington
(401) 277-2601

United Way of Rhode Island
229 Waterman Street
Providence, RI 02908
Ms. Florence Dzija
(401) 351-6500

South Carolina

Division of Research and Statistical
Services
South Carolina Budget and Control
Board
Rembert Dennis Bldg. Room 425
Columbia, SC 29201
Mr. Bobby Bowers
*Mr. Mike Macfarlane
(803) 734-3780

South Carolina State Library
P.O. Box 11469
Columbia, SC 29211
Ms. Mary Bostick
(803) 734-8666

South Dakota

Business Research Bureau
School of Business
University of South Dakota
414 East Clark
Vermillion, SD 57069
*Ms DeVee Dykstra
(605) 677-5287

Documents Department
South Dakota State Library
Department of Education and
Cultural Affairs
800 Governors Drive
Pierre, SD 57501-2294
Ms. Margaret Bezpaletz
(605) 773-3131

Labor Market Information Center
South Dakota Department of Labor
420 S. Rosevelt   Box 4730
Aberdeen, SD 57402-4730
Ms. Mary Susan Vickers
(605) 622-2314

Center for Health Policy & Statistics
South Dakota Department of Health
Foss Building 523 E Capitol
Pierre, SD 57501
Ms. Jan Smith
(605) 773-3355

Tennessee

Tennessee State Planning Office
John Sevier State Office Bldg.
500 Charlotte Ave. Suite 307
Nashville, TN 37219
*Mr. Charles Brown
(615) 741-1676

Center for Business and Economic
Research
College of Business Administration
University of Tennessee
Room 100, Glocker Hall
Knoxville, TN 37996-4170
Ms. Betty Vickers
(615) 974-5441

Texas

State Data Center
Texas Department of Commerce
9th and Congress Streets
(mailing address)
P.O. Box 12728
Capitol Station
Austin, TX 78711
*Ms. Susan Tully
(512) 472-5059

Department of Rural Sociology
Texas A & M University System
Special Services Building
College Station, TX 77843
Dr. Steve Murdock
(409) 845-5115 or 5332

Texas Natural Resources Information
System (TNRIS)
P.O. Box 133231
Austin, TX 78711
Mr. Charles Palmer
(512) 463-8402

Texas State Library and Archive
Commission
P.O. Box 12927
Capitol Station
Austin, TX 78711
Ms. Bonnie Grobar
(512) 463-5427

Utah

Office of Planning & Budget
State Capitol, Rm. 116
Salt Lake City, UT 84114
Mr. Brad Barber, Director
*Ms. Linda Smith
(801) 538-1036

*Denotes key contact SDC
+ Denotes key contact BIDC*

Bureau of Economic and Business
Research
401 Garff Building
University of Utah
Salt Lake City, UT 84112
Ms. Frank Hachman
(801) 581-6333

Population Research Laboratory
Utah State University, UMC 07
Logan, UT 84322
Mr. Yun Kim
(801) 750-1231

Department of Employment Security
174 Social Hall Avenue
P.O. Box 11249
Salt Lake City, UT 84147
Mr. Ken Jensen
(801) 533-2372

Vermont

Office of Policy Research and
Coordination
Pavilion Office Building
109 State Street
Montpelier, VT 05602
*Mr. Ken Jones
(802) 828-3326

Center for Rural Studies
University of Vermont
207 Morrill Hall
Burlington, VT 05405-0106
Ms. Cathleen Gent
(802) 656-3021

Vermont Department of Libraries
111 State Street
Montpelier, VT 05602
Ms. Patricia Klinck, State Librarian
(802) 828-3265

Vermont Agency of Development
and Community Affairs
Pavilion Office Building
109 State Street
Montpelier, VT 05602
Mr. Jed Guertin
(802) 828-3211

Virginia

Virginia Employment Commission
703 East Main Street
Richmond, VA 23219
*Mr. Larry Robinson
(804) 786-8624

Center for Public Service
University of Virginia
Dynamics Bldg., 4th Floor
2015 Ivy Road
Charlottesville, VA 22903
Dr. Michael Spar
(804) 971-2661

Virginia State Library
12th and Capitol Streets
Richmond, VA 23219
Ms. Linda Morrissett
(804) 786-2175

Virgin Islands

University of the Virgin Islands
Caribbean Research Institute
Charlotte Amalie
St. Thomas, VI 00802
*Dr. Frank Mills
(809) 776-9200

Virgin Islands Department of
Economic Development
P.O. Box 6400
Charlotte Amalie
St. Thomas, VI 00801
Mr. Richard Moore
(809) 774-8784

Washington (BIDC)

Estimation & Forecasting Unit
Office of Financial Management
Insurance Bldg., AQ-44
Olympia, WA 98504-0202
*+Mr. Michael Knight
(206) 586-2504

Documents Section
Washington State Library
AJ-11
Olympia, WA 98504
Ms. Ann Bregent
(206) 753-4027

Puget Sound Council of Govts.
216 1st Avenue South
Seattle, WA 98104
Mr. Deana Dryden
(206) 464-7532

Social Research Center
Department of Rural Sociology
Washington State Univeristy
Pullman, WA 99164
Dr. Annabel Cook
(509) 335-4519

Department of Sociology
Demographic Research Laboratory
Western Washington University
Bellingham, WA 98225
Mr. Lucky Tedrow, Director
(206) 676-3617

Applied Social Data Center
Department of Sociology
Central Washington University
Ellensburg, WA 98926
Mr. David Kaufman
(509) 963-3131

West Virginia (BIDC)

Community Development Division
Governor's Office of Community and
Industrial Development
Capitol Complex
Building 6, Room 553
Charleston, WV 25305
*Ms. Mary C. Harless
(304) 348-4010

The Center for Economic Research
West Virginia University
209 Armstrong Hall
Morgantown, WV 26506-6025
Dr. Tom Witt, Director
+Ms. Linda Culp
(304) 293-5837

Reference Library
West Virginia State Library
Commission
Science and Cultural Center
Capitol Complex
Charleston, WV 25305
Ms. Karen Goff
(304) 348-2045

Office of Health Services Research
Department of Community Health
West Virginia University
900 Chestnut Ridge Road
Morgantown, WV 26505
Ms. Stephanie Pratt
(304) 293-2601

Wisconsin (BIDC)

Demographic Services Center
Department of Administration
101 S. Webster St., 6th Floor
P.O. Box 7868
Madison, WI 53707-7868
Ms. Nadene Roenspies
*Mr. Robert Naylor
(608) 266-1927

Department of Rural Sociology
University of Wisconsin
1450 Linden Drive, Rm. 316
Madison, WI 53706
Ms. Doris Slesinger
Mr. Robert Wilger
(608) 262-1515

* *Denotes key contact SDC*
+ *Denotes key contact BIDC*

Applied Population Laboratory
Department of Rural Sociology
University of Wisconsin
316 Agriculture Hall
Madison, WI 53706
+Ms. Judy Suchman
(608) 262-9526

Wyoming

Department of Administration and
Fiscal Control
Research & Statistics Division
Emerson Building
Cheyenne, WY 82002-0060
*Ms. Mary Byrnes, Director
(307) 777-7505

Survey Research Center
University of Wyoming
P.O. Box 3925
Laramie, WY 82071
Mr. G. Fred Doll
(307) 766-5141

Denotes key contact SDC
+ *Denotes key contact BIDC*

Appendix P

Acronyms

Acronyms

ASVAB	Armed Services Vocational Aptitude Battery
BLS	U.S. Bureau of Labor Statistics
CES	Current Employment Statistics Program
CEW	Covered Employment and Wages Program
CIDS	Career Information Delivery Systems
CPS	Current Population Survey
DOL	U.S. Department of Labor
DOT	*Dictionary of Occupational Titles*
ECDP	Employee Career Development Project
EEO	Equal Employment Opportunity Commission
GOE	*Guide for Occupational Exploration*
ICDM	Improved Career Decision Making
LAUS	Local Area Unemployment Statistics
LMA	Labor Market Area
LMI	Labor Market Information
MLS	Mass Layoff Statistics Program
MSA	Metropolitan Statistical Area
NCDA	National Career Development Association
NOICC	National Occupational Information Coordinating Committee
OES	Occupational Employment Statistics
OIS	Occupational Information Systems
OOH	*Occupational Outlook Handbook*
OOQ	*Occupational Outlook Quarterly*
SESA	State Employment Security Agency
SIC	*Standard Occupational Classification*
SOICC	State Occupational Information Coordinating committee
OVAE	U.S. Office of Vocational and Adult Education